TOKYO GHOUL

SUI ISHIDA

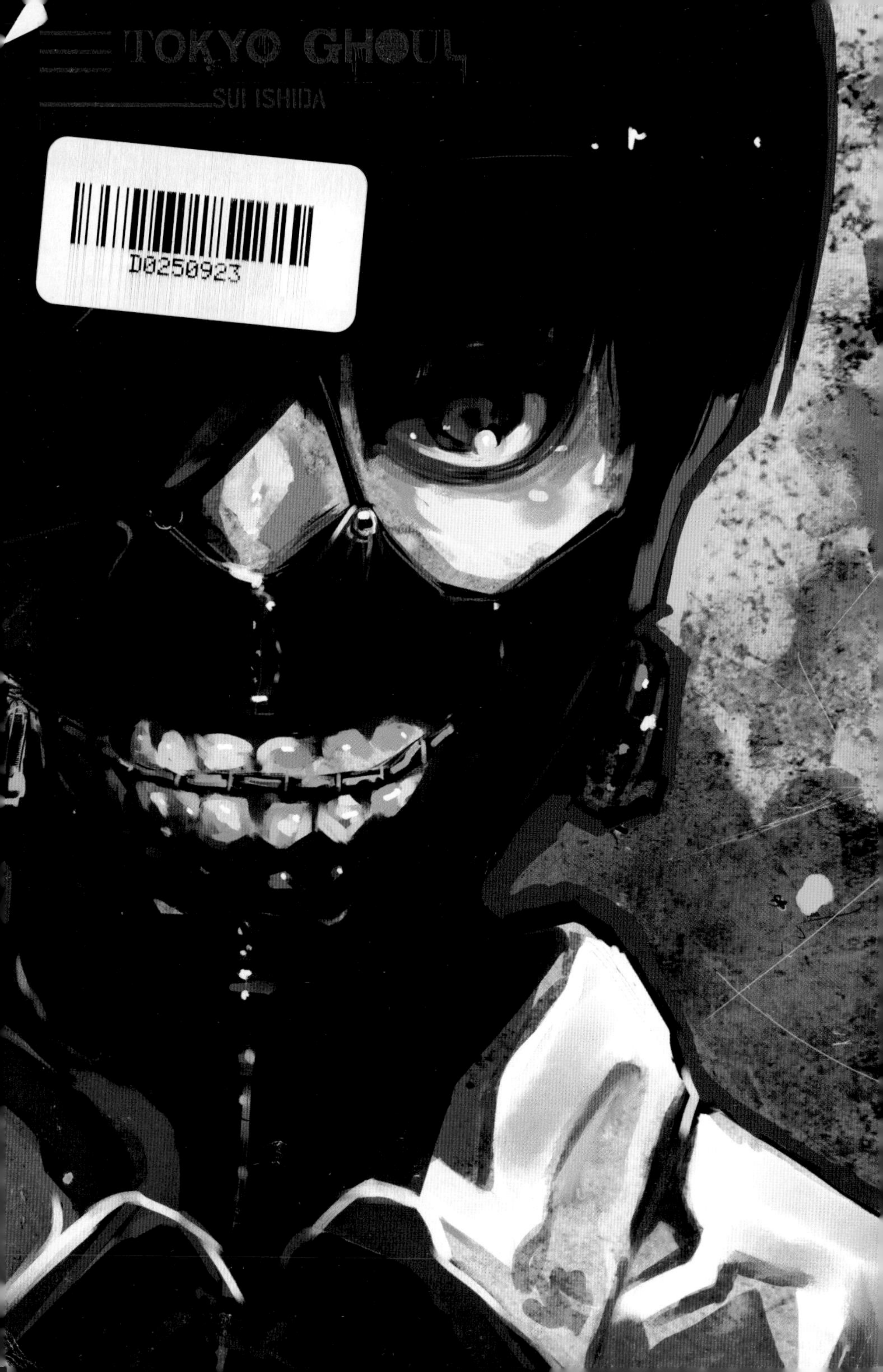

SUI ISHIDA was born in Fukuoka, Japan. He is the author of ***Tokyo Ghoul*** and several ***Tokyo Ghoul*** one-shots, including one that won him second place in the *Weekly Young Jump* 113th Grand Prix award in 2010. ***Tokyo Ghoul*** began serialization in *Weekly Young Jump* in 2011 and was adapted into an anime series in 2014.

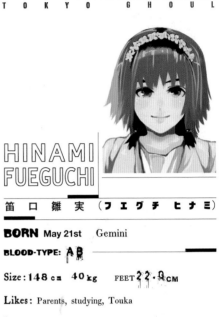

HINAMI FUEGUCHI

笛口雛実（フエグチ ヒナミ）

BORN May 21st Gemini

BLOOD-TYPE: AB

Size: 148 cm 40 kg FEET 22.0 CM

Likes: Parents, studying, Touka

Interests: Sen Takatsuki books, human society, Kaneki

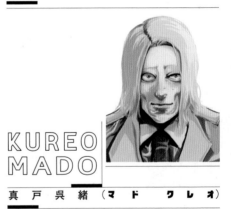

KUREO MADO

真戸呉緒（マド クレオ）

BORN January 24th Aquarius

CCG Main Office Senior Investigator

BLOOD-TYPE: A

Size: 177 cm 47 kg FEET 26.5 CM

Likes: Wife and daughter, hard-earned weapons

Quinques: **Fueguchi 1: Rinkaku**
A spinal cord-like design.
A sharp, high-speed combat Quinque.

Fueguchi 2: Kokaku
The petals that spread out in all directions block Kagune attacks. An offensive and defensive Quinque.

Plus 20 other types...

東京喰種

TOKYO GHOUL

TOKYO GHOUL

SUI
ISHIDA

T O K Y O G H O U L

sui ishida

3

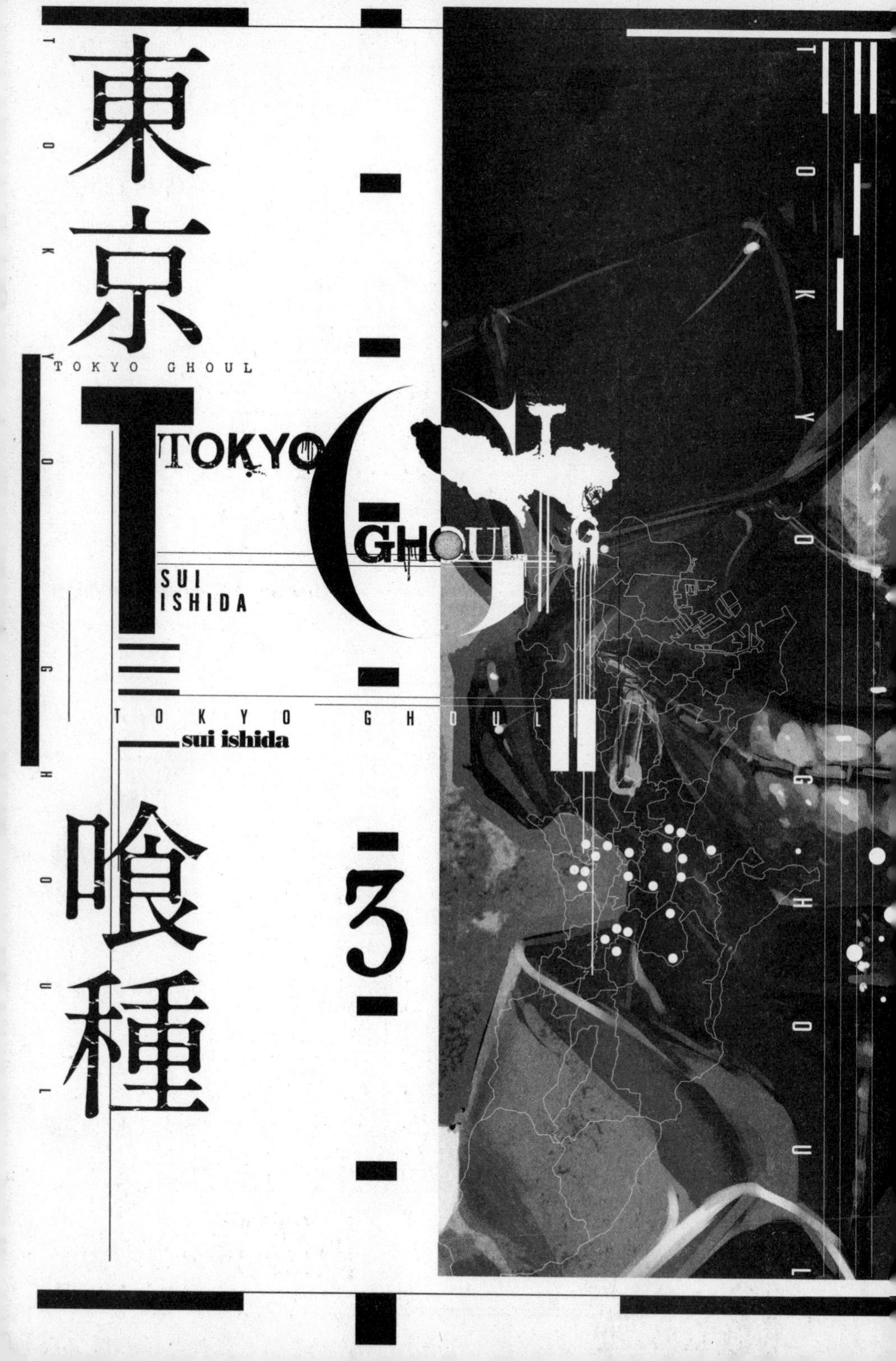

T O K Y O G H O U L

東

京

喰

種

TOKYO GHOUL

SUI
ISHIDA

C O N T E N T S

3

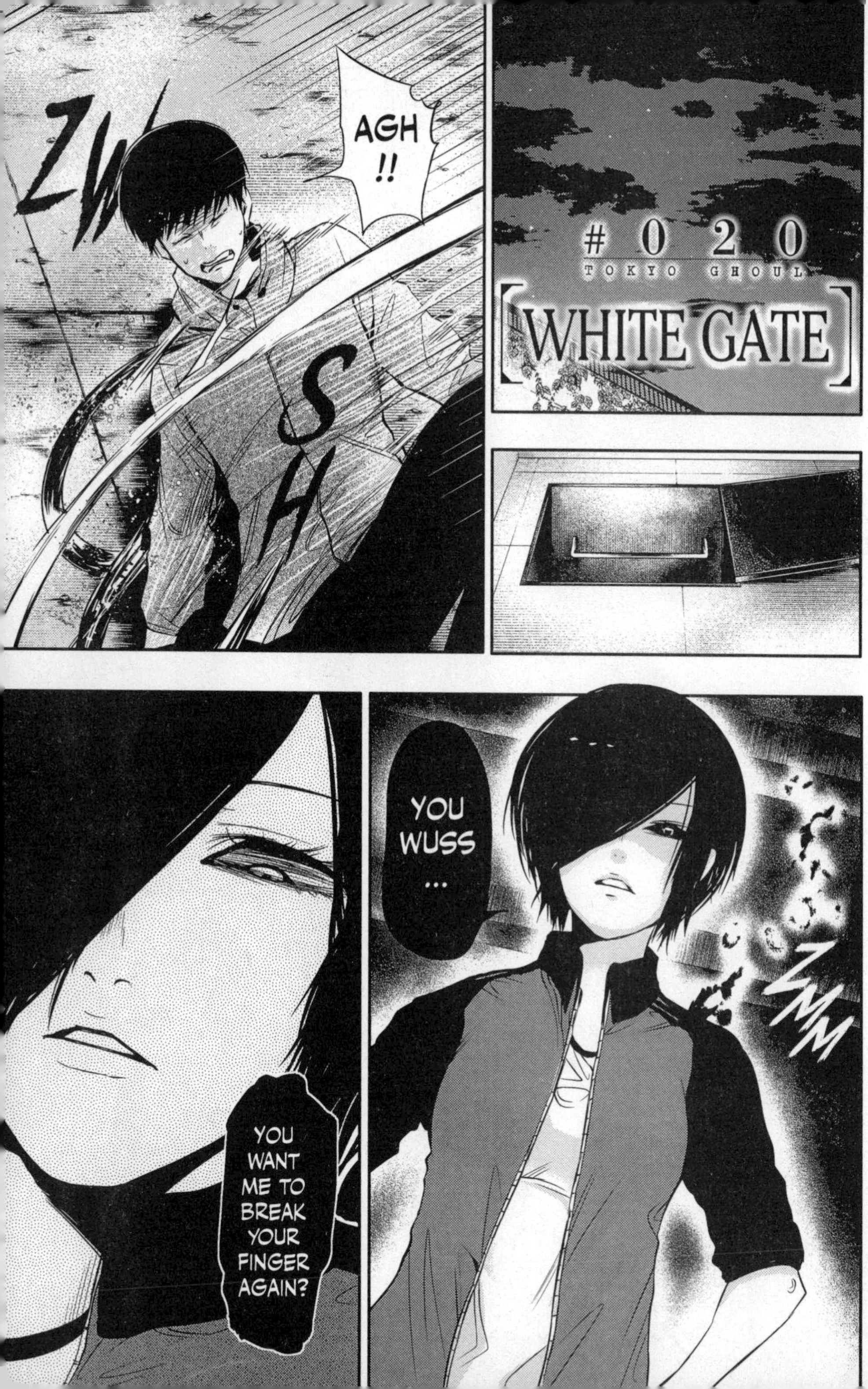

#020
TOKYO GHOUL
[WHITE GATE]
ZWSH
AGH !!
YOU WUSS ...
ZMM
YOU WANT ME TO BREAK YOUR FINGER AGAIN?

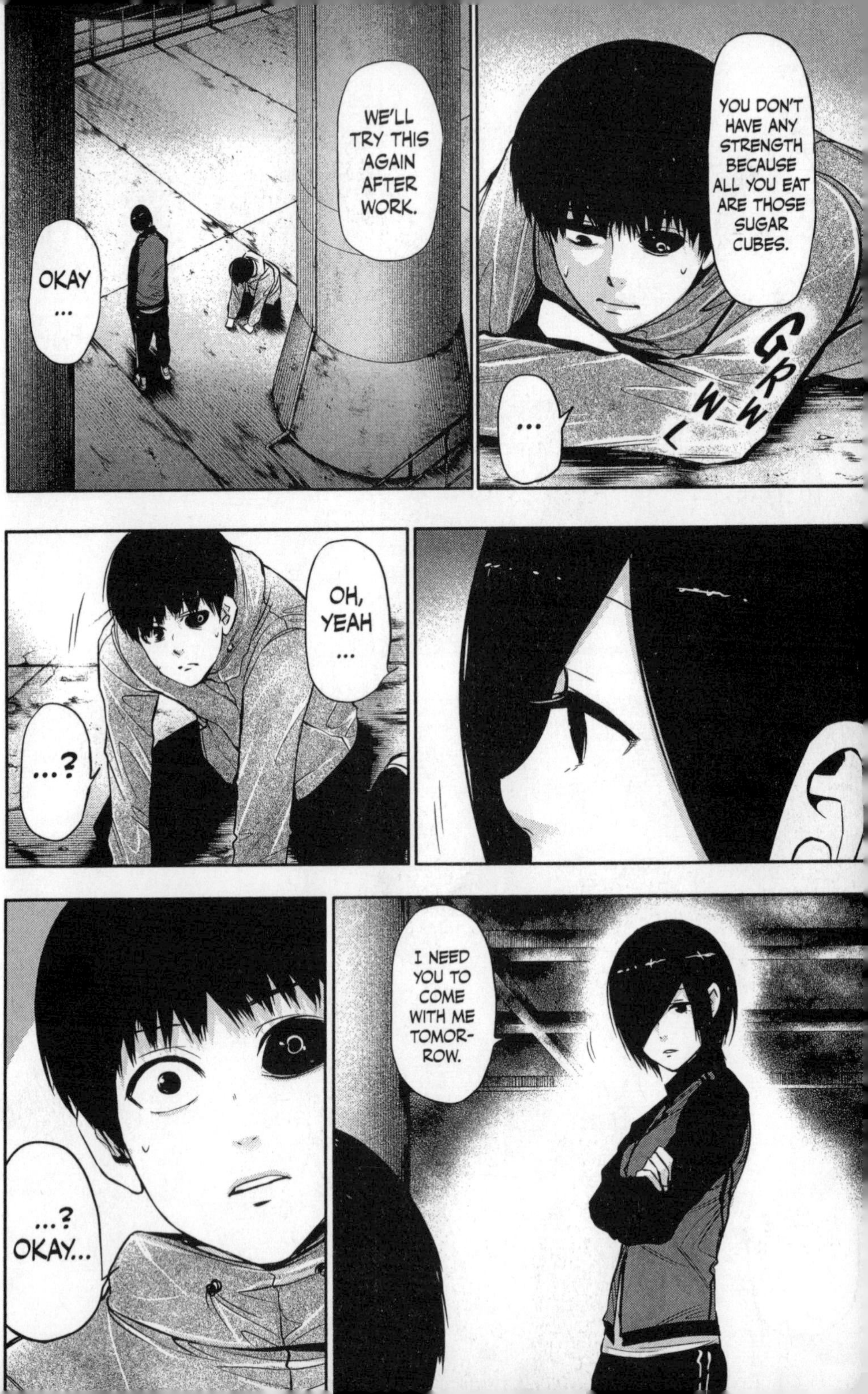
YOU DON'T HAVE ANY STRENGTH BECAUSE ALL YOU EAT ARE THOSE SUGAR CUBES.
GRWL
...
WE'LL TRY THIS AGAIN AFTER WORK.
OKAY ...
OH, YEAH ...
...?
I NEED YOU TO COME WITH ME TOMOR-ROW.
...? OKAY...

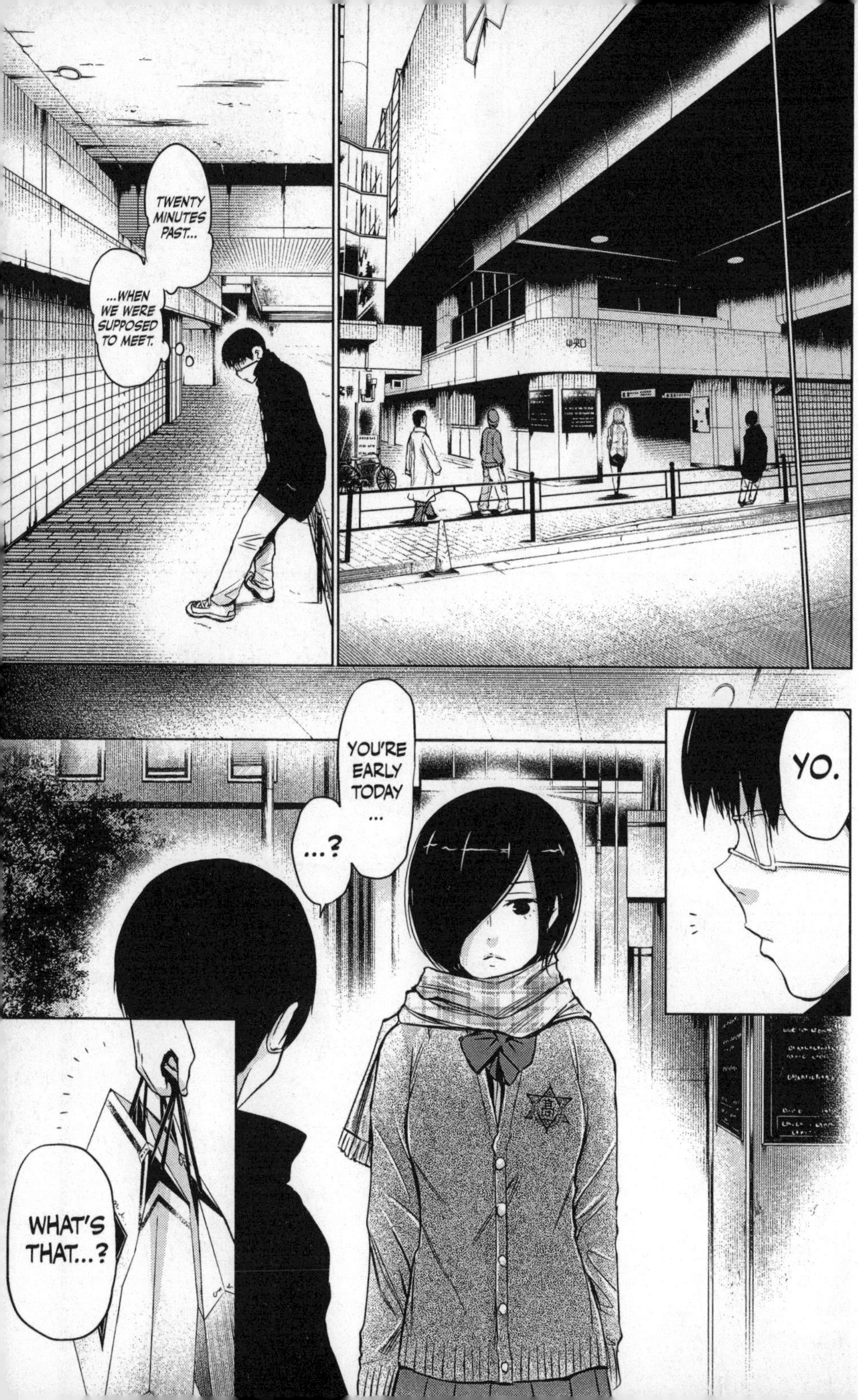
TWENTY MINUTES PAST...
...WHEN WE WERE SUPPOSED TO MEET.
YO.
YOU'RE EARLY TODAY...
...?
WHAT'S THAT...?

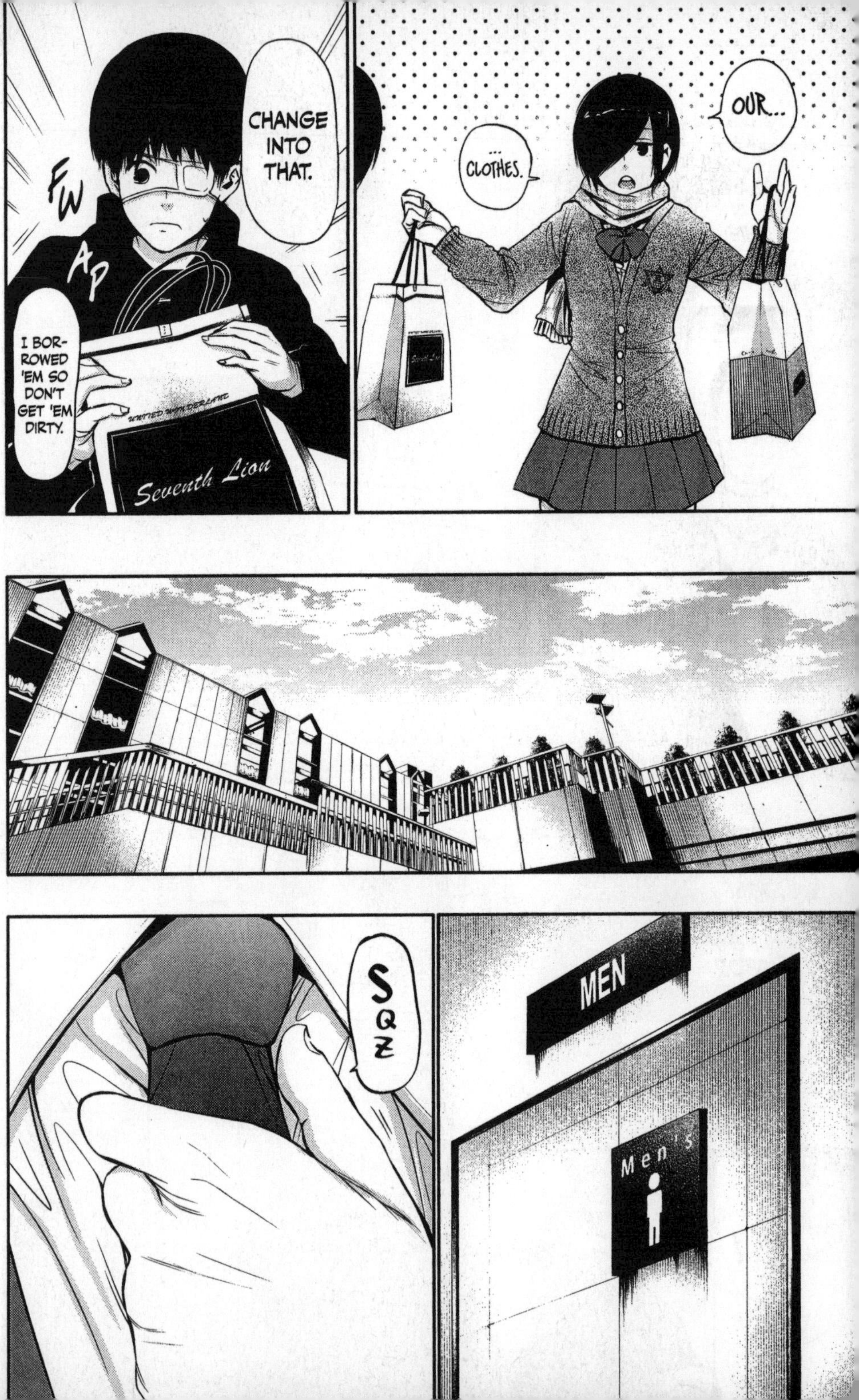
OUR...
...CLOTHES.
CHANGE INTO THAT.
FWAP
I BORROWED 'EM SO DON'T GET 'EM DIRTY.
Seventh Lion
MEN
Men's
SQZ

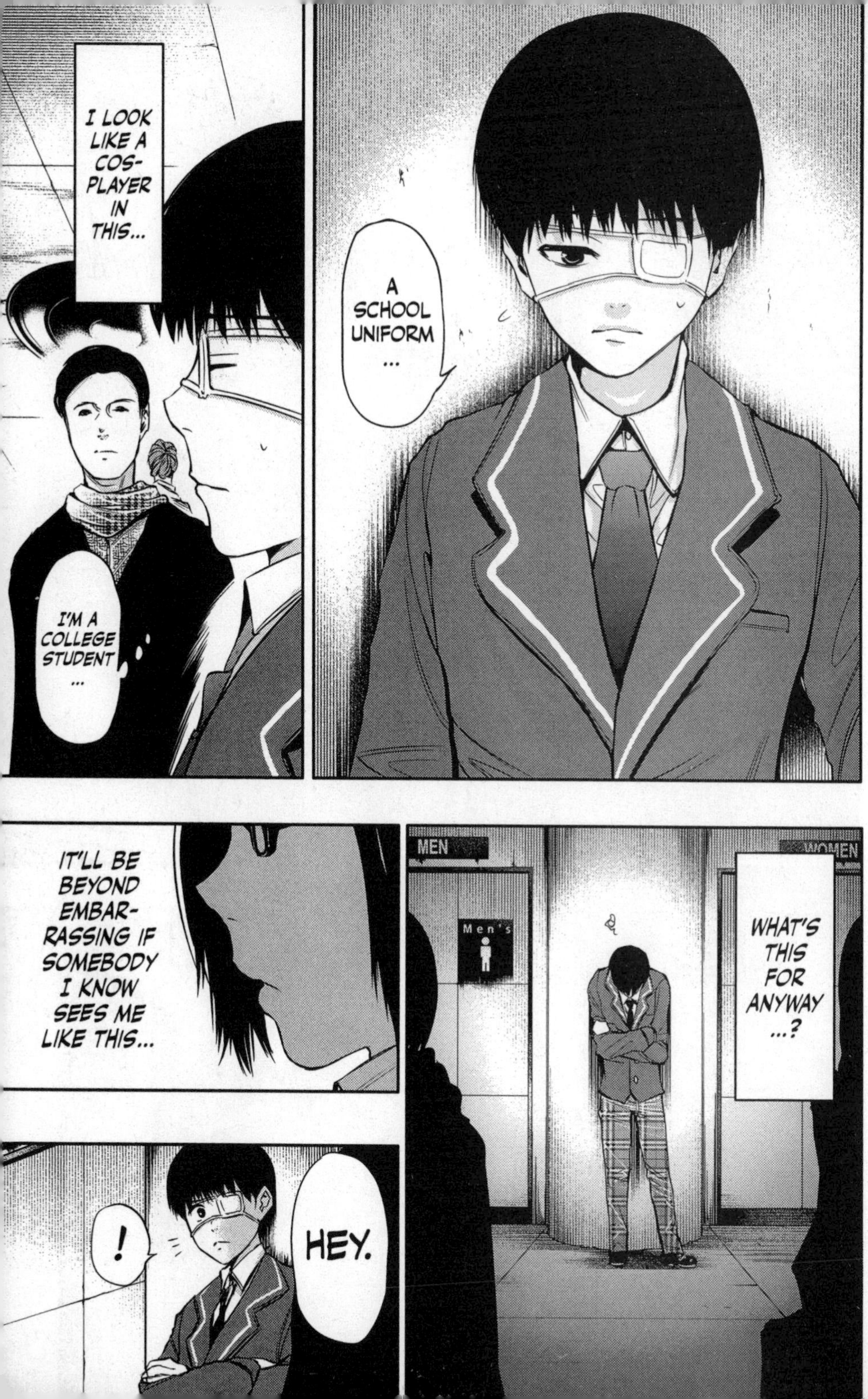
A SCHOOL UNIFORM ...
I LOOK LIKE A COS-PLAYER IN THIS...
I'M A COLLEGE STUDENT ...
WOMEN
MEN
Men's
WHAT'S THIS FOR ANYWAY ...?
IT'LL BE BEYOND EMBAR-RASSING IF SOMEBODY I KNOW SEES ME LIKE THIS...
HEY.
!

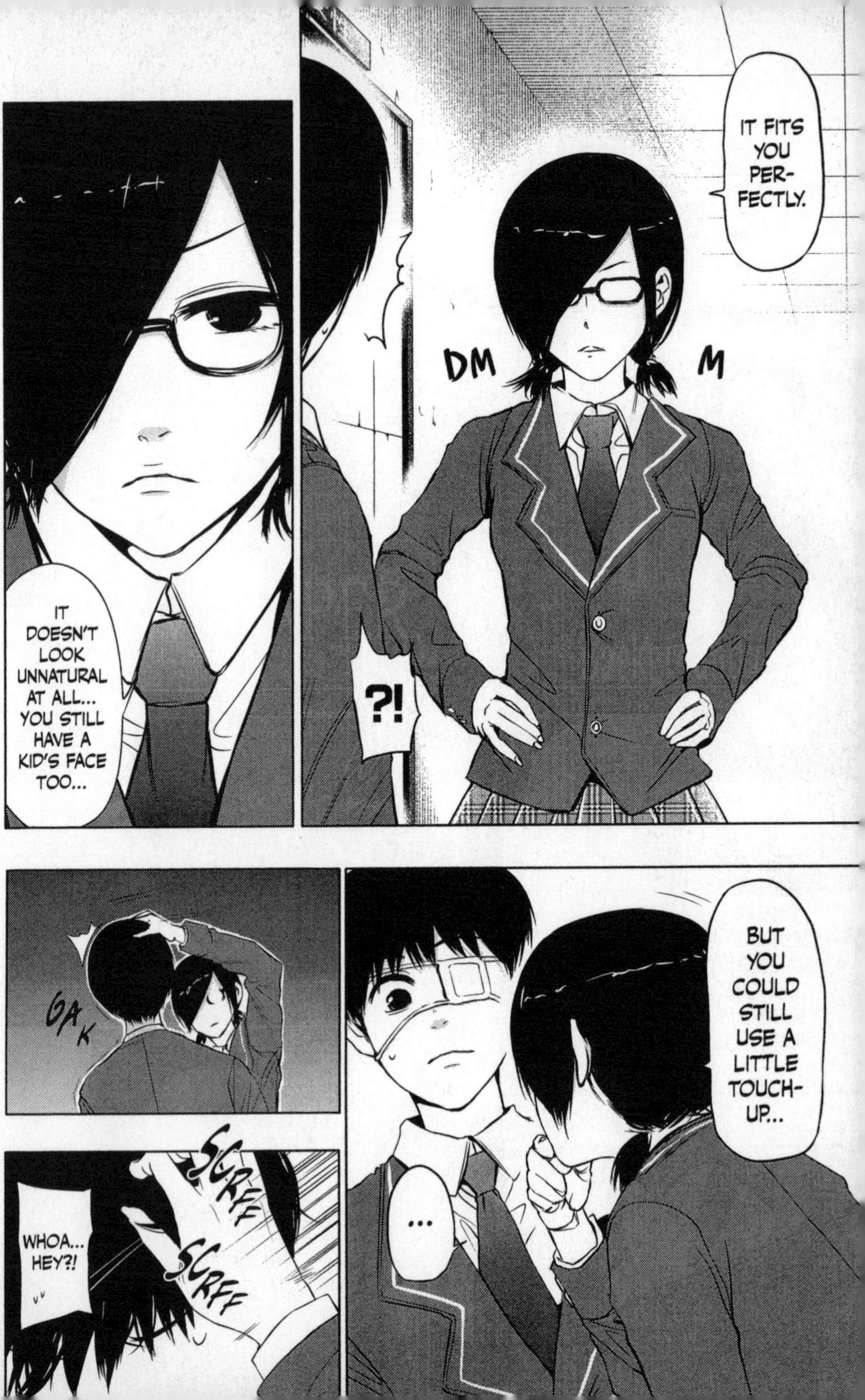
IT FITS YOU PER-FECTLY.
DM M
?!
IT DOESN'T LOOK UNNATURAL AT ALL... YOU STILL HAVE A KID'S FACE TOO...
BUT YOU COULD STILL USE A LITTLE TOUCH-UP...
...
GAK
SCRFF
SCRFF
WHOA... HEY?!

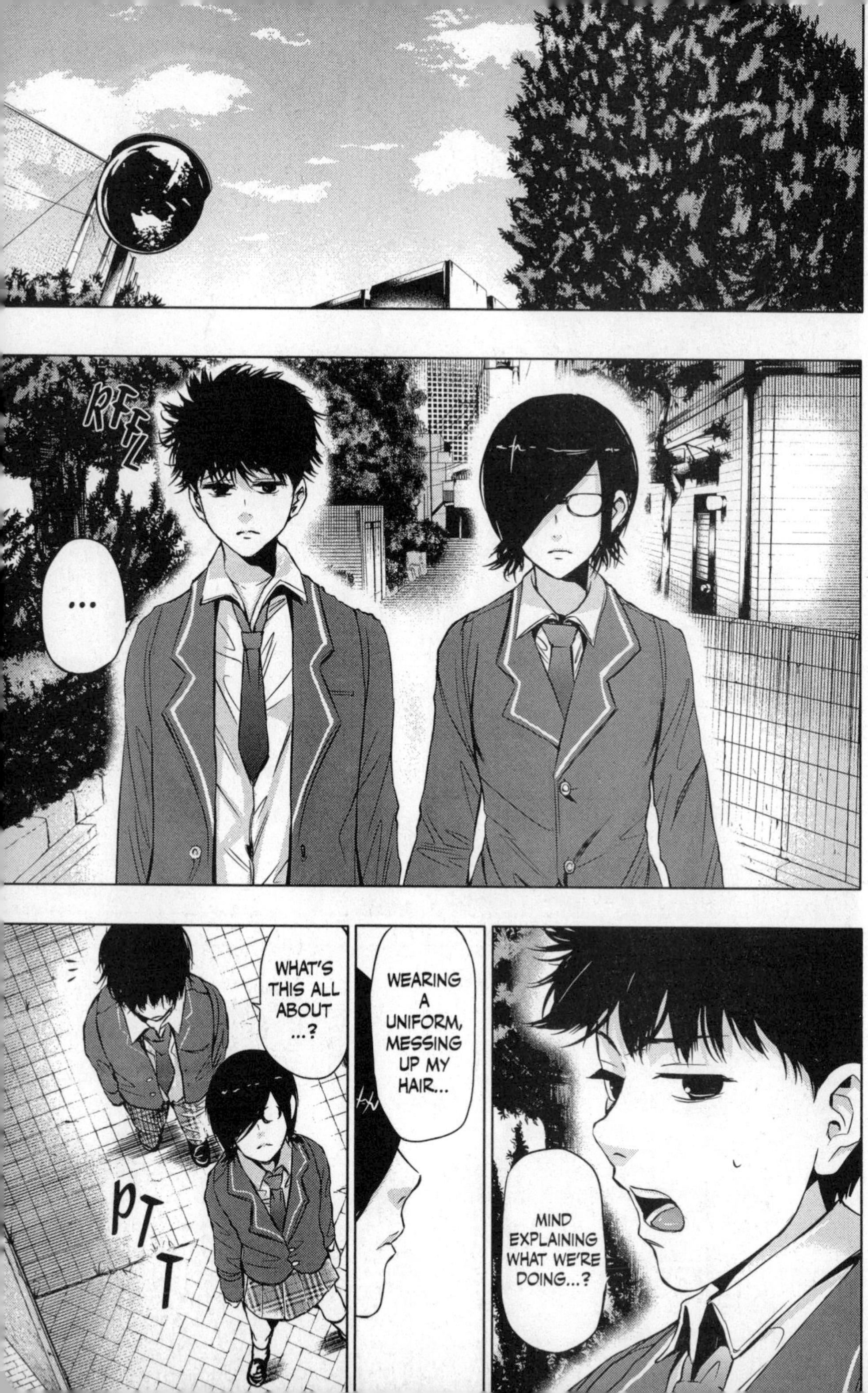
RFFL
...
MIND EXPLAINING WHAT WE'RE DOING...?
WEARING A UNIFORM, MESSING UP MY HAIR...
WHAT'S THIS ALL ABOUT ...?
PTT

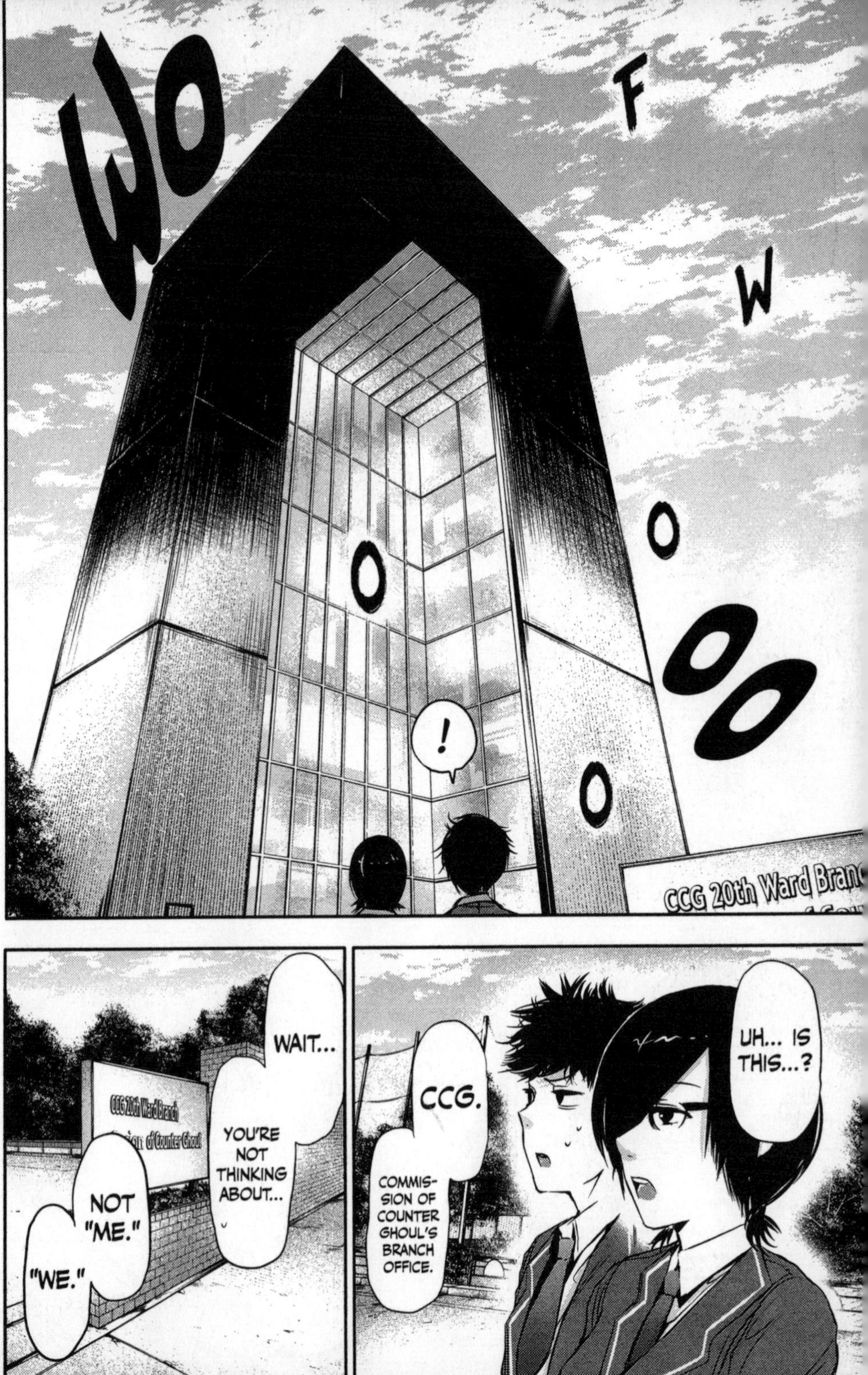
WO
F
W
O
O
OO
O
!
CCG 20th Ward Bran
UH... IS THIS...?
CCG.
COMMISSION OF COUNTER GHOUL'S BRANCH OFFICE.
CCG 20th Ward Branch
WAIT...
YOU'RE NOT THINKING ABOUT...
NOT "ME."
"WE."

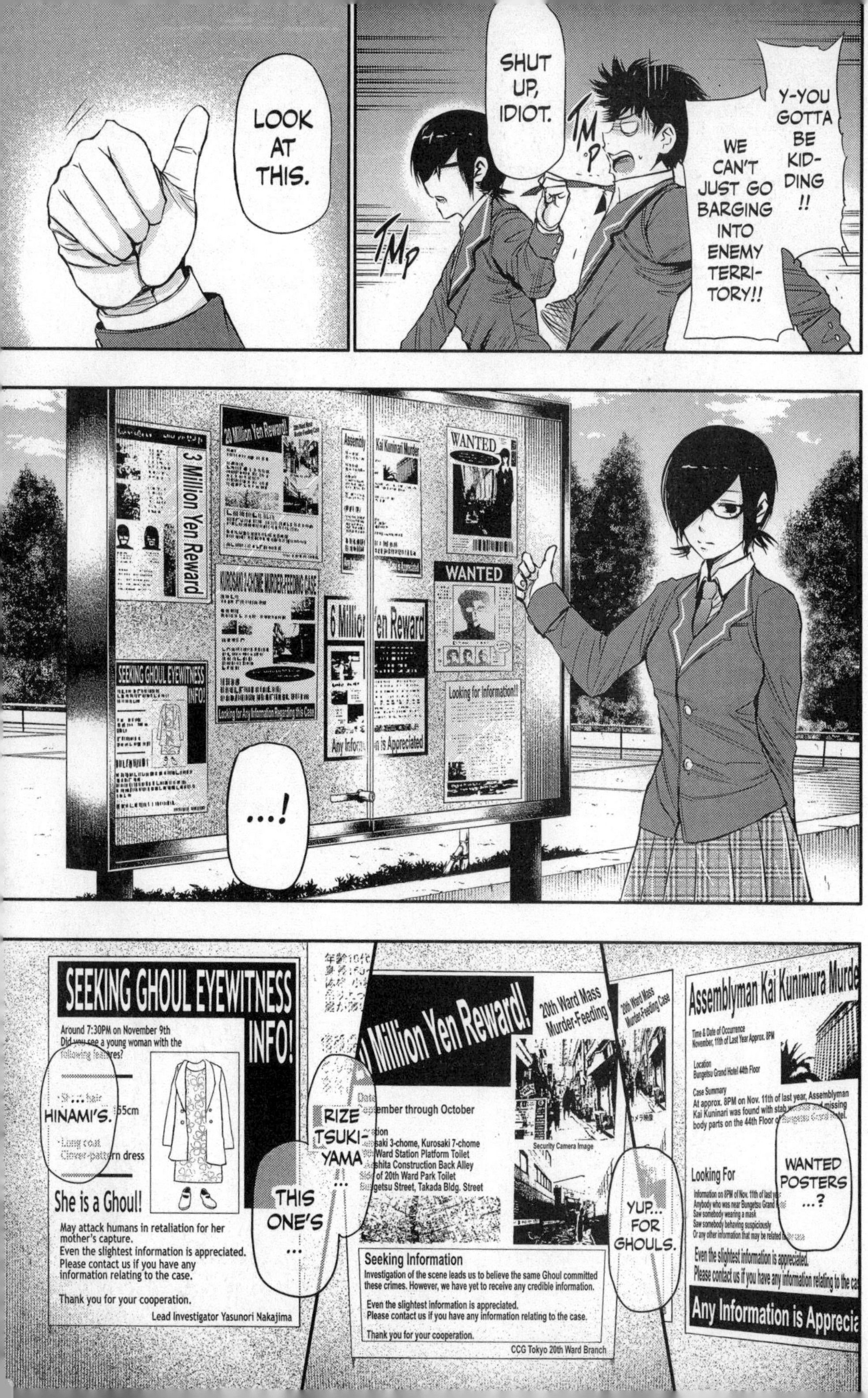

Y-YOU GOTTA BE KID-DING!!
WE CAN'T JUST GO BARGING INTO ENEMY TERRI-TORY!!
SHUT UP, IDIOT.
TMP
TMP
TMP
LOOK AT THIS.
...!
20 Million Yen Reward!
3 Million Yen Reward
Kai Kuninari Murder
WANTED
WANTED
KUROSAKI 7-CHOME MURDER-FEEDING CASE
6 Million Yen Reward
Any Information is Appreciated
SEEKING GHOUL EYEWITNESS INFO!
Looking for Information!!
Looking for Any Information Regarding this Case
Assemblyman Kai Kunimura Murde
Time & Date of Occurrence
November, 11th of Last Year Approx. 8PM
Location
Bungetsu Grand Hotel 44th Floor
Case Summary
Looking For
Even the slightest information is appreciated.
Any Information is Apprecia
WANTED POSTERS ...?
20th Ward Mass Murder-Feeding Case
20th Ward Mass Murder-Feeding
Security Camera Image
YUP... FOR GHOULS.
Million Yen Reward!
September through October
Seeking Information
Investigation of the scene leads us to believe the same Ghoul committed these crimes. However, we have yet to receive any credible information.
Even the slightest information is appreciated.
Please contact us if you have any information relating to the case.
Thank you for your cooperation.
CCG Tokyo 20th Ward Branch
RIZE TSUKI-YAMA...
THIS ONE'S ...
SEEKING GHOUL EYEWITNESS INFO!
Around 7:30PM on November 9th
Did you see a young woman with the following features?
...HINAMI'S.
She is a Ghoul!
May attack humans in retaliation for her mother's capture.
Even the slightest information is appreciated.
Please contact us if you have any information relating to the case.
Thank you for your cooperation.
Lead Investigator Yasunori Nakajima

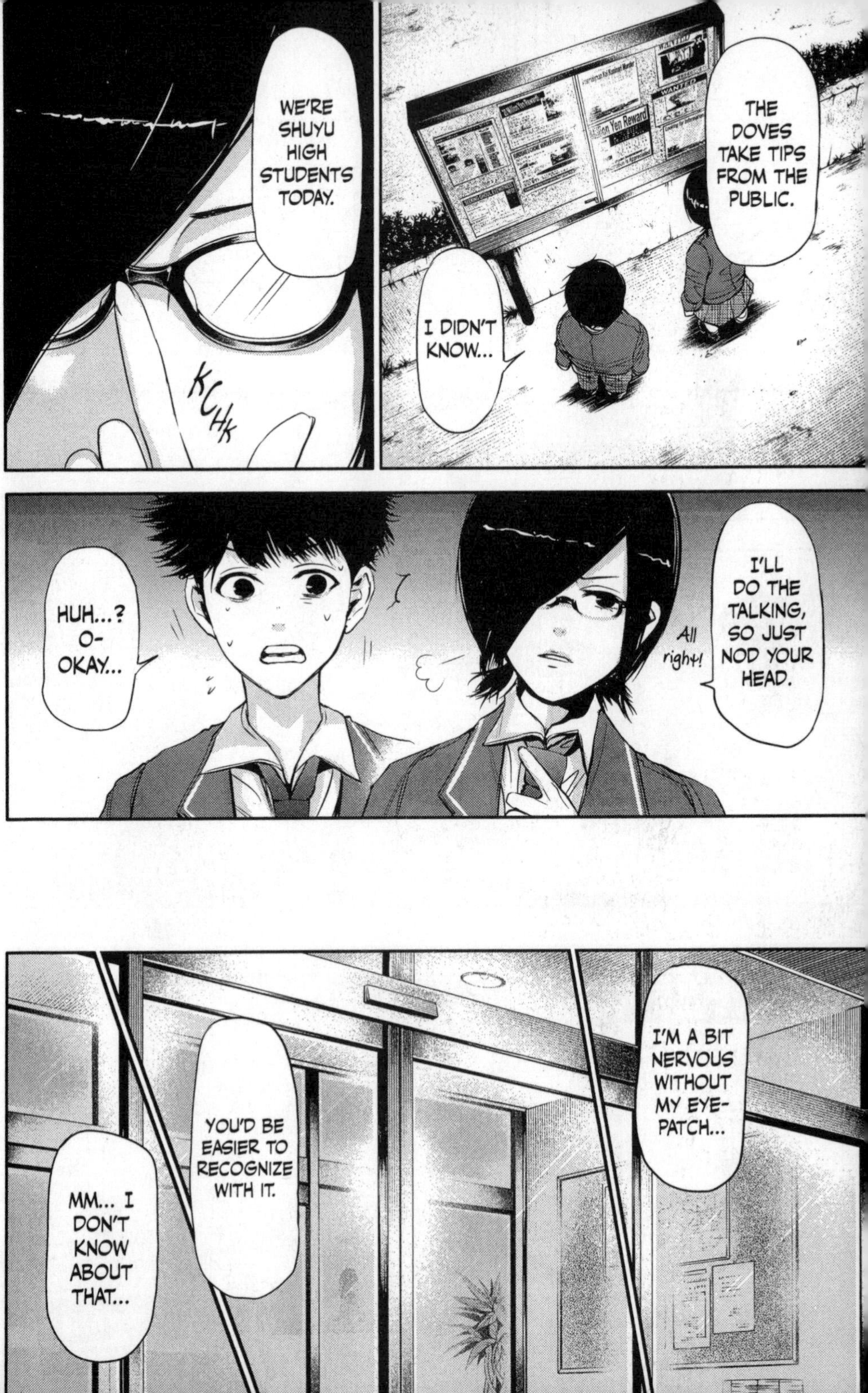
THE DOVES TAKE TIPS FROM THE PUBLIC.
I DIDN'T KNOW...
WE'RE SHUYU HIGH STUDENTS TODAY.
KCHK
I'LL DO THE TALKING, SO JUST NOD YOUR HEAD.
All right!
HUH...? O-OKAY...
I'M A BIT NERVOUS WITHOUT MY EYE-PATCH...
YOU'D BE EASIER TO RECOGNIZE WITH IT.
MM... I DON'T KNOW ABOUT THAT...

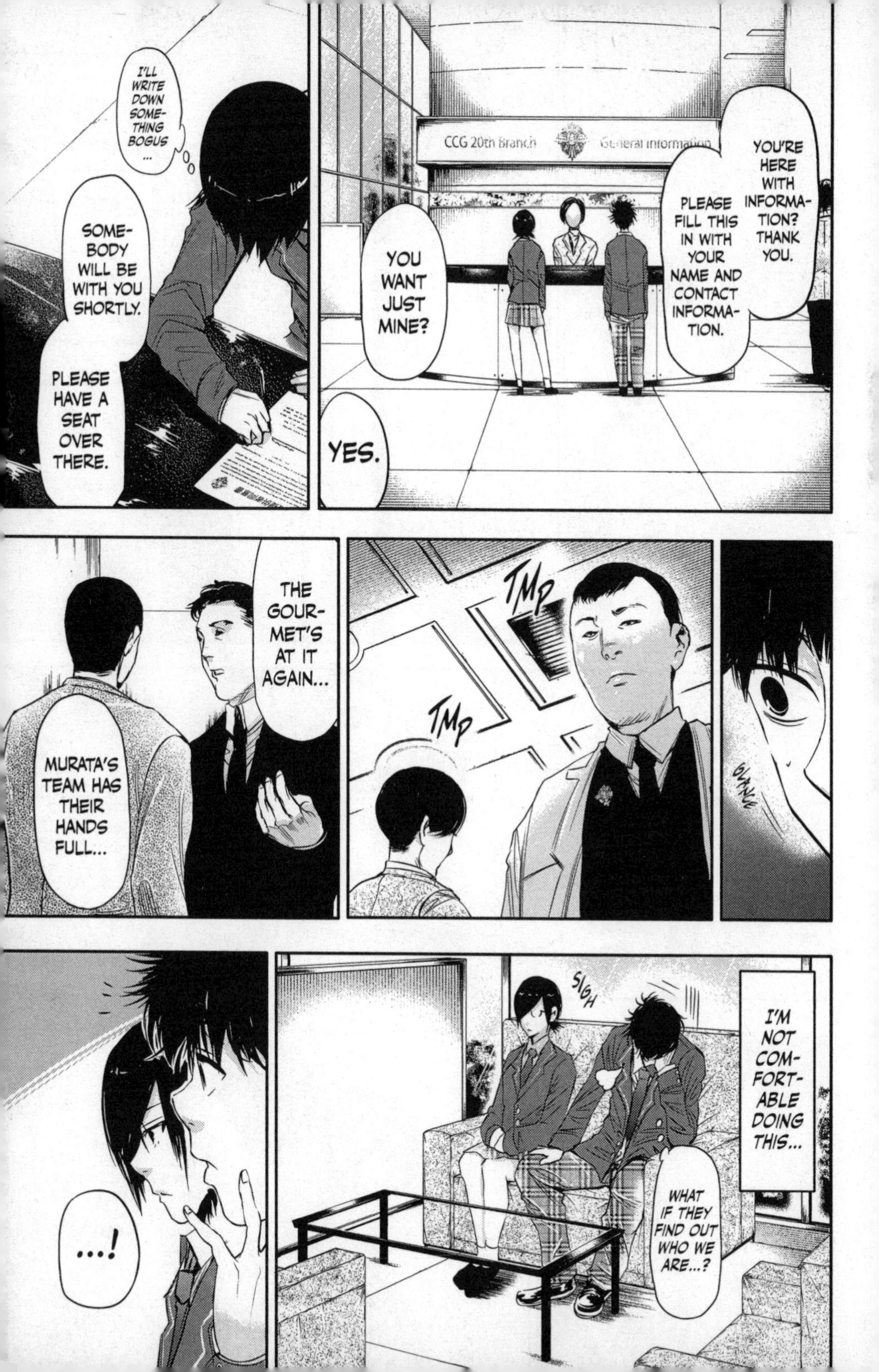
CCG 20th Branch
YOU'RE HERE WITH INFORMATION? THANK YOU.
PLEASE FILL THIS IN WITH YOUR NAME AND CONTACT INFORMATION.
YOU WANT JUST MINE?
YES.
I'LL WRITE DOWN SOMETHING BOGUS...
SOMEBODY WILL BE WITH YOU SHORTLY.
PLEASE HAVE A SEAT OVER THERE.
TMP
TMP
THE GOURMET'S AT IT AGAIN...
MURATA'S TEAM HAS THEIR HANDS FULL...
I'M NOT COMFORTABLE DOING THIS...
SIGH
WHAT IF THEY FIND OUT WHO WE ARE...?
...!

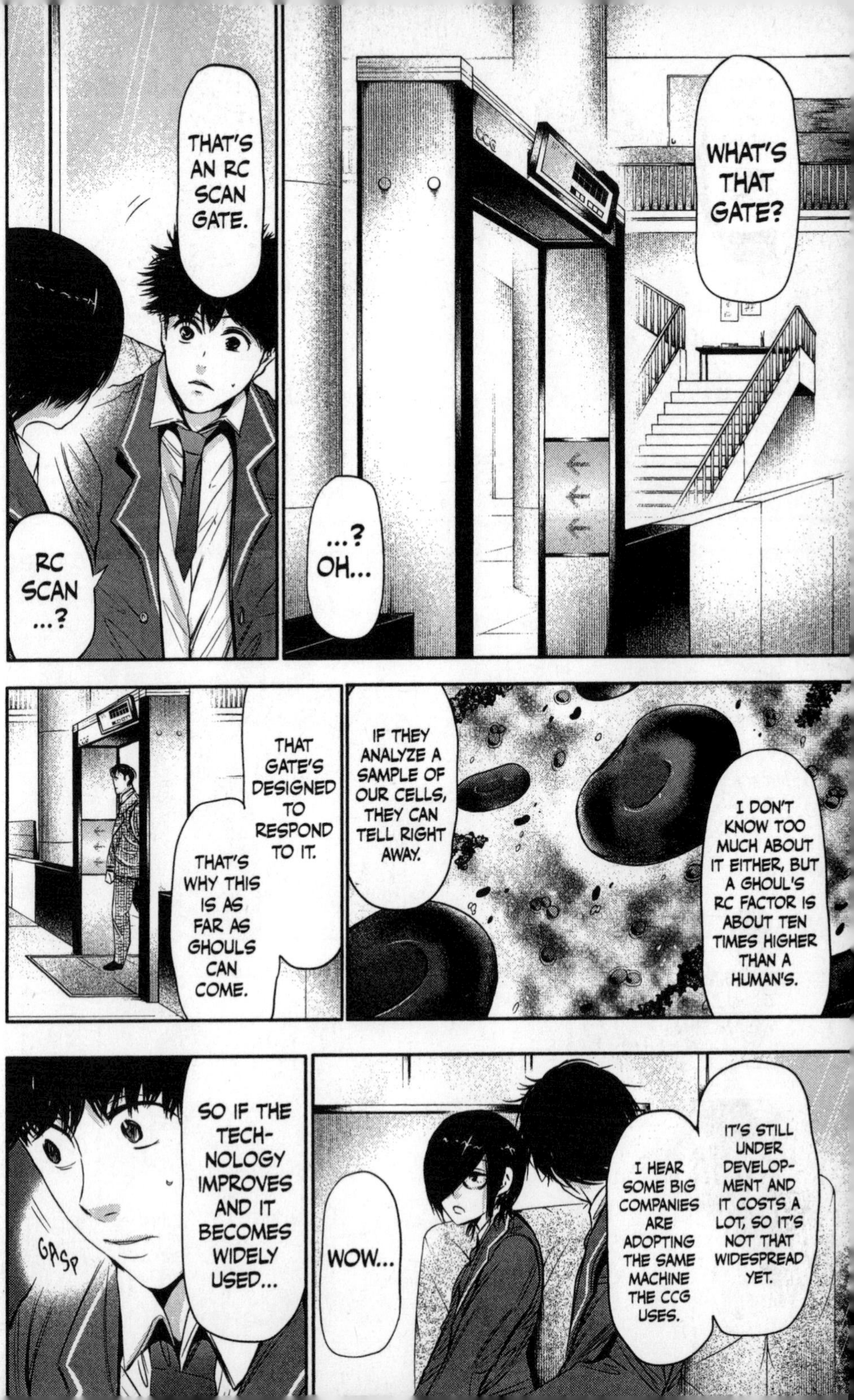
WHAT'S THAT GATE?
...? OH...
THAT'S AN RC SCAN GATE.
RC SCAN ...?
I DON'T KNOW TOO MUCH ABOUT IT EITHER, BUT A GHOUL'S RC FACTOR IS ABOUT TEN TIMES HIGHER THAN A HUMAN'S.
IF THEY ANALYZE A SAMPLE OF OUR CELLS, THEY CAN TELL RIGHT AWAY.
THAT GATE'S DESIGNED TO RESPOND TO IT.
THAT'S WHY THIS IS AS FAR AS GHOULS CAN COME.
IT'S STILL UNDER DEVELOPMENT AND IT COSTS A LOT, SO IT'S NOT THAT WIDESPREAD YET.
I HEAR SOME BIG COMPANIES ARE ADOPTING THE SAME MACHINE THE CCG USES.
WOW...
SO IF THE TECHNOLOGY IMPROVES AND IT BECOMES WIDELY USED...
GASP

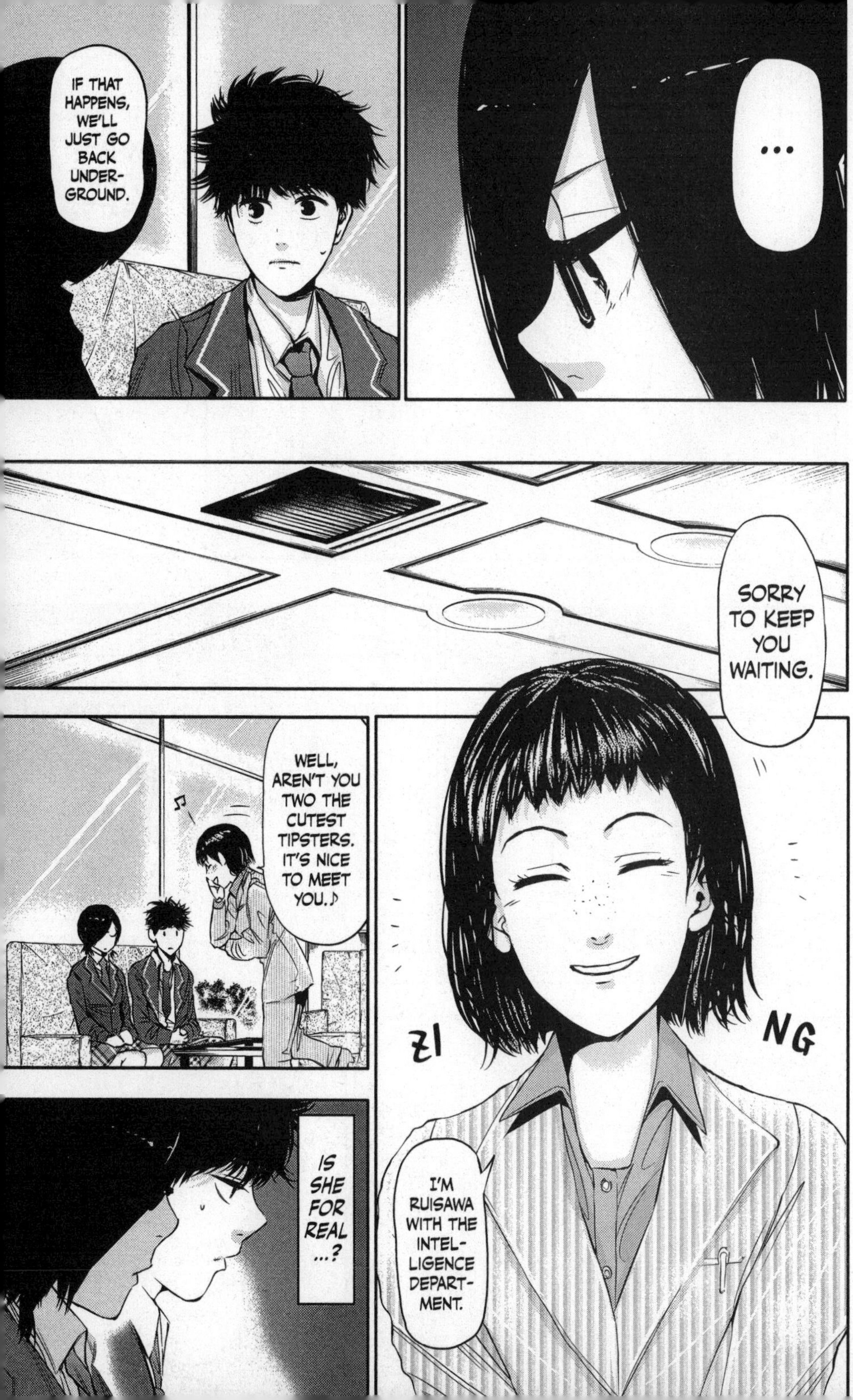
...
IF THAT HAPPENS, WE'LL JUST GO BACK UNDER-GROUND.
SORRY TO KEEP YOU WAITING.
ZI NG
I'M RUISAWA WITH THE INTEL-LIGENCE DEPART-MENT.
WELL, AREN'T YOU TWO THE CUTEST TIPSTERS. IT'S NICE TO MEET YOU.♪
IS SHE FOR REAL ...?

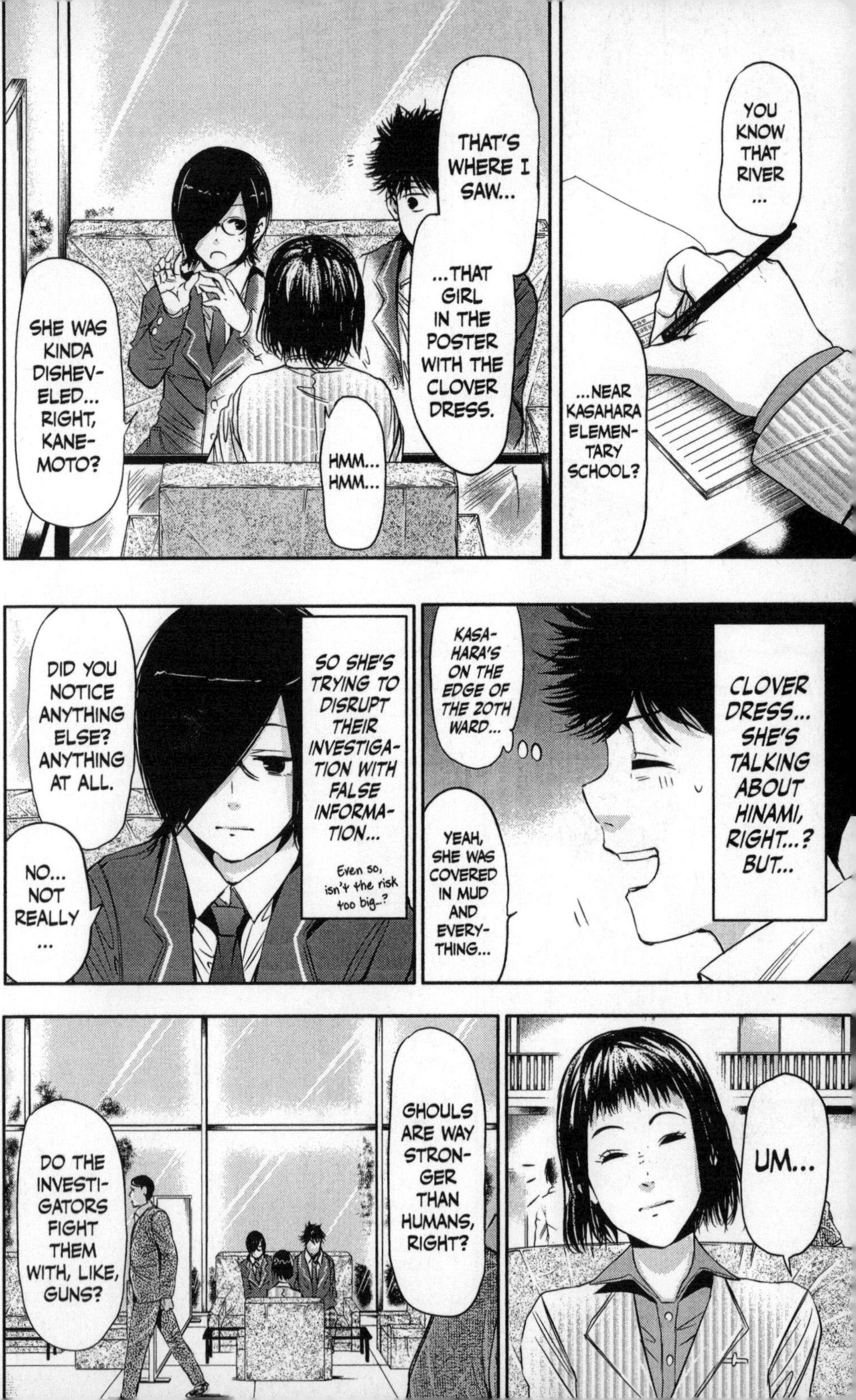
YOU KNOW THAT RIVER ...
...NEAR KASAHARA ELEMENTARY SCHOOL?
THAT'S WHERE I SAW...
...THAT GIRL IN THE POSTER WITH THE CLOVER DRESS.
SHE WAS KINDA DISHEVELED... RIGHT, KANEMOTO?
HMM... HMM...
CLOVER DRESS... SHE'S TALKING ABOUT HINAMI, RIGHT...? BUT...
KASAHARA'S ON THE EDGE OF THE 20TH WARD...
YEAH, SHE WAS COVERED IN MUD AND EVERYTHING...
SO SHE'S TRYING TO DISRUPT THEIR INVESTIGATION WITH FALSE INFORMATION...
Even so, isn't the risk too big...?
DID YOU NOTICE ANYTHING ELSE? ANYTHING AT ALL.
NO... NOT REALLY ...
UM...
GHOULS ARE WAY STRONGER THAN HUMANS, RIGHT?
DO THE INVESTIGATORS FIGHT THEM WITH, LIKE, GUNS?

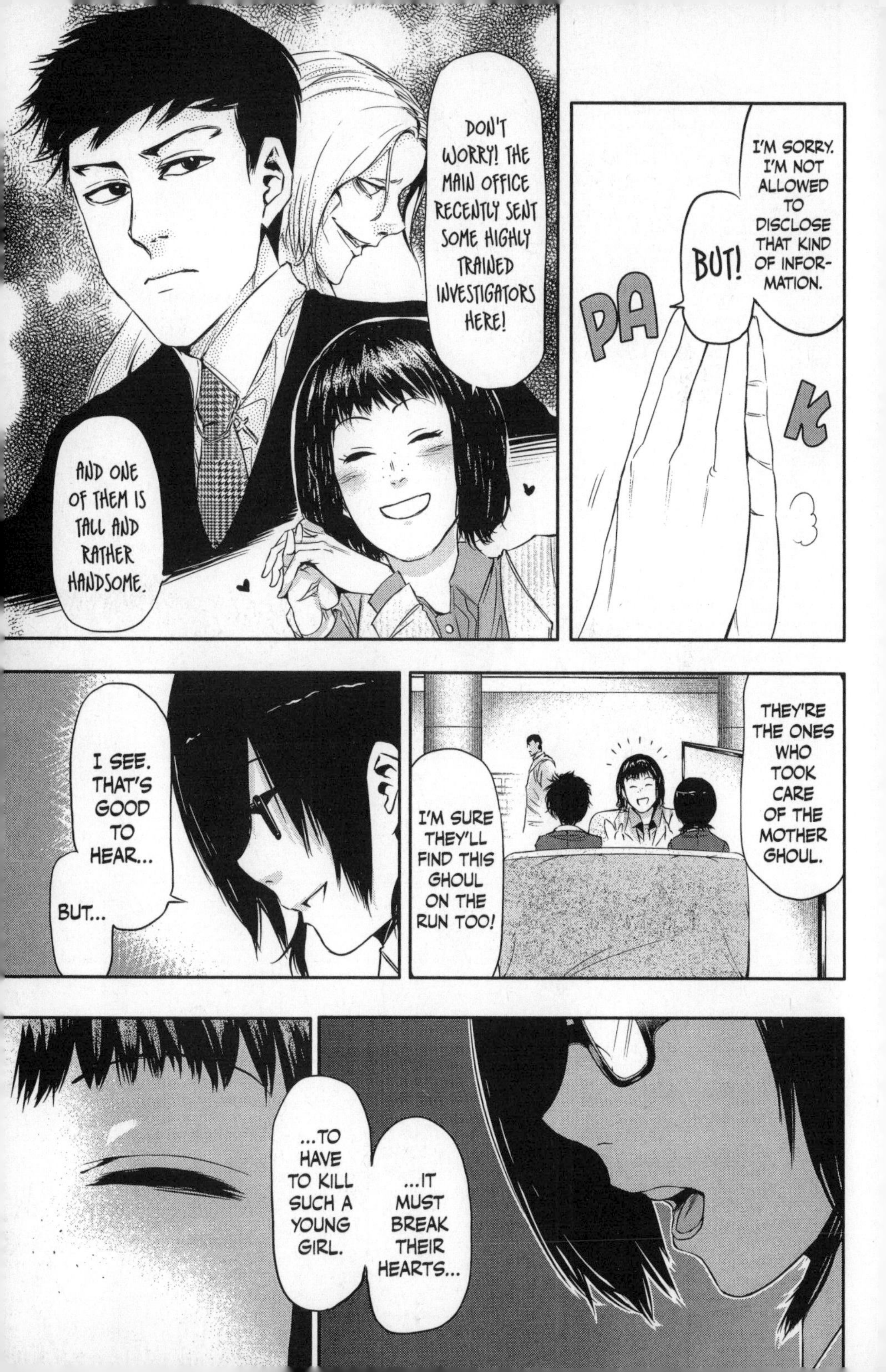
I'M SORRY. I'M NOT ALLOWED TO DISCLOSE THAT KIND OF INFORMATION.
BUT!
PA
K
DON'T WORRY! THE MAIN OFFICE RECENTLY SENT SOME HIGHLY TRAINED INVESTIGATORS HERE!
AND ONE OF THEM IS TALL AND RATHER HANDSOME.
THEY'RE THE ONES WHO TOOK CARE OF THE MOTHER GHOUL.
I'M SURE THEY'LL FIND THIS GHOUL ON THE RUN TOO!
I SEE. THAT'S GOOD TO HEAR...
BUT...
...TO HAVE TO KILL SUCH A YOUNG GIRL.
...IT MUST BREAK THEIR HEARTS...

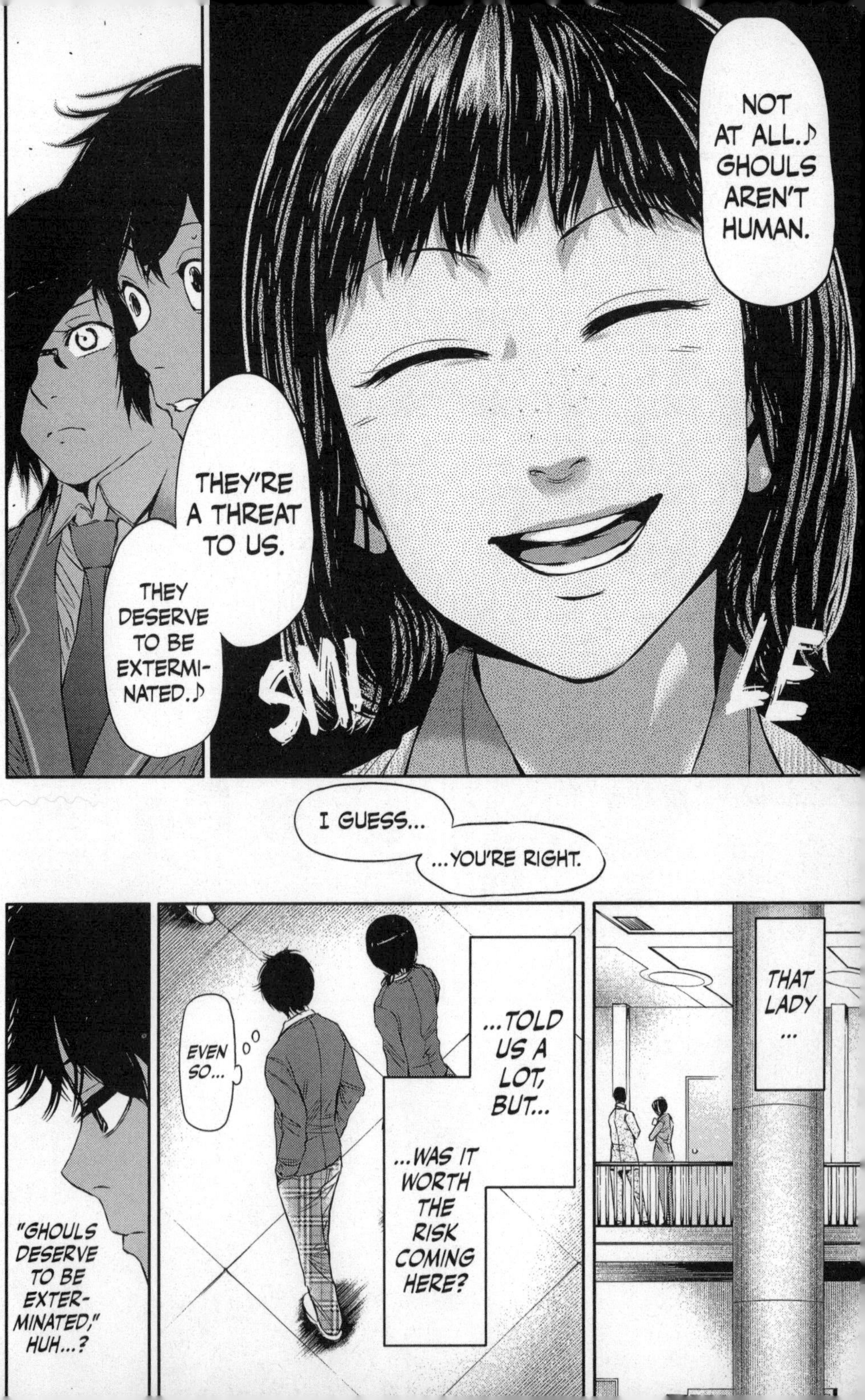
NOT AT ALL.♪ GHOULS AREN'T HUMAN.
THEY'RE A THREAT TO US.
THEY DESERVE TO BE EXTERMINATED.♪
SMILE
I GUESS...
...YOU'RE RIGHT.
THAT LADY ...
...TOLD US A LOT, BUT...
...WAS IT WORTH THE RISK COMING HERE?
EVEN SO...
"GHOULS DESERVE TO BE EXTERMINATED," HUH...?

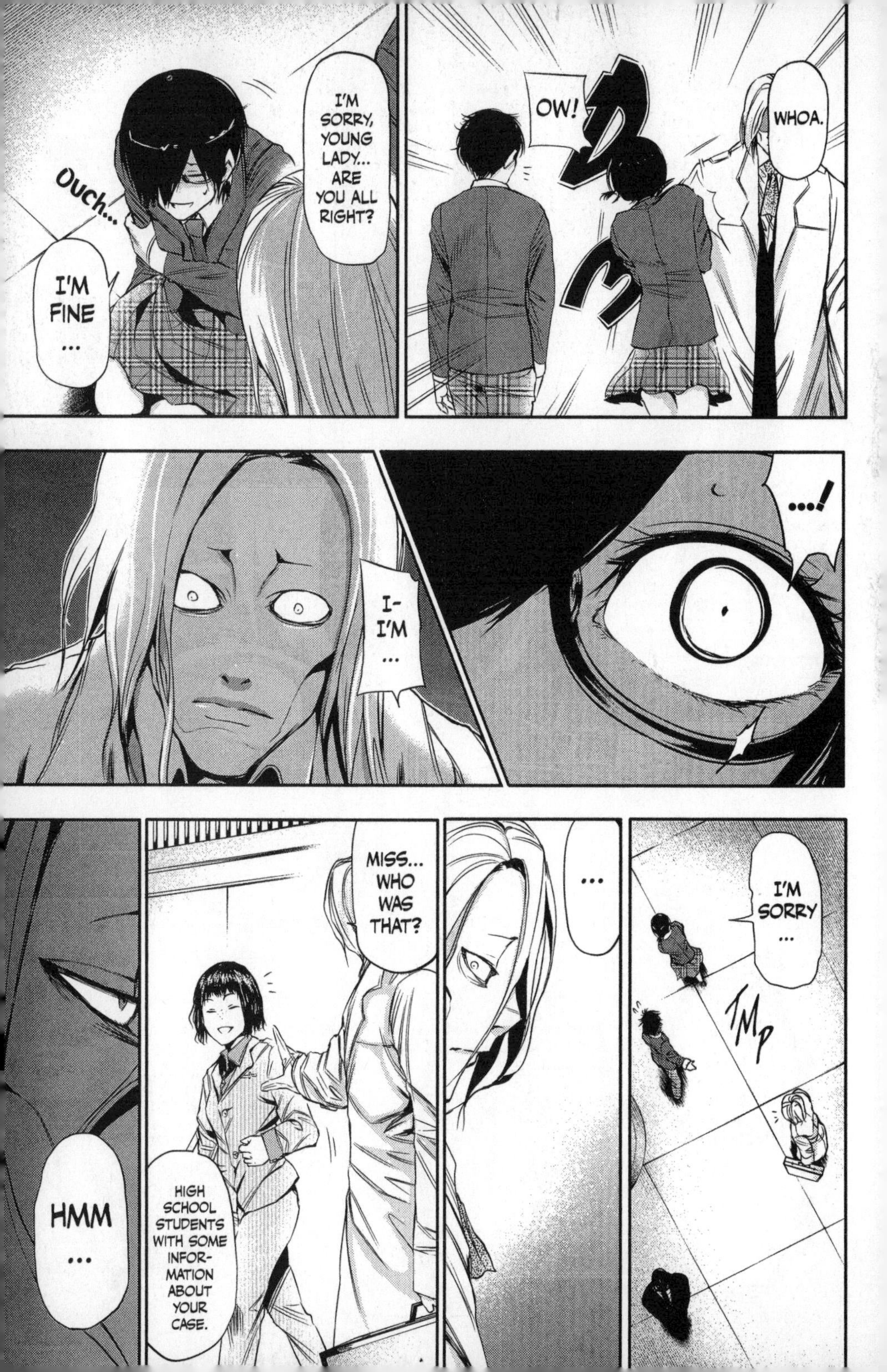
WHOA.
OW!
I'M SORRY, YOUNG LADY... ARE YOU ALL RIGHT?
Ouch...
I'M FINE ...
...!
I- I'M ...
I'M SORRY ...
TMP
...
MISS... WHO WAS THAT?
HIGH SCHOOL STUDENTS WITH SOME INFOR-MATION ABOUT YOUR CASE.
HMM ...

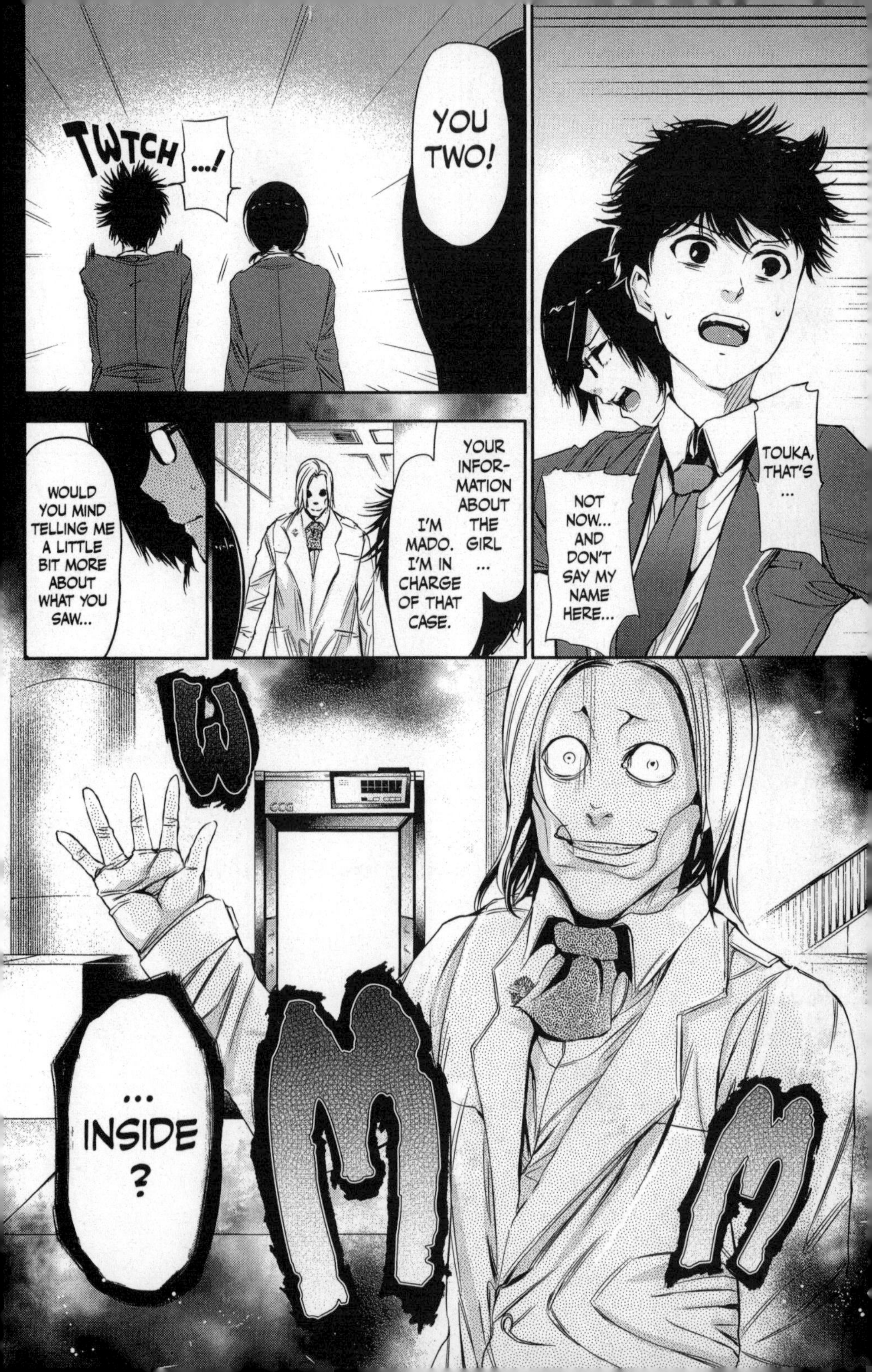
TOUKA, THAT'S ...
NOT NOW... AND DON'T SAY MY NAME HERE...
YOU TWO!
...!
TWTCH
YOUR INFORMATION ABOUT THE GIRL ...
I'M MADO. I'M IN CHARGE OF THAT CASE.
WOULD YOU MIND TELLING ME A LITTLE BIT MORE ABOUT WHAT YOU SAW...
... INSIDE ?

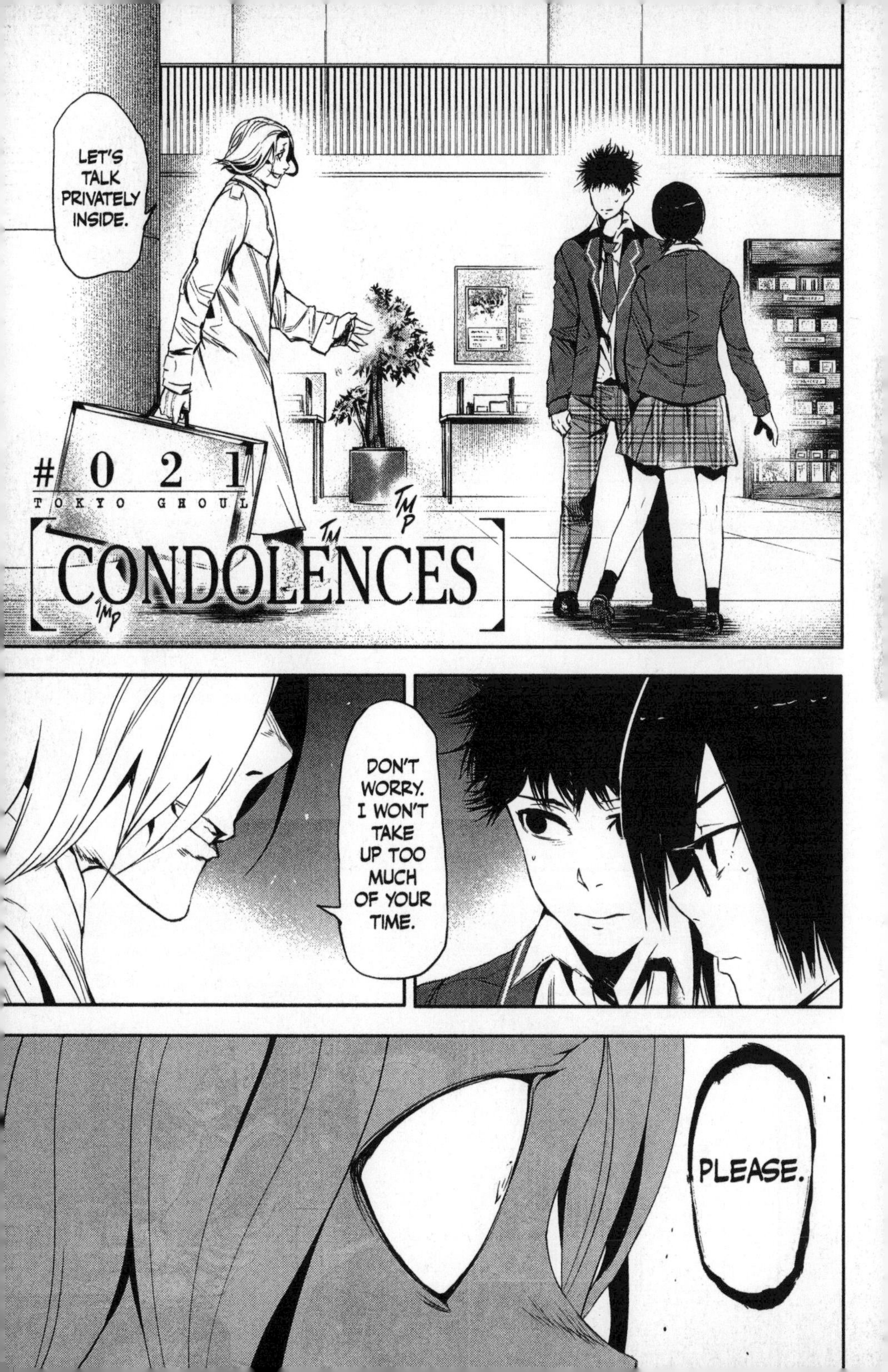

LET'S TALK PRIVATELY INSIDE.
TMP
TM
TMP
#021
TOKYO GHOUL
CONDOLENCES
DON'T WORRY. I WON'T TAKE UP TOO MUCH OF YOUR TIME.
PLEASE.

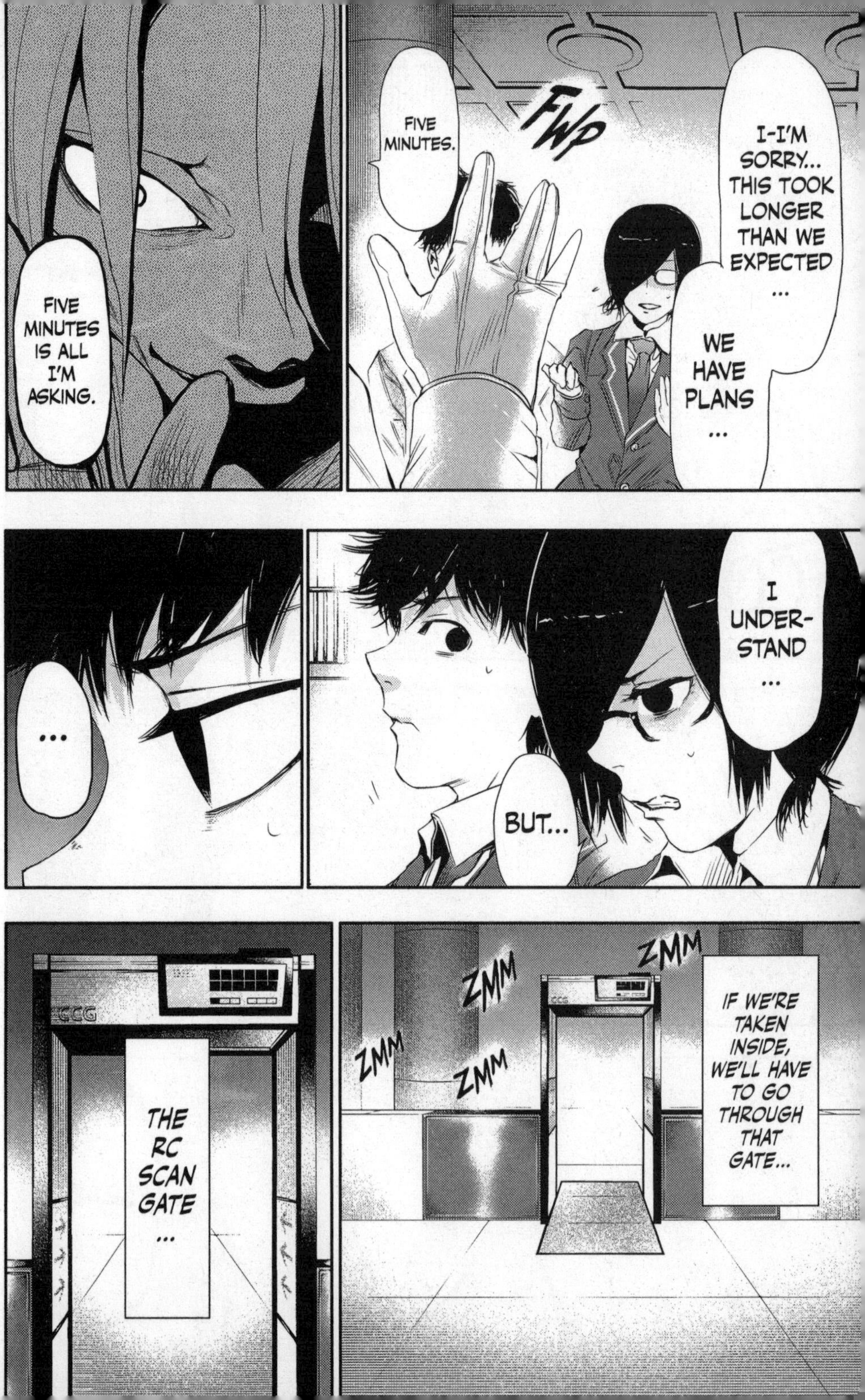
I-I'M SORRY... THIS TOOK LONGER THAN WE EXPECTED ...
WE HAVE PLANS ...
FWP
FIVE MINUTES.
FIVE MINUTES IS ALL I'M ASKING.
I UNDER-STAND ...
BUT...
...
ZMM
ZMM
ZMM
ZMM
CCG
IF WE'RE TAKEN INSIDE, WE'LL HAVE TO GO THROUGH THAT GATE...
CCG
THE RC SCAN GATE ...

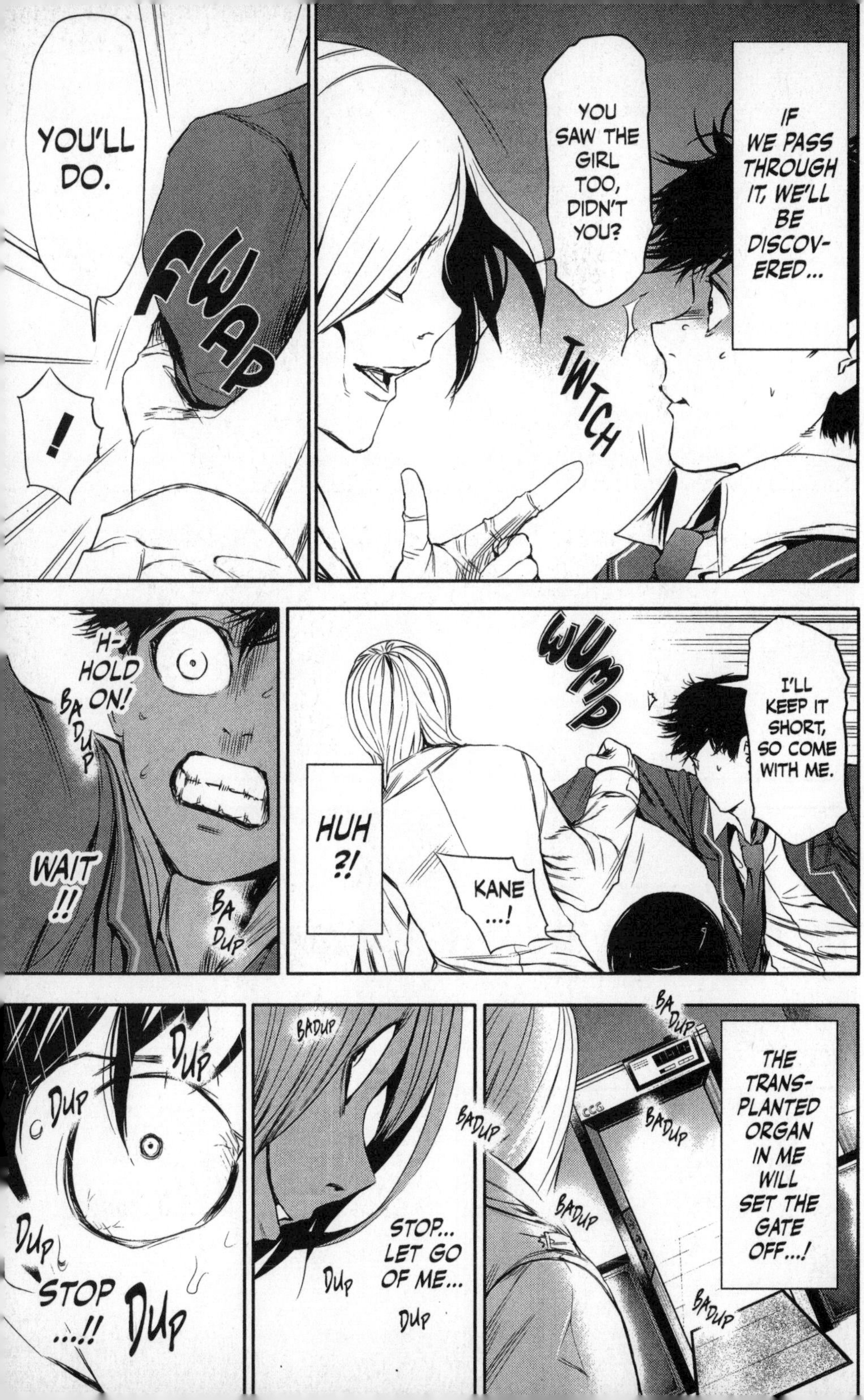
IF WE PASS THROUGH IT, WE'LL BE DISCOVERED...
YOU SAW THE GIRL TOO, DIDN'T YOU?
TWTCH
YOU'LL DO.
FWAP
!
I'LL KEEP IT SHORT, SO COME WITH ME.
WUMP
HUH ?!
KANE ...!
H-HOLD ON!
BADUP
WAIT !!
BA DUP
BADUP
THE TRANS-PLANTED ORGAN IN ME WILL SET THE GATE OFF...!
BADUP
BADUP
BADUP
BADUP
BADUP
STOP... LET GO OF ME...
DUP
DUP
DUP
DUP
DUP
STOP ...!!
DUP

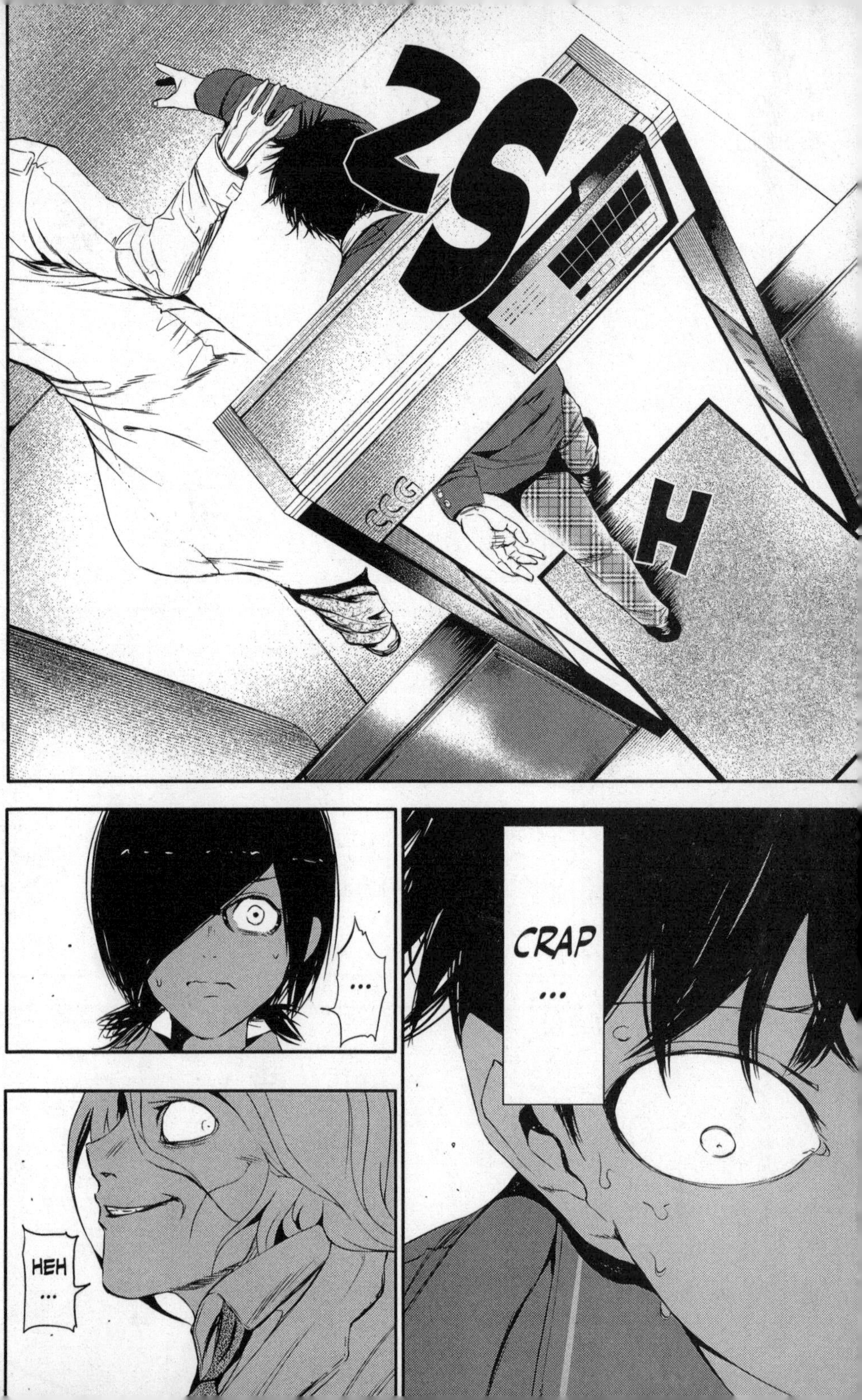
CRAP ...
...
HEH ...

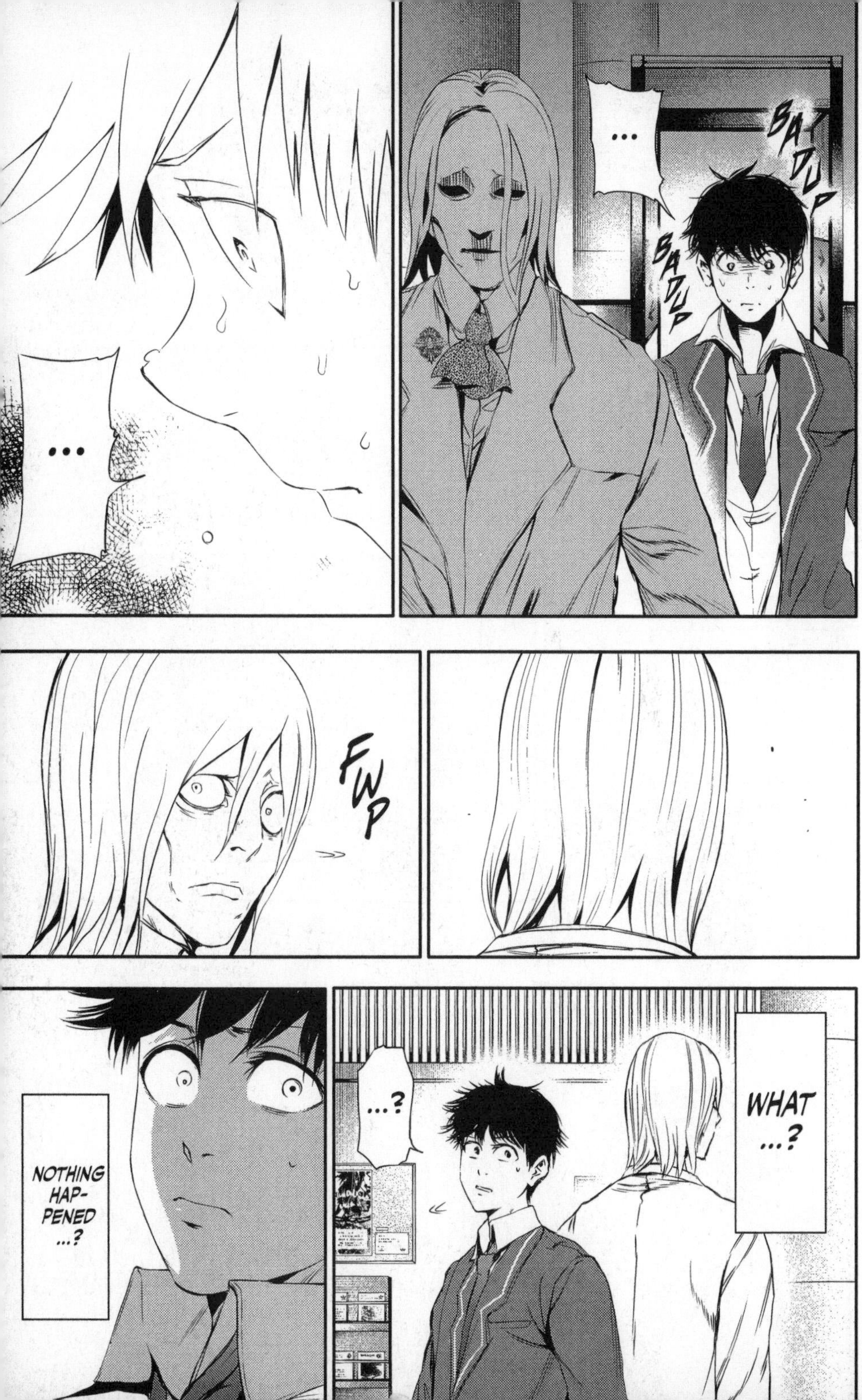
...
BADUP
BADUP
...
FWP
WHAT ...?
...?
NOTHING HAP-PENED ...?

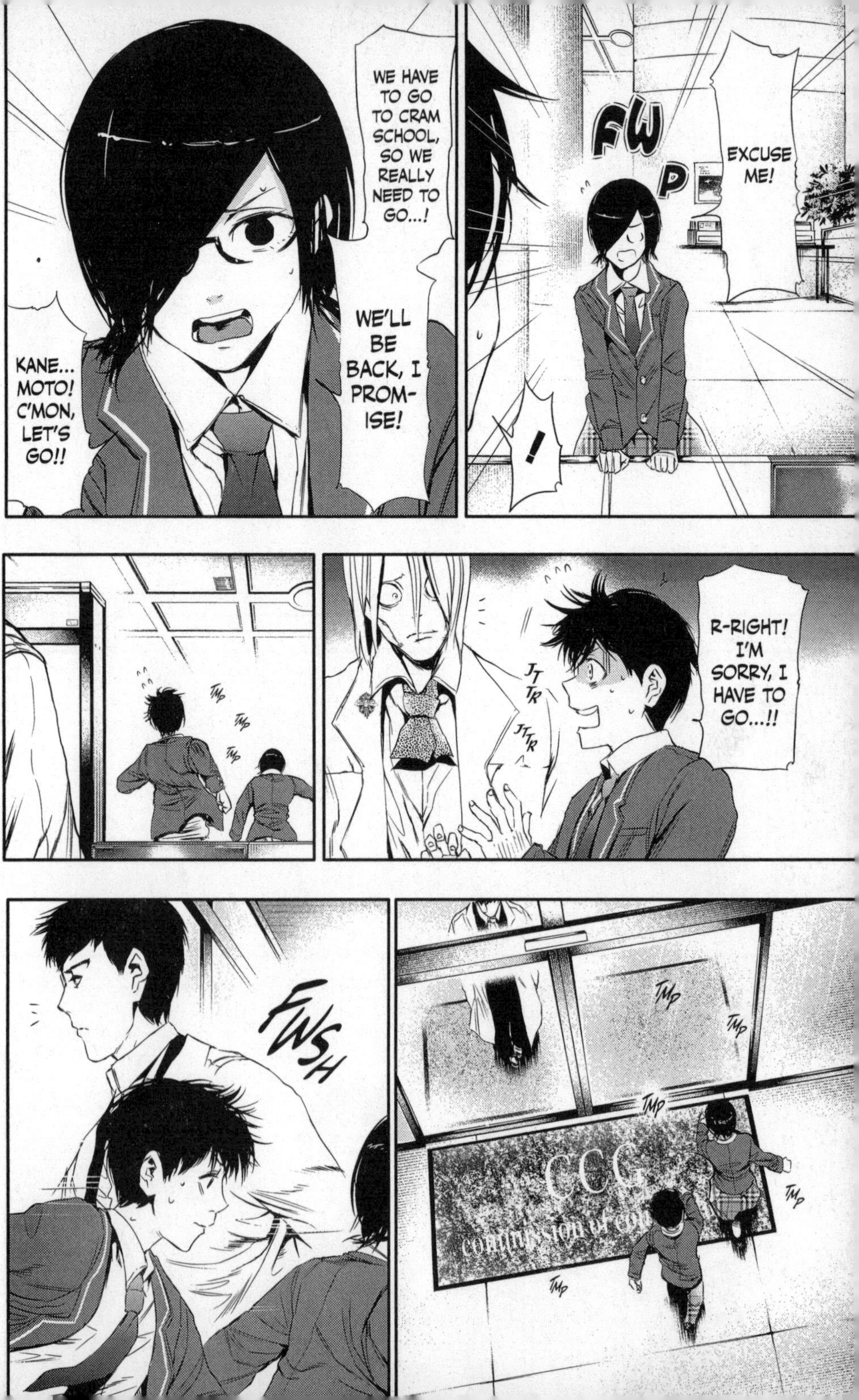
FWP
EXCUSE ME!
!
WE HAVE TO GO TO CRAM SCHOOL, SO WE REALLY NEED TO GO...!
WE'LL BE BACK, I PROMISE!
KANE... MOTO! C'MON, LET'S GO!!
R-RIGHT! I'M SORRY, I HAVE TO GO...!!
JTTR
JTTR
TMP
TMP
TMP
TMP
TMP
TMP
TMP
TMP
FWSH

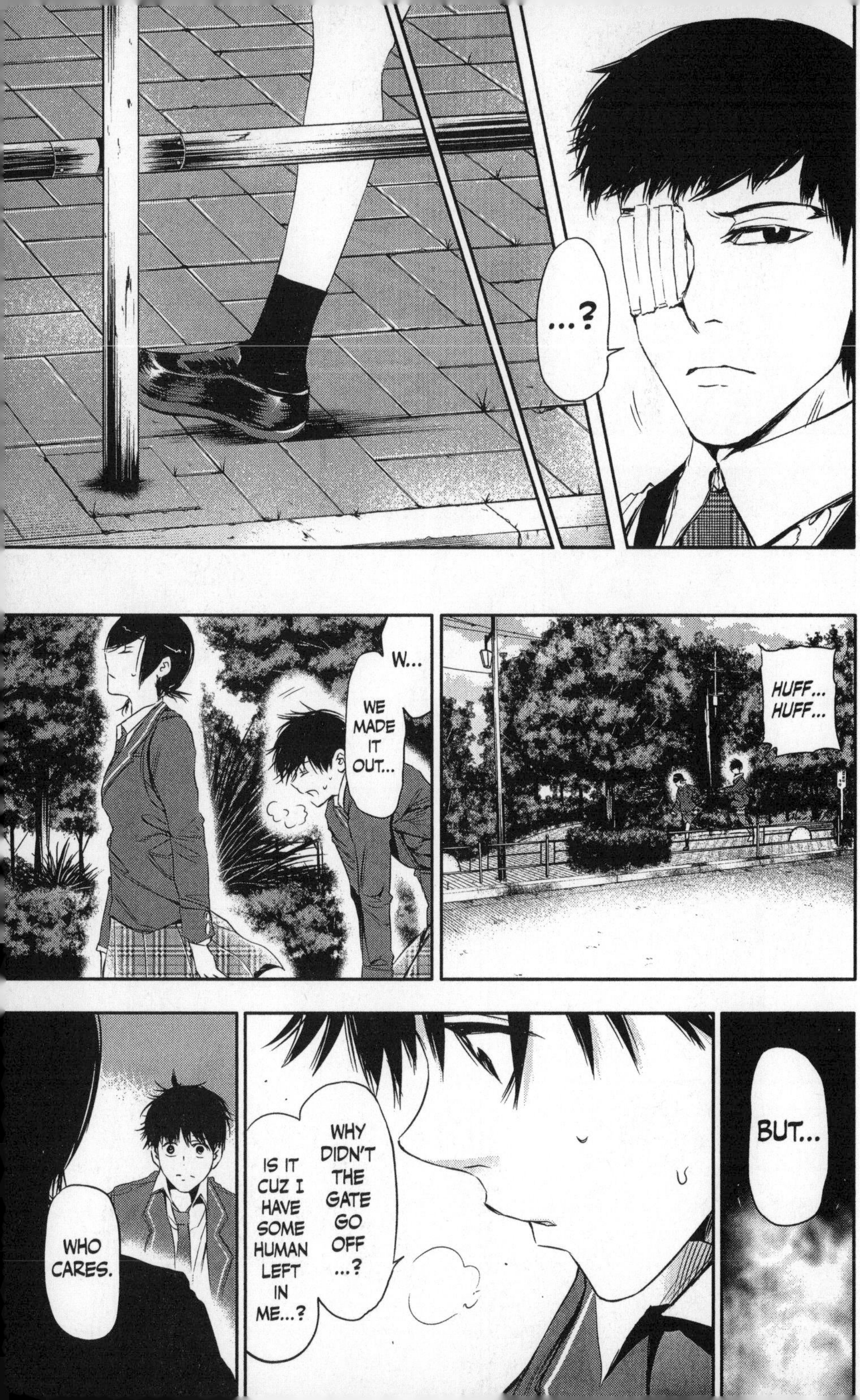
...?
HUFF... HUFF...
W...
WE MADE IT OUT...
BUT...
WHY DIDN'T THE GATE GO OFF...?
IS IT CUZ I HAVE SOME HUMAN LEFT IN ME...?
WHO CARES.

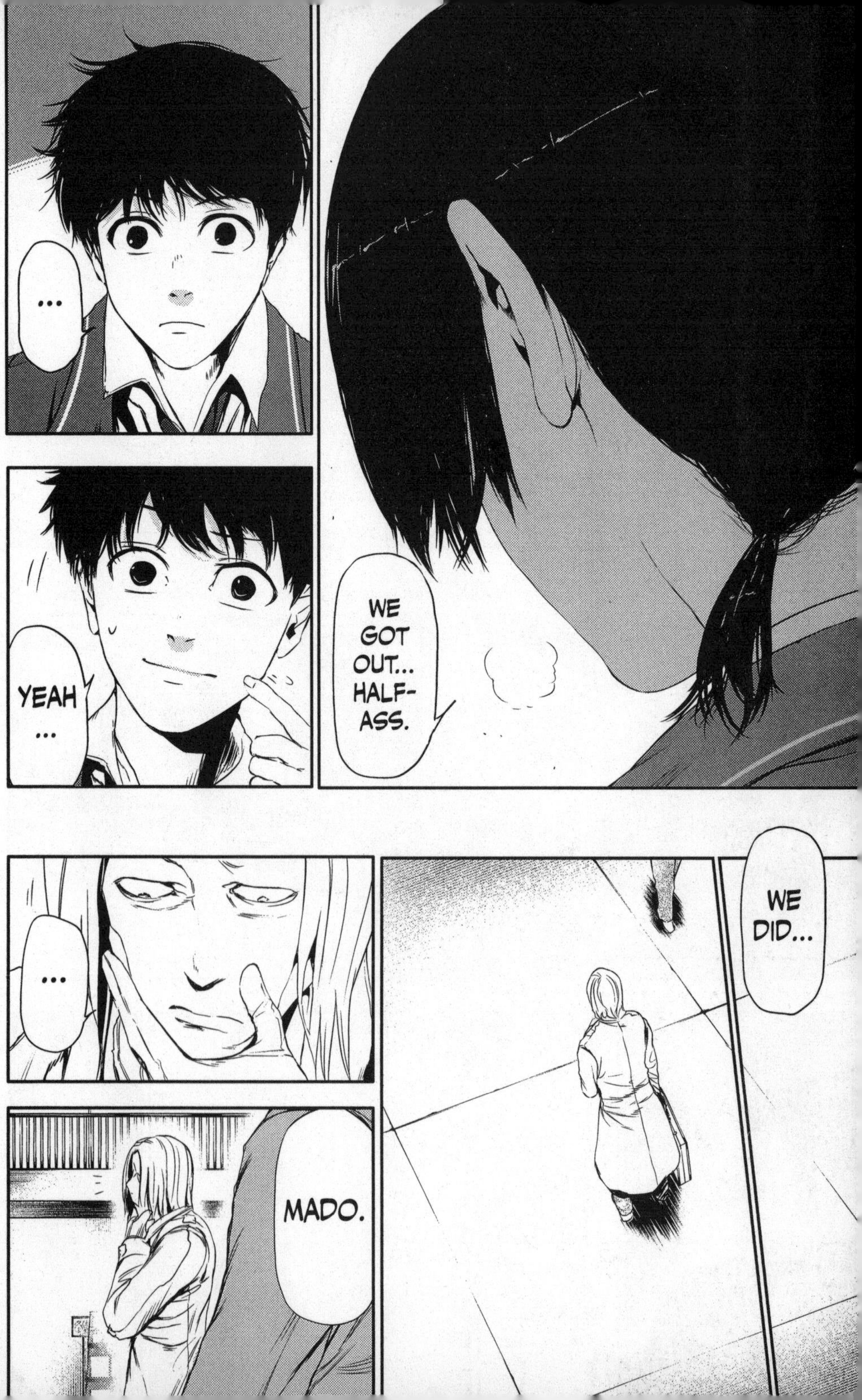

WE GOT OUT... HALF-ASS.
...
YEAH ...
WE DID...
...
MADO.

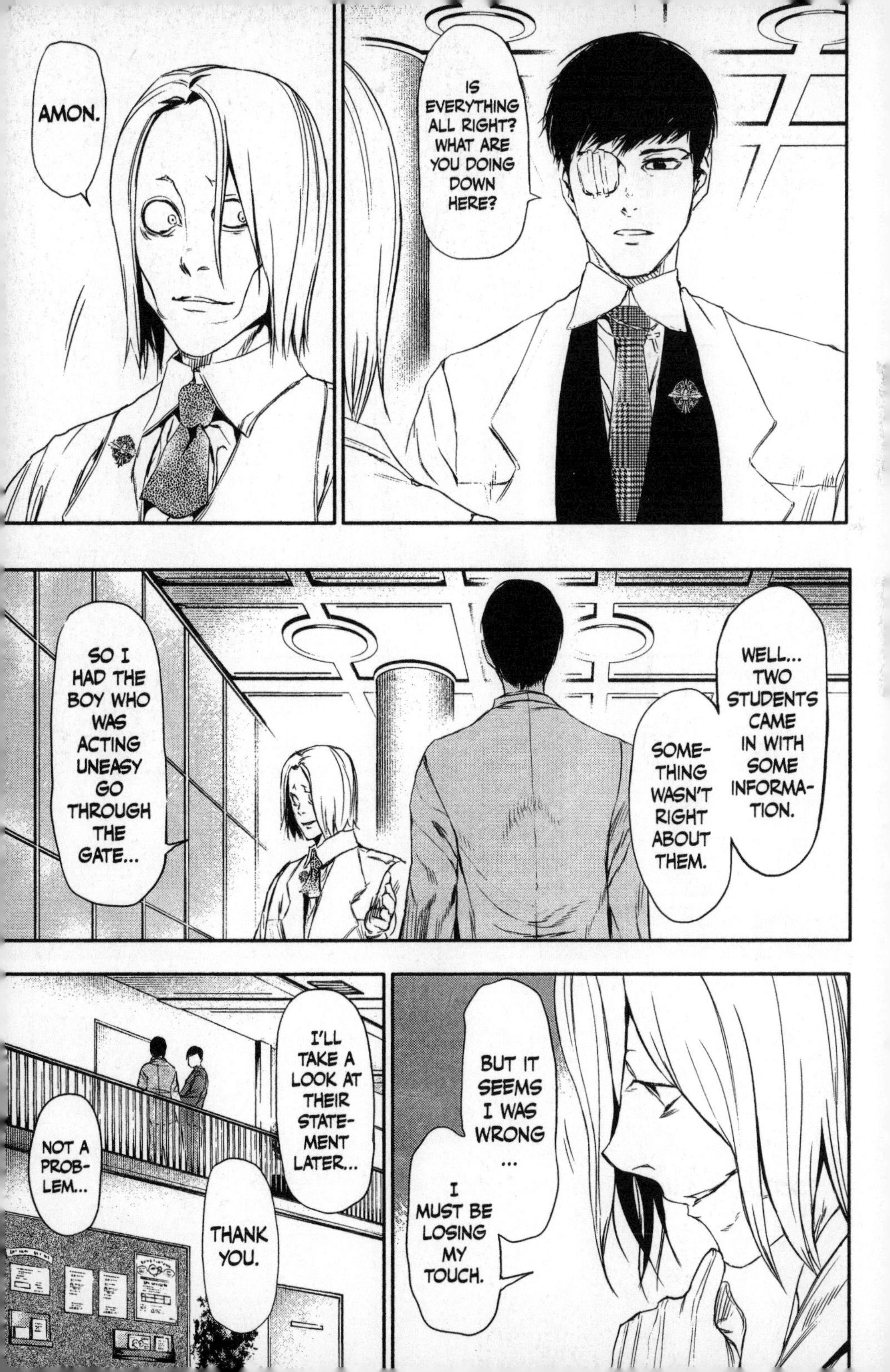
IS EVERYTHING ALL RIGHT? WHAT ARE YOU DOING DOWN HERE?
AMON.
WELL... TWO STUDENTS CAME IN WITH SOME INFORMATION.
SOMETHING WASN'T RIGHT ABOUT THEM.
SO I HAD THE BOY WHO WAS ACTING UNEASY GO THROUGH THE GATE...
BUT IT SEEMS I WAS WRONG ...
I MUST BE LOSING MY TOUCH.
I'LL TAKE A LOOK AT THEIR STATEMENT LATER...
NOT A PROBLEM...
THANK YOU.

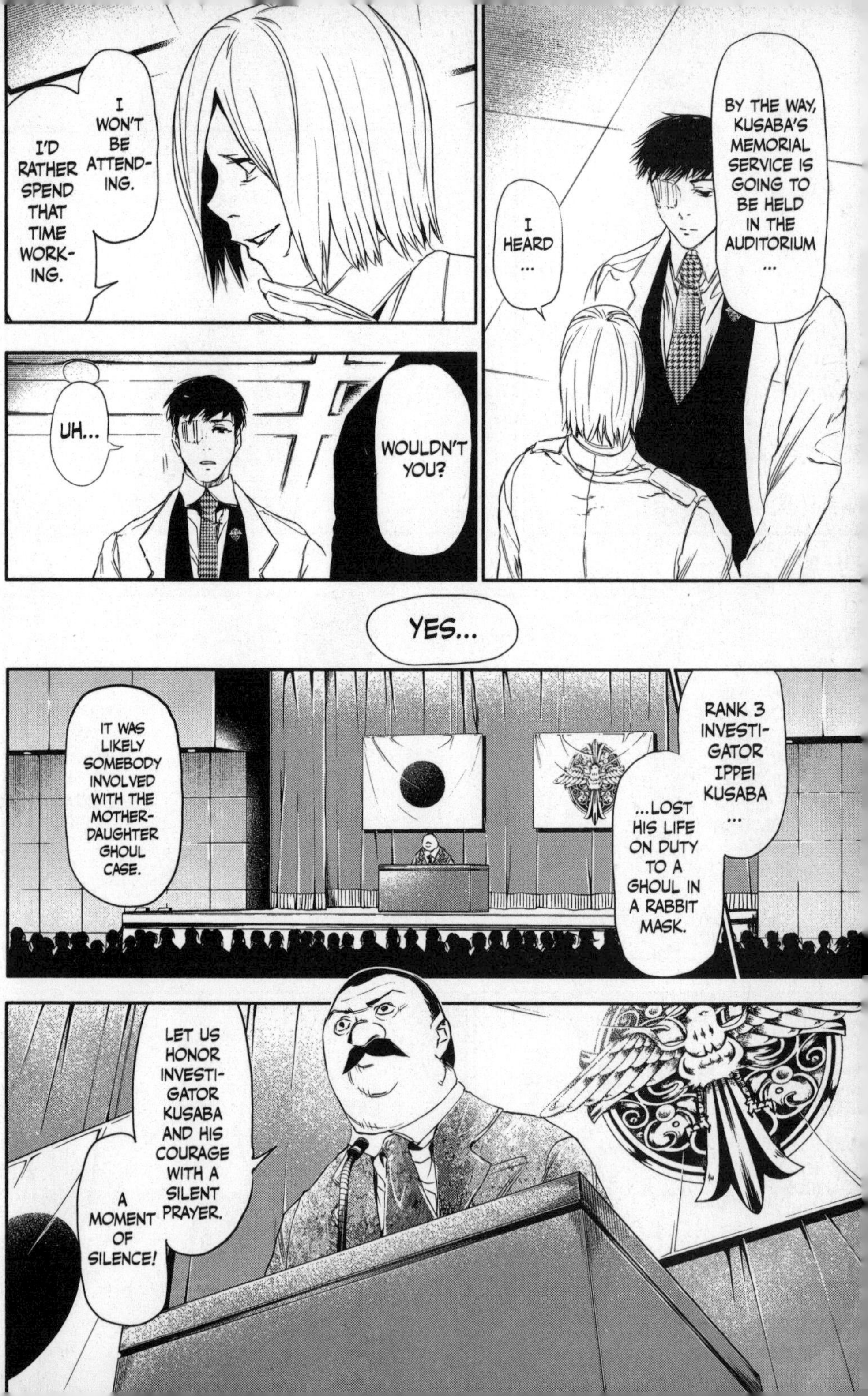
BY THE WAY, KUSABA'S MEMORIAL SERVICE IS GOING TO BE HELD IN THE AUDITORIUM...
I HEARD...
I WON'T BE ATTENDING.
I'D RATHER SPEND THAT TIME WORKING.
WOULDN'T YOU?
UH...
YES...
RANK 3 INVESTIGATOR IPPEI KUSABA...
...LOST HIS LIFE ON DUTY TO A GHOUL IN A RABBIT MASK.
IT WAS LIKELY SOMEBODY INVOLVED WITH THE MOTHER-DAUGHTER GHOUL CASE.
LET US HONOR INVESTIGATOR KUSABA AND HIS COURAGE WITH A SILENT PRAYER.
A MOMENT OF SILENCE!

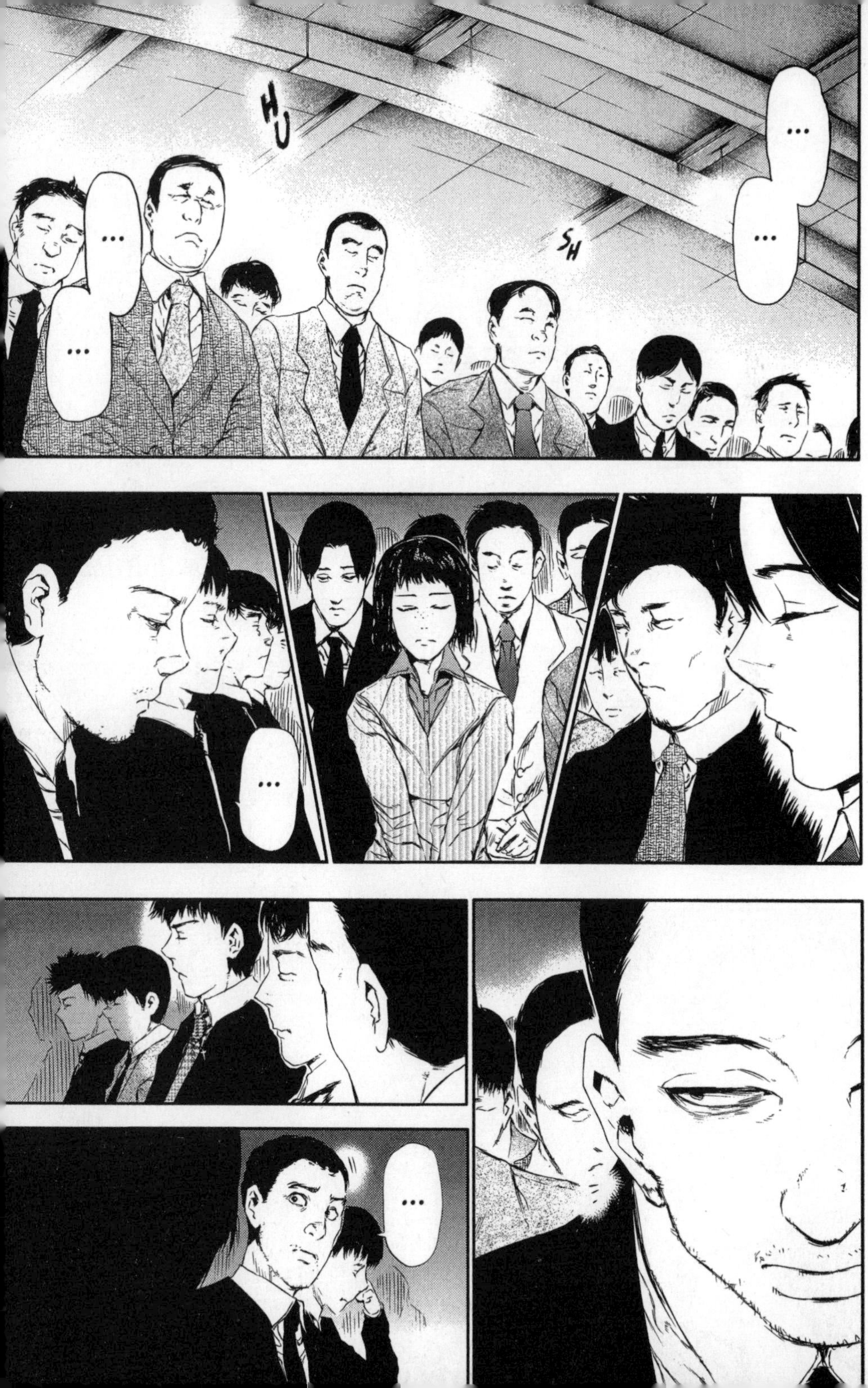
...
...
HU
SH
...
...
...
...

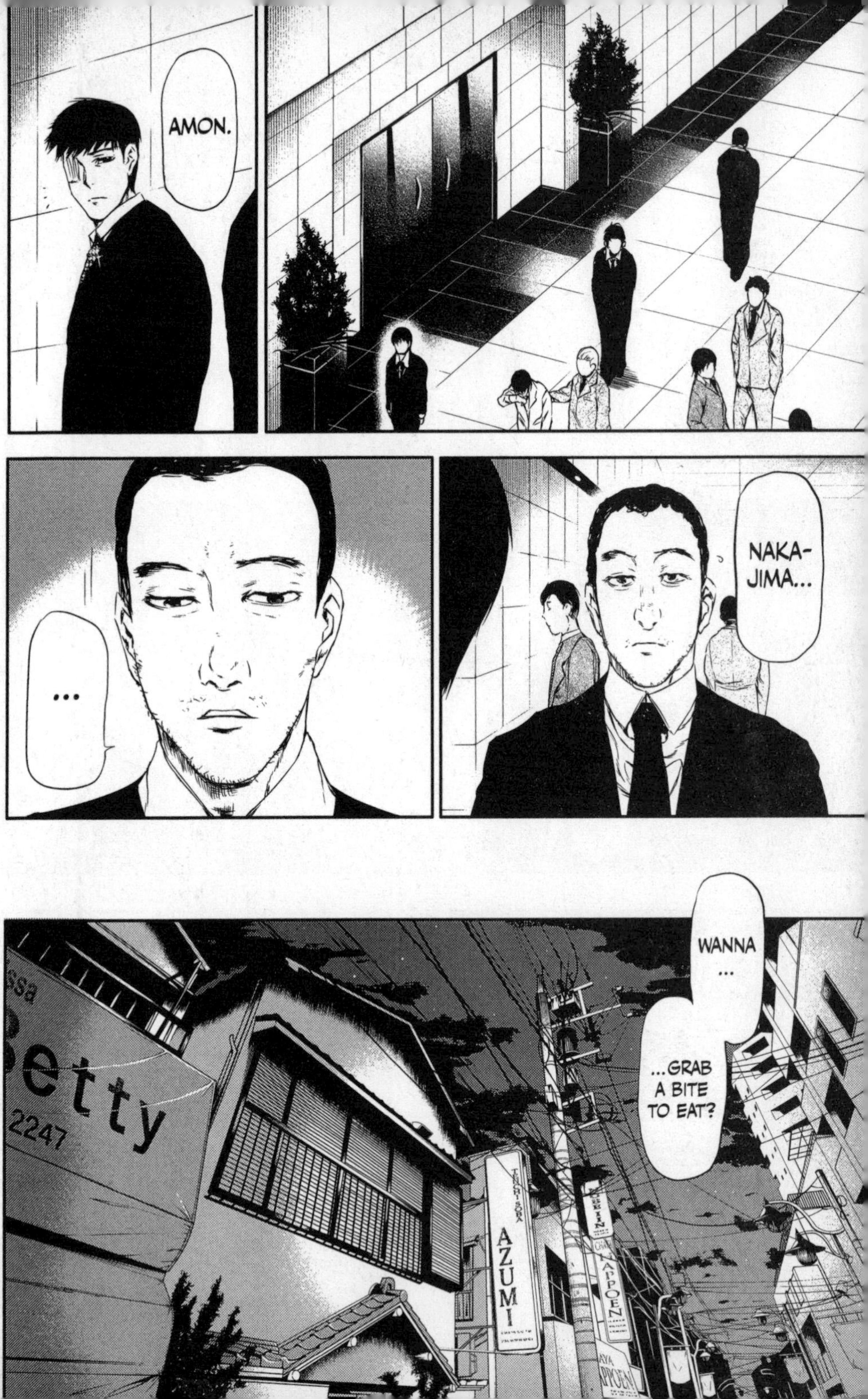
AMON.
NAKA-JIMA...
...
WANNA ...
...GRAB A BITE TO EAT?
AZUMI

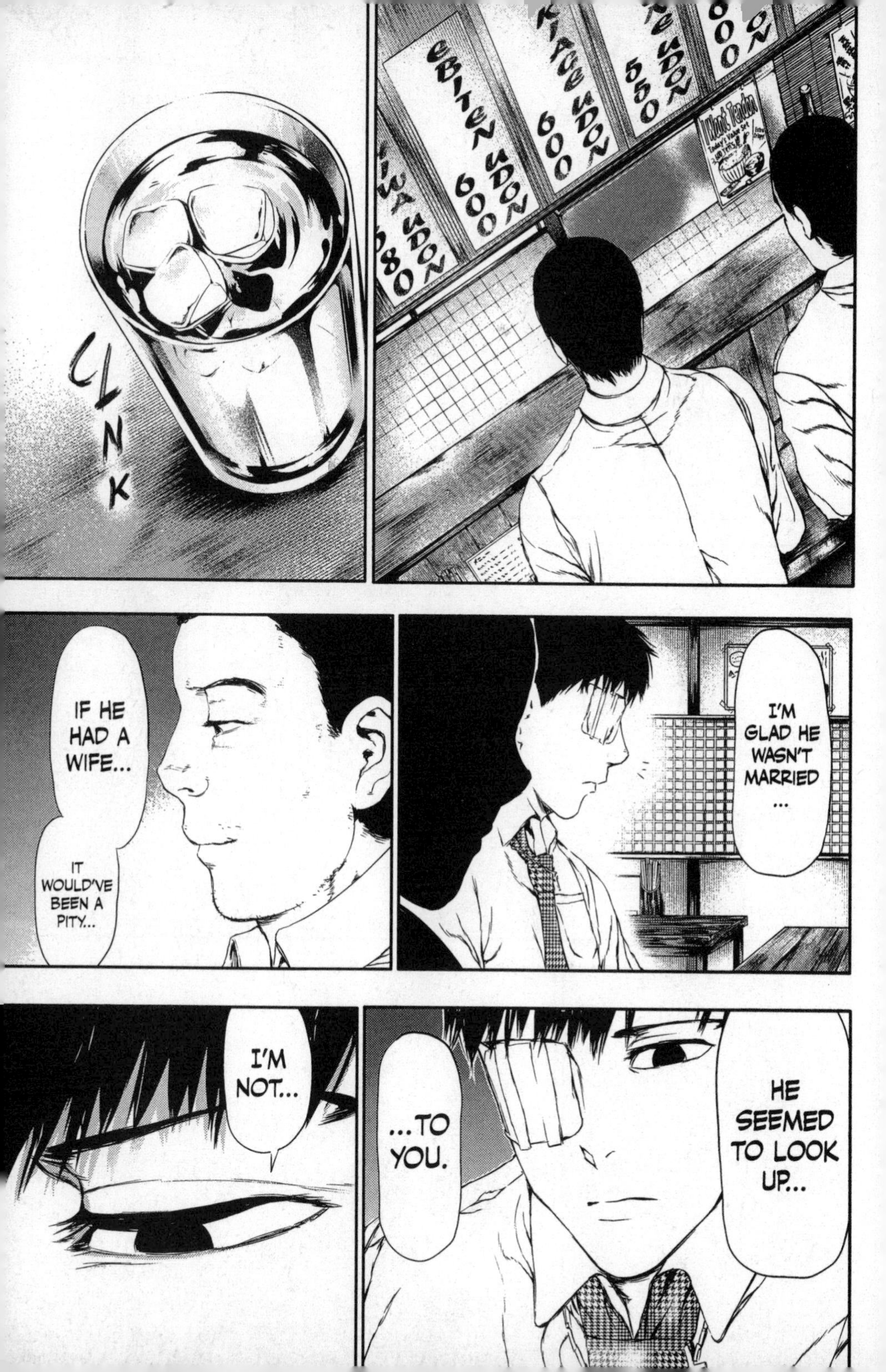
EBITEN UDON 600
KIAGE UDON 600
CLNK
I'M GLAD HE WASN'T MARRIED...
IF HE HAD A WIFE...
IT WOULD'VE BEEN A PITY...
HE SEEMED TO LOOK UP...
...TO YOU.
I'M NOT...

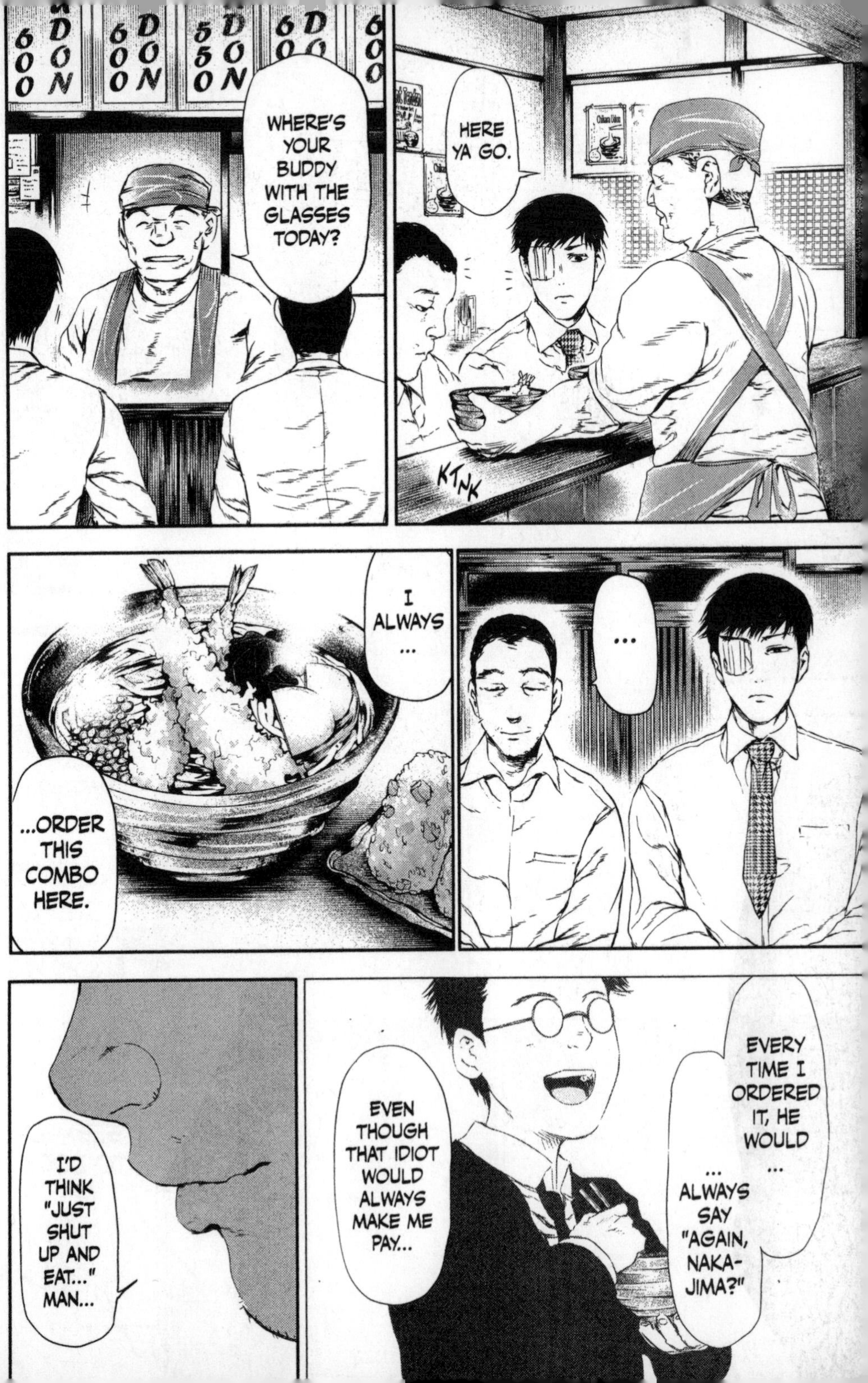
HERE YA GO.
KTNK
WHERE'S YOUR BUDDY WITH THE GLASSES TODAY?
...
I ALWAYS ...
...ORDER THIS COMBO HERE.
EVERY TIME I ORDERED IT, HE WOULD ...
... ALWAYS SAY "AGAIN, NAKA-JIMA?"
EVEN THOUGH THAT IDIOT WOULD ALWAYS MAKE ME PAY...
I'D THINK "JUST SHUT UP AND EAT..." MAN...

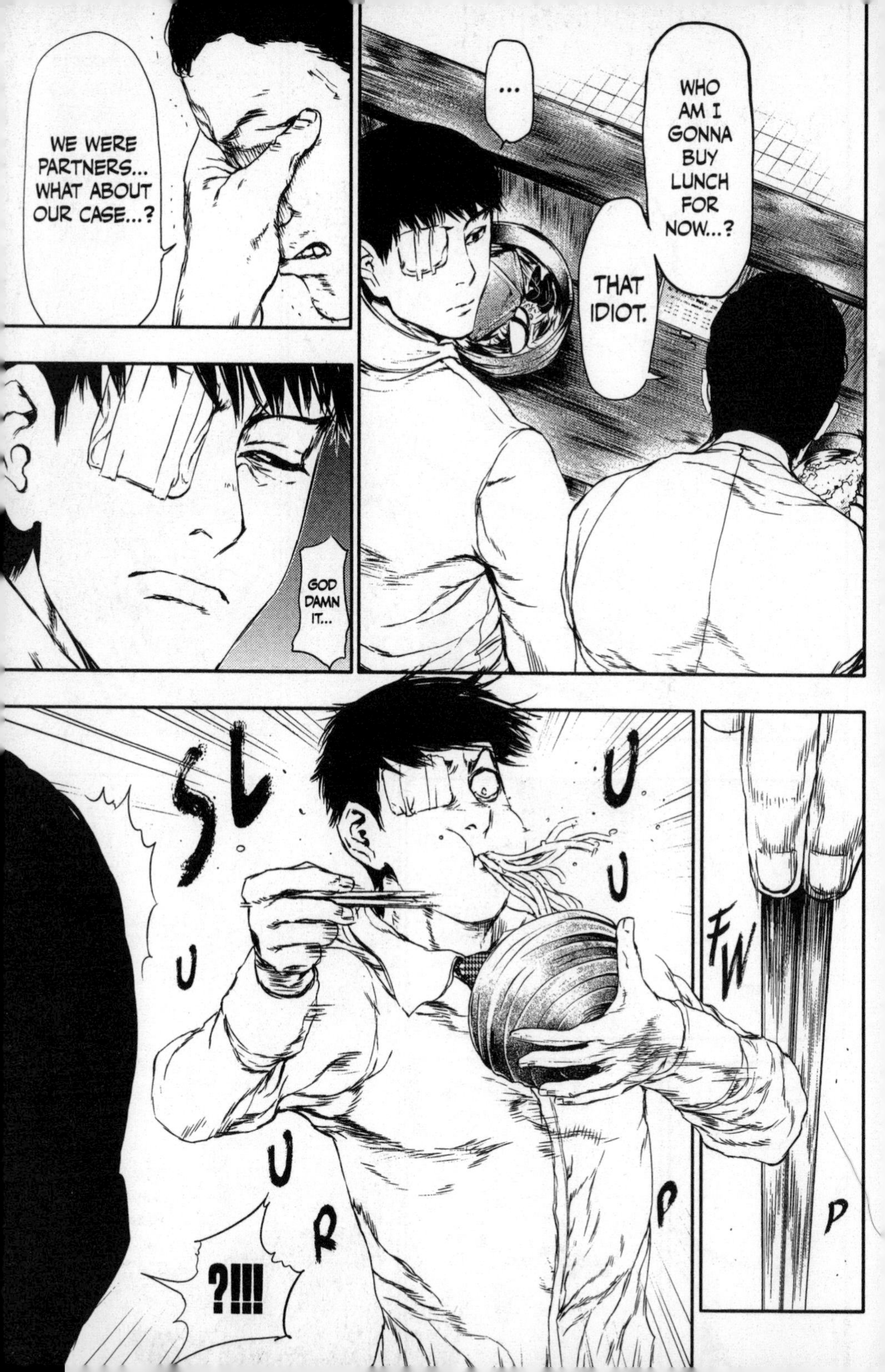
WHO AM I GONNA BUY LUNCH FOR NOW...?
...
THAT IDIOT.
WE WERE PARTNERS... WHAT ABOUT OUR CASE...?
GOD DAMN IT...
FWP
SLUUUURP
?!!!

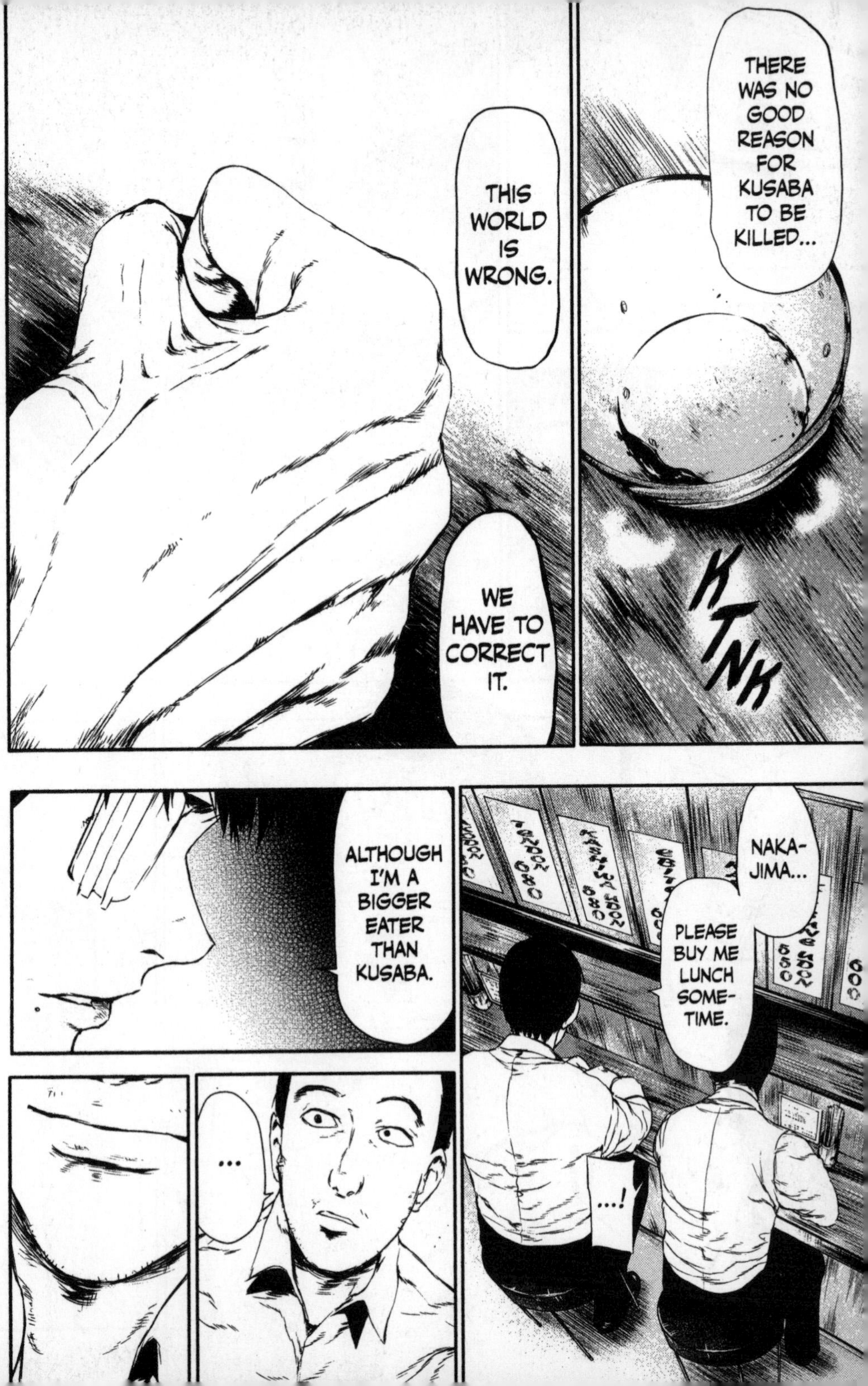
THERE WAS NO GOOD REASON FOR KUSABA TO BE KILLED...
KTNK
THIS WORLD IS WRONG.
WE HAVE TO CORRECT IT.
NAKAJIMA...
PLEASE BUY ME LUNCH SOMETIME.
TENDON 680
KASHIWA UDON 580
...!
ALTHOUGH I'M A BIGGER EATER THAN KUSABA.
...

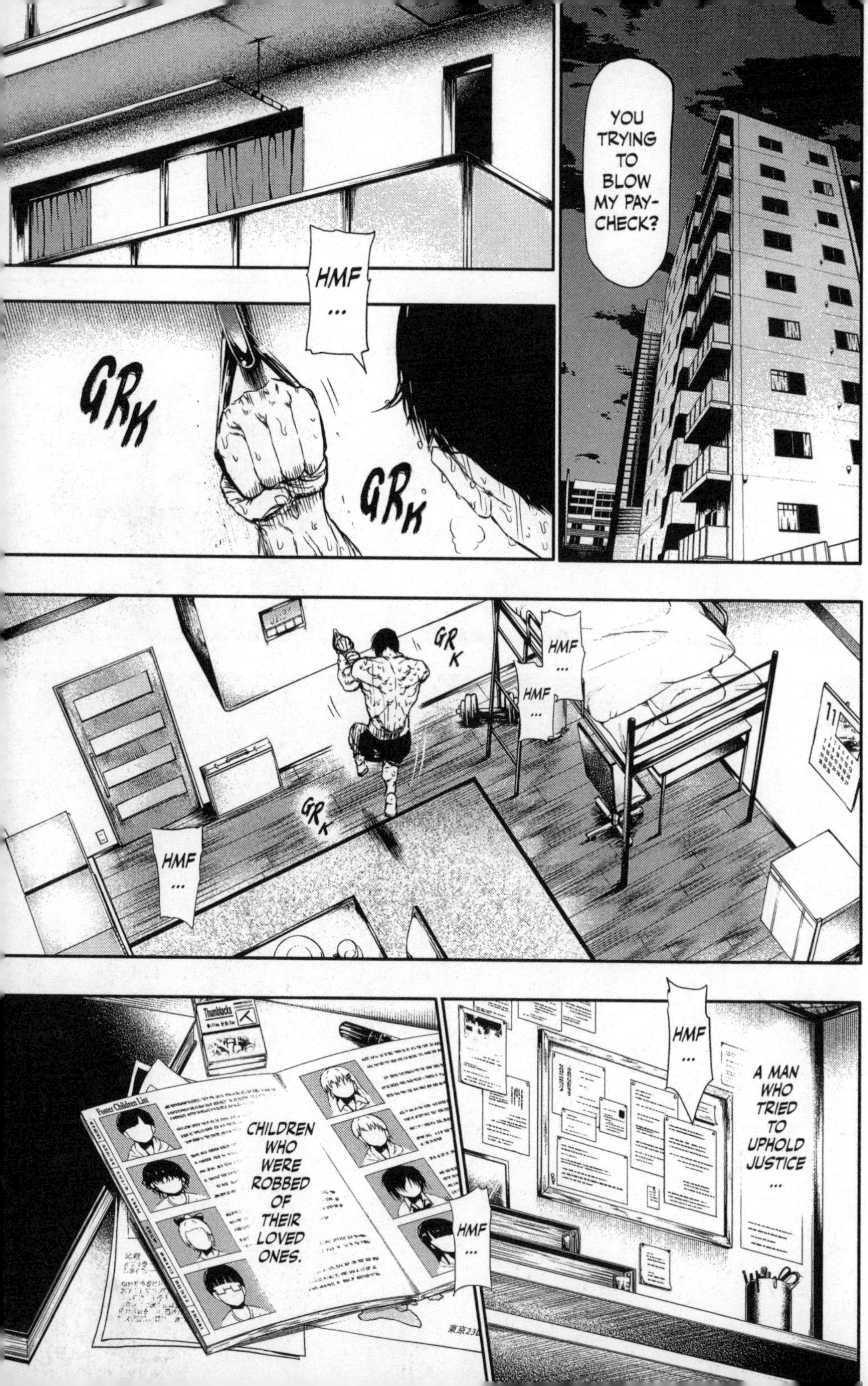

YOU TRYING TO BLOW MY PAY-CHECK?
HMF ...
GRK
GRK
HMF ...
HMF ...
GRK
GRK
HMF ...
HMF ...
A MAN WHO TRIED TO UPHOLD JUSTICE ...
Thumbtacks
Foster Children List
HMF ...
CHILDREN WHO WERE ROBBED OF THEIR LOVED ONES.
東京23

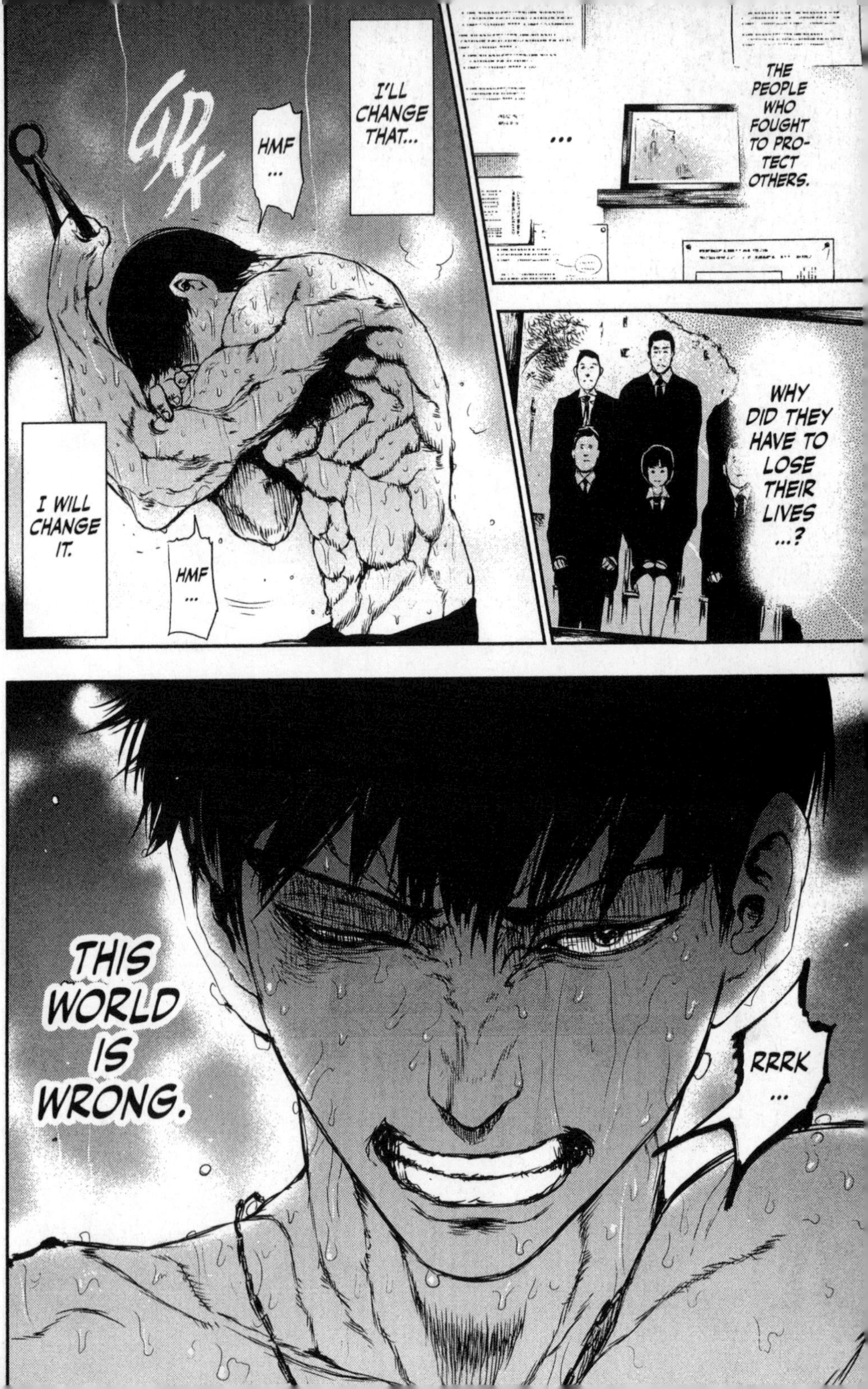
THE PEOPLE WHO FOUGHT TO PRO-TECT OTHERS.
...
WHY DID THEY HAVE TO LOSE THEIR LIVES ...?
I'LL CHANGE THAT...
HMF ...
GRK
I WILL CHANGE IT.
HMF ...
RRRK ...
THIS WORLD IS WRONG.

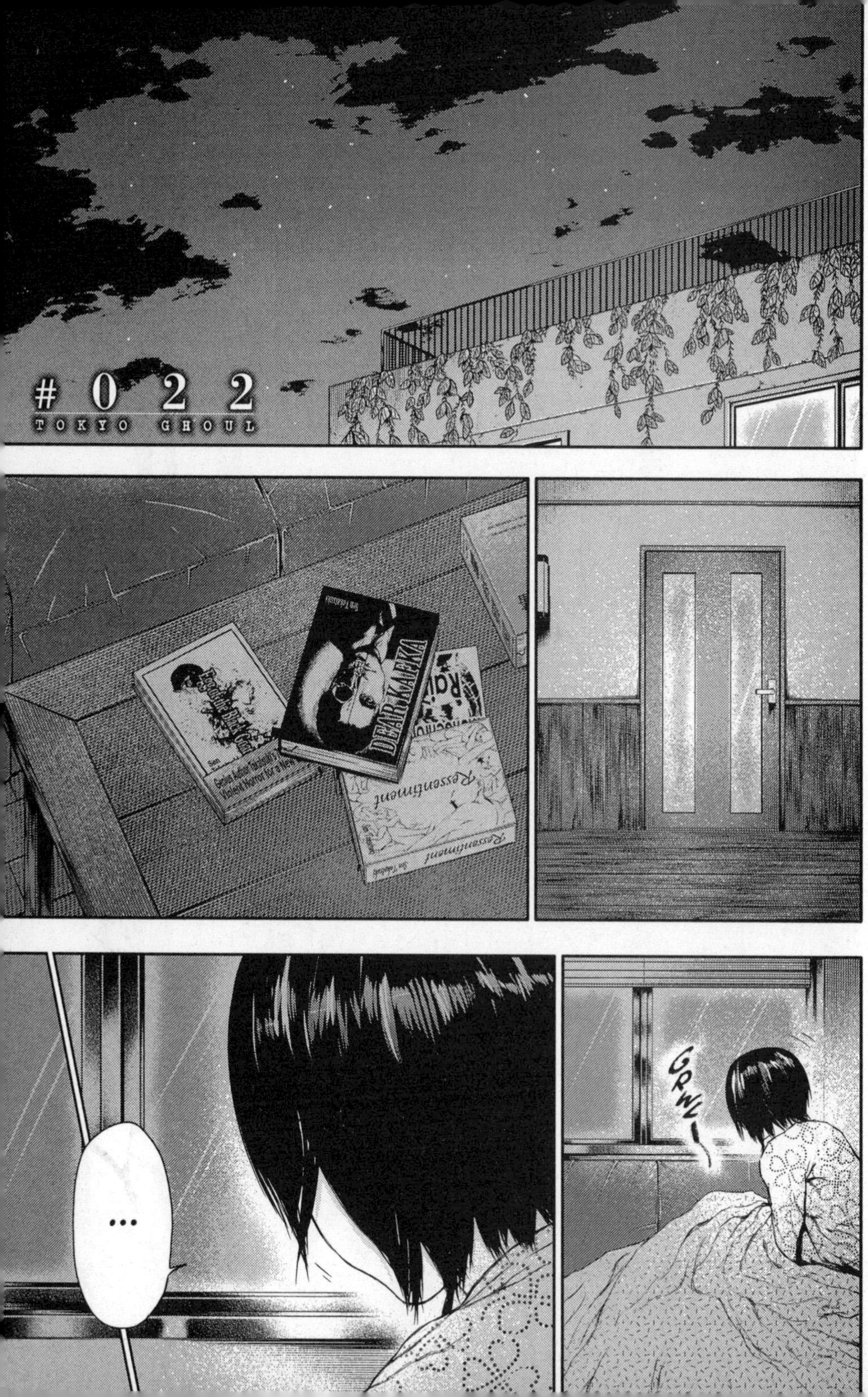

#022
TOKYO GHOUL
DEAR KAFKA
Ressentiment
Ressentiment
GRWL
...

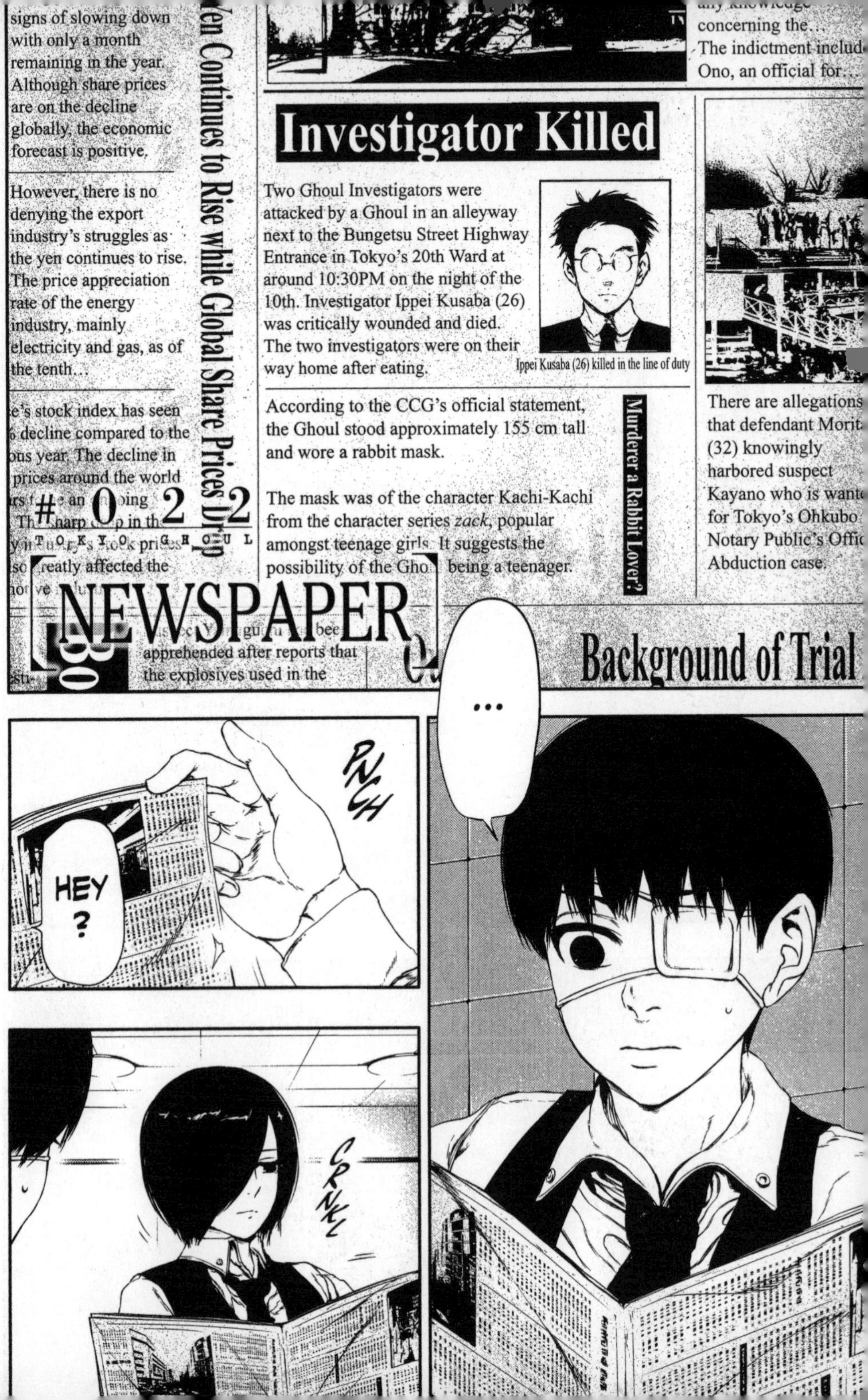
Investigator Killed
Two Ghoul Investigators were attacked by a Ghoul in an alleyway next to the Bungetsu Street Highway Entrance in Tokyo's 20th Ward at around 10:30PM on the night of the 10th. Investigator Ippei Kusaba (26) was critically wounded and died. The two investigators were on their way home after eating.
Ippei Kusaba (26) killed in the line of duty
According to the CCG's official statement, the Ghoul stood approximately 155 cm tall and wore a rabbit mask.
The mask was of the character Kachi-Kachi from the character series *zack*, popular amongst teenage girls. It suggests the possibility of the Gho being a teenager.
Murderer a Rabbit Lover?
concerning the...
The indictment includ
Ono, an official for...
There are allegations that defendant Morit (32) knowingly harbored suspect Kayano who is want for Tokyo's Ohkubo Notary Public's Offic Abduction case.
Background of Trial
signs of slowing down with only a month remaining in the year. Although share prices are on the decline globally, the economic forecast is positive.
However, there is no denying the export industry's struggles as the yen continues to rise. The price appreciation rate of the energy industry, mainly electricity and gas, as of the tenth...
Yen Continues to Rise while Global Share Prices Drop
#022 TOKYO GHOUL
NEWSPAPER
apprehended after reports that the explosives used in the
...
PNCH
HEY?
CRNKL

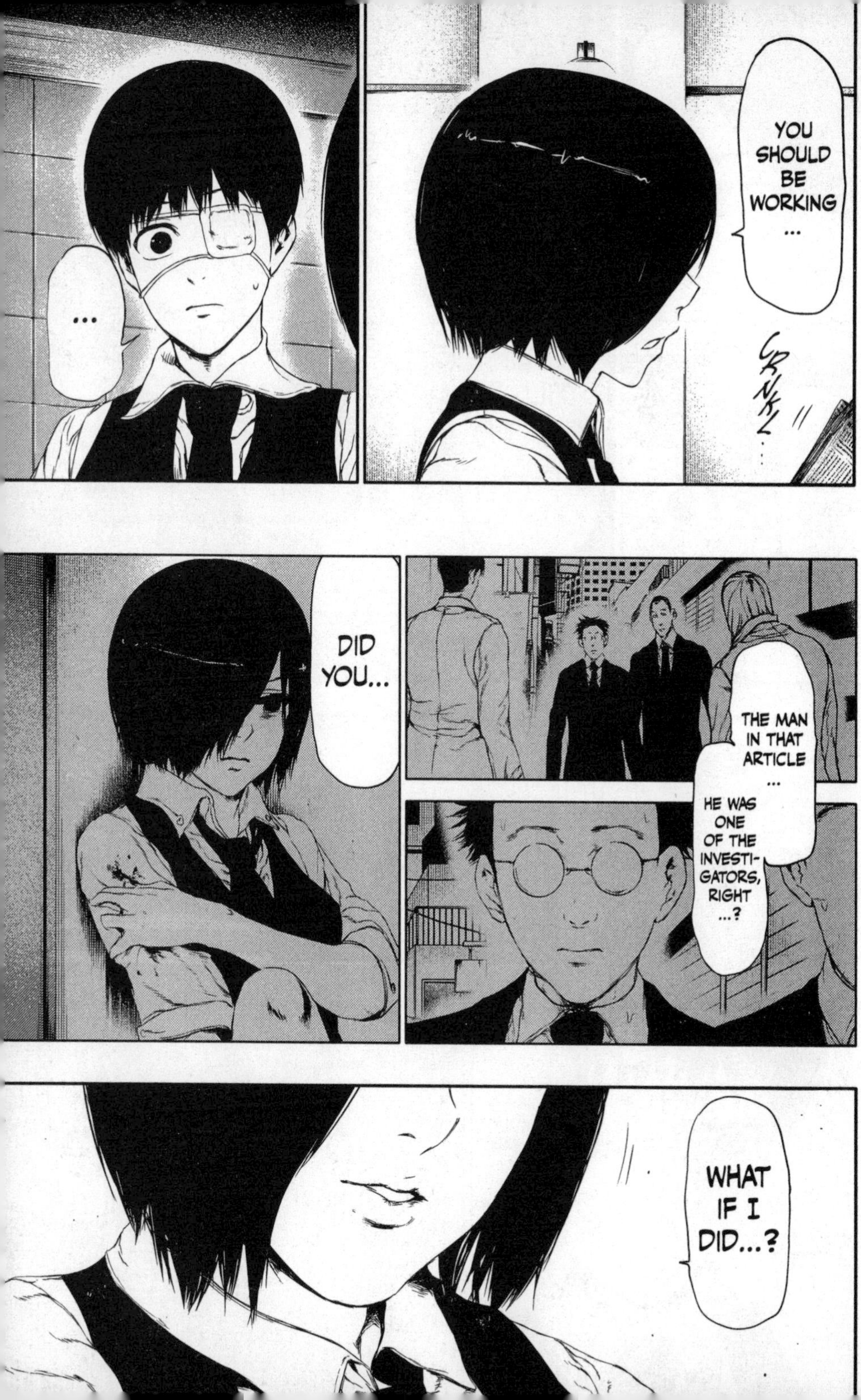

YOU SHOULD BE WORKING ...
CRNKL...
...
THE MAN IN THAT ARTICLE ...
HE WAS ONE OF THE INVESTI-GATORS, RIGHT ...?
DID YOU...
WHAT IF I DID...?

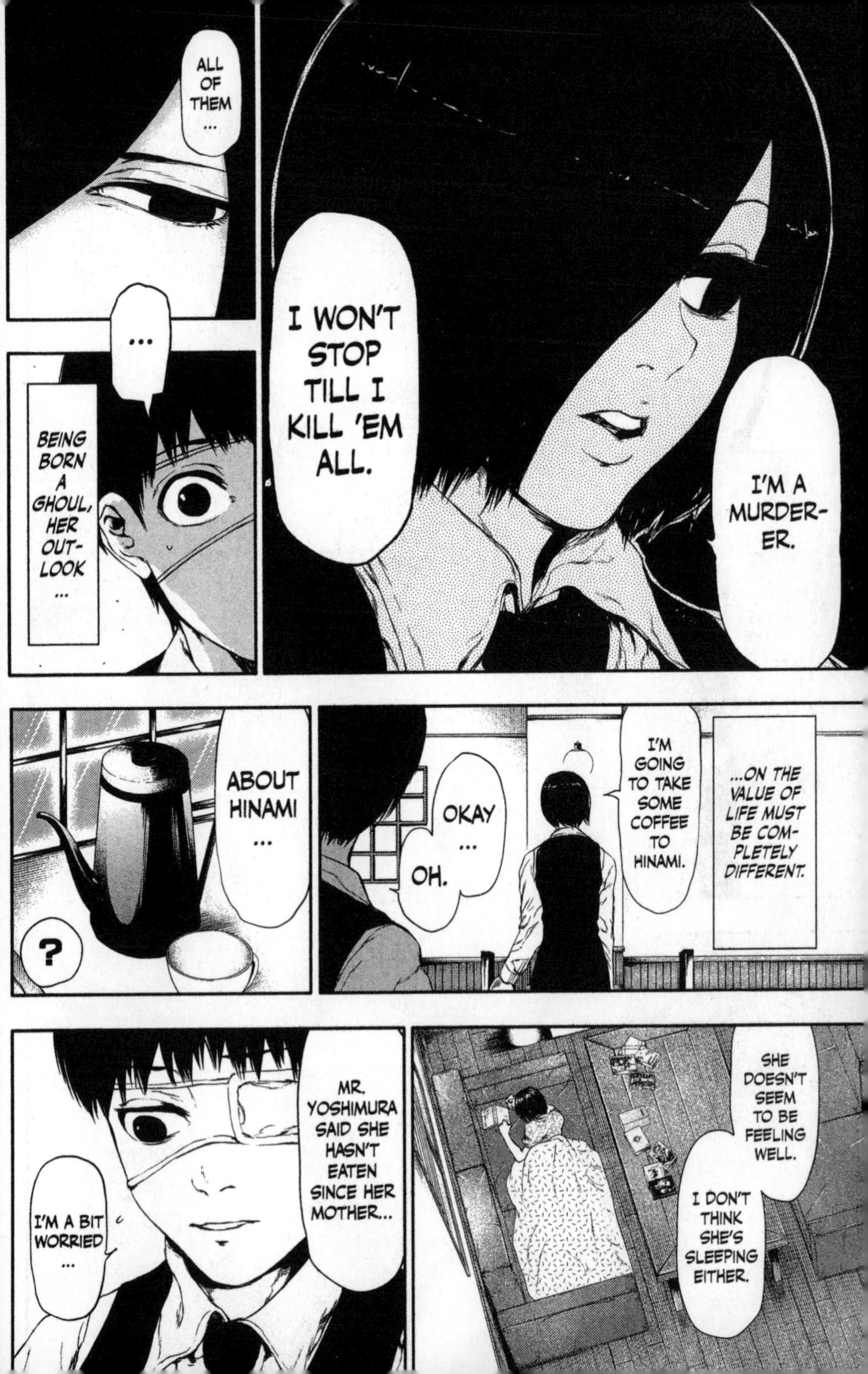

I'M A MURDERER.
I WON'T STOP TILL I KILL 'EM ALL.
ALL OF THEM ...
...
BEING BORN A GHOUL, HER OUTLOOK ...
...ON THE VALUE OF LIFE MUST BE COMPLETELY DIFFERENT.
I'M GOING TO TAKE SOME COFFEE TO HINAMI.
OKAY ...
OH.
ABOUT HINAMI ...
?
SHE DOESN'T SEEM TO BE FEELING WELL.
I DON'T THINK SHE'S SLEEPING EITHER.
MR. YOSHIMURA SAID SHE HASN'T EATEN SINCE HER MOTHER...
I'M A BIT WORRIED ...

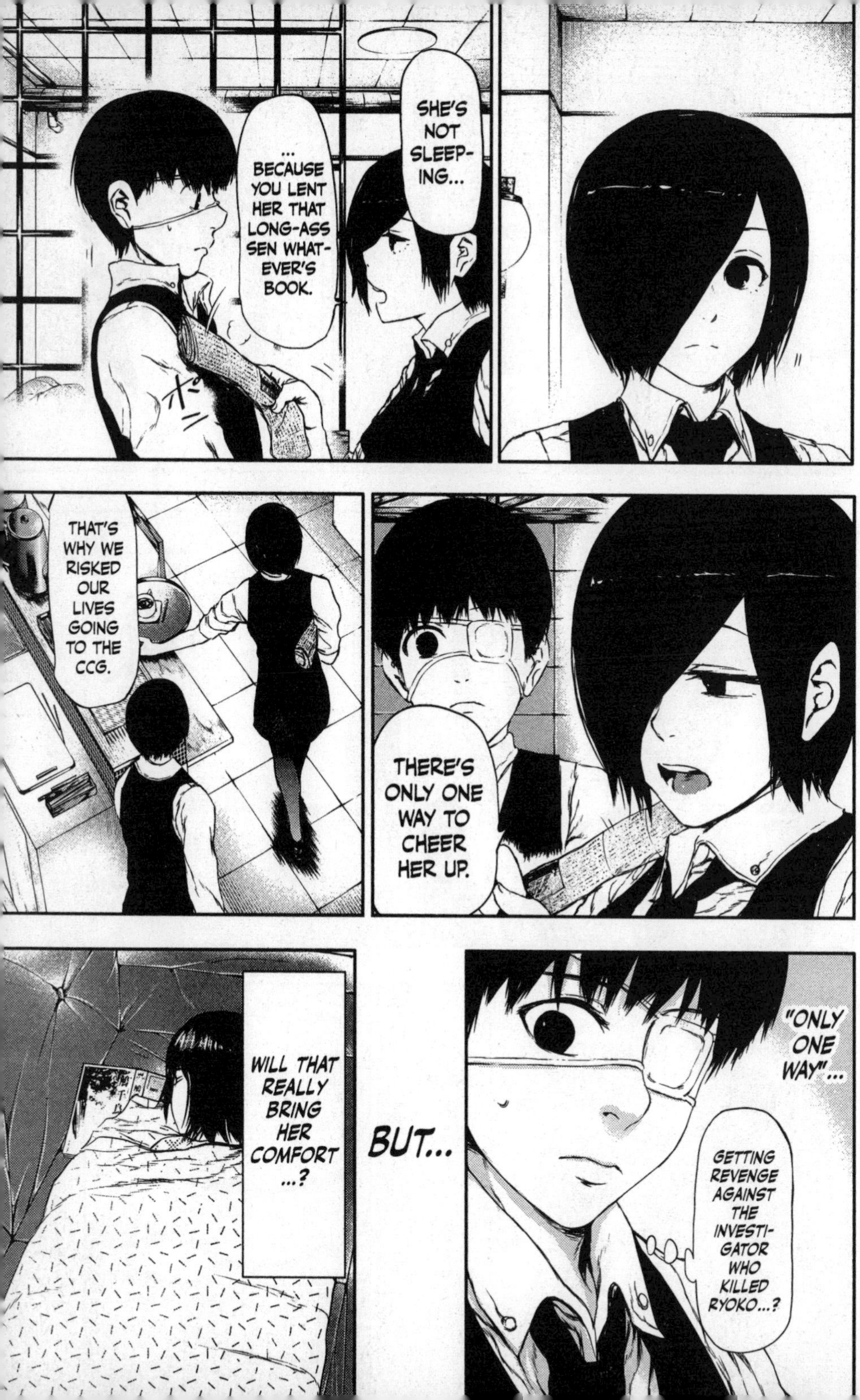
SHE'S NOT SLEEPING...
...BECAUSE YOU LENT HER THAT LONG-ASS SEN WHATEVER'S BOOK.
THERE'S ONLY ONE WAY TO CHEER HER UP.
THAT'S WHY WE RISKED OUR LIVES GOING TO THE CCG.
"ONLY ONE WAY"...
GETTING REVENGE AGAINST THE INVESTIGATOR WHO KILLED RYOKO...?
BUT...
WILL THAT REALLY BRING HER COMFORT...?

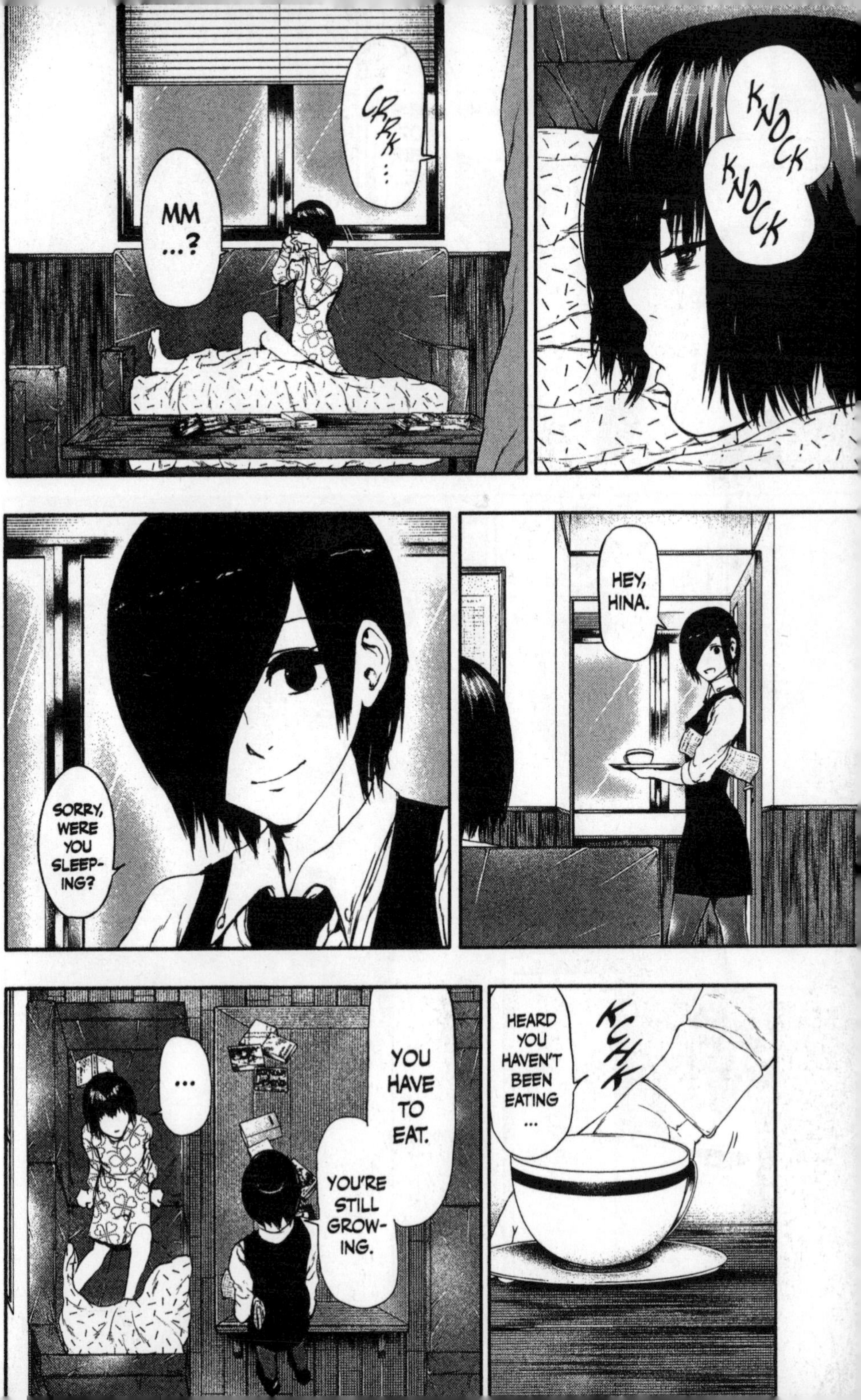
KNOCK KNOCK
CRRK...
MM ...?
HEY, HINA.
SORRY, WERE YOU SLEEP-ING?
KCHK
HEARD YOU HAVEN'T BEEN EATING ...
YOU HAVE TO EAT.
YOU'RE STILL GROW-ING.
...

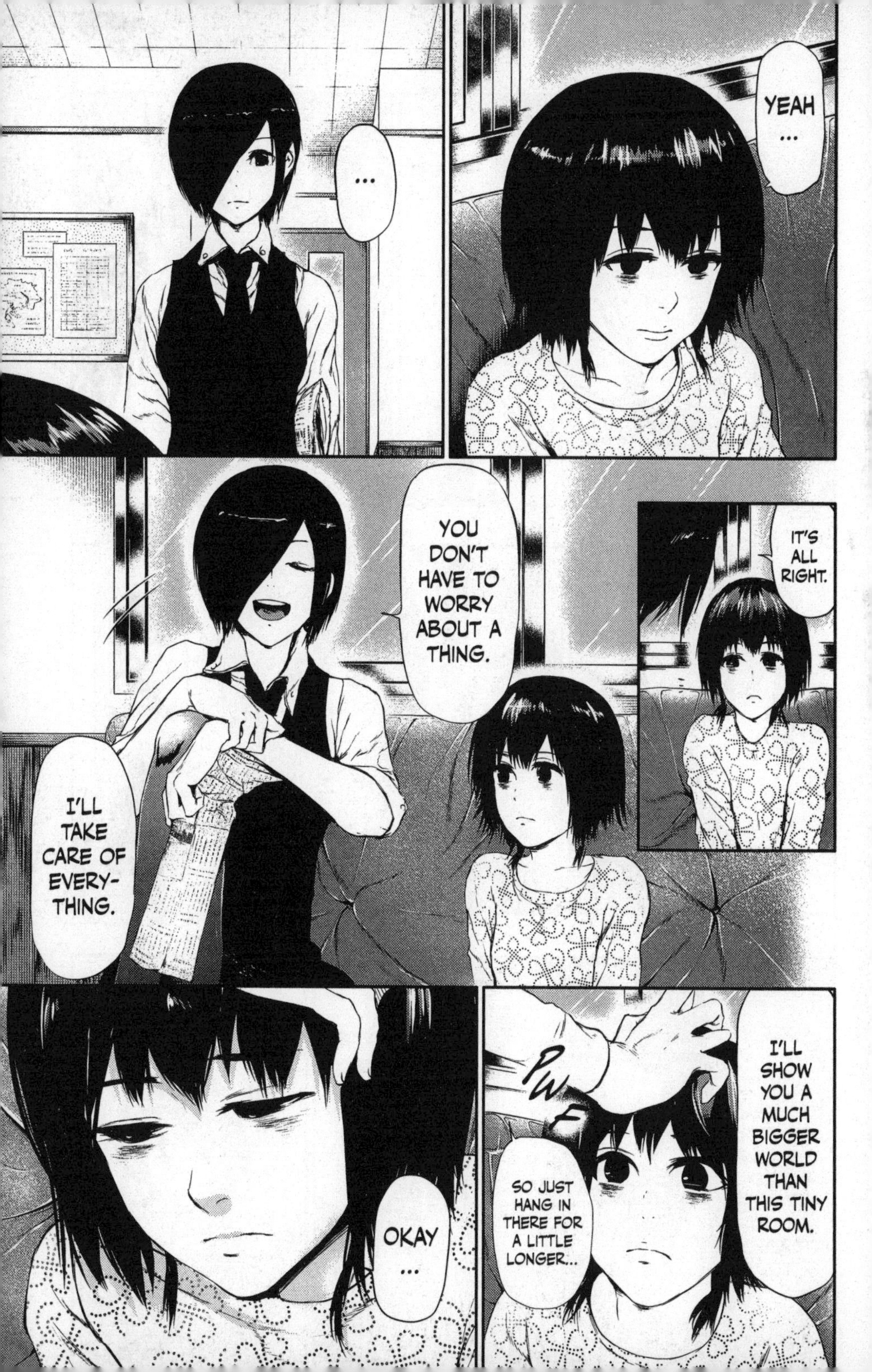
YEAH ...
...
IT'S ALL RIGHT.
YOU DON'T HAVE TO WORRY ABOUT A THING.
I'LL TAKE CARE OF EVERY-THING.
PWF
I'LL SHOW YOU A MUCH BIGGER WORLD THAN THIS TINY ROOM.
SO JUST HANG IN THERE FOR A LITTLE LONGER...
OKAY ...

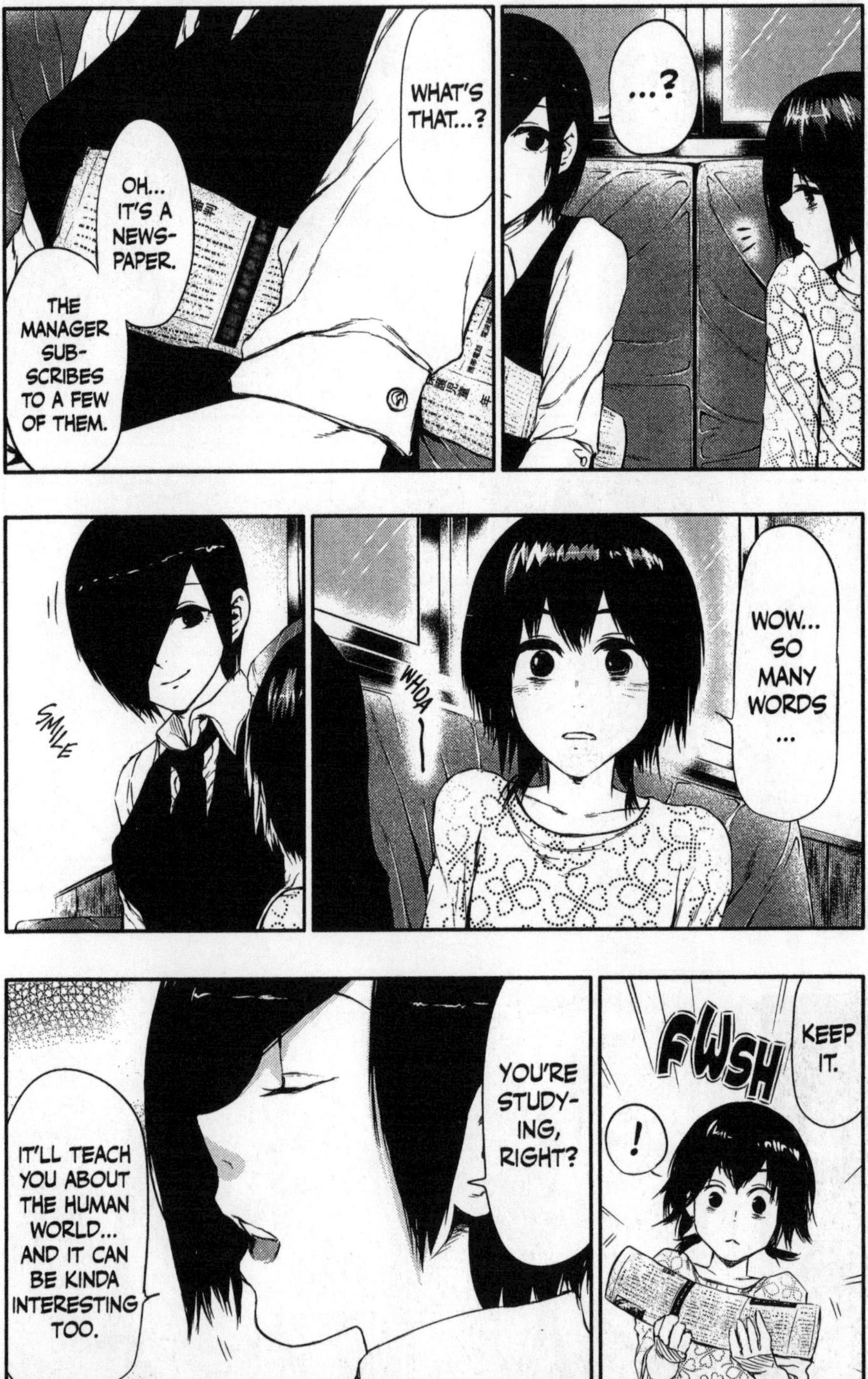
...?
WHAT'S THAT...?
OH... IT'S A NEWS-PAPER.
THE MANAGER SUB-SCRIBES TO A FEW OF THEM.
WOW... SO MANY WORDS ...
WHOA
SMILE
KEEP IT.
FWSH
!
YOU'RE STUDY-ING, RIGHT?
IT'LL TEACH YOU ABOUT THE HUMAN WORLD... AND IT CAN BE KINDA INTERESTING TOO.

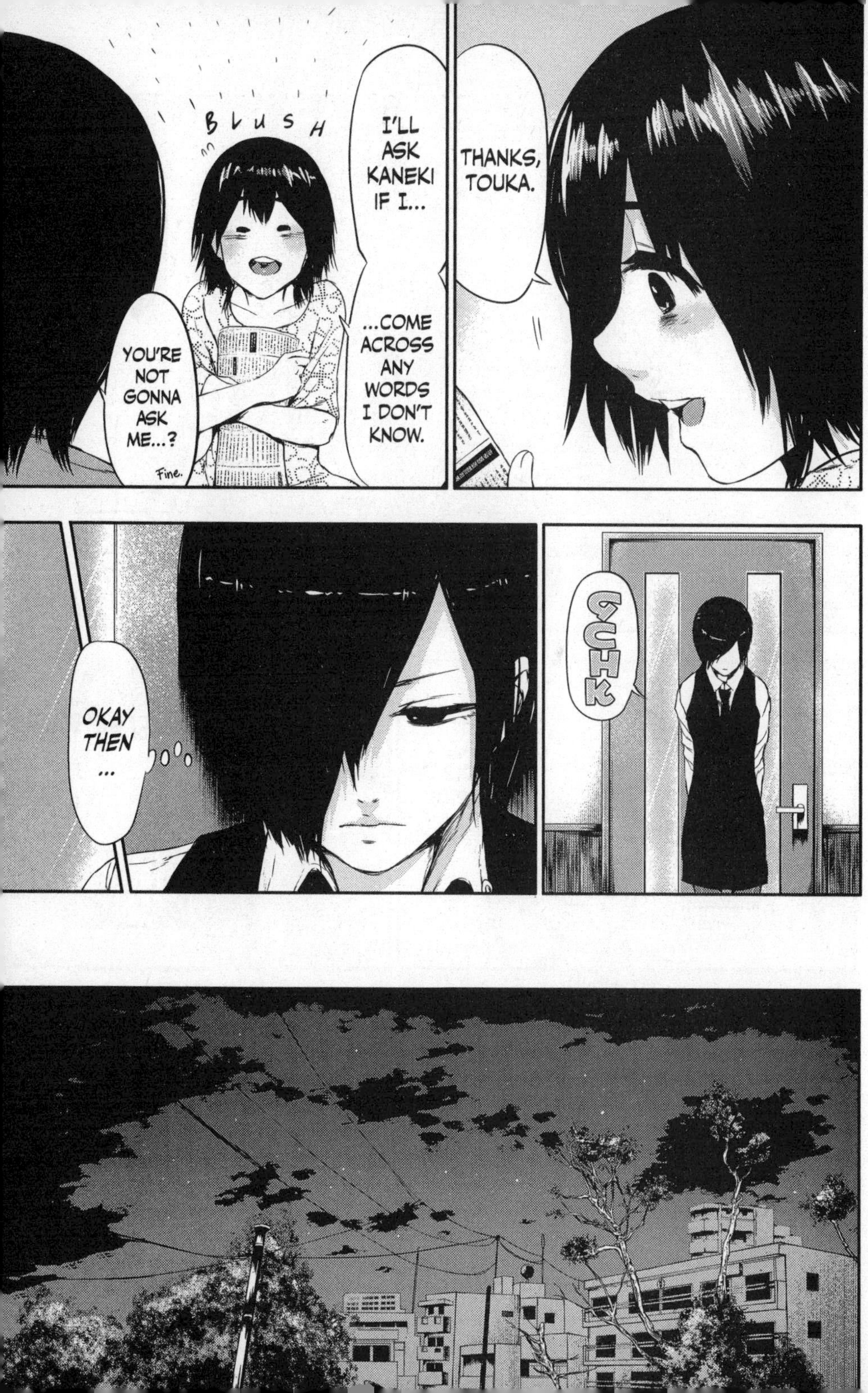
THANKS, TOUKA.
I'LL ASK KANEKI IF I...
...COME ACROSS ANY WORDS I DON'T KNOW.
BLUSH
YOU'RE NOT GONNA ASK ME...?
Fine.
GCHK
OKAY THEN...

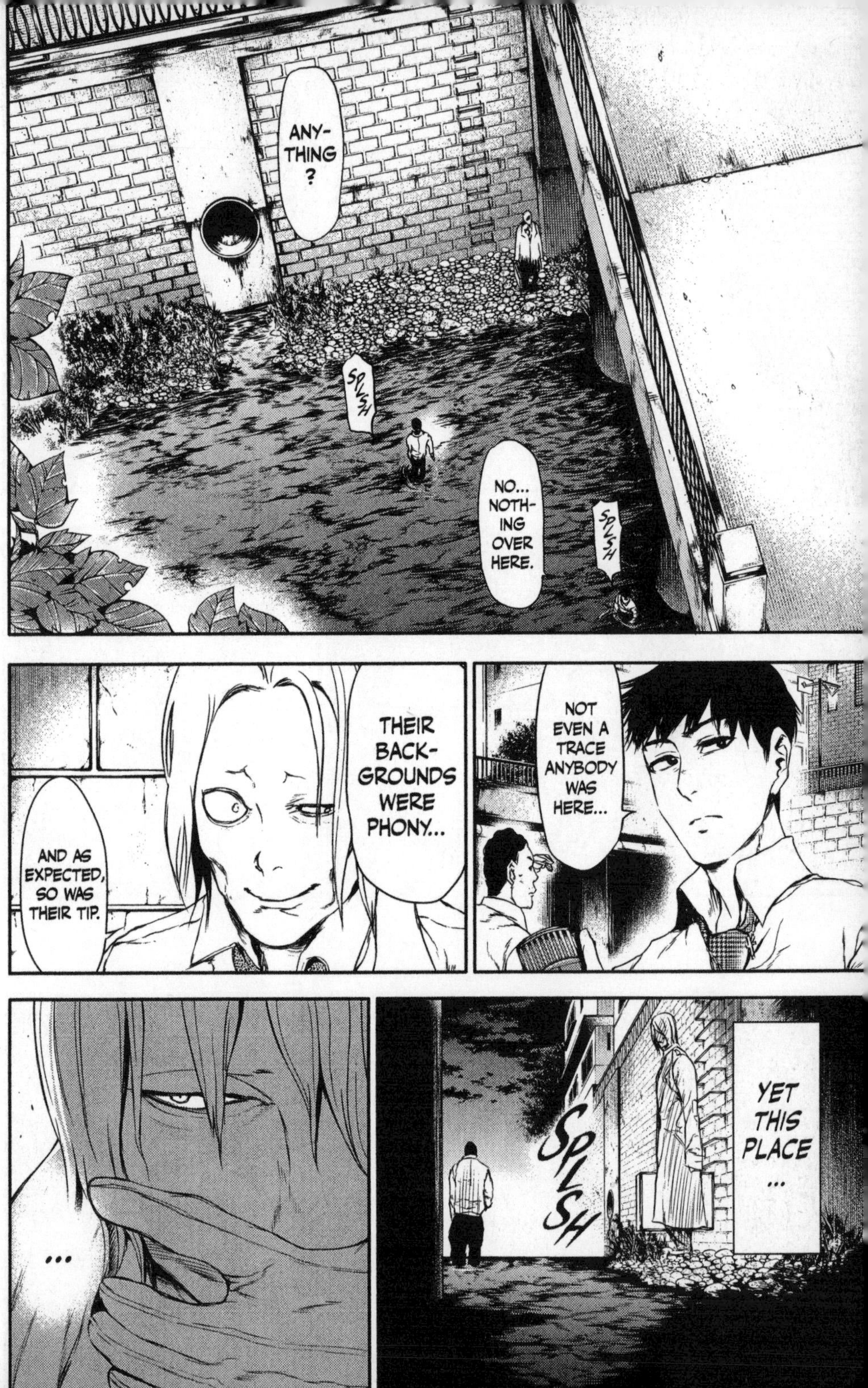
ANY-THING?
SPLSH
NO... NOTH-ING OVER HERE.
SPLSH
NOT EVEN A TRACE ANYBODY WAS HERE...
THEIR BACK-GROUNDS WERE PHONY...
AND AS EXPECTED, SO WAS THEIR TIP.
YET THIS PLACE ...
SPLSH
...

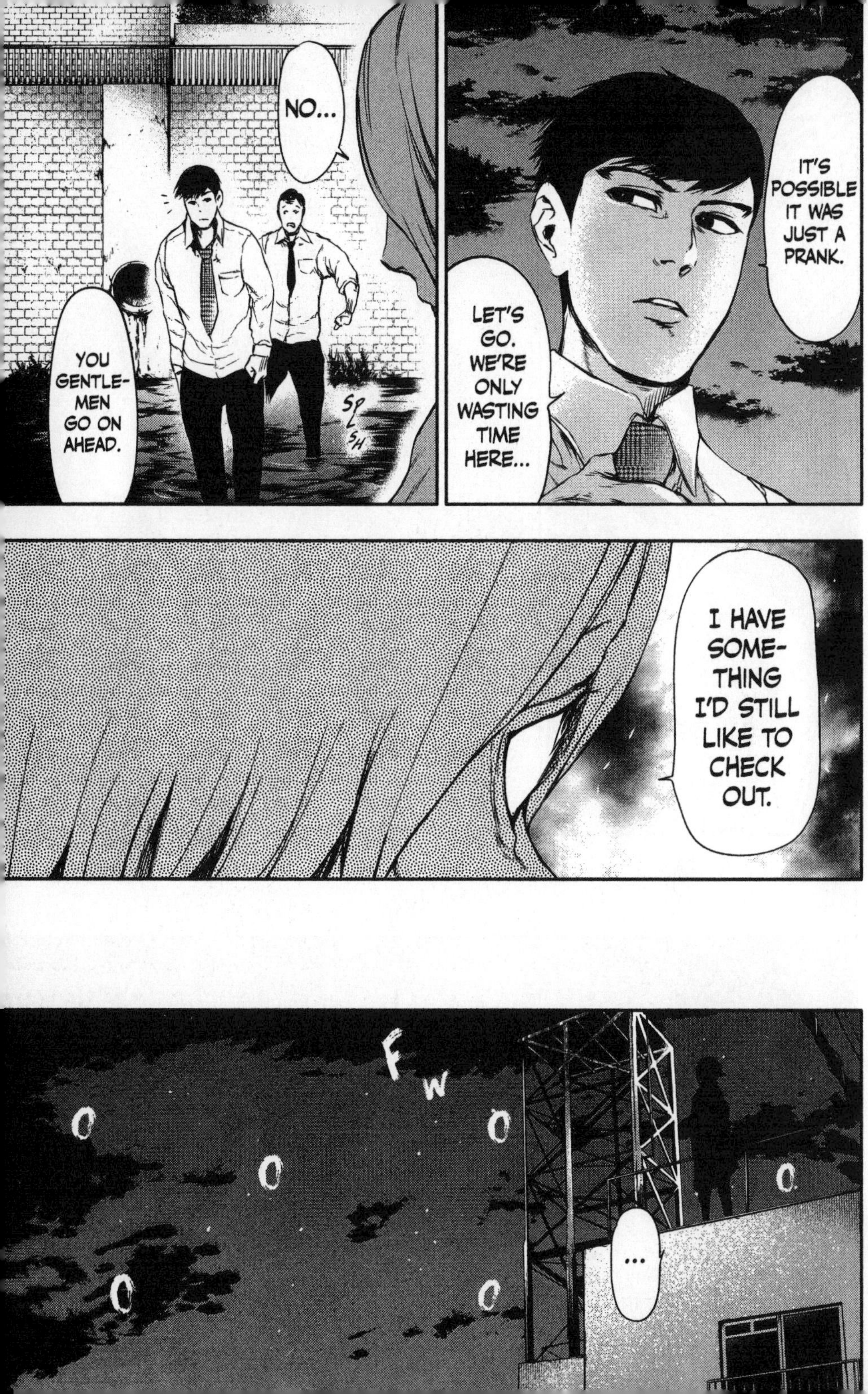
IT'S POSSIBLE IT WAS JUST A PRANK.
LET'S GO. WE'RE ONLY WASTING TIME HERE...
NO...
SPLSH
YOU GENTLE-MEN GO ON AHEAD.
I HAVE SOME-THING I'D STILL LIKE TO CHECK OUT.
FWOOOOOO
...

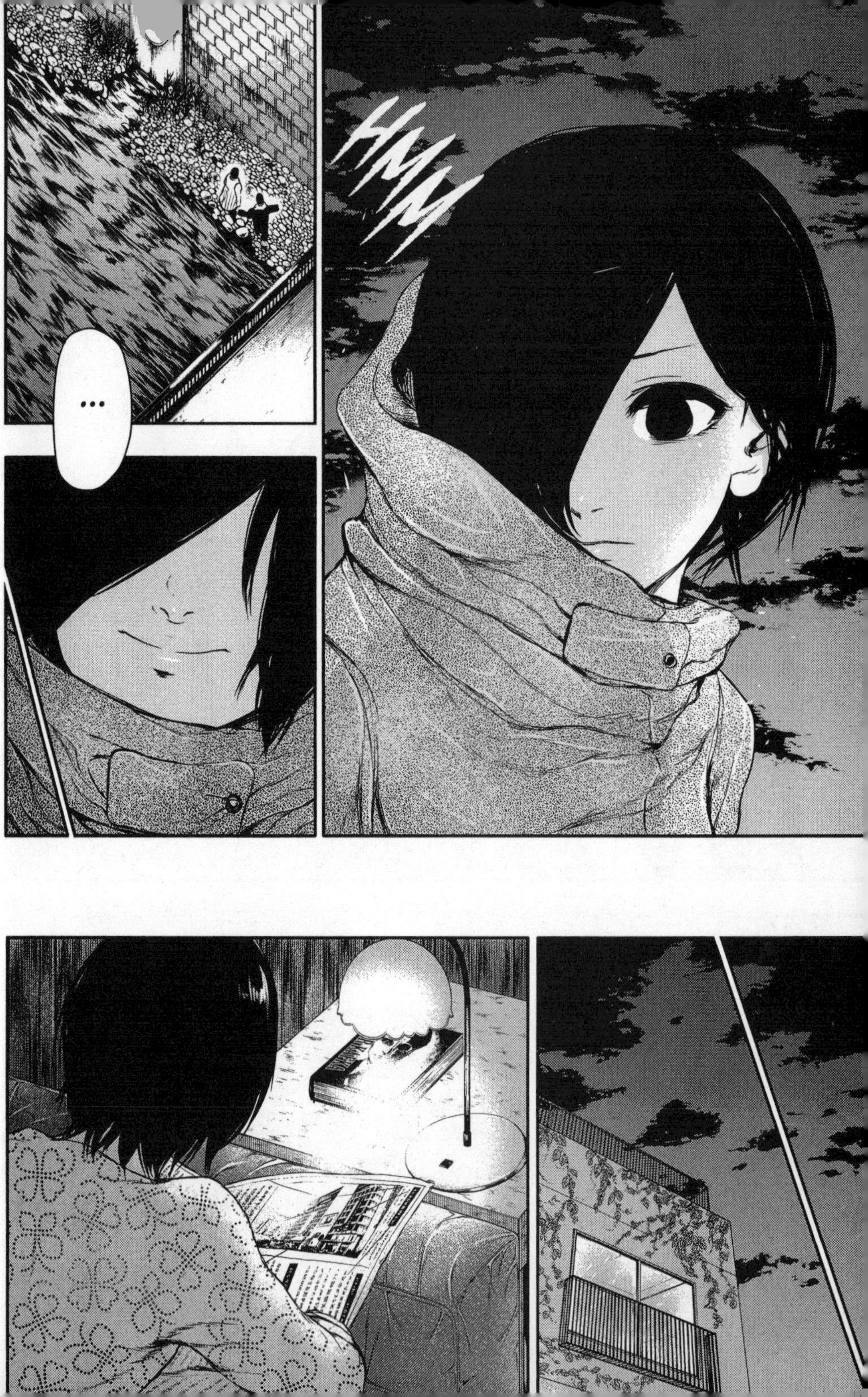
HMM
...

It was with
great sorrow
we learned the
offer our
est condole
We pray

...?

CONDO-
LENCES
...?

What
does
that
mean...?

DA

EXPRES-
SION OF
SYMPATHY,
SADNESS
...

"CONDO-
LENCES"
...

FSH

...

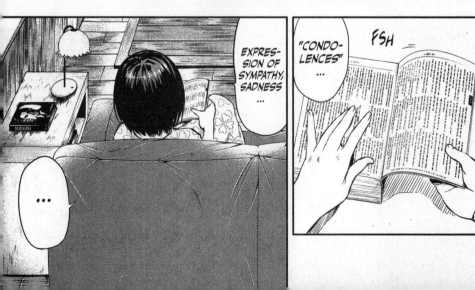

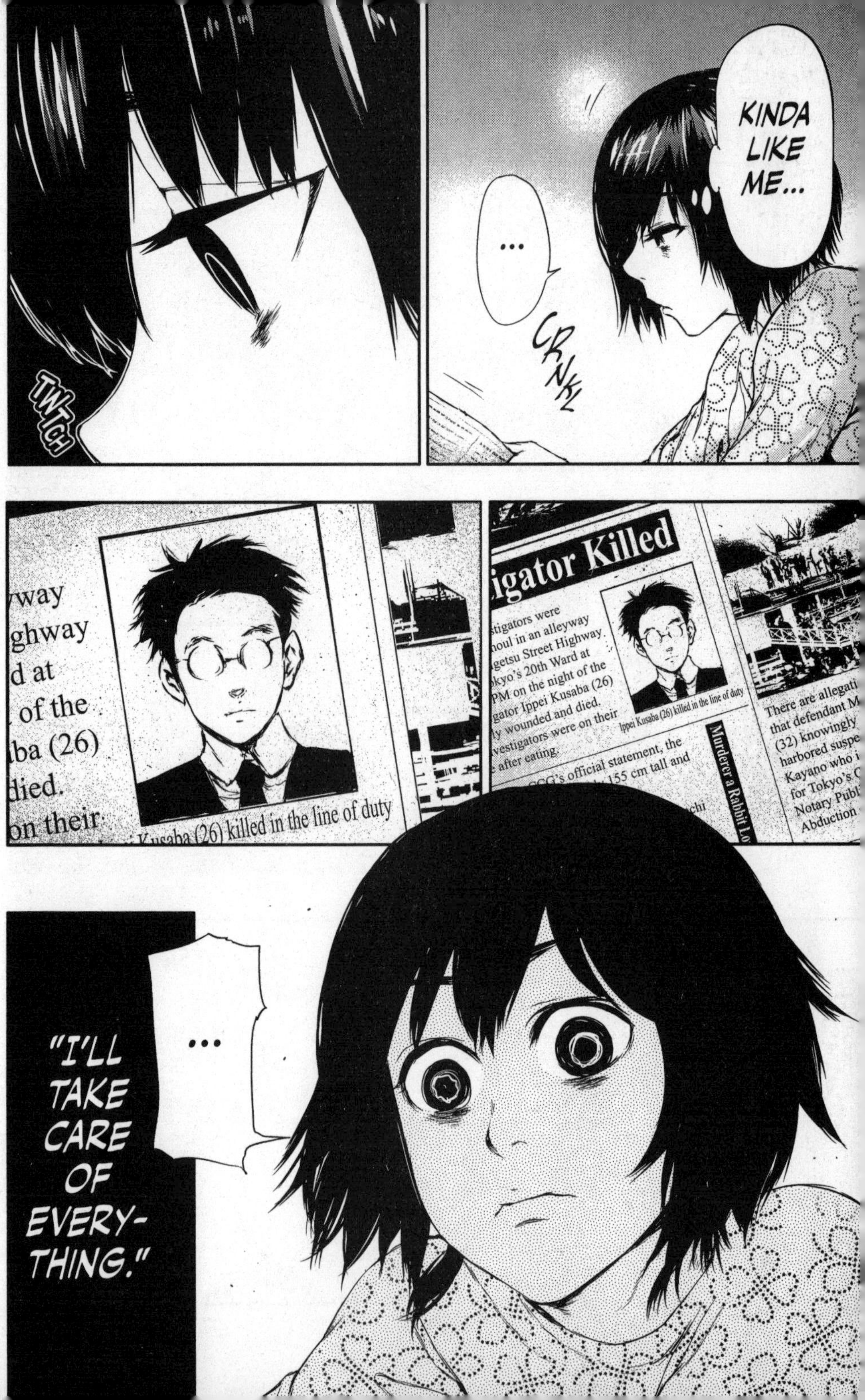
KINDA LIKE ME...
...
CRNKL
TWITCH
igator Killed
stigators were
houl in an alleyway
getsu Street Highway
kyo's 20th Ward at
PM on the night of the
gator Ippei Kusaba (26)
ly wounded and died.
vestigators were on their
after eating.
Ippei Kusaba (26) killed in the line of duty
CCG's official statement, the
155 cm tall and
Murderer a Rabbit
There are allegat
that defendant M
(32) knowingly
harbored suspe
Kayano who
for Tokyo's
Notary Publ
Abduction
yway
ghway
d at
of the
ba (26)
died.
on their
Kusaba (26) killed in the line of duty
...
"I'LL TAKE CARE OF EVERY-THING."

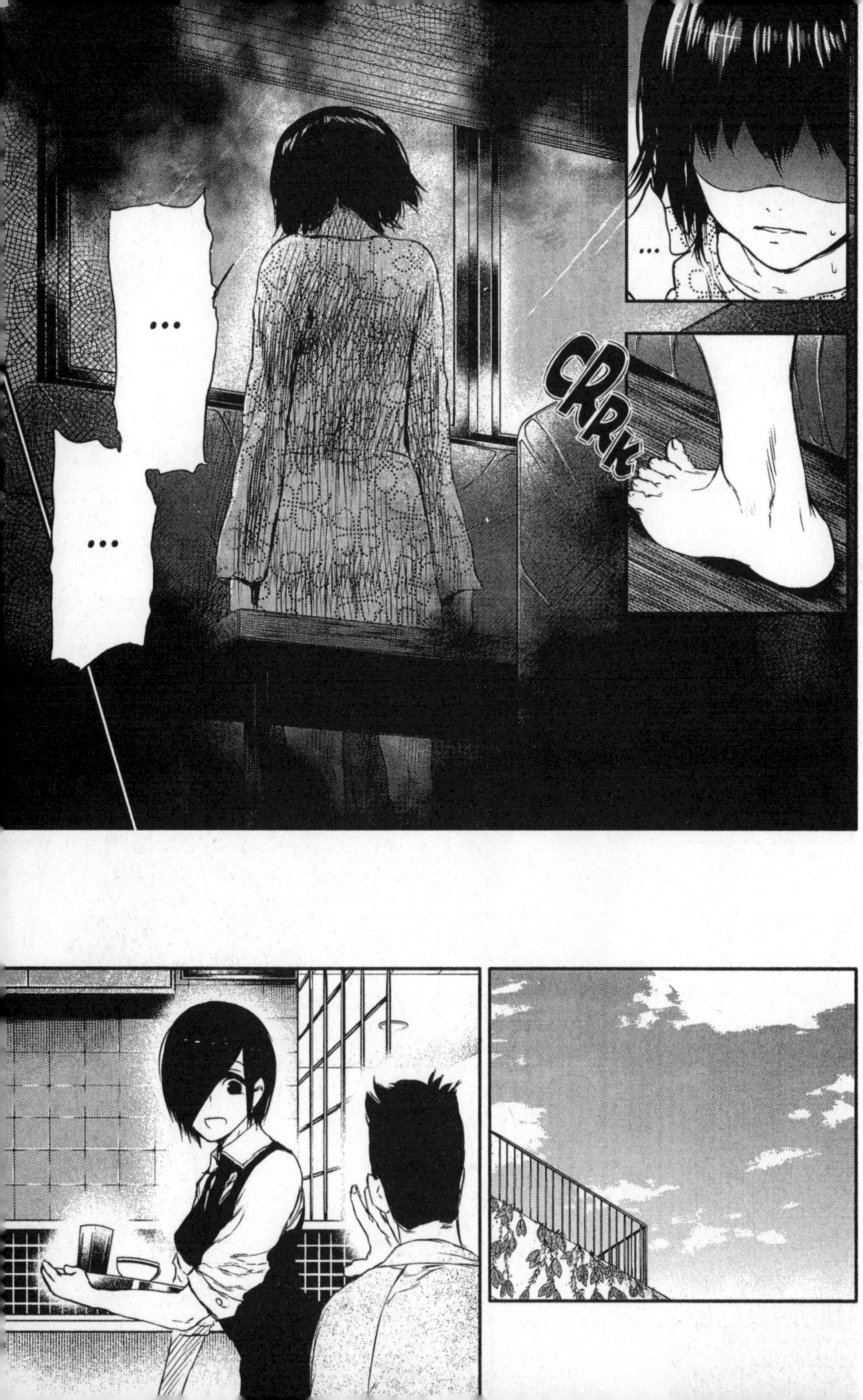
...
CRRK
...
...

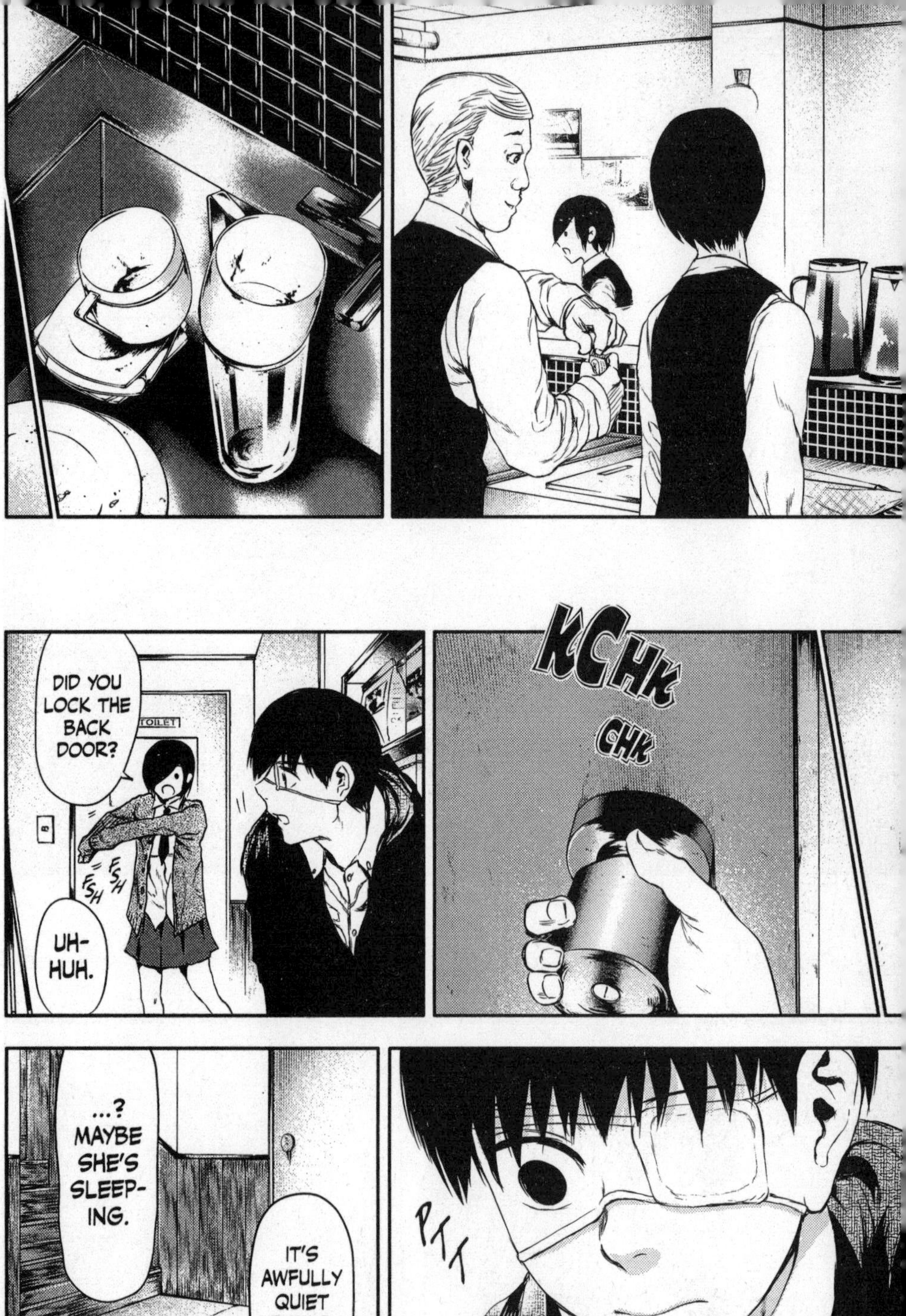
KCHK
CHK
DID YOU LOCK THE BACK DOOR?
TOILET
FSH FSH
UH-HUH.
PTTT
IT'S AWFULLY QUIET UPSTAIRS ...
...? MAYBE SHE'S SLEEP-ING.

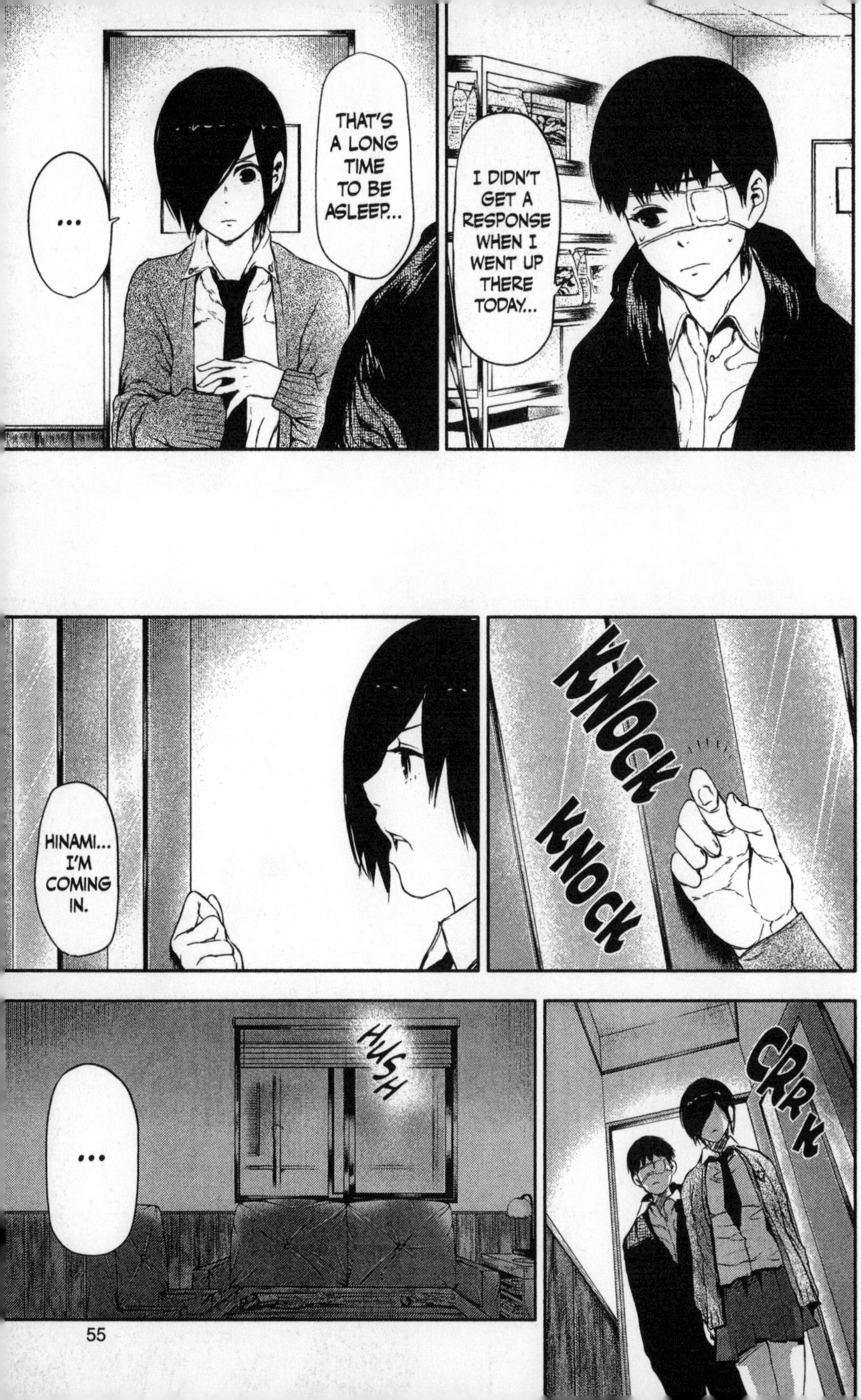
I DIDN'T GET A RESPONSE WHEN I WENT UP THERE TODAY...
THAT'S A LONG TIME TO BE ASLEEP...
...
KNOCK KNOCK
HINAMI... I'M COMING IN.
CRRK
HUSH
...

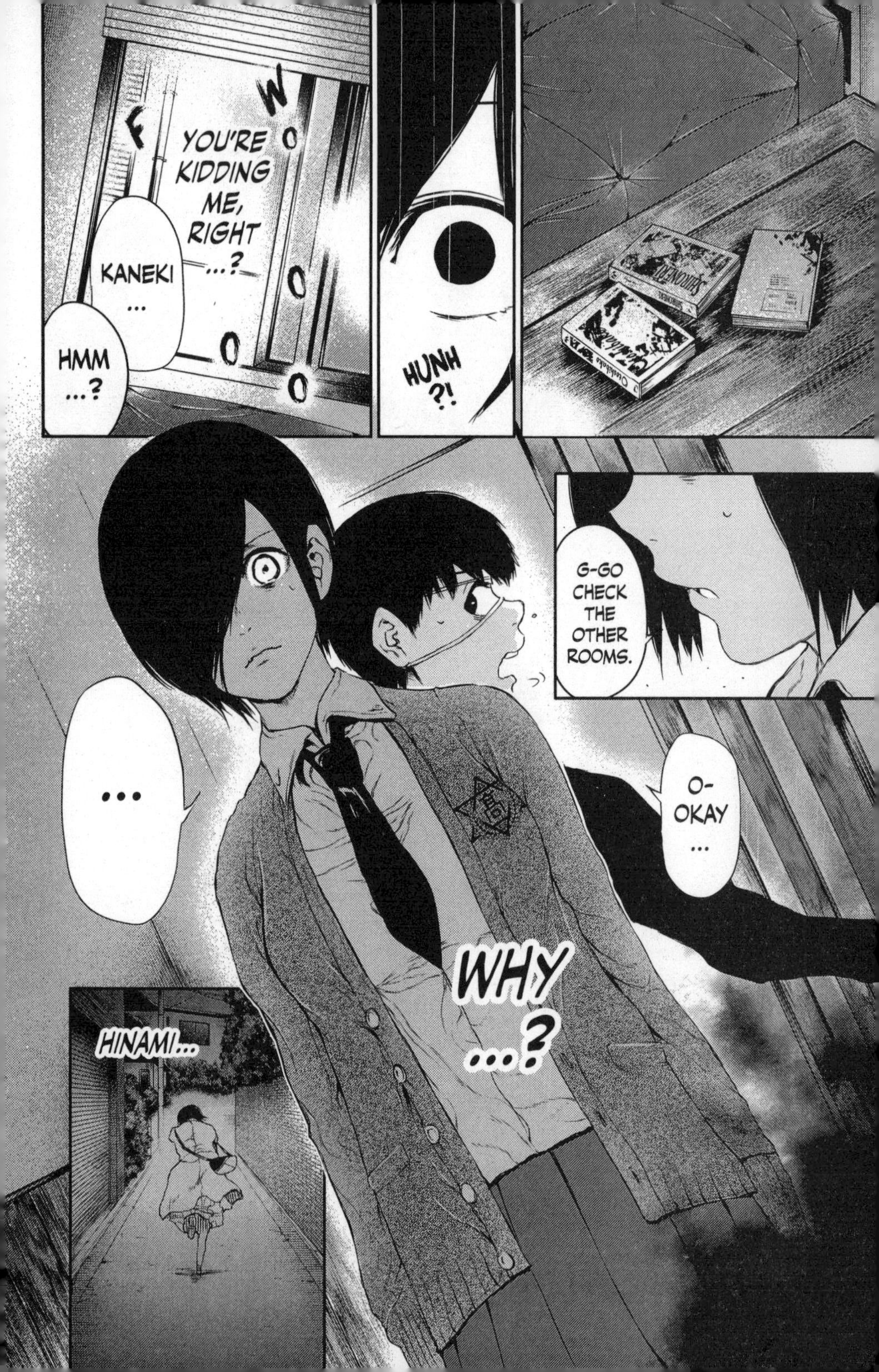
HUNH ?!
FWOOOO
YOU'RE KIDDING ME, RIGHT ...?
KANEKI ...
HMM ...?
G-GO CHECK THE OTHER ROOMS.
O-OKAY ...
...
WHY ...?
HINAMI...

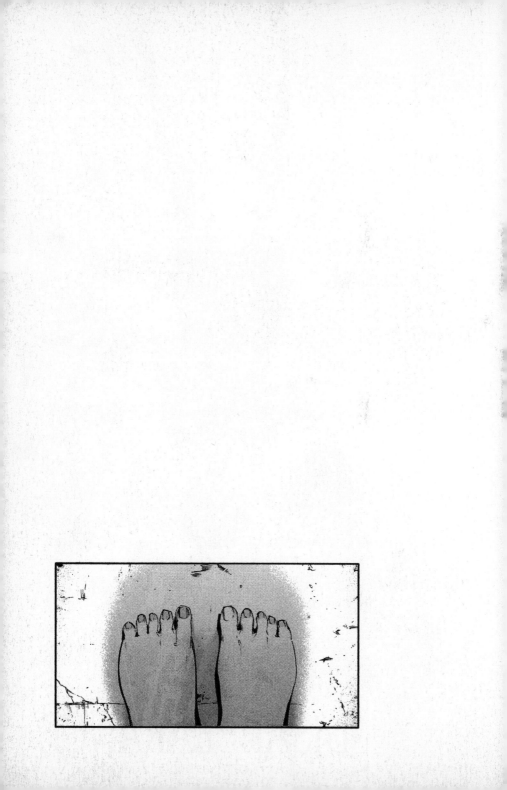

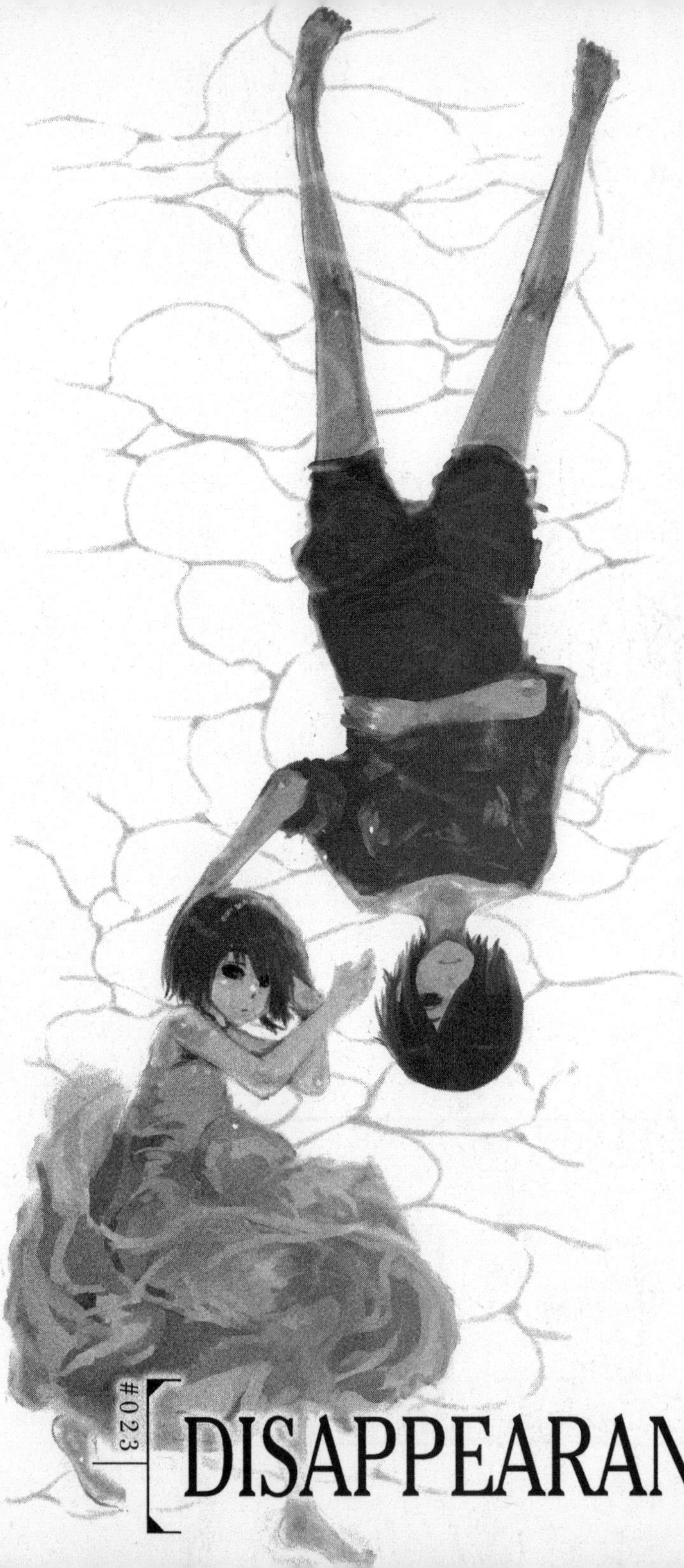

#023 DISAPPEARANCE

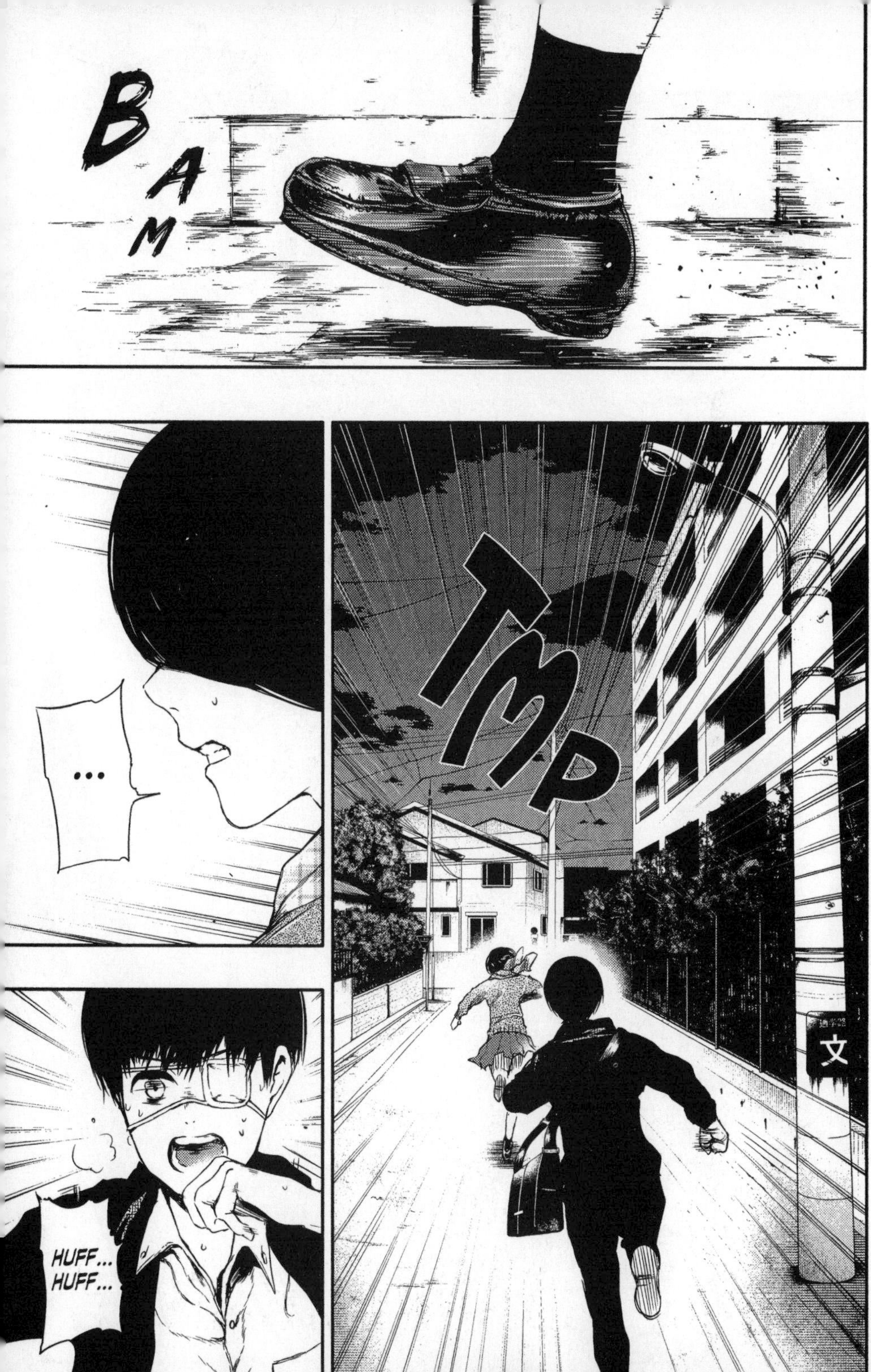
BAM
TMP
文
...
HUFF... HUFF...

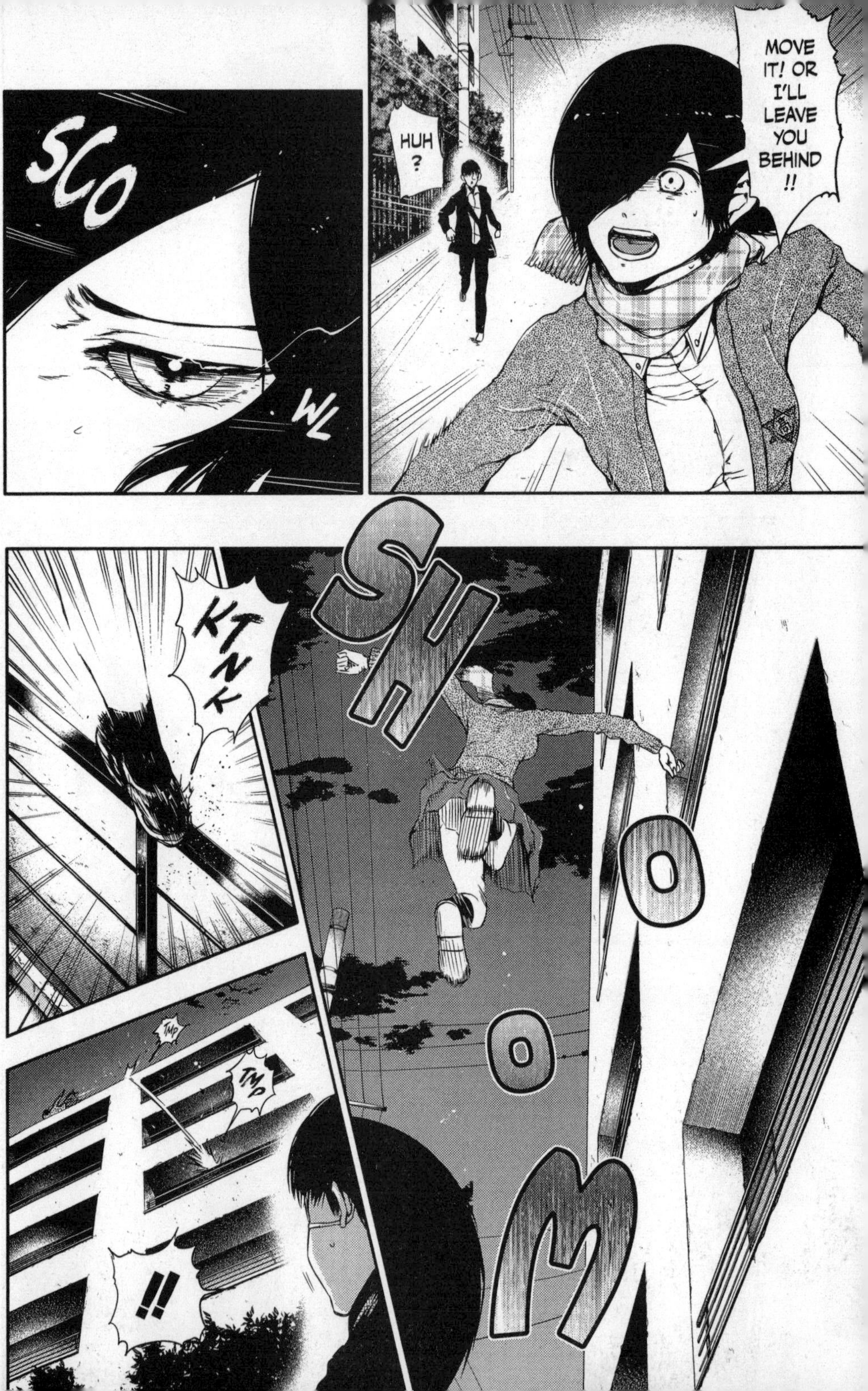
MOVE IT! OR I'LL LEAVE YOU BEHIND!!
HUH?
SCO
WL
SH
O
O
M
KTINK
TMP
TMP
!!

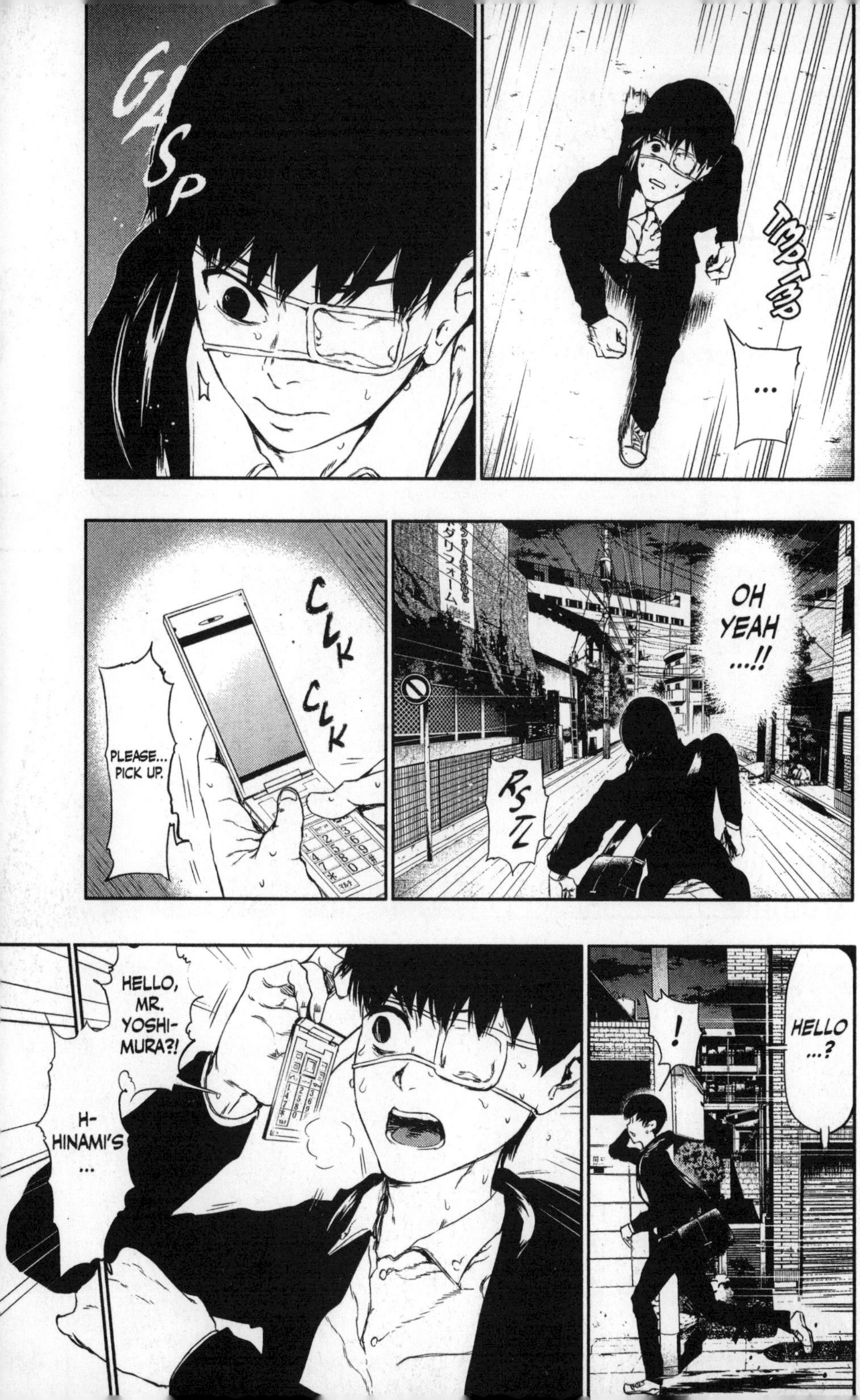
TMPTMP
...
GASP
OH YEAH ...!!
RSTL
CLK
CLK
PLEASE... PICK UP.
HELLO ...?
!
HELLO, MR. YOSHI-MURA?!
H-HINAMI'S ...

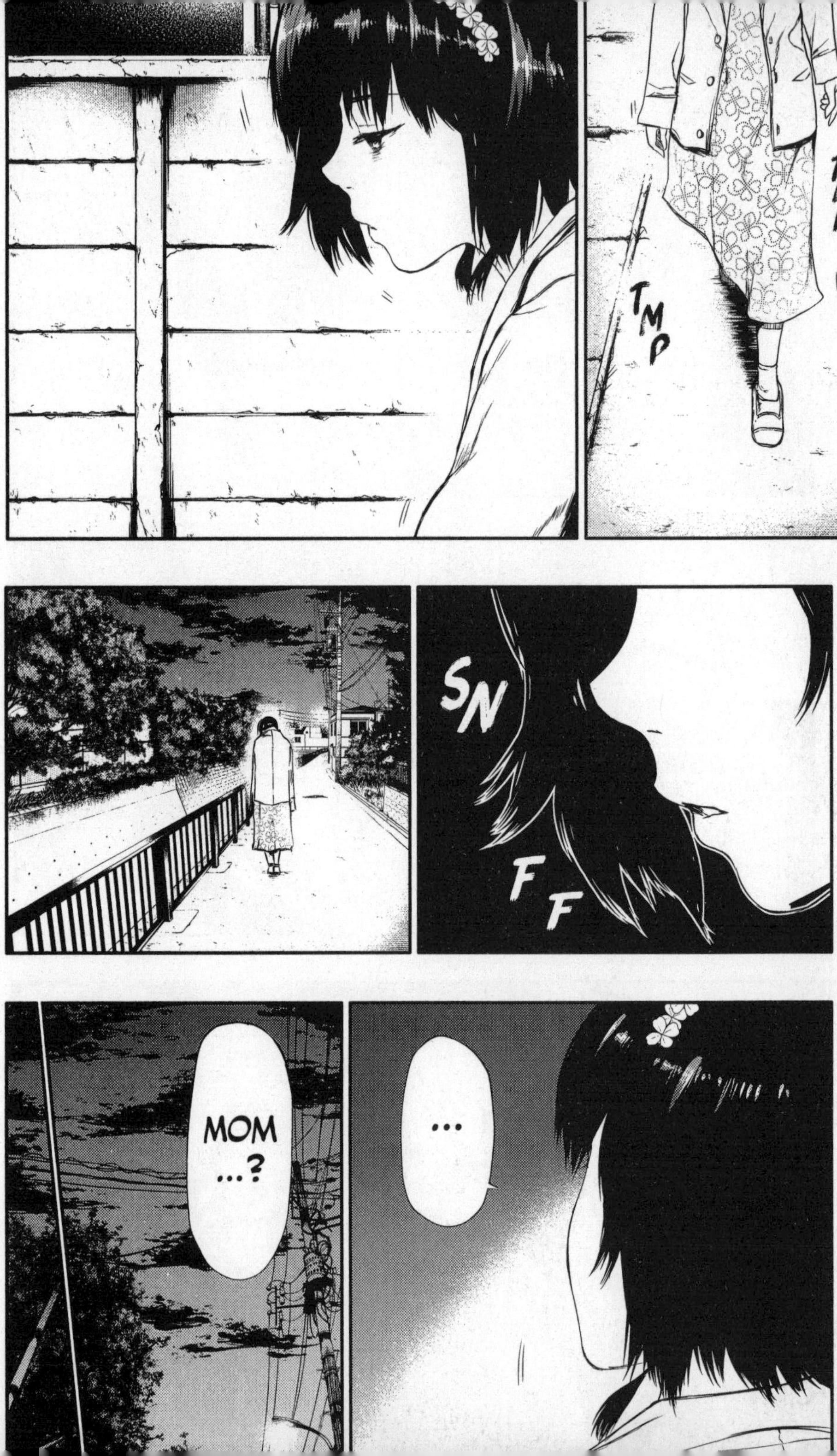
TMP
TMP
SNFF
...
MOM ...?

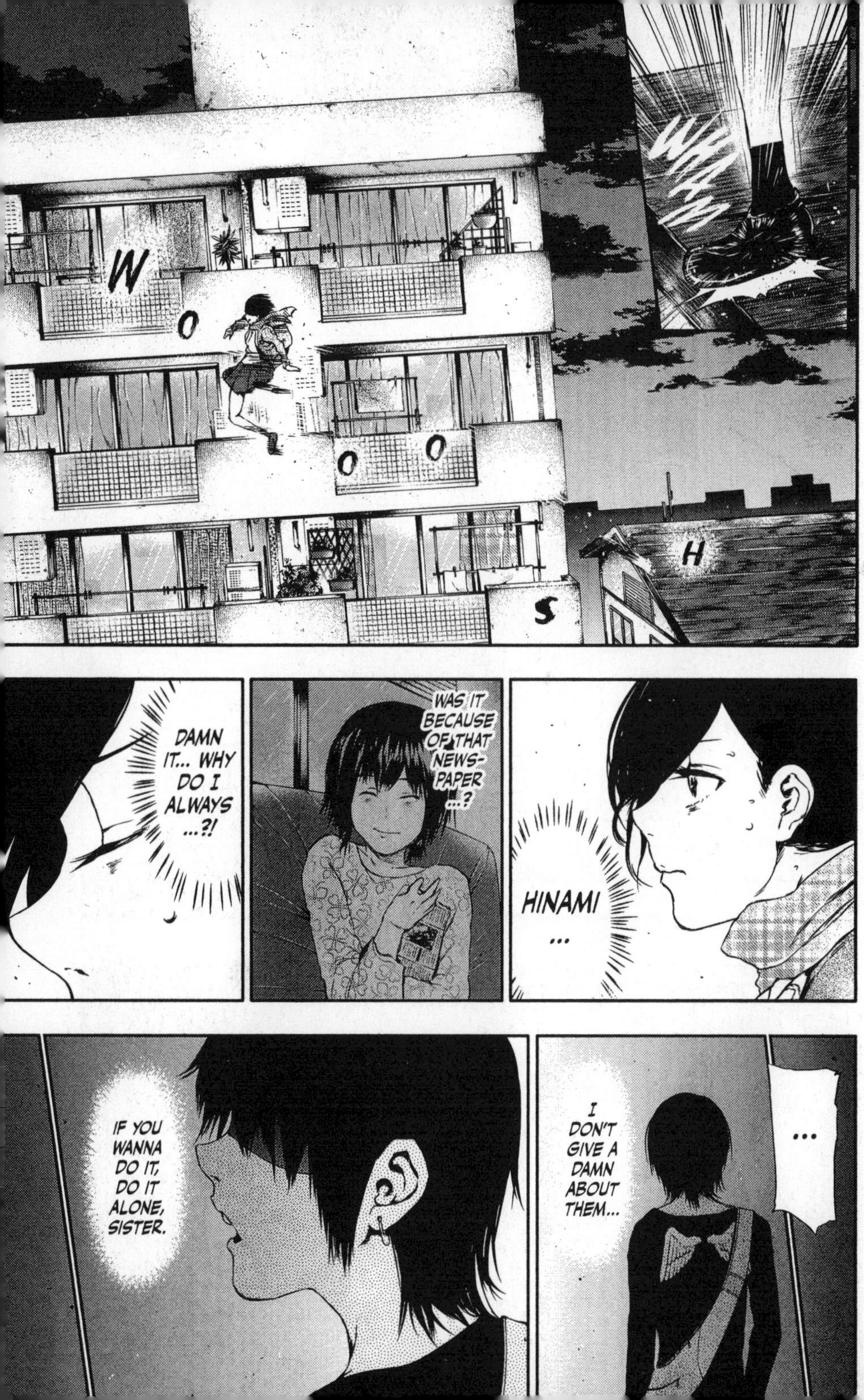
WHAM
WOOOSH
HINAMI ...
WAS IT BECAUSE OF THAT NEWS-PAPER ...?
DAMN IT... WHY DO I ALWAYS ...?!
...
I DON'T GIVE A DAMN ABOUT THEM...
IF YOU WANNA DO IT, DO IT ALONE, SISTER.

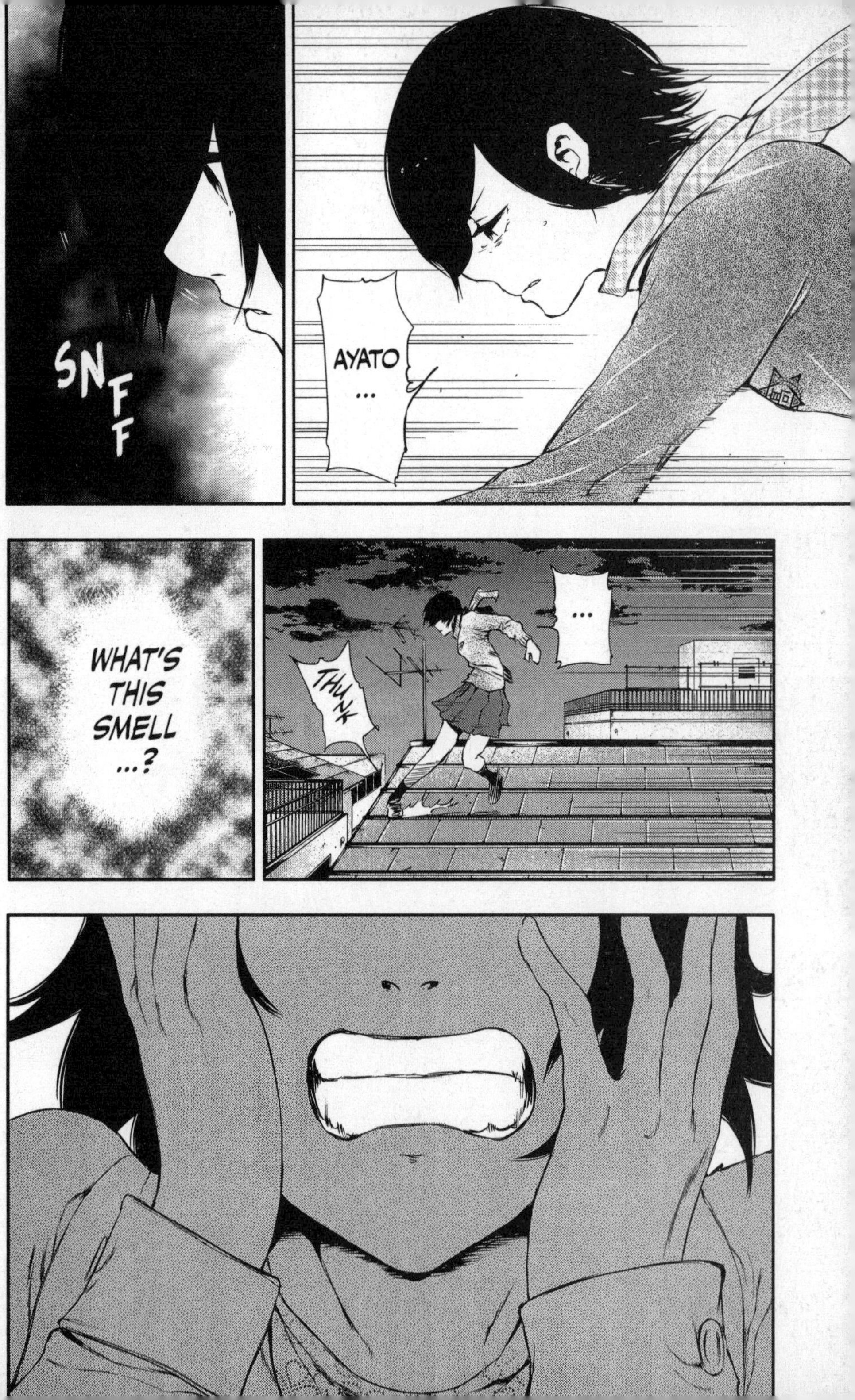
AYATO
...
SNFF
...
THUNK
WHAT'S THIS SMELL ...?

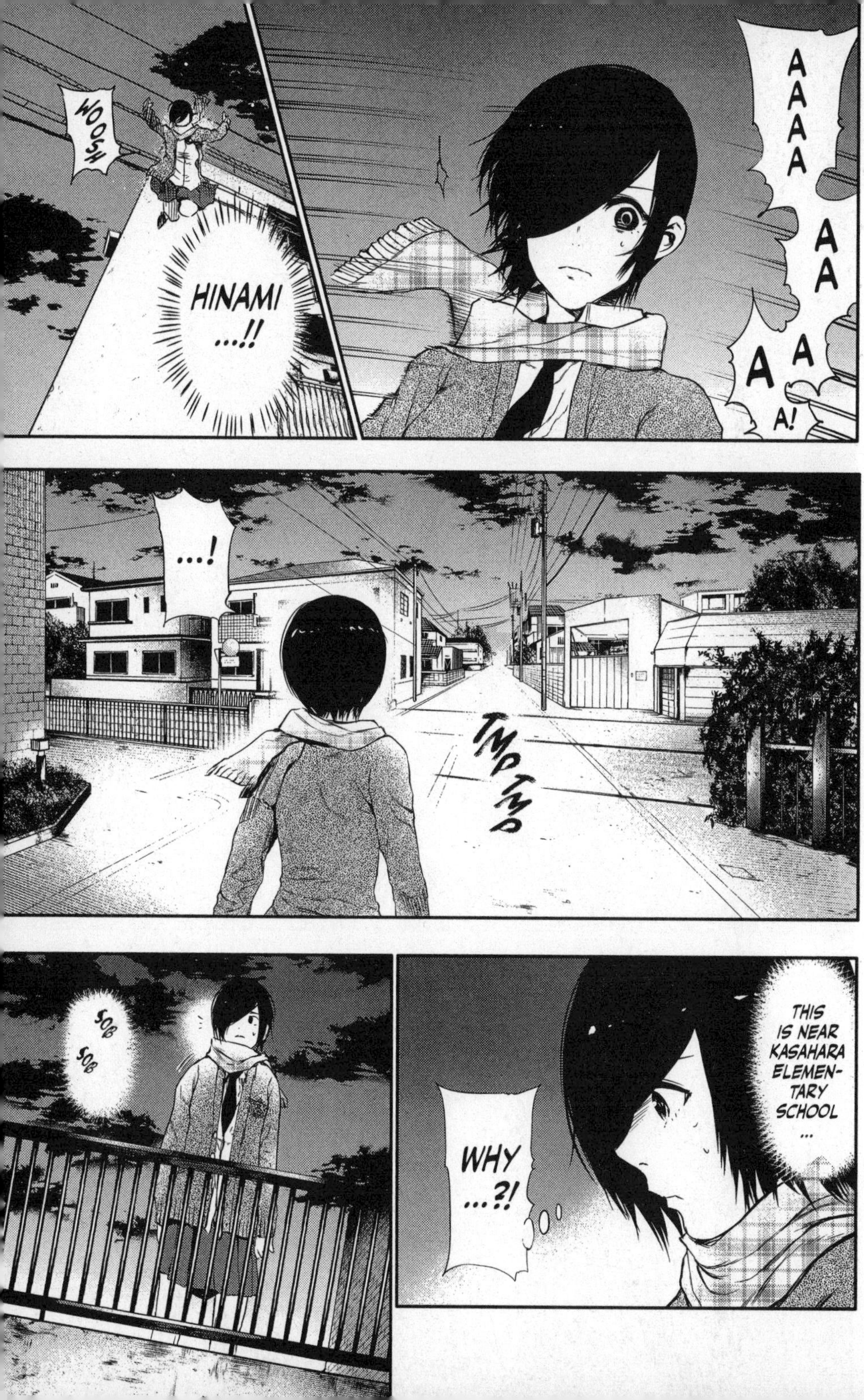
AAAAAAAAA!
WOOSH
HINAMI ...!!
...!
TMP TMP
THIS IS NEAR KASAHARA ELEMENTARY SCHOOL ...
WHY ...?!
SOB SOB

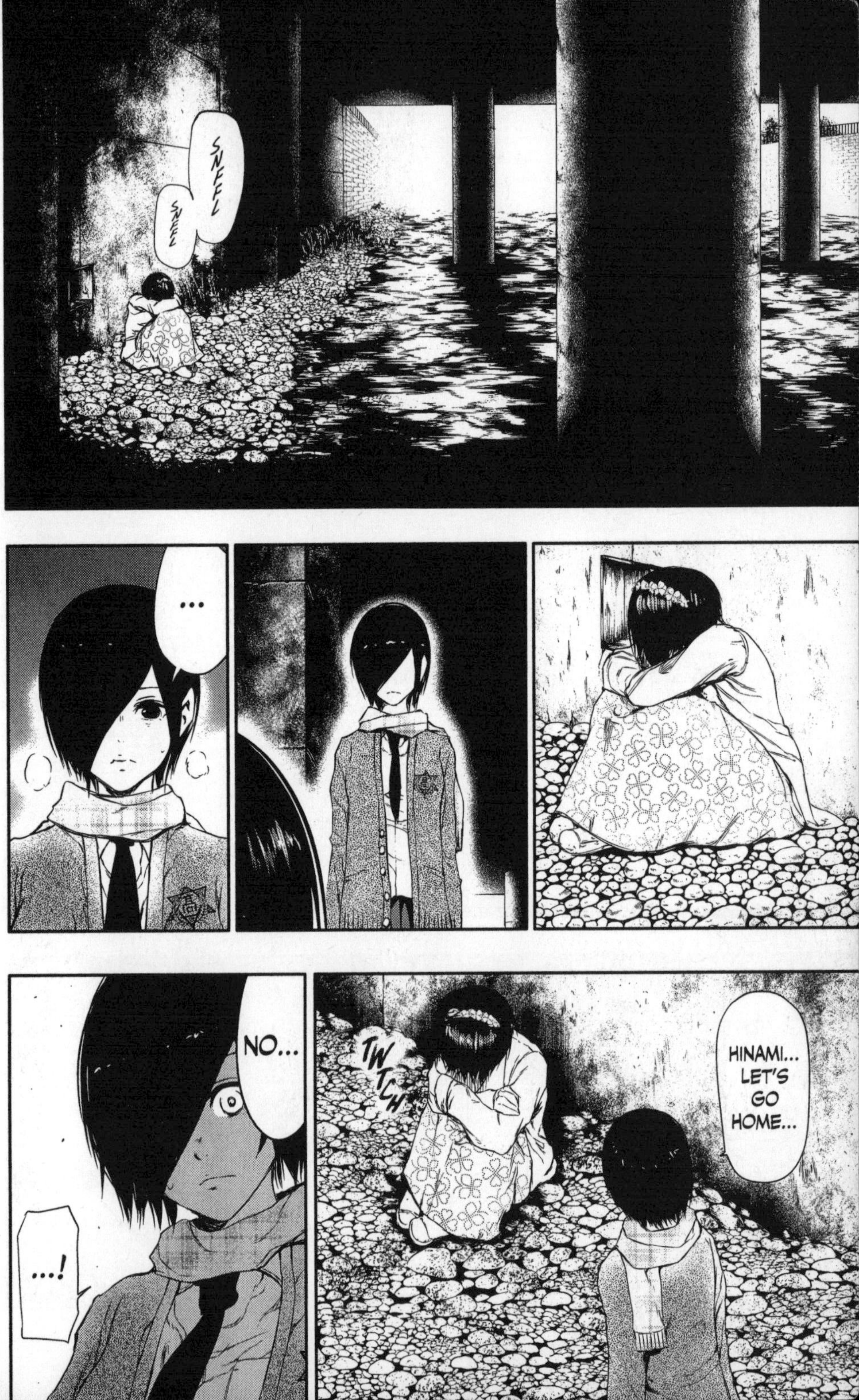
SNFFL
SNFFL
...
HINAMI... LET'S GO HOME...
TWTCH
NO...
...!

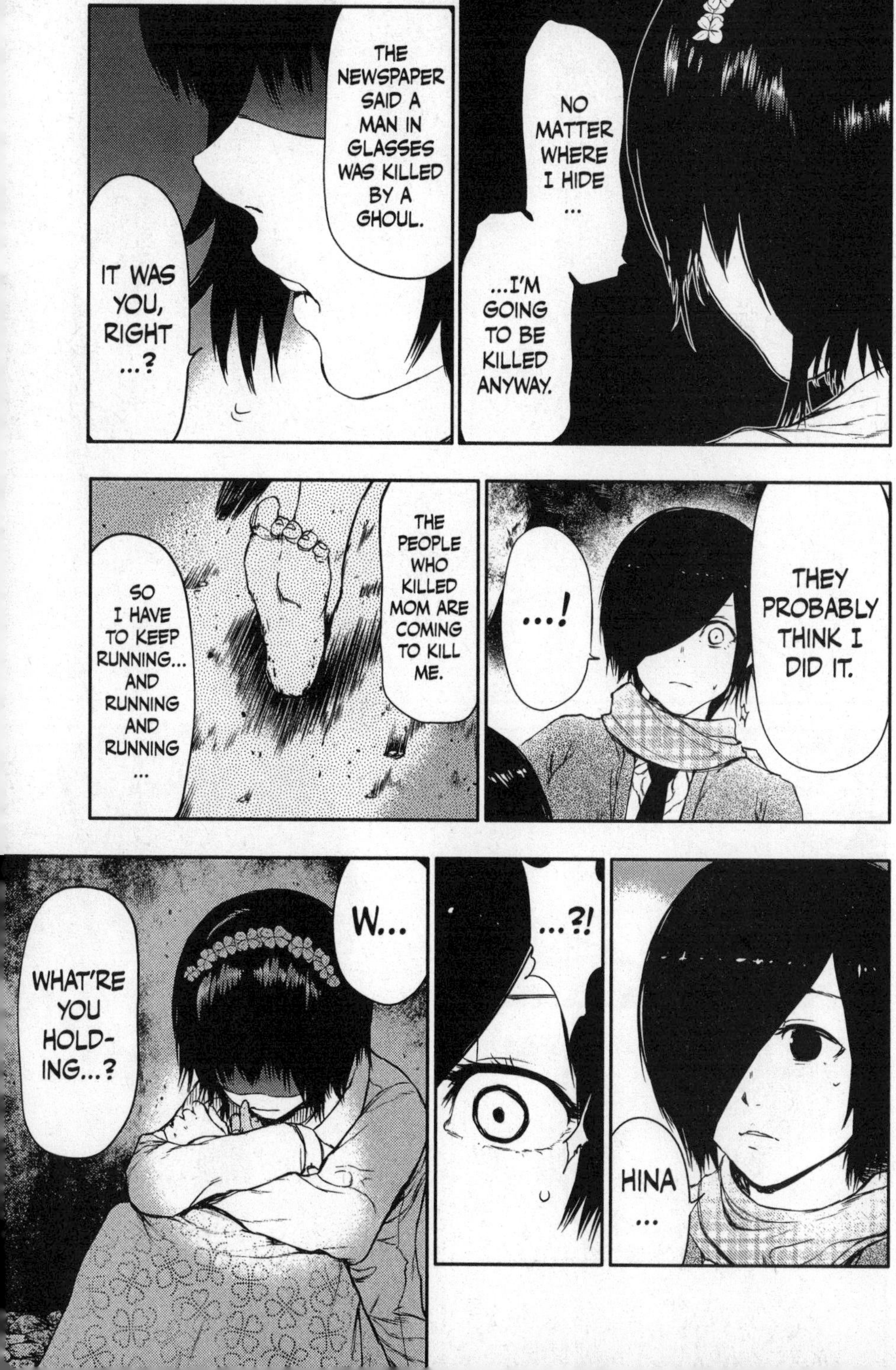
NO MATTER WHERE I HIDE ...
...I'M GOING TO BE KILLED ANYWAY.
THE NEWSPAPER SAID A MAN IN GLASSES WAS KILLED BY A GHOUL.
IT WAS YOU, RIGHT ...?
THEY PROBABLY THINK I DID IT.
...!
THE PEOPLE WHO KILLED MOM ARE COMING TO KILL ME.
SO I HAVE TO KEEP RUNNING... AND RUNNING AND RUNNING ...
HINA ...
...?!
W...
WHAT'RE YOU HOLDING...?

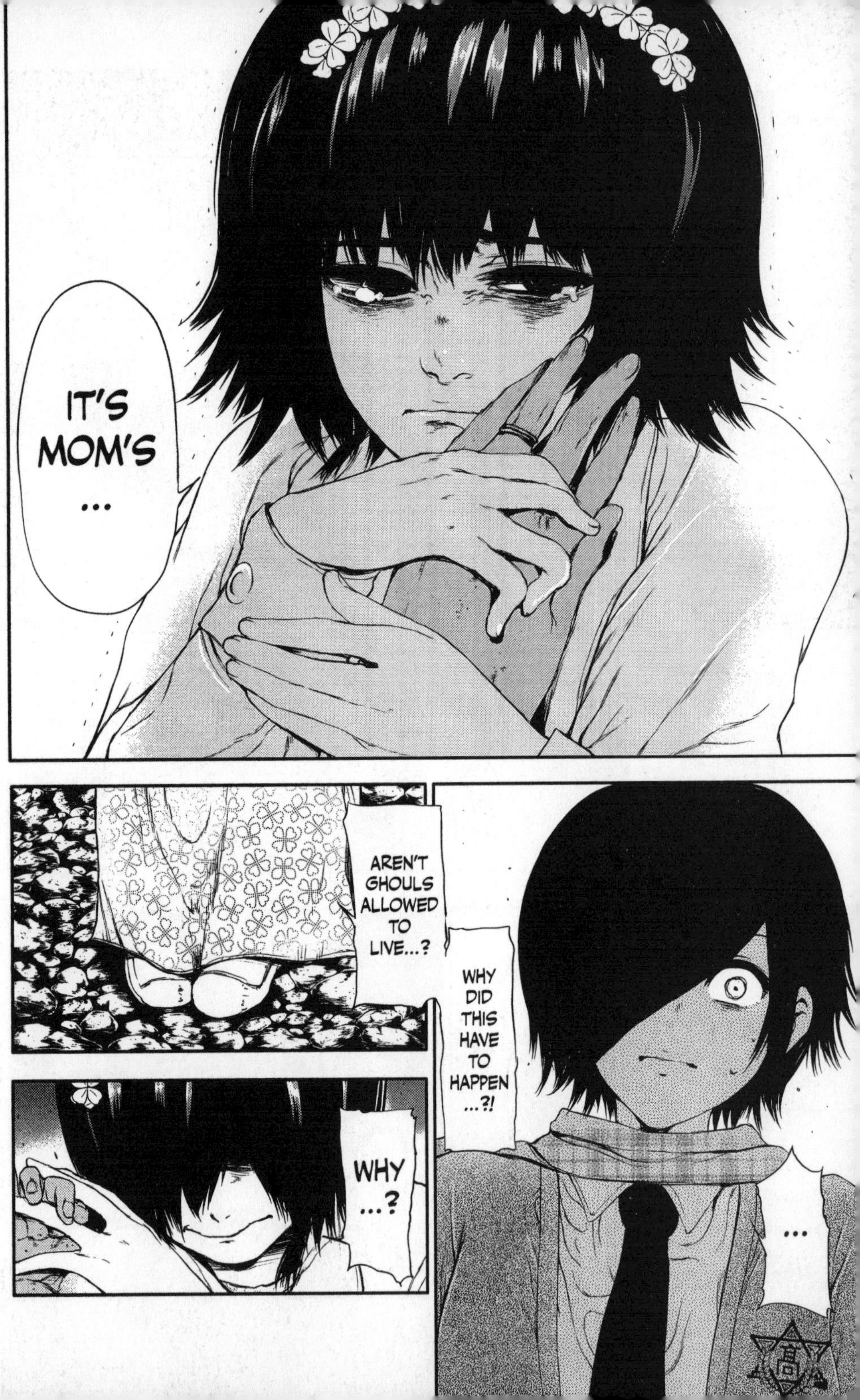
IT'S MOM'S ...
WHY DID THIS HAVE TO HAPPEN ...?!
...
AREN'T GHOULS ALLOWED TO LIVE...?
WHY ...?

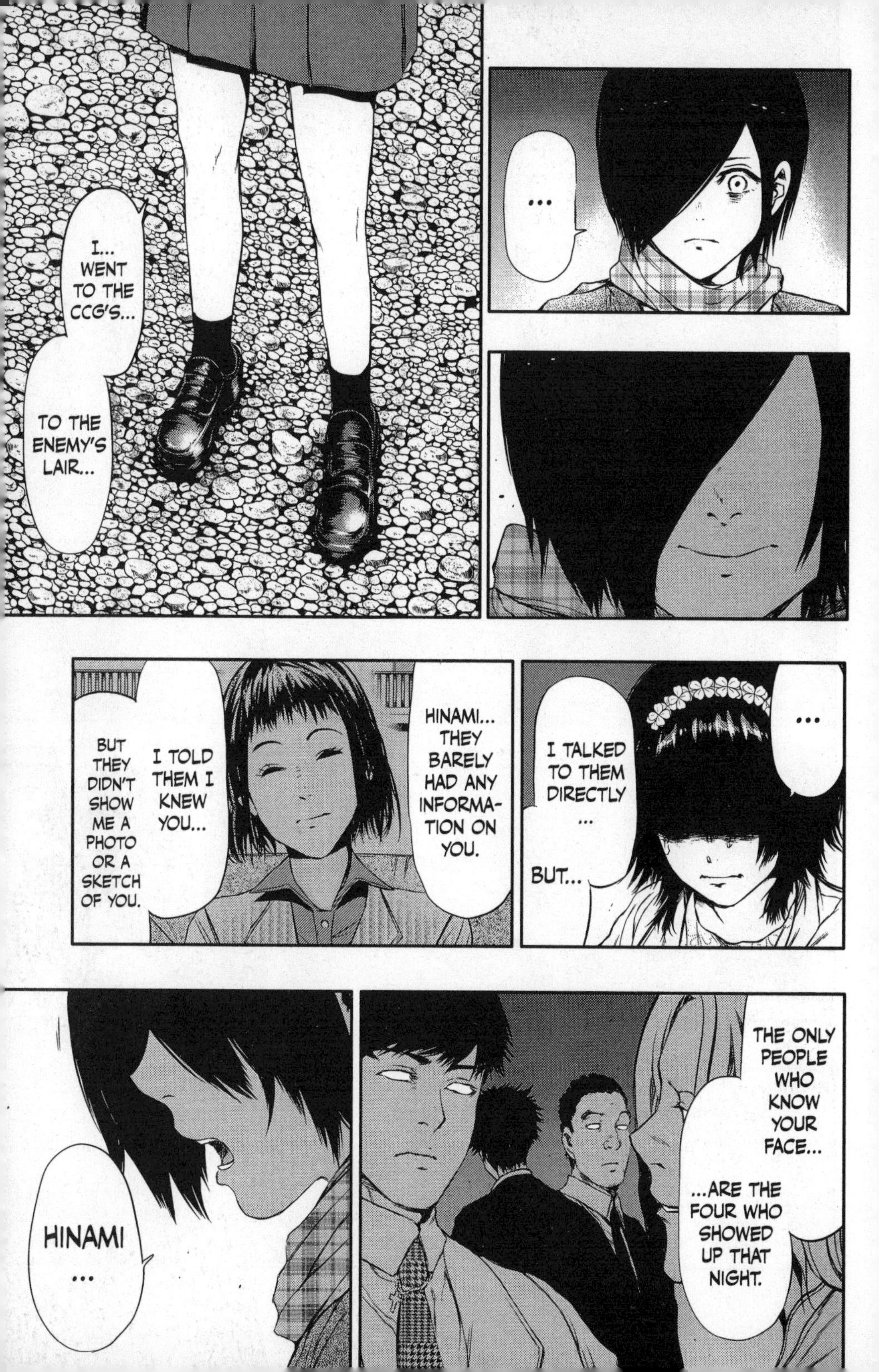
...
I... WENT TO THE CCG'S...
TO THE ENEMY'S LAIR...
...
I TALKED TO THEM DIRECTLY ...
BUT...
HINAMI... THEY BARELY HAD ANY INFORMATION ON YOU.
I TOLD THEM I KNEW YOU...
BUT THEY DIDN'T SHOW ME A PHOTO OR A SKETCH OF YOU.
THE ONLY PEOPLE WHO KNOW YOUR FACE...
...ARE THE FOUR WHO SHOWED UP THAT NIGHT.
HINAMI ...

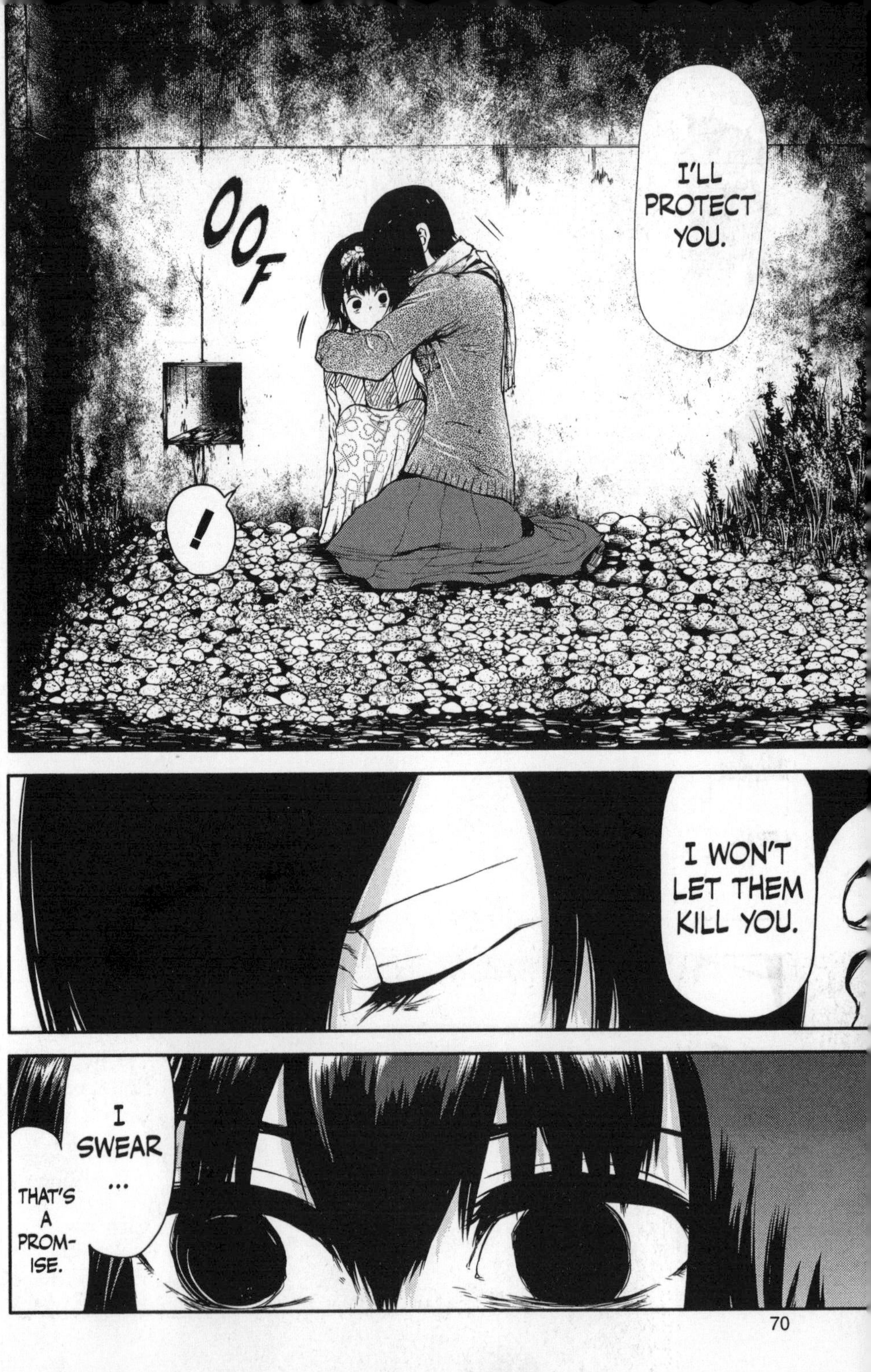
I'LL PROTECT YOU.
OOF
!
I WON'T LET THEM KILL YOU.
I SWEAR ...
THAT'S A PROM-ISE.

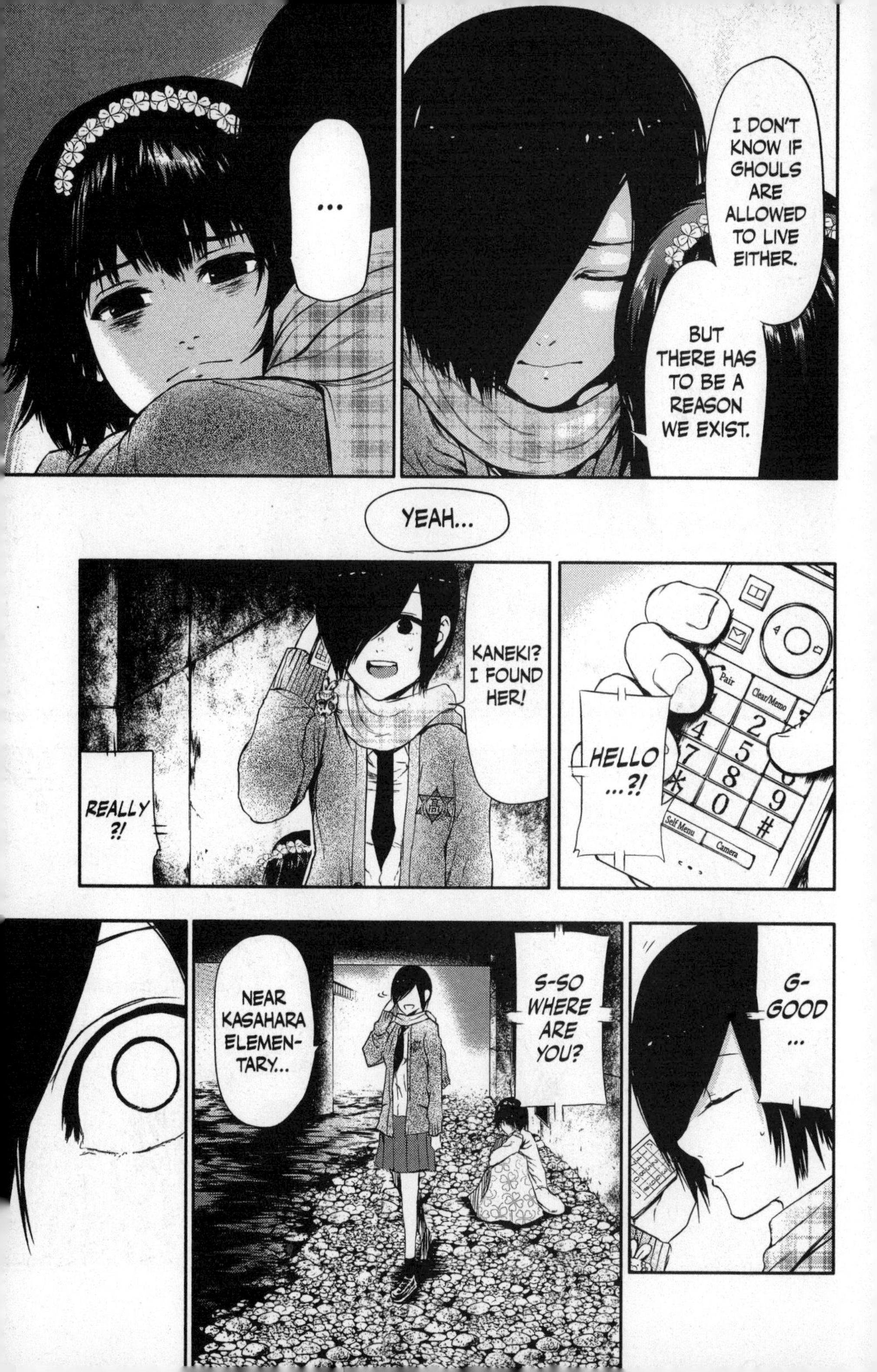

I DON'T KNOW IF GHOULS ARE ALLOWED TO LIVE EITHER.
BUT THERE HAS TO BE A REASON WE EXIST.
...
YEAH...
HELLO ...?!
Pair
Clear/Memo
Self Menu
Camera
KANEKI? I FOUND HER!
REALLY ?!
G- GOOD ...
S-SO WHERE ARE YOU?
NEAR KASAHARA ELEMEN- TARY...

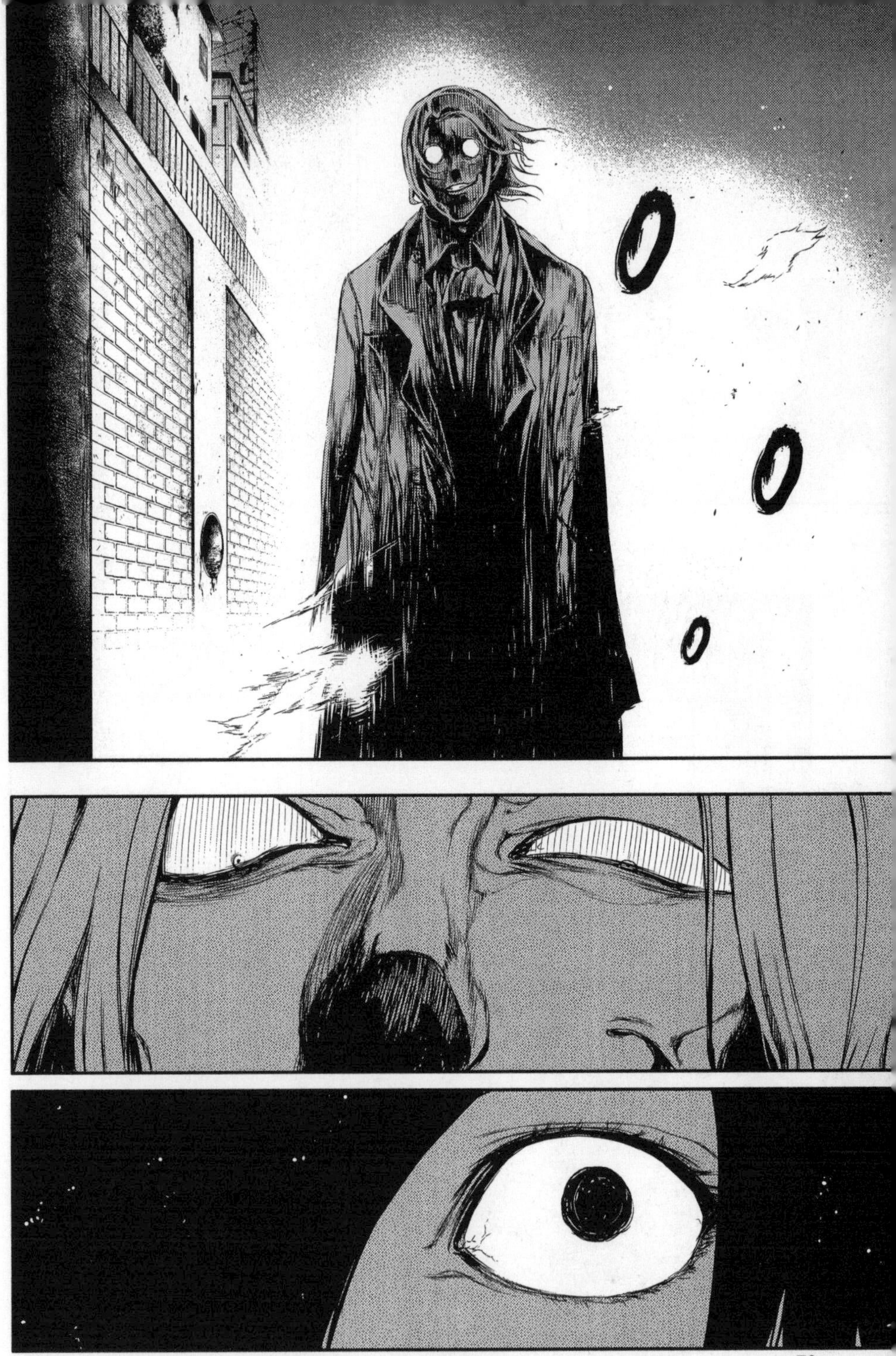

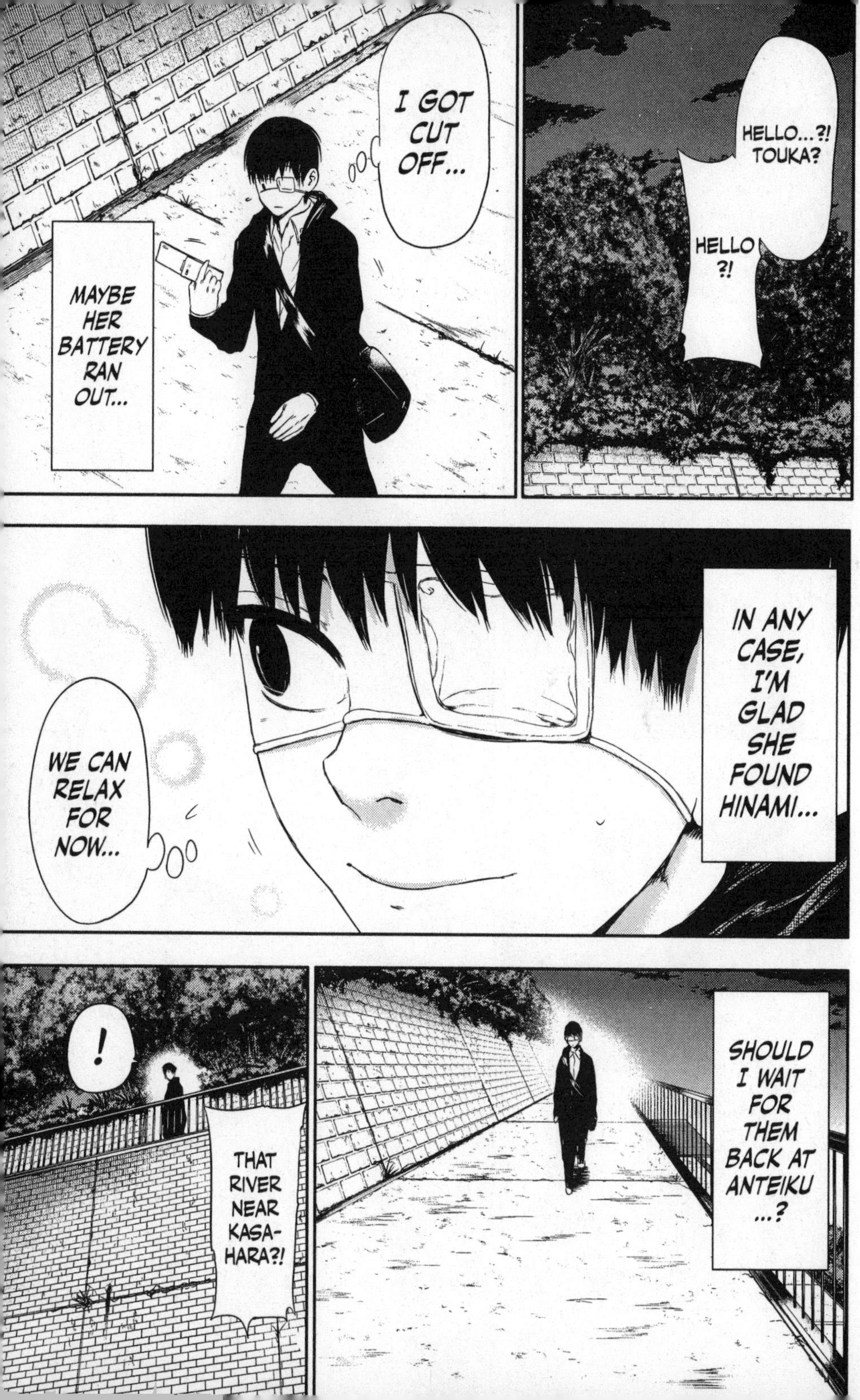
HELLO...?! TOUKA?
HELLO ?!
I GOT CUT OFF...
MAYBE HER BATTERY RAN OUT...
IN ANY CASE, I'M GLAD SHE FOUND HINAMI...
WE CAN RELAX FOR NOW...
SHOULD I WAIT FOR THEM BACK AT ANTEIKU ...?
!
THAT RIVER NEAR KASA-HARA?!

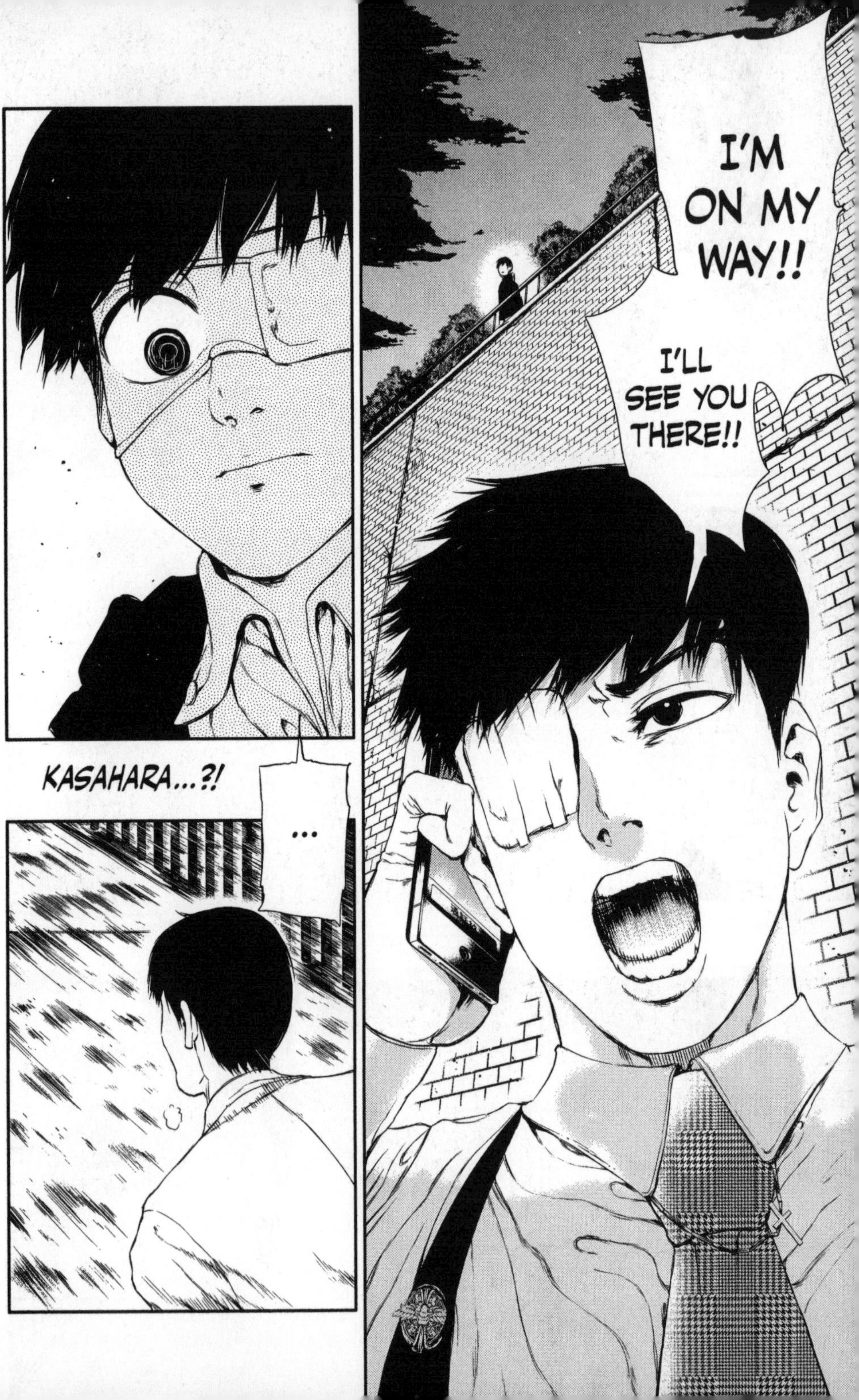
I'M ON MY WAY!!
I'LL SEE YOU THERE!!
KASAHARA...?!
...

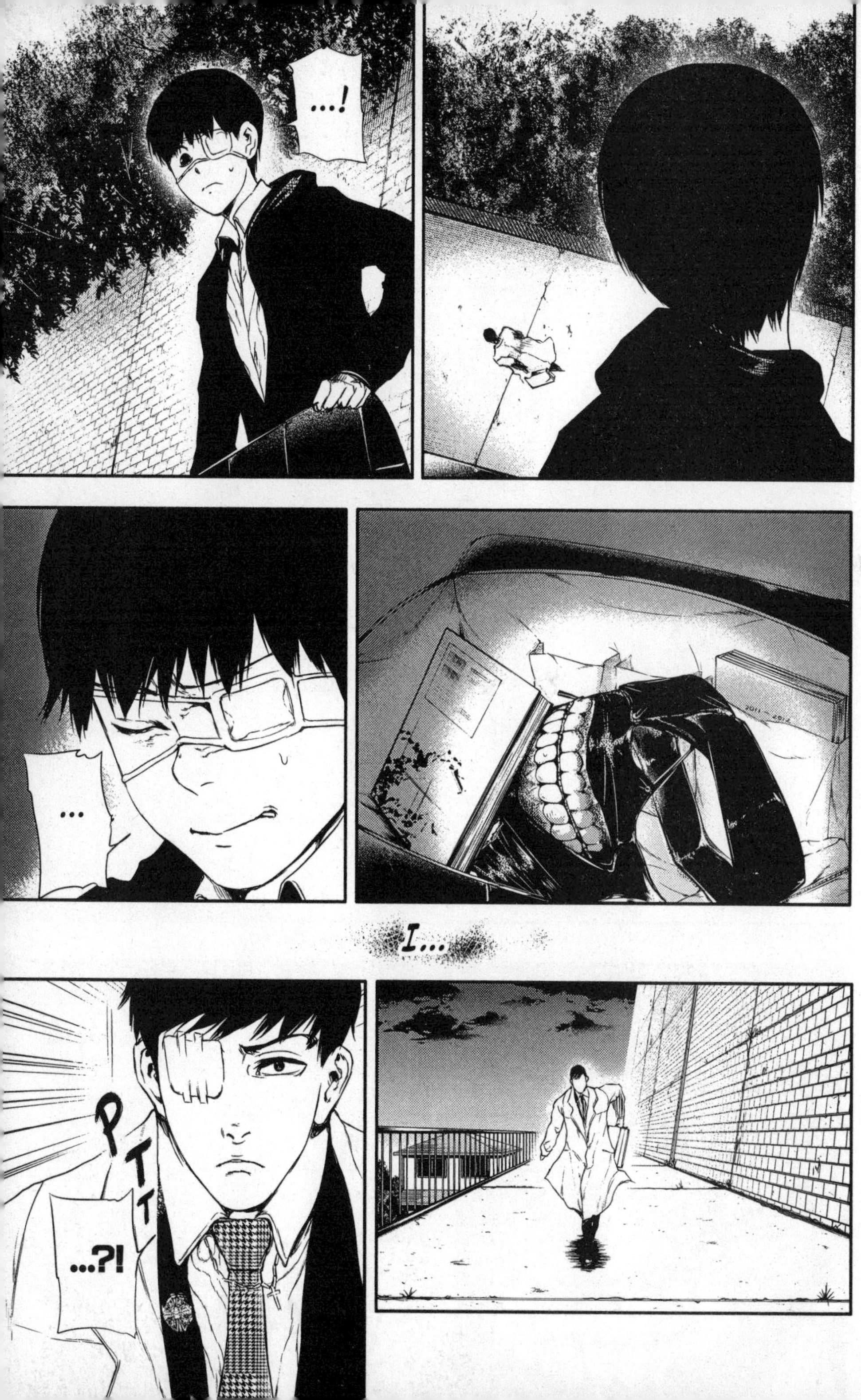
...!
...
I...
PTT
...?!

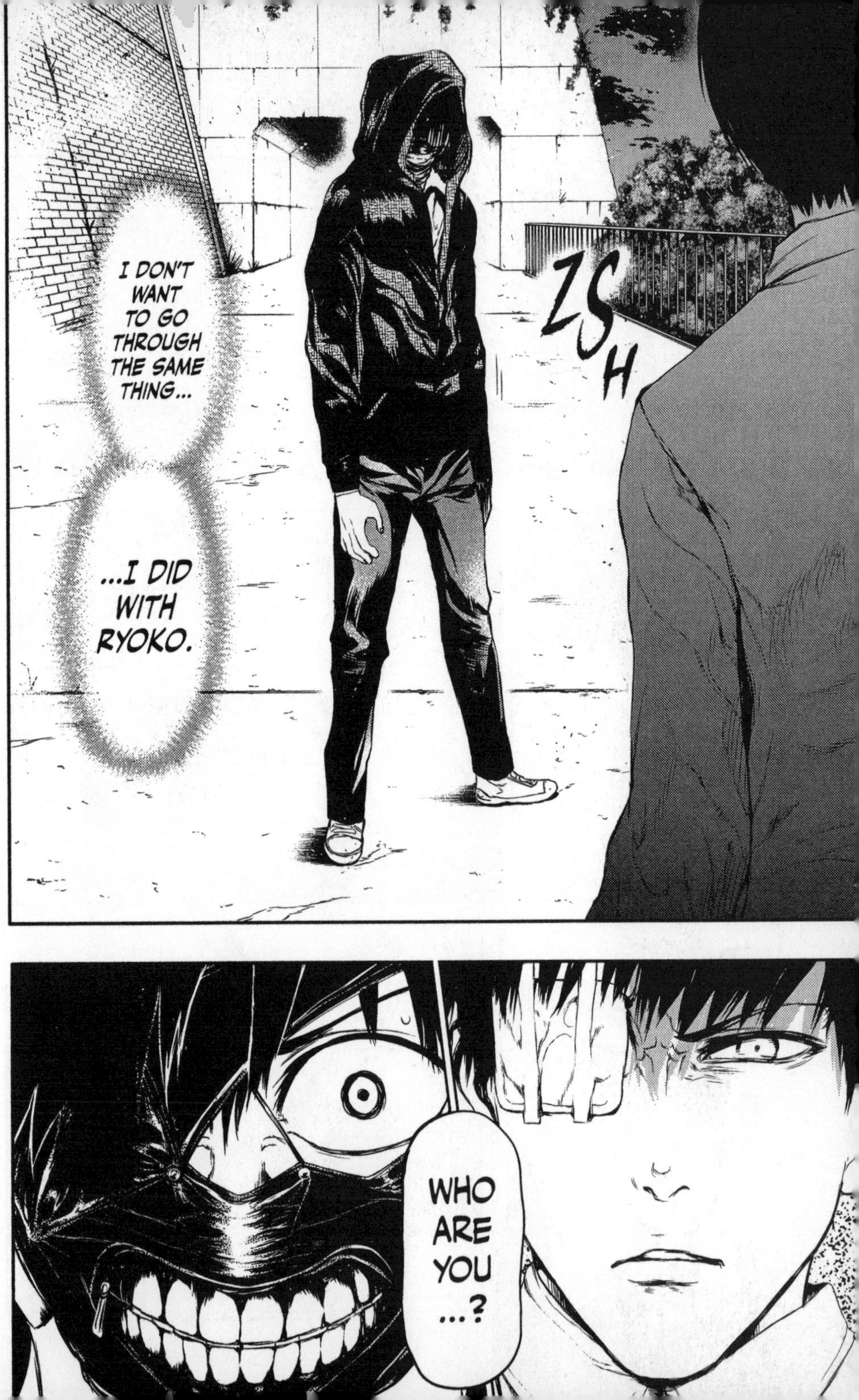
ZSH
I DON'T WANT TO GO THROUGH THE SAME THING...
...I DID WITH RYOKO.
WHO ARE YOU ...?

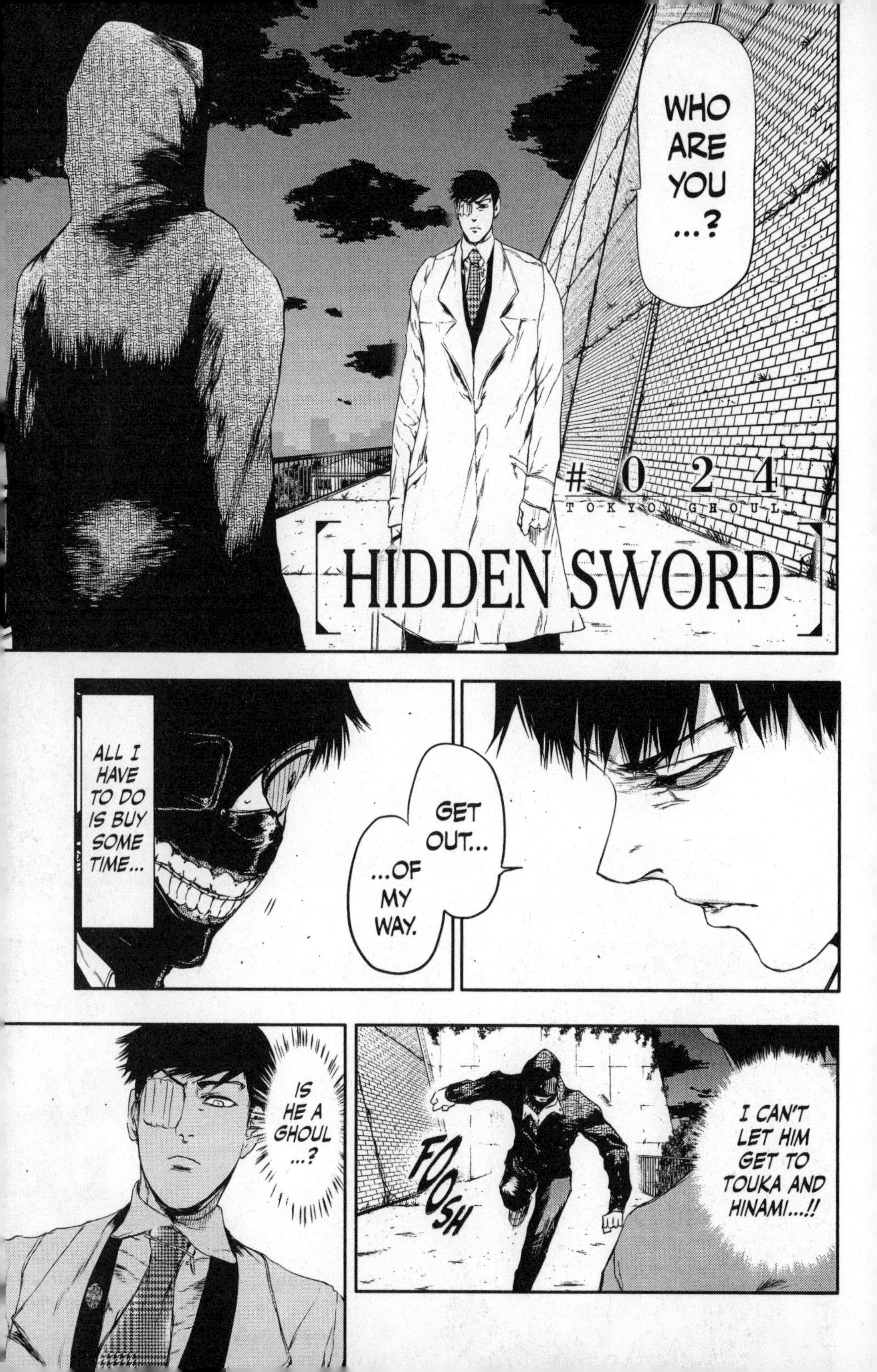
WHO ARE YOU ...?
#024
TOKYO GHOUL
HIDDEN SWORD
GET OUT...
...OF MY WAY.
ALL I HAVE TO DO IS BUY SOME TIME...
I CAN'T LET HIM GET TO TOUKA AND HINAMI...!!
FOOSH
IS HE A GHOUL ...?

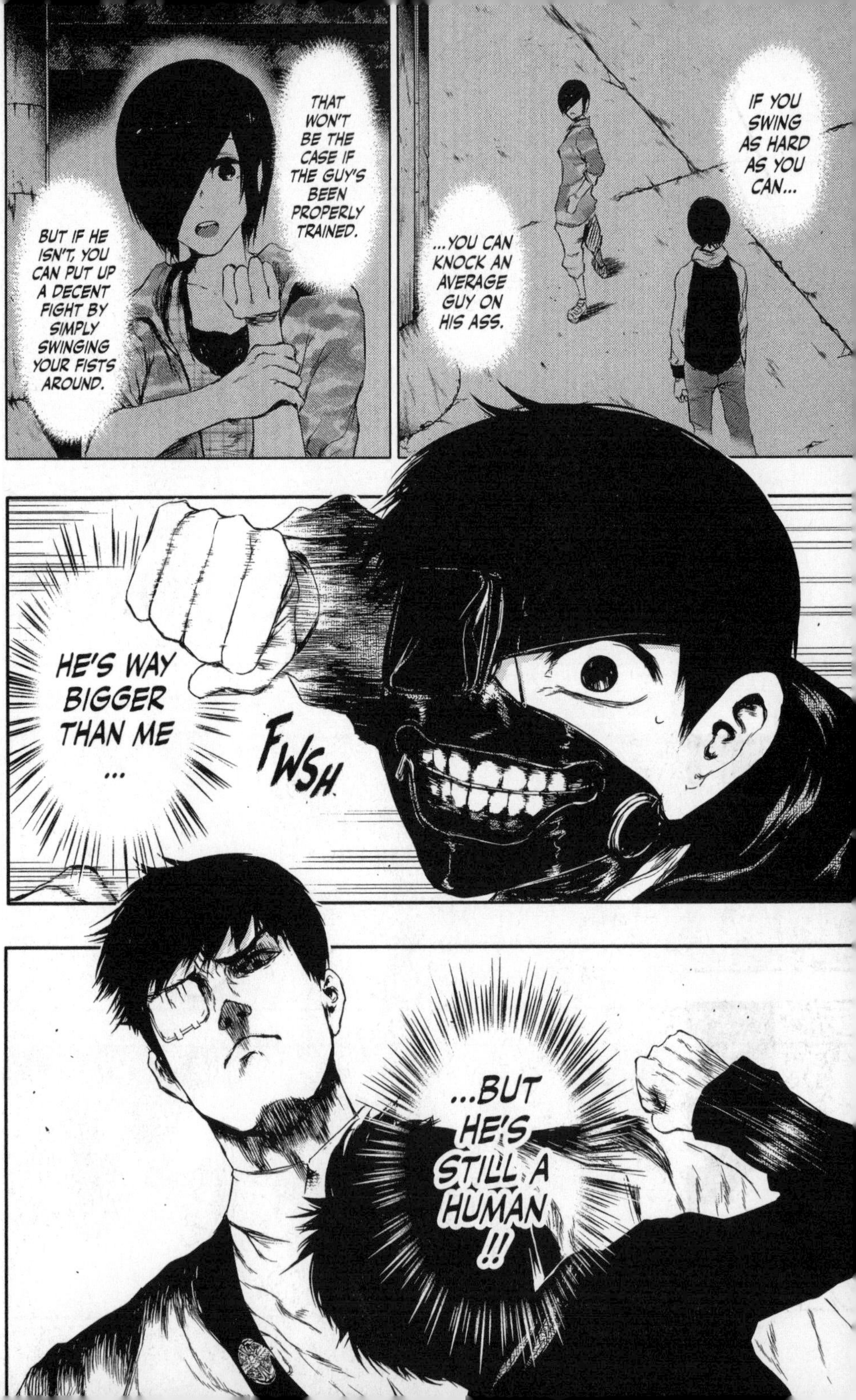
IF YOU SWING AS HARD AS YOU CAN...
...YOU CAN KNOCK AN AVERAGE GUY ON HIS ASS.
THAT WON'T BE THE CASE IF THE GUY'S BEEN PROPERLY TRAINED.
BUT IF HE ISN'T, YOU CAN PUT UP A DECENT FIGHT BY SIMPLY SWINGING YOUR FISTS AROUND.
HE'S WAY BIGGER THAN ME ...
FWSH
...BUT HE'S STILL A HUMAN!!

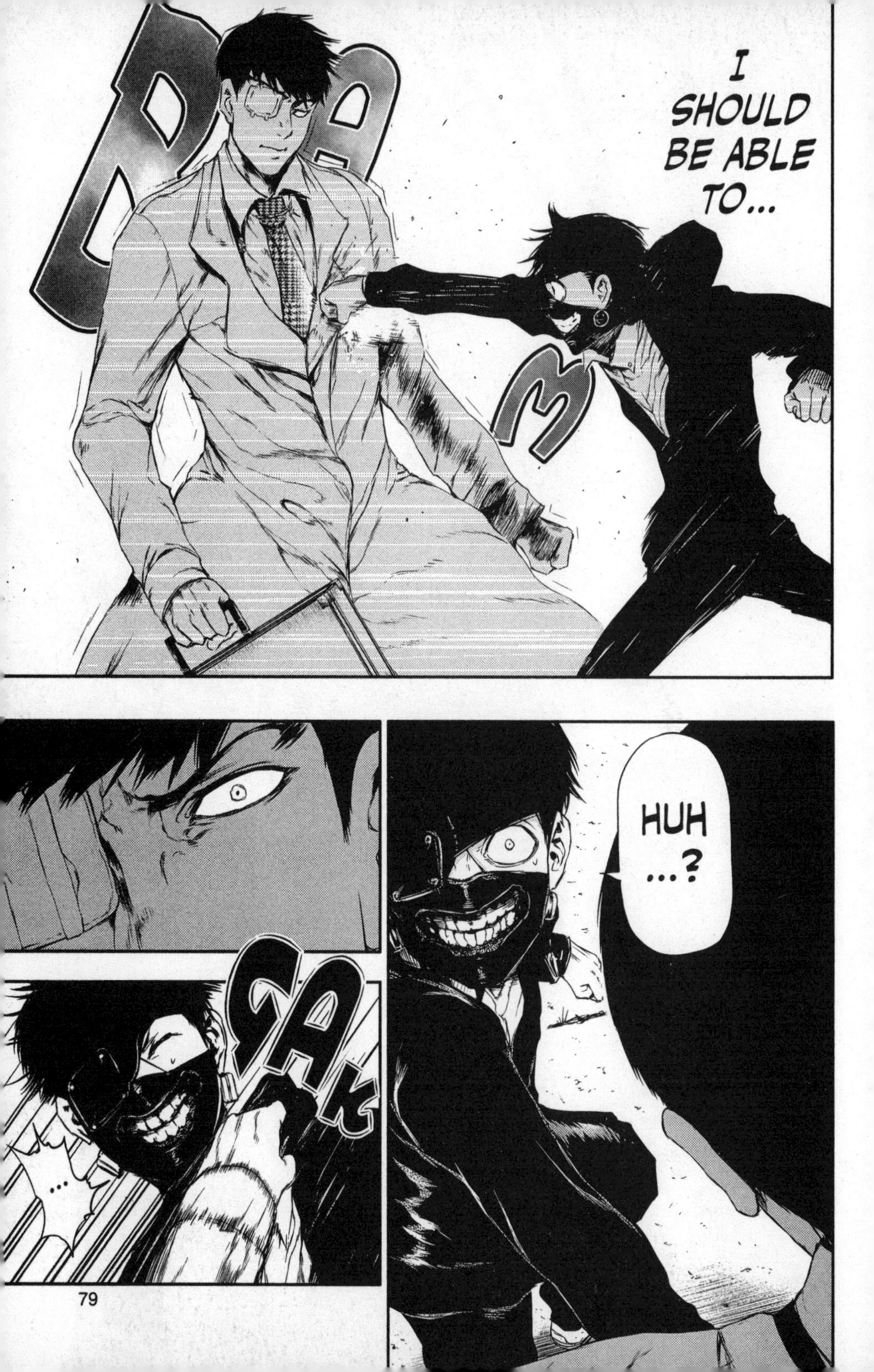
BA
M
I SHOULD BE ABLE TO...
HUH ...?
GAK
...

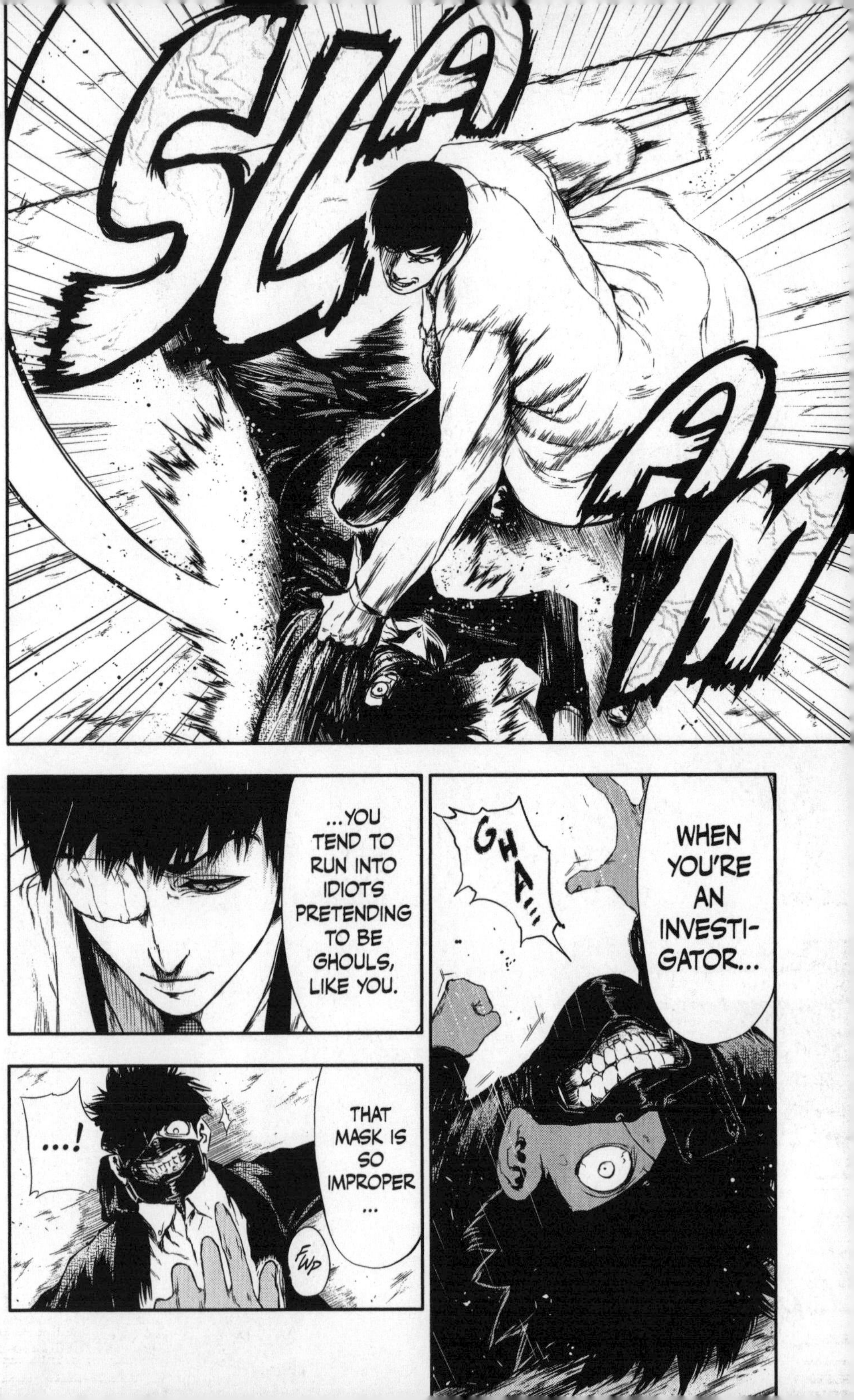
SLAM
WHEN YOU'RE AN INVESTI-GATOR...
GHA!!!
...YOU TEND TO RUN INTO IDIOTS PRETENDING TO BE GHOULS, LIKE YOU.
THAT MASK IS SO IMPROPER ...
FWP
...!

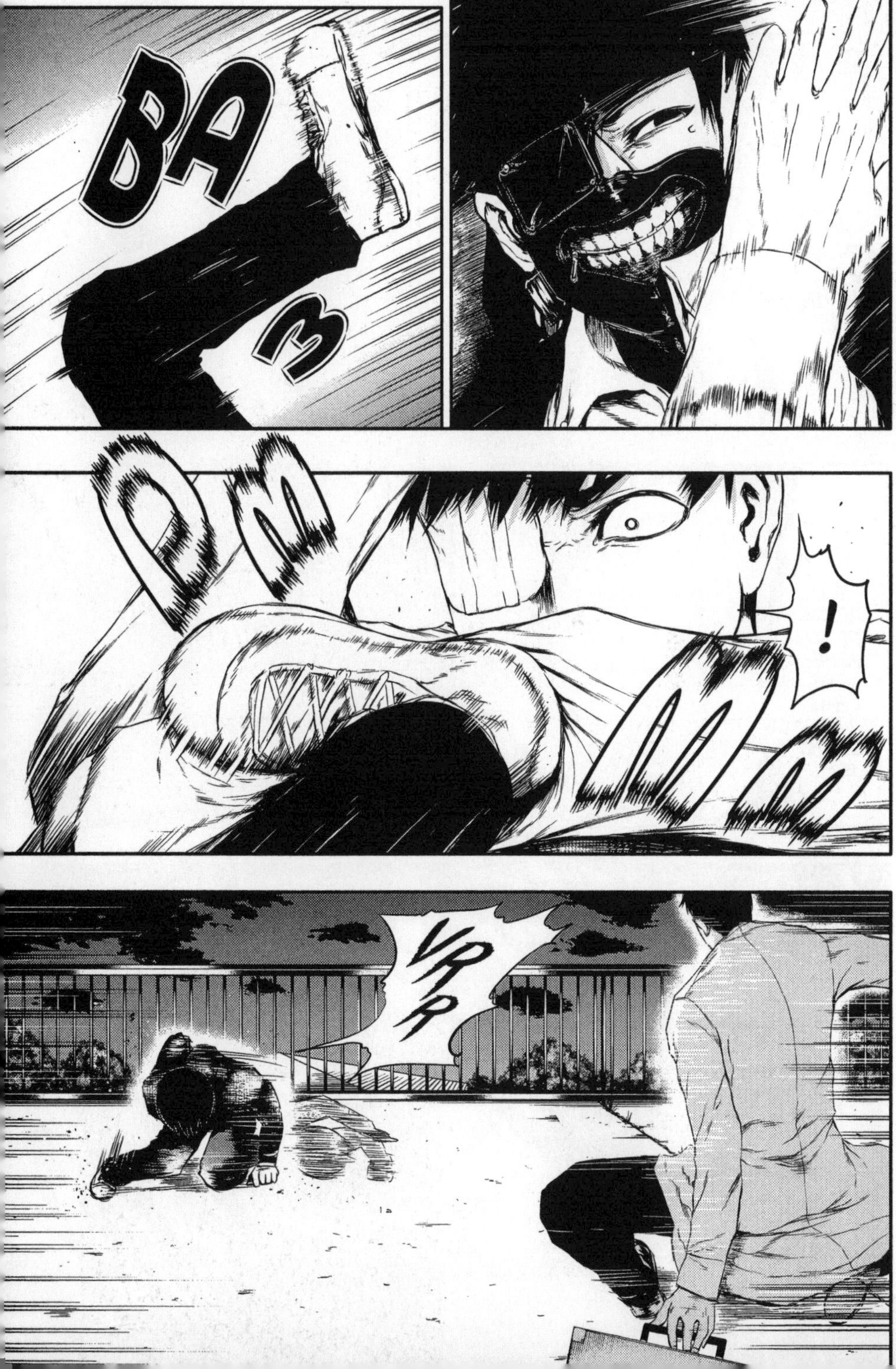
BAM
DMMMM
!
VRR

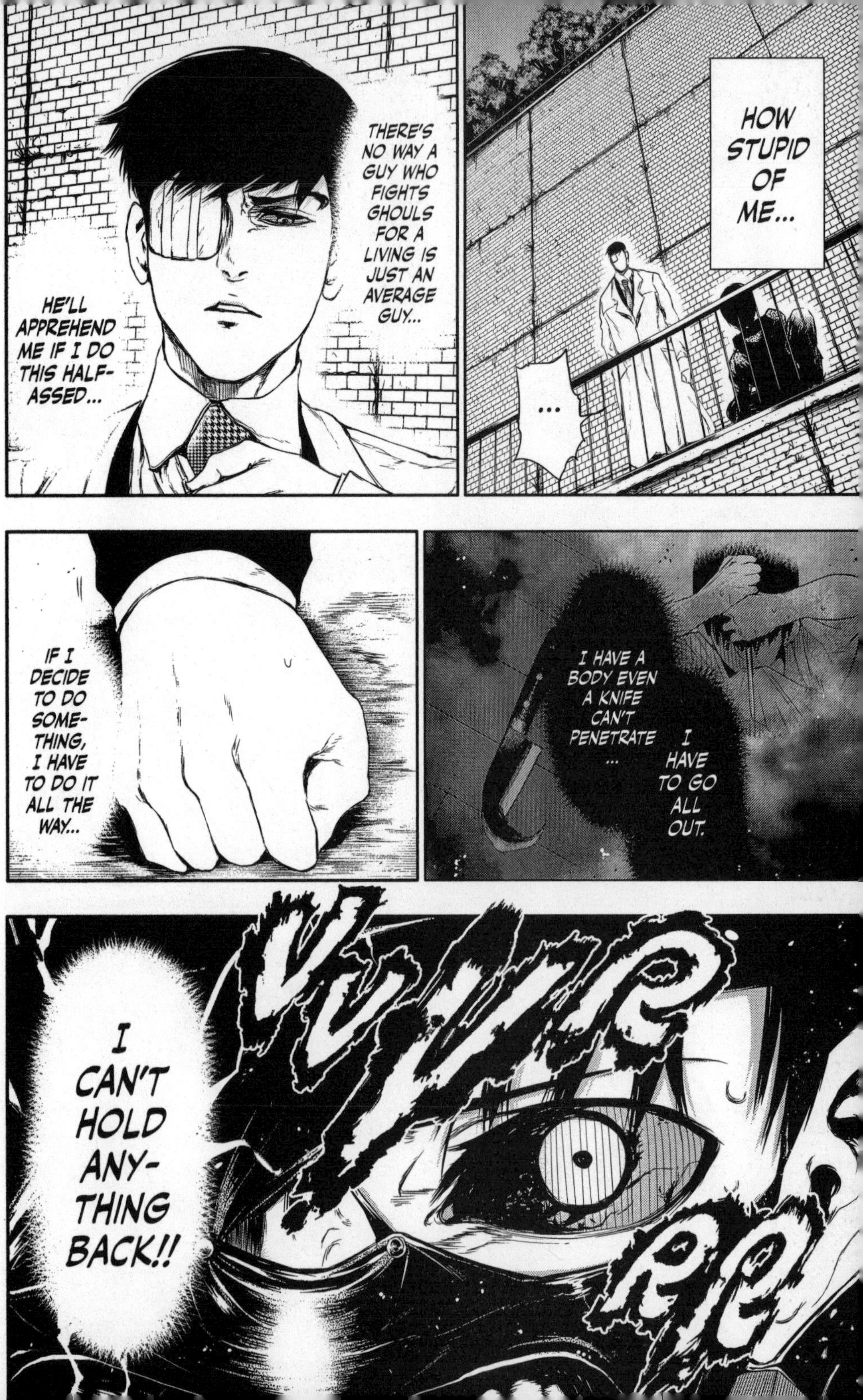
HOW STUPID OF ME...
...
THERE'S NO WAY A GUY WHO FIGHTS GHOULS FOR A LIVING IS JUST AN AVERAGE GUY...
HE'LL APPREHEND ME IF I DO THIS HALF-ASSED...
I HAVE A BODY EVEN A KNIFE CAN'T PENETRATE...
I HAVE TO GO ALL OUT.
IF I DECIDE TO DO SOMETHING, I HAVE TO DO IT ALL THE WAY...
I CAN'T HOLD ANYTHING BACK!!

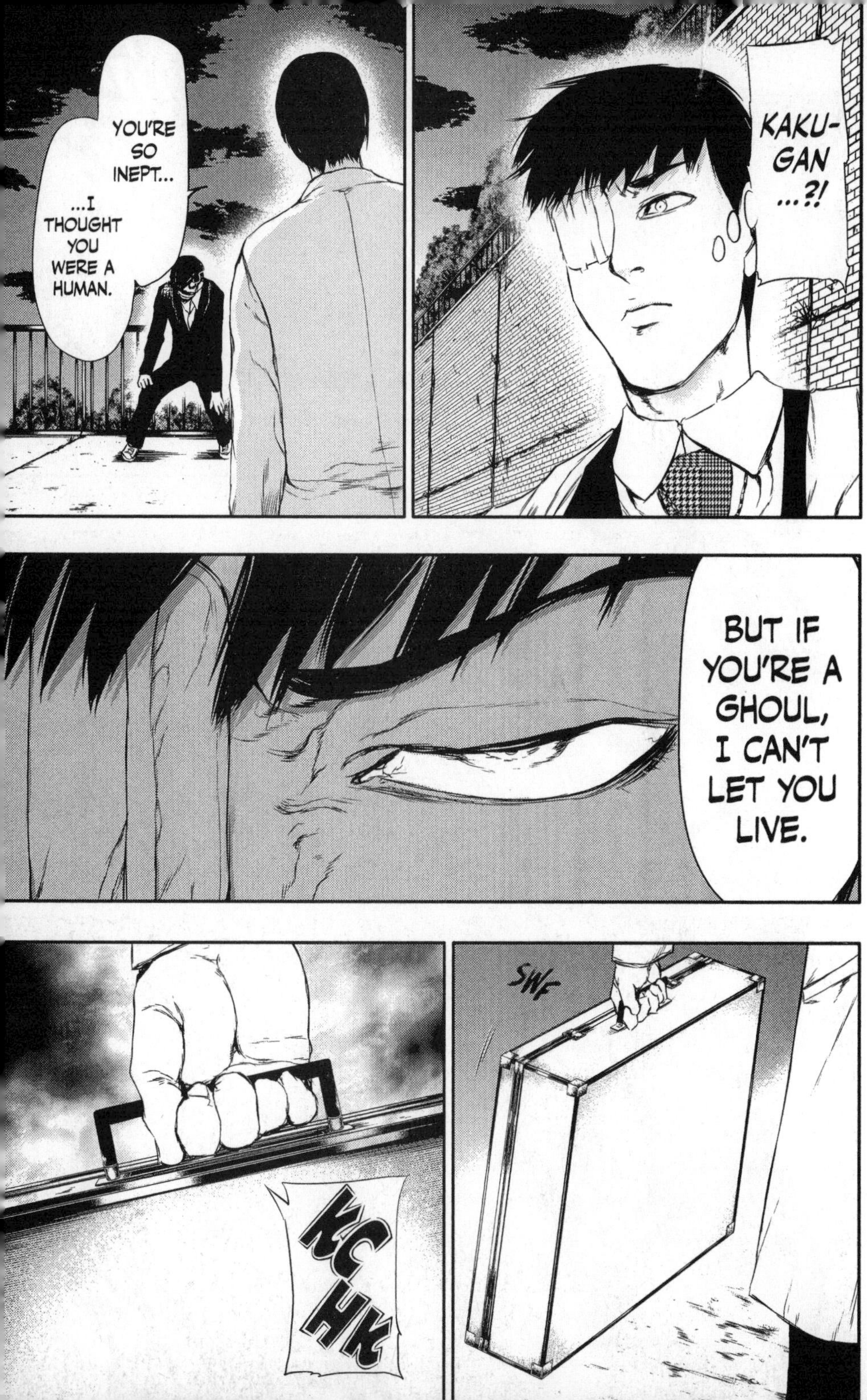
KAKU-GAN ...?!
YOU'RE SO INEPT...
...I THOUGHT YOU WERE A HUMAN.
BUT IF YOU'RE A GHOUL, I CAN'T LET YOU LIVE.
SWF
KCHK

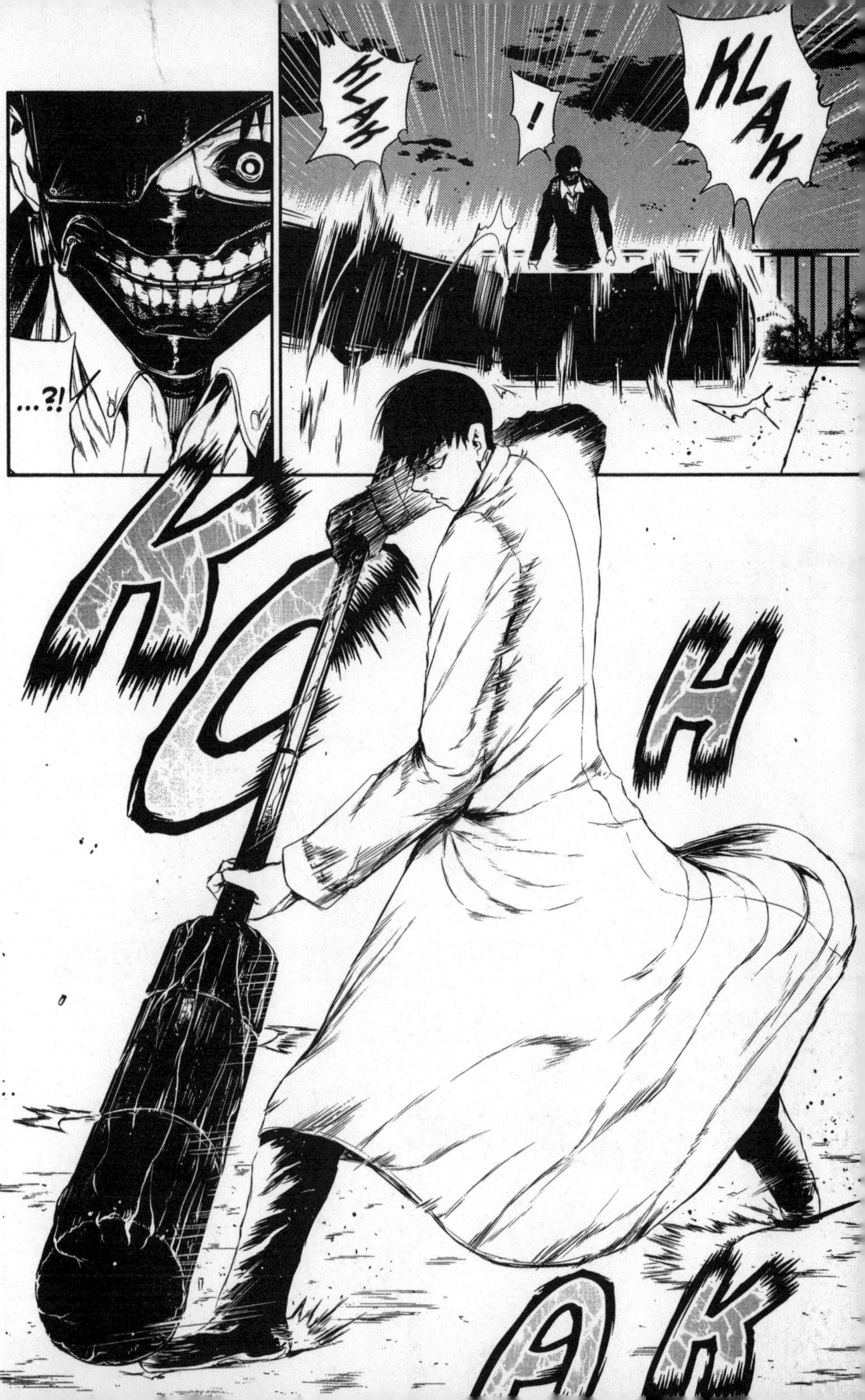
KLAK
!
KLAK
...?!
KCHAK

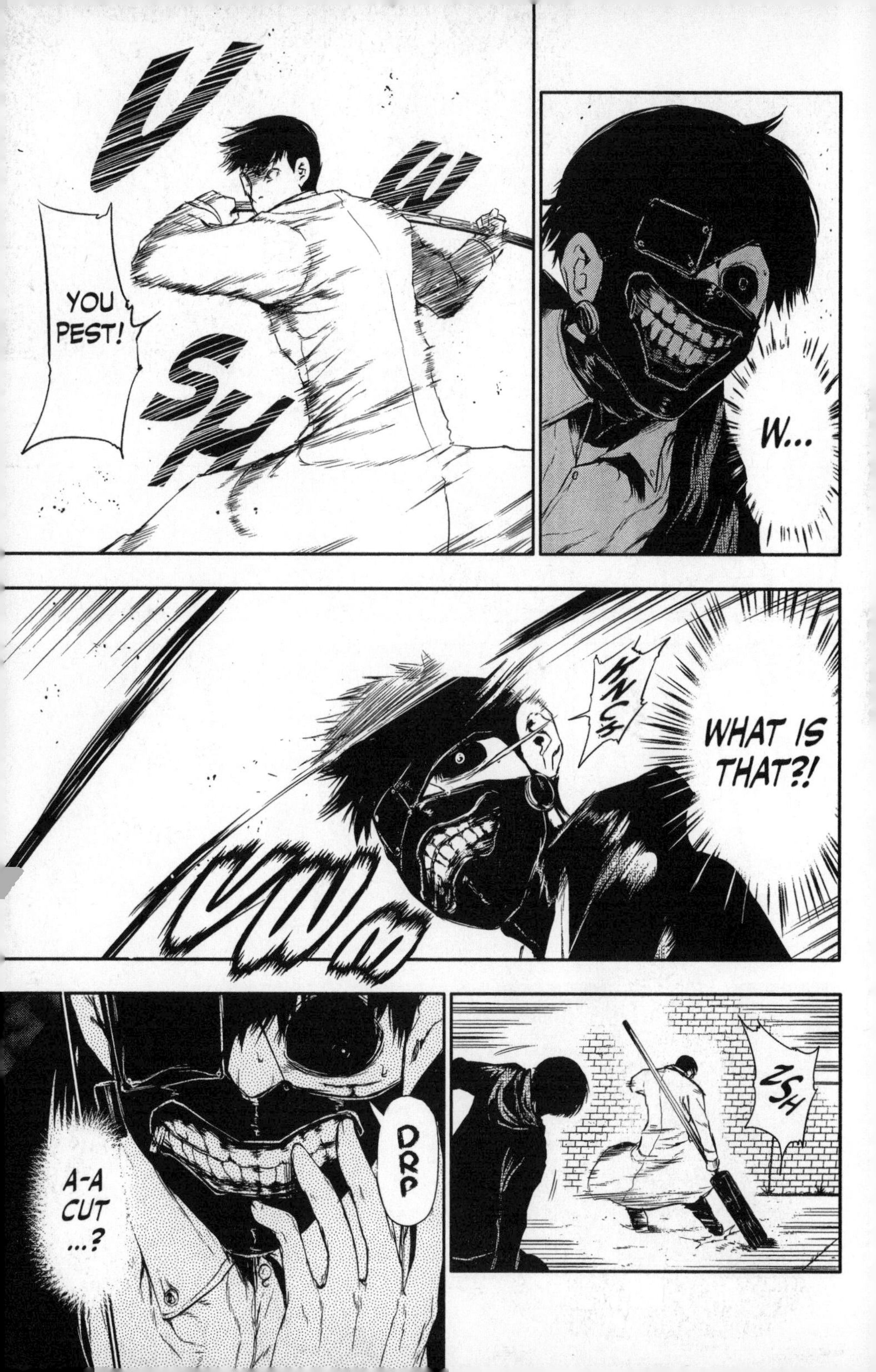
W...
YOU PEST!
KNCH
WHAT IS THAT?!
ZSH
DRP
A-A CUT ...?

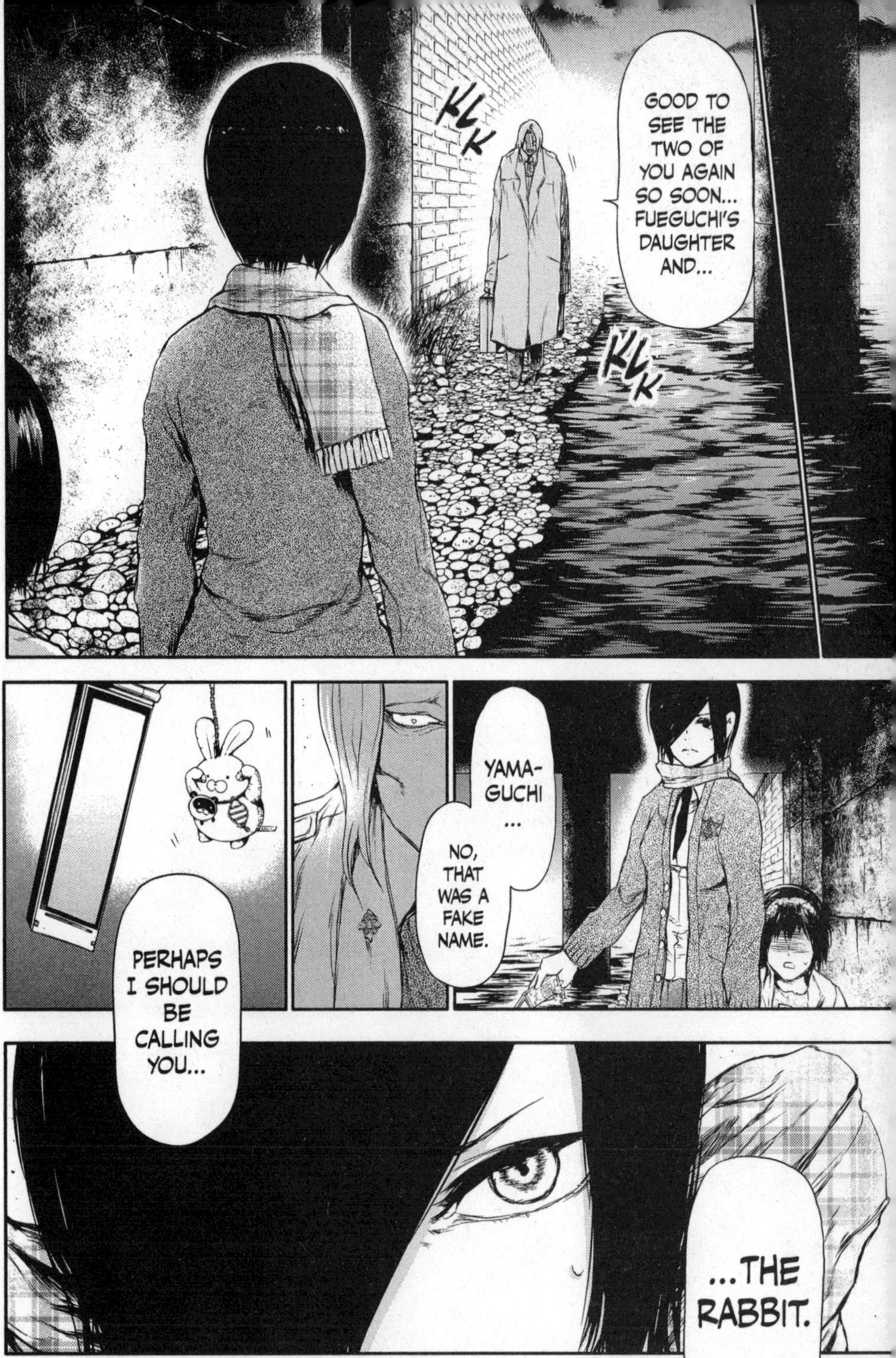
GOOD TO SEE THE TWO OF YOU AGAIN SO SOON... FUEGUCHI'S DAUGHTER AND...
KLK
KLK
YAMA-GUCHI...
NO, THAT WAS A FAKE NAME.
PERHAPS I SHOULD BE CALLING YOU...
...THE RABBIT.

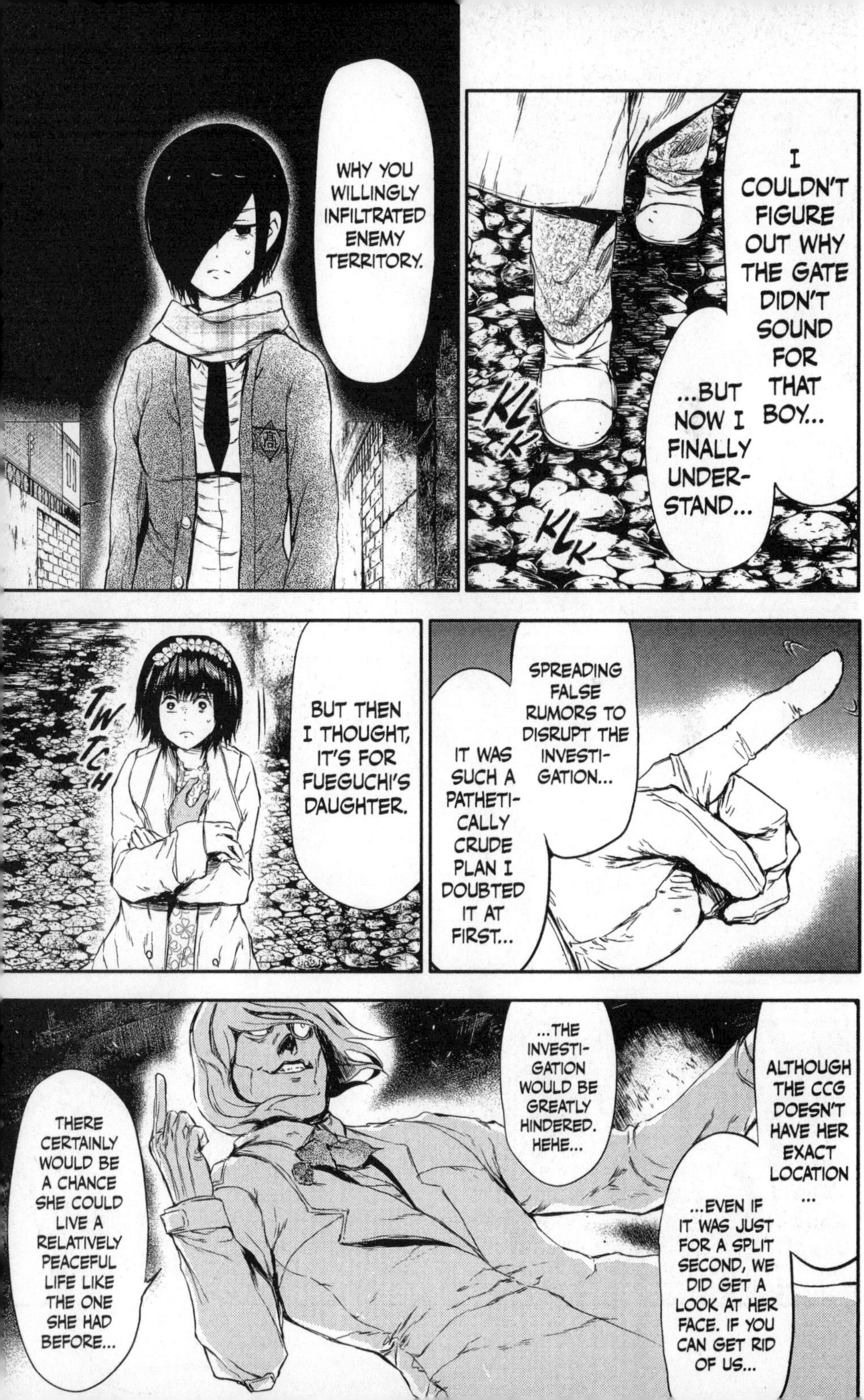
I COULDN'T FIGURE OUT WHY THE GATE DIDN'T SOUND FOR THAT BOY...
...BUT NOW I FINALLY UNDER-STAND...
KLK
KLK
WHY YOU WILLINGLY INFILTRATED ENEMY TERRITORY.
SPREADING FALSE RUMORS TO DISRUPT THE INVESTI-GATION...
IT WAS SUCH A PATHETI-CALLY CRUDE PLAN I DOUBTED IT AT FIRST...
TWTCH
BUT THEN I THOUGHT, IT'S FOR FUEGUCHI'S DAUGHTER.
ALTHOUGH THE CCG DOESN'T HAVE HER EXACT LOCATION ...
...EVEN IF IT WAS JUST FOR A SPLIT SECOND, WE DID GET A LOOK AT HER FACE. IF YOU CAN GET RID OF US...
...THE INVESTI-GATION WOULD BE GREATLY HINDERED. HEHE...
THERE CERTAINLY WOULD BE A CHANCE SHE COULD LIVE A RELATIVELY PEACEFUL LIFE LIKE THE ONE SHE HAD BEFORE...

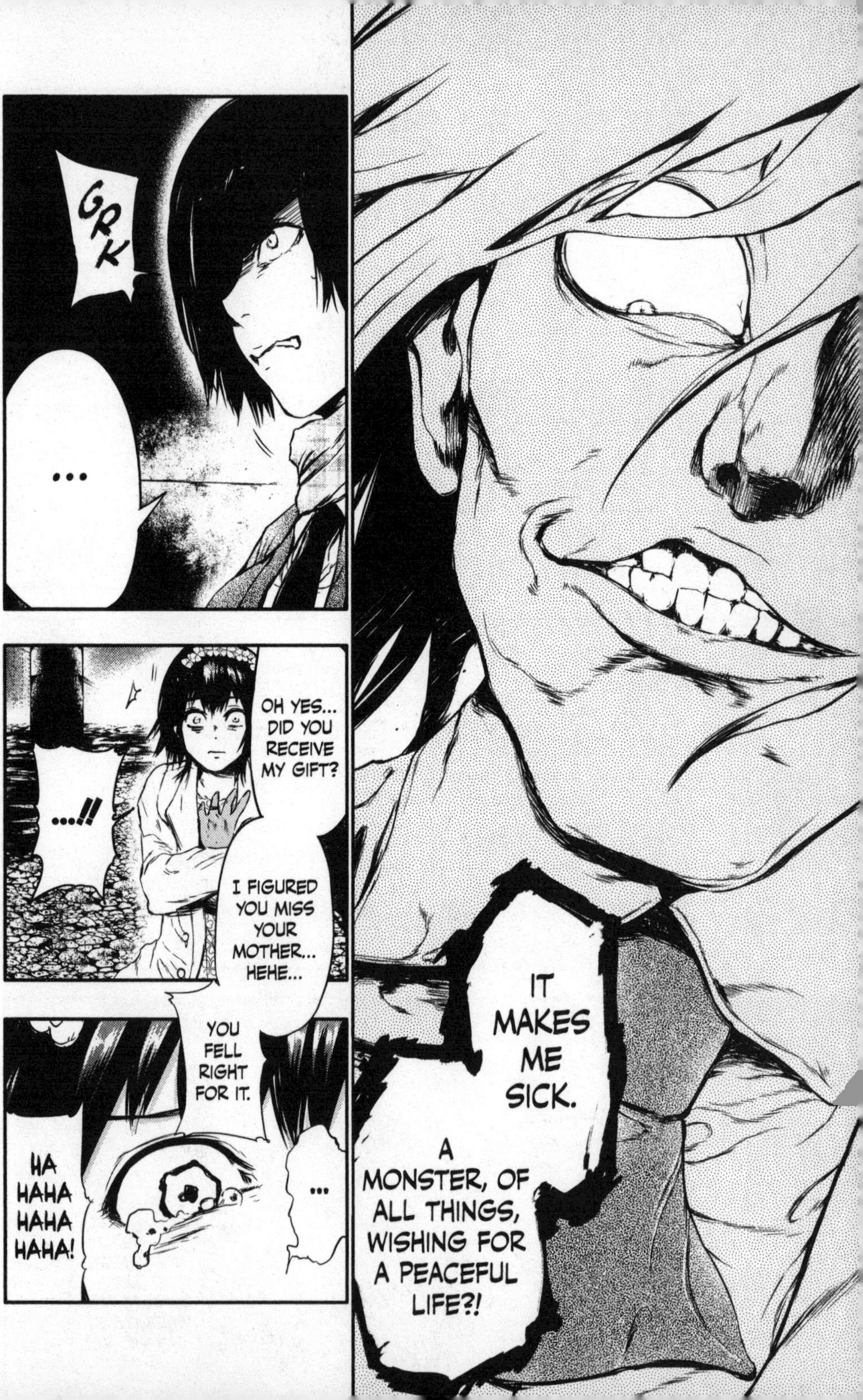
IT MAKES ME SICK.
A MONSTER, OF ALL THINGS, WISHING FOR A PEACEFUL LIFE?!
GRK
...
OH YES... DID YOU RECEIVE MY GIFT?
...!!
I FIGURED YOU MISS YOUR MOTHER... HEHE...
YOU FELL RIGHT FOR IT.
...
HA HAHA HAHA HAHA!

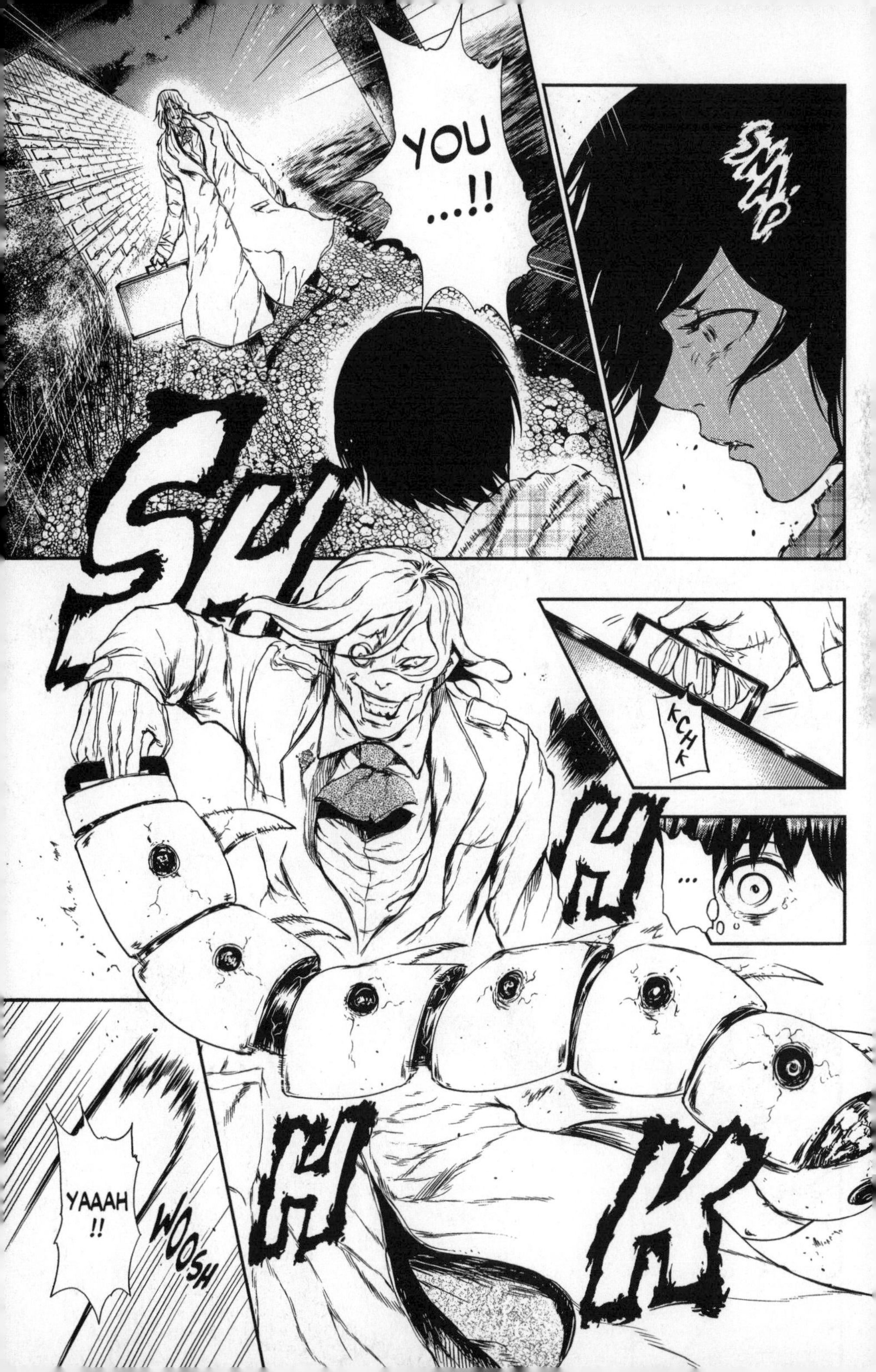
SNAP
YOU ...!!
KCHK
...
SHHHK
YAAAH!!
WOOSH

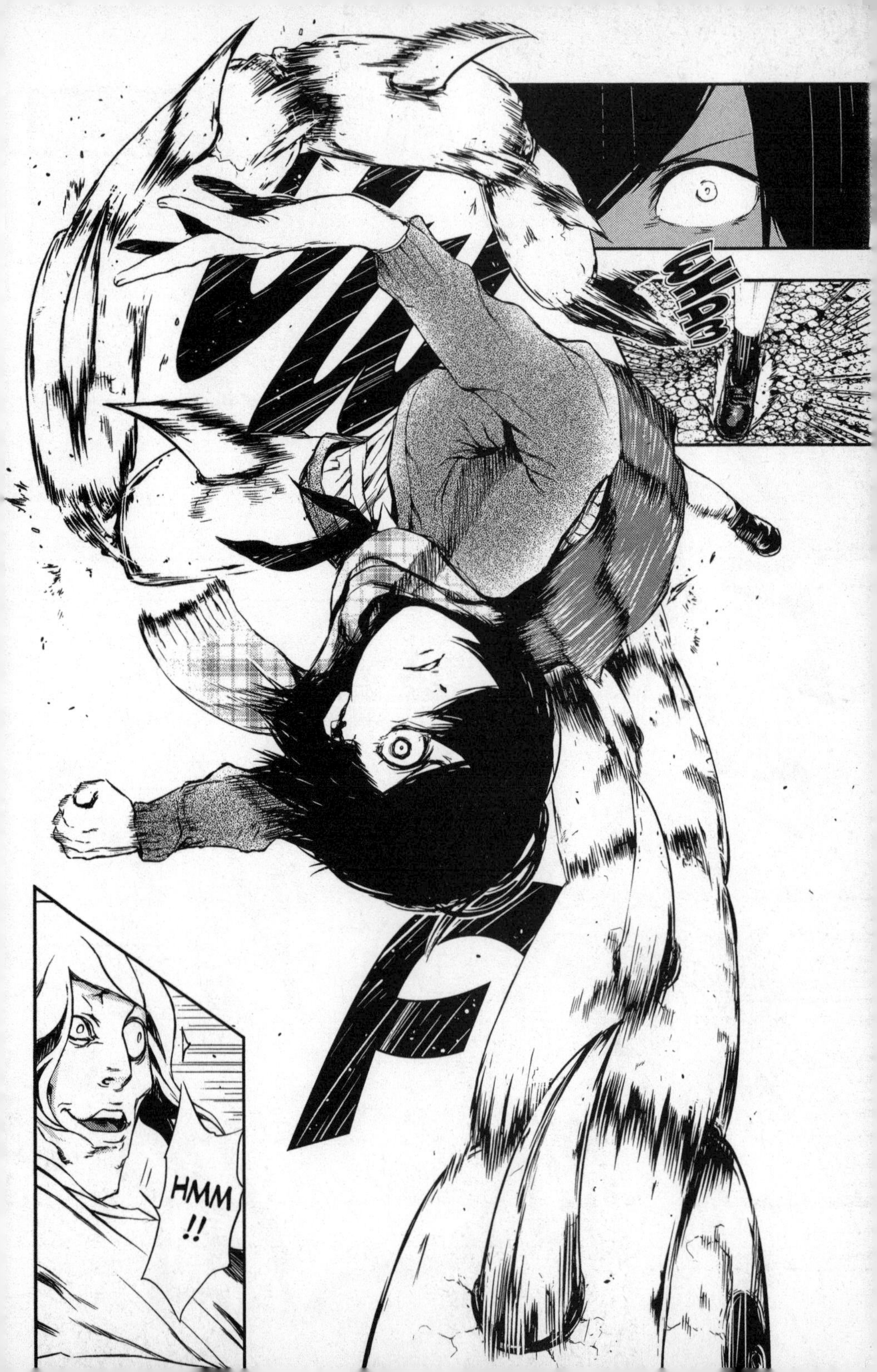
WHAM
HMM
!!

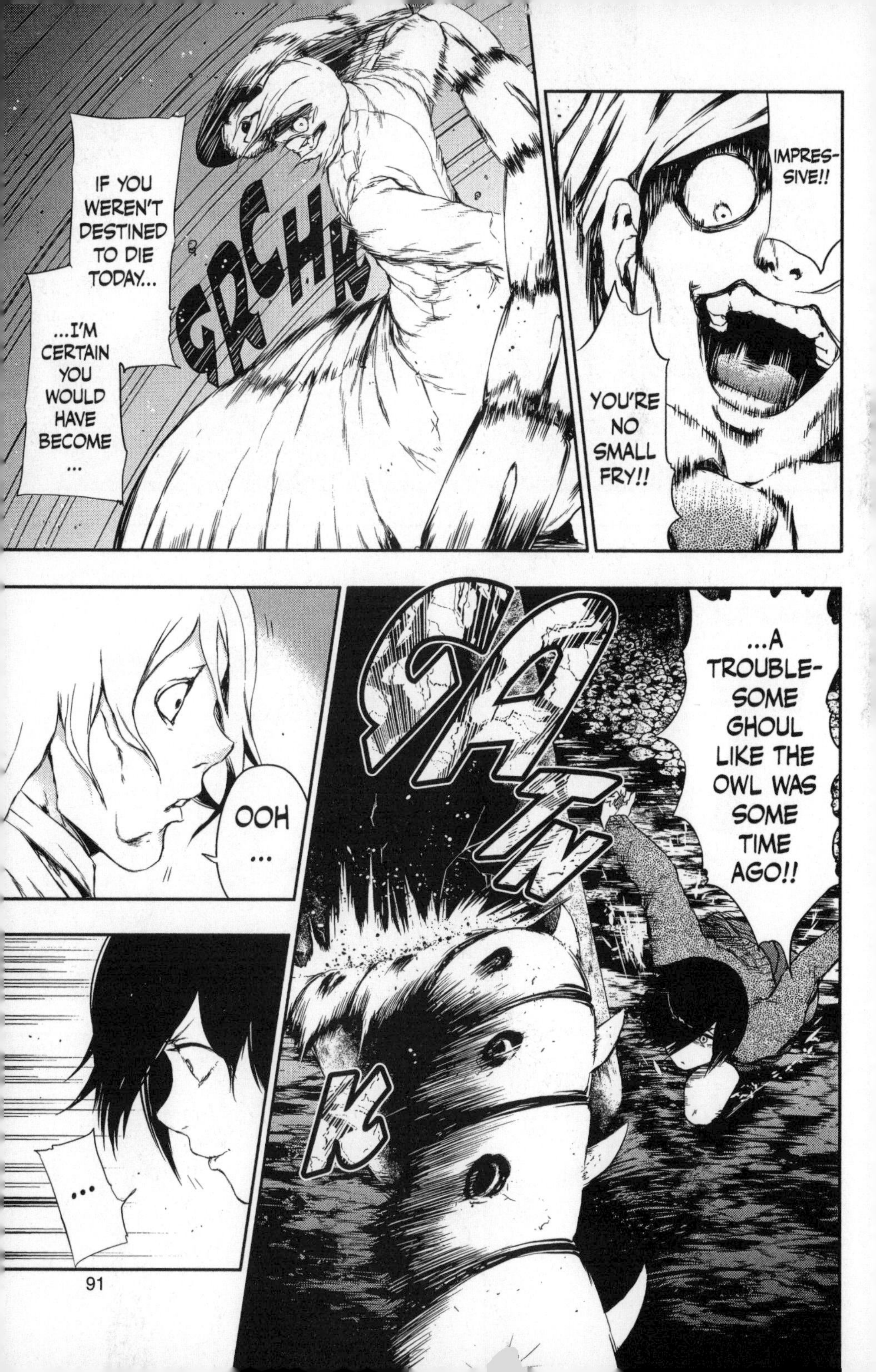
IMPRES-SIVE!!
YOU'RE NO SMALL FRY!!
IF YOU WEREN'T DESTINED TO DIE TODAY...
...I'M CERTAIN YOU WOULD HAVE BECOME ...
GRCHK
...A TROUBLE-SOME GHOUL LIKE THE OWL WAS SOME TIME AGO!!
OOH ...
...

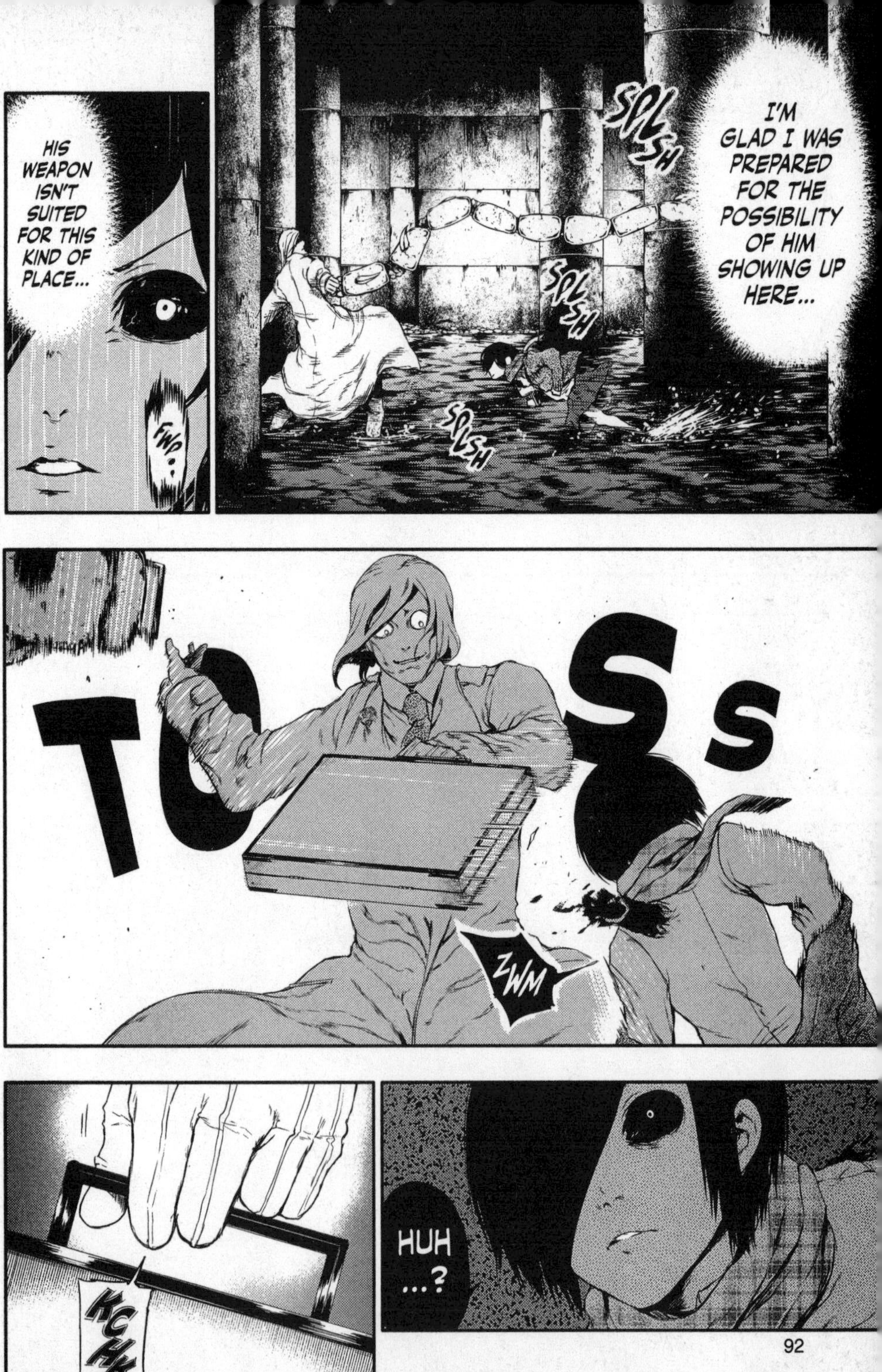
SPLSH
I'M GLAD I WAS PREPARED FOR THE POSSIBILITY OF HIM SHOWING UP HERE...
SPLSH
SPLSH
HIS WEAPON ISN'T SUITED FOR THIS KIND OF PLACE...
FWP
TOSS
ZWM
HUH ...?
KCHK

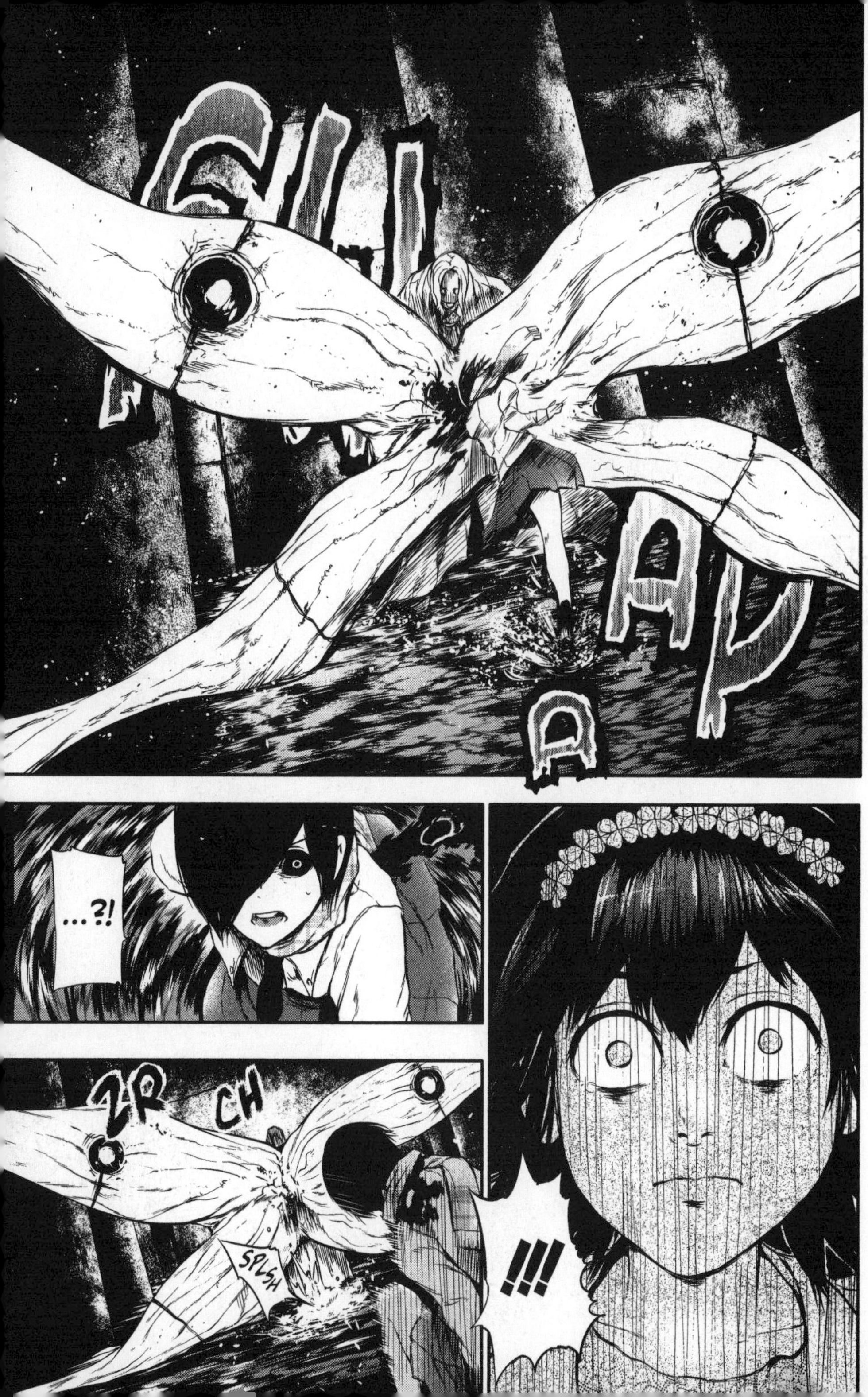
!!!
...?!
ZRCH
SPLSH

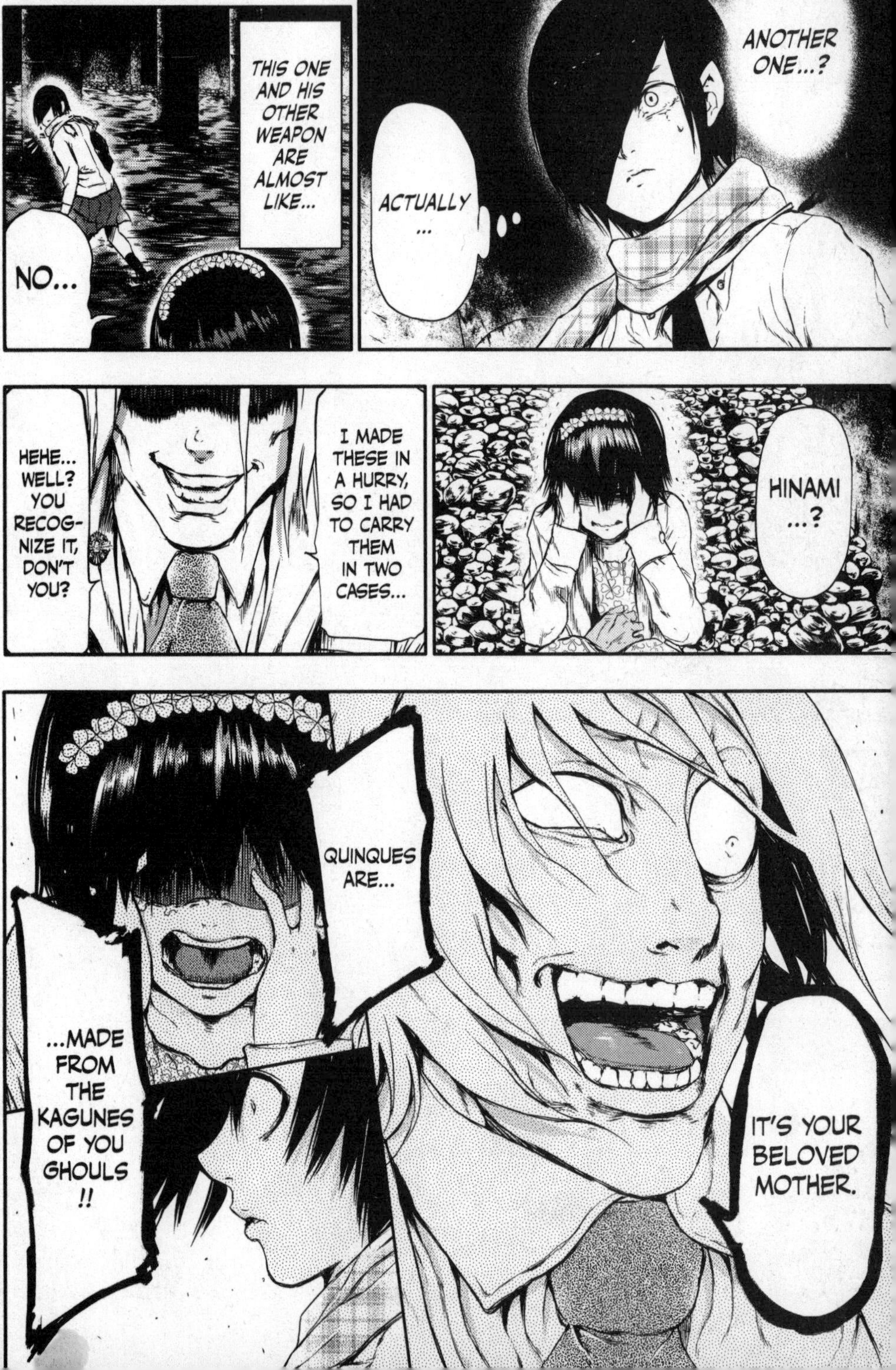
ANOTHER ONE...?
ACTUALLY ...
THIS ONE AND HIS OTHER WEAPON ARE ALMOST LIKE...
NO...
HINAMI ...?
I MADE THESE IN A HURRY, SO I HAD TO CARRY THEM IN TWO CASES...
HEHE... WELL? YOU RECOGNIZE IT, DON'T YOU?
IT'S YOUR BELOVED MOTHER.
QUINQUES ARE...
...MADE FROM THE KAGUNES OF YOU GHOULS !!

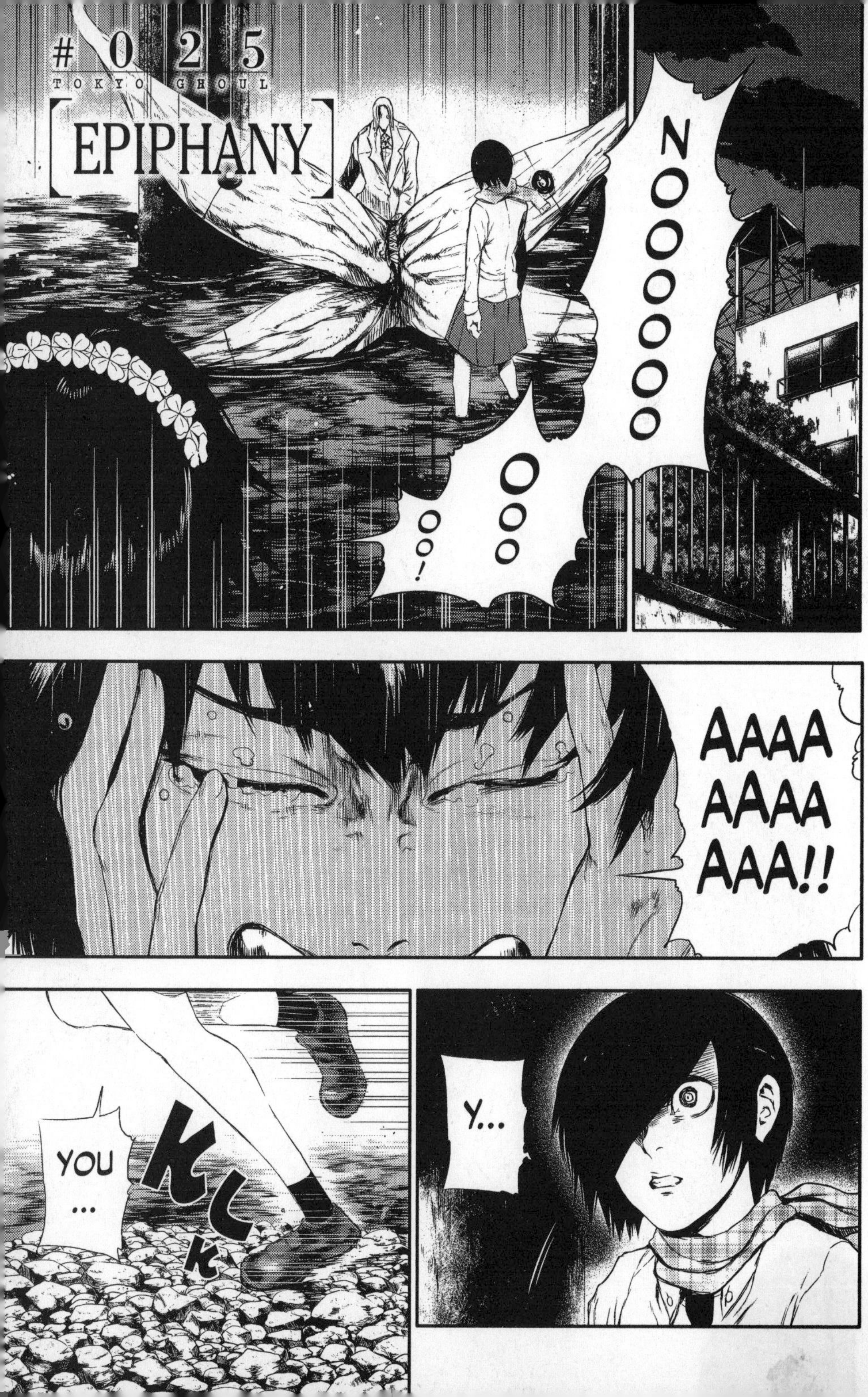
NOOOOOOOOOOO!
#025
TOKYO GHOUL
[EPIPHANY]
AAAAAAAAAAA!!
Y...
YOU...
KLK

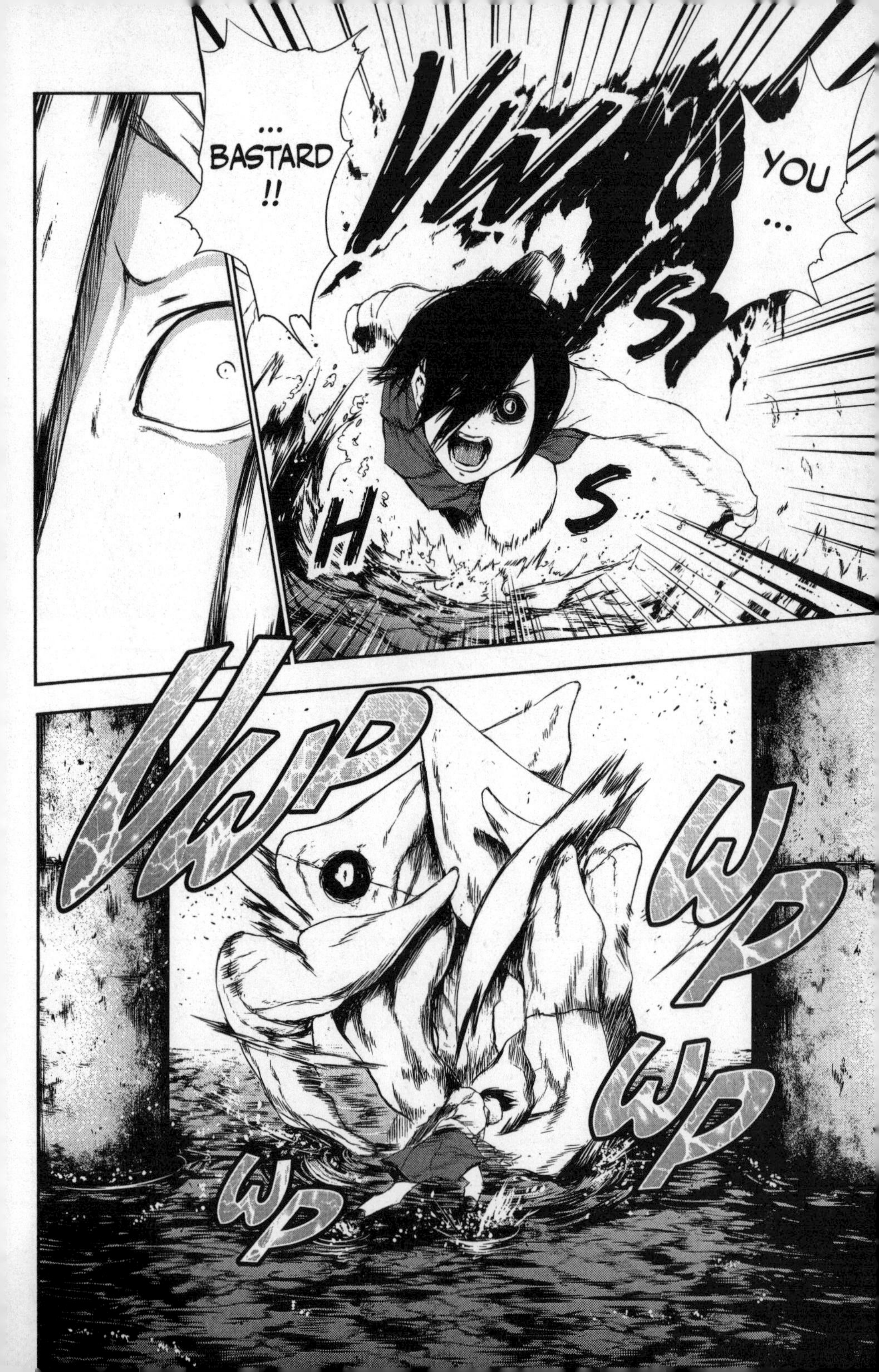
YOU ...
... BASTARD !!
VWP
WP
WP
WP

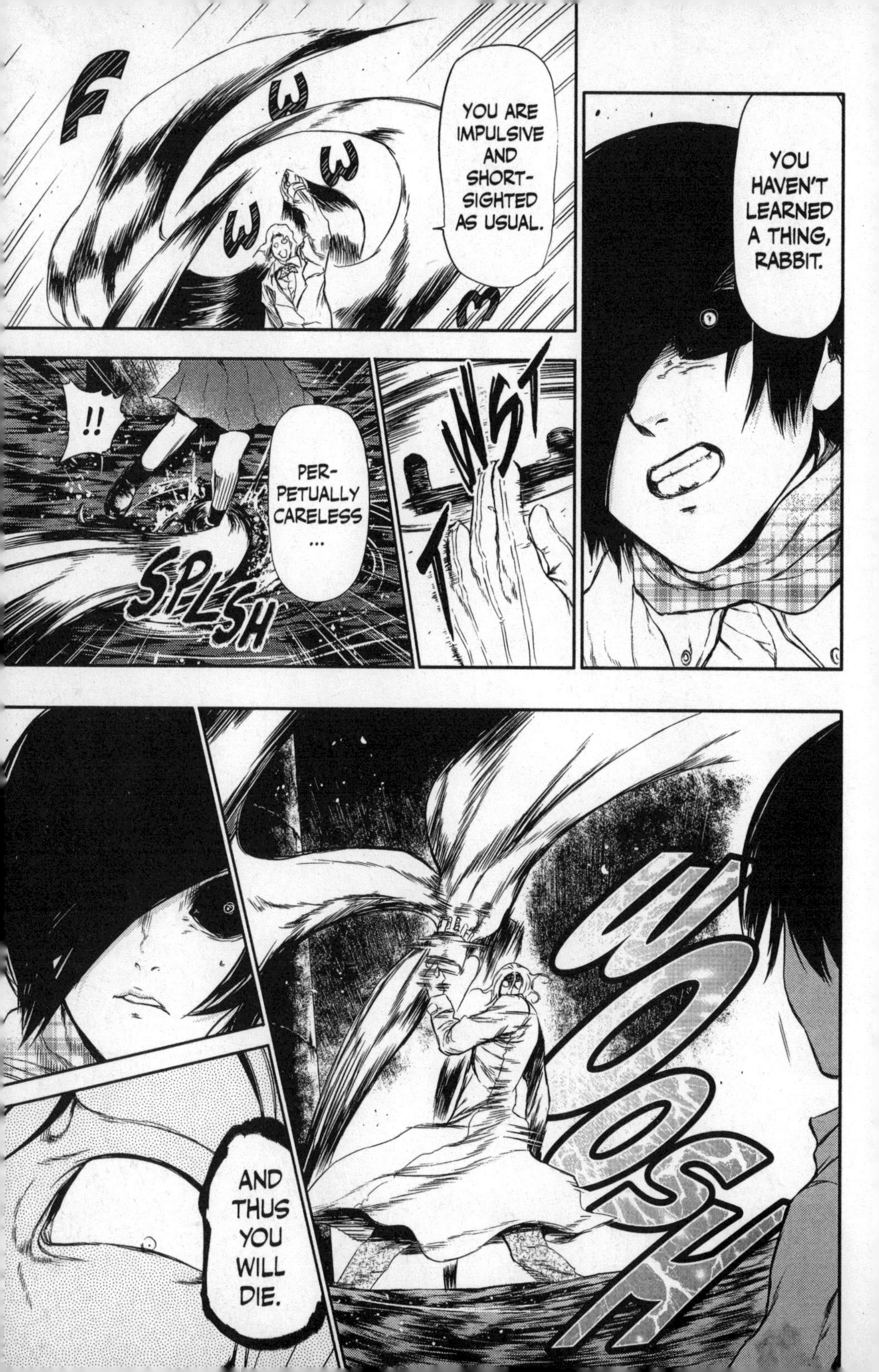
YOU HAVEN'T LEARNED A THING, RABBIT.
FWWWB
YOU ARE IMPULSIVE AND SHORT-SIGHTED AS USUAL.
TWIST
!!
PER-PETUALLY CARELESS ...
SPLSH
WOOSH
AND THUS YOU WILL DIE.

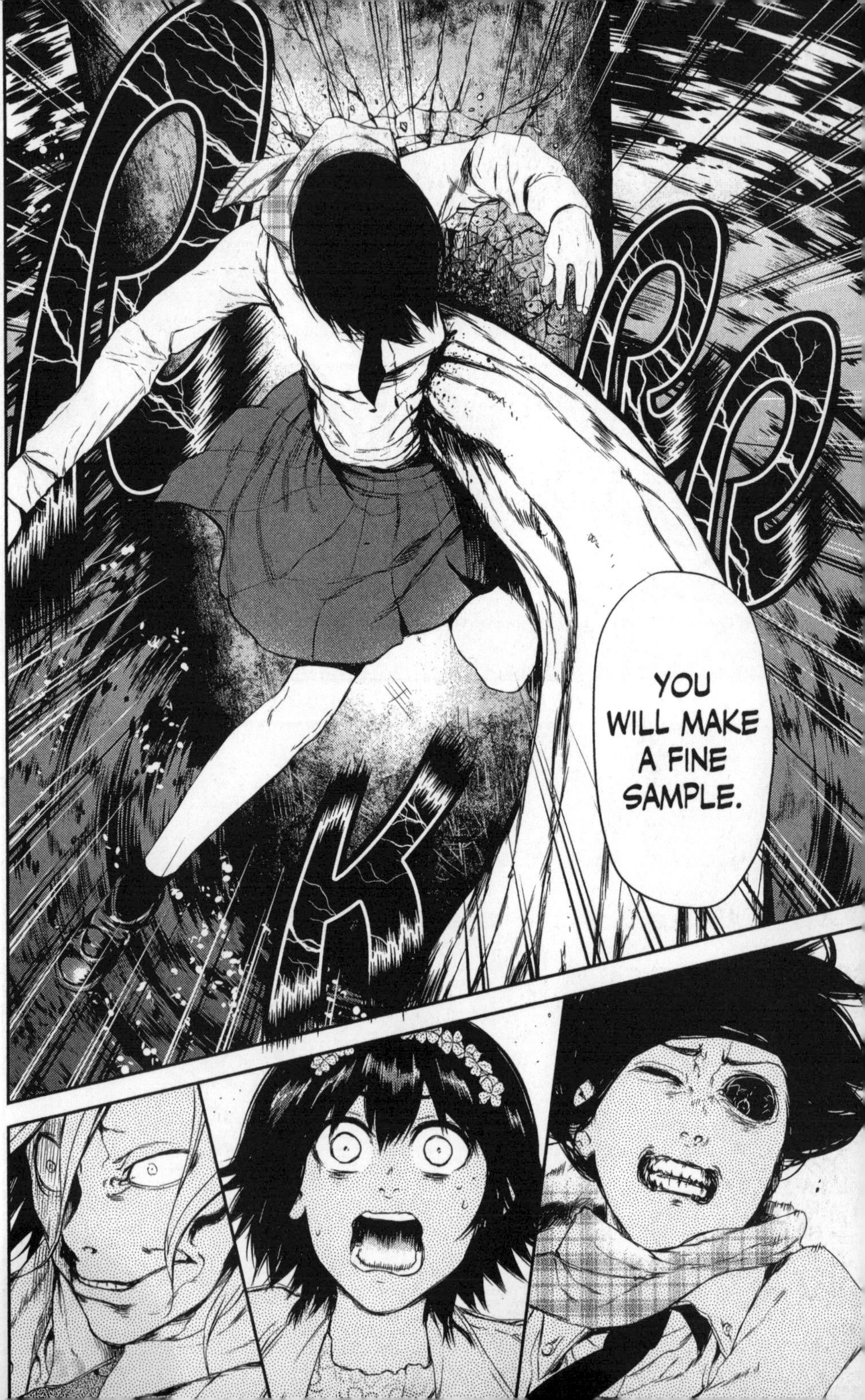
YOU WILL MAKE A FINE SAMPLE.

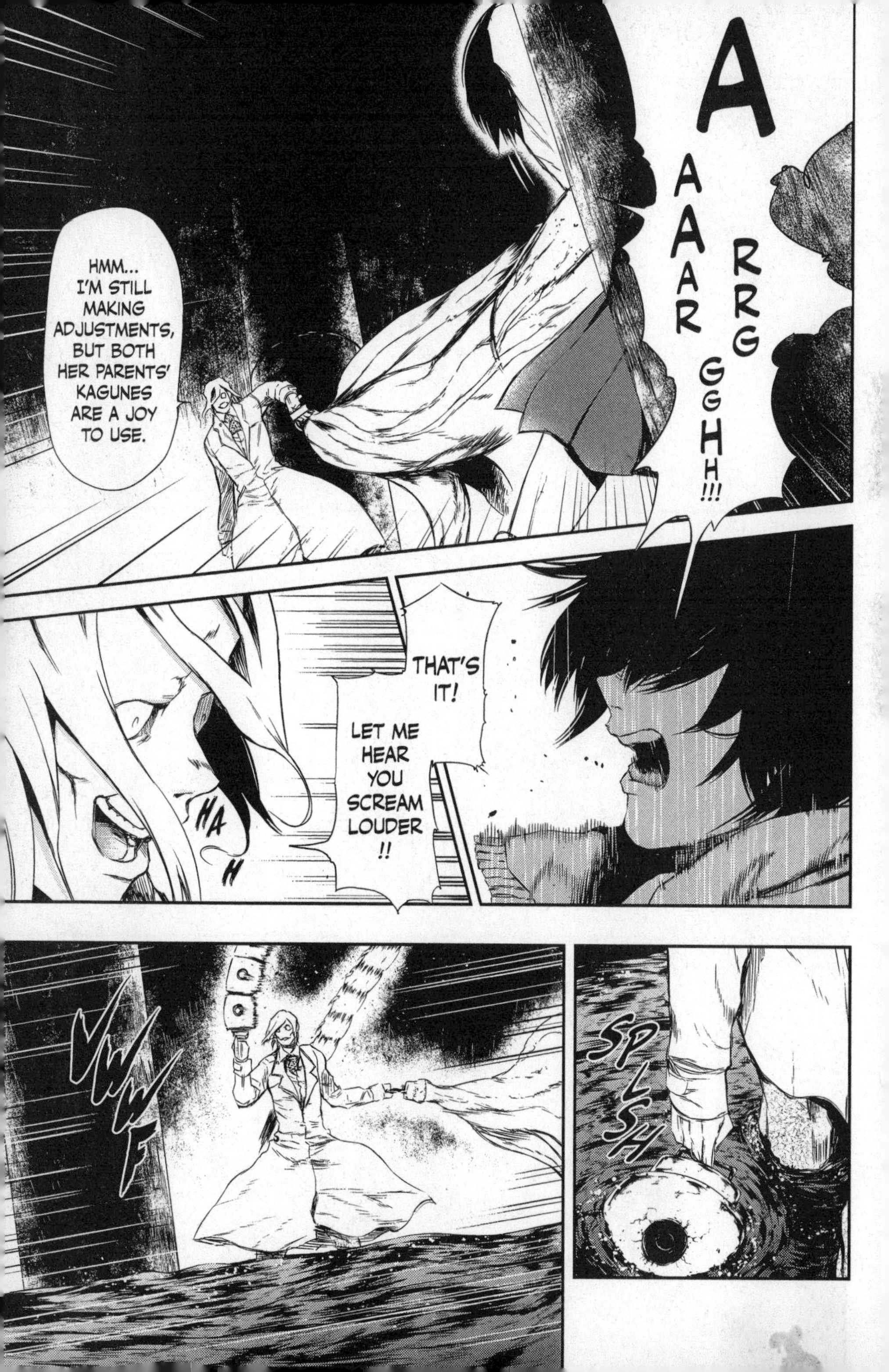

AAAARRRGGGHH!!!
HMM... I'M STILL MAKING ADJUSTMENTS, BUT BOTH HER PARENTS' KAGUNES ARE A JOY TO USE.
THAT'S IT! LET ME HEAR YOU SCREAM LOUDER!!
HA H
SPLSH
VWWF

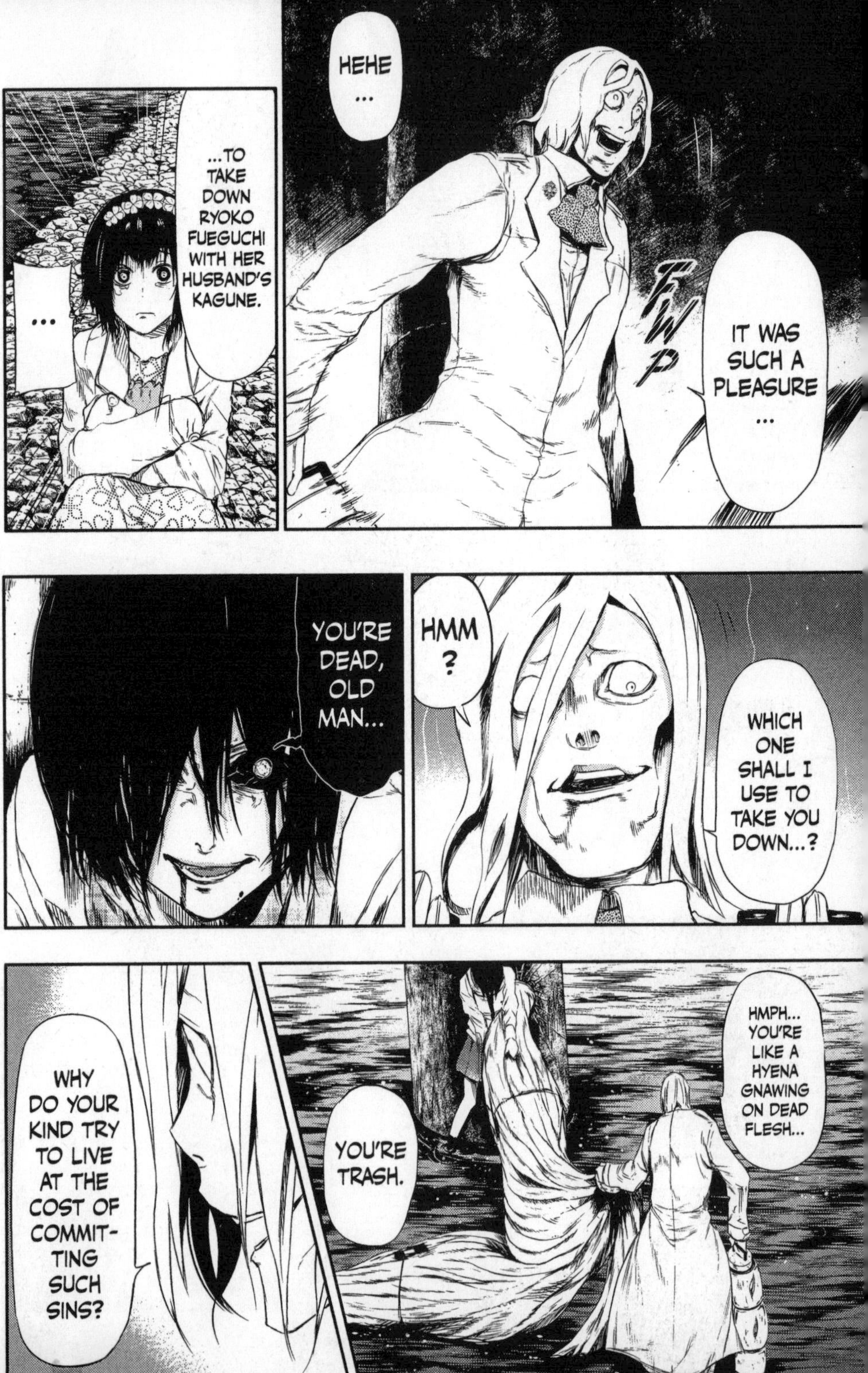
HEHE...
FWP
IT WAS SUCH A PLEASURE...
...TO TAKE DOWN RYOKO FUEGUCHI WITH HER HUSBAND'S KAGUNE.
...
HMM?
WHICH ONE SHALL I USE TO TAKE YOU DOWN...?
YOU'RE DEAD, OLD MAN...
HMPH... YOU'RE LIKE A HYENA GNAWING ON DEAD FLESH...
YOU'RE TRASH.
WHY DO YOUR KIND TRY TO LIVE AT THE COST OF COMMITTING SUCH SINS?

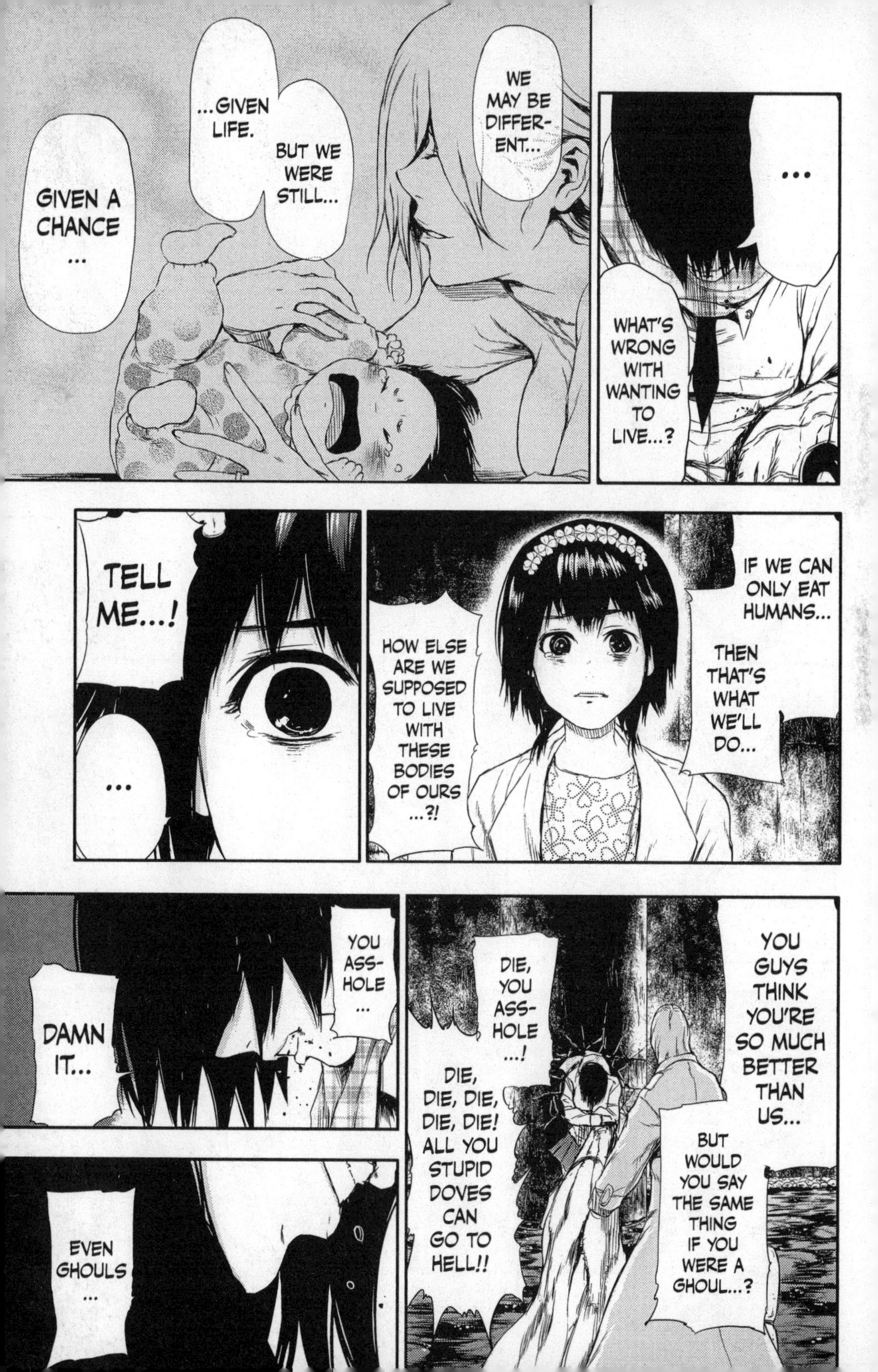
...
WHAT'S WRONG WITH WANTING TO LIVE...?
WE MAY BE DIFFERENT...
BUT WE WERE STILL...
...GIVEN LIFE.
GIVEN A CHANCE...
IF WE CAN ONLY EAT HUMANS...
THEN THAT'S WHAT WE'LL DO...
HOW ELSE ARE WE SUPPOSED TO LIVE WITH THESE BODIES OF OURS...?!
TELL ME...!
...
YOU GUYS THINK YOU'RE SO MUCH BETTER THAN US...
BUT WOULD YOU SAY THE SAME THING IF YOU WERE A GHOUL...?
DIE, YOU ASSHOLE...!
DIE, DIE, DIE, DIE, DIE! ALL YOU STUPID DOVES CAN GO TO HELL!!
YOU ASSHOLE...
DAMN IT...
EVEN GHOULS...

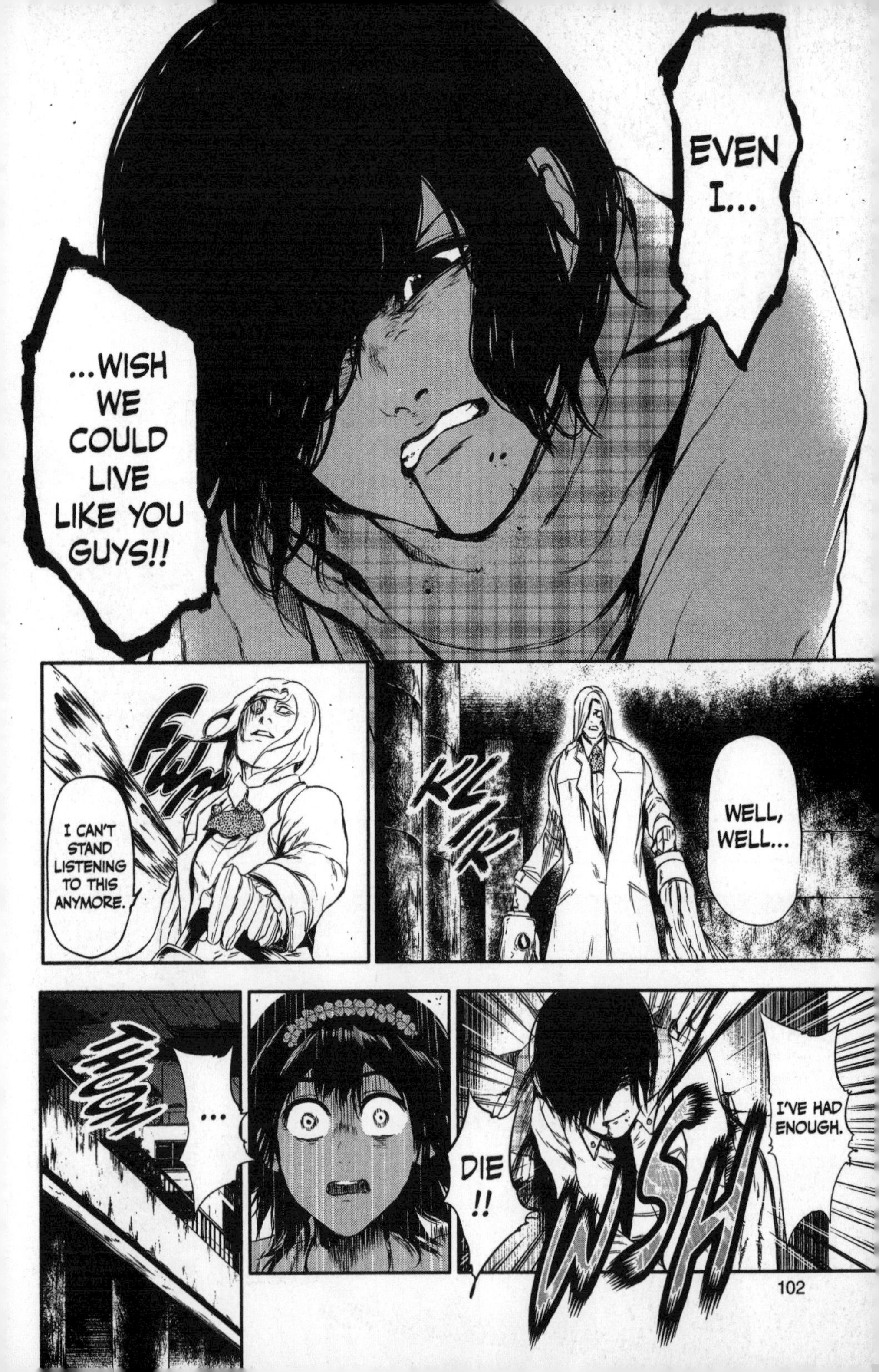
EVEN I...
...WISH WE COULD LIVE LIKE YOU GUYS!!
KLIK
WELL, WELL...
FWM
I CAN'T STAND LISTENING TO THIS ANYMORE.
I'VE HAD ENOUGH.
DIE!!
WSH
THOOM
...

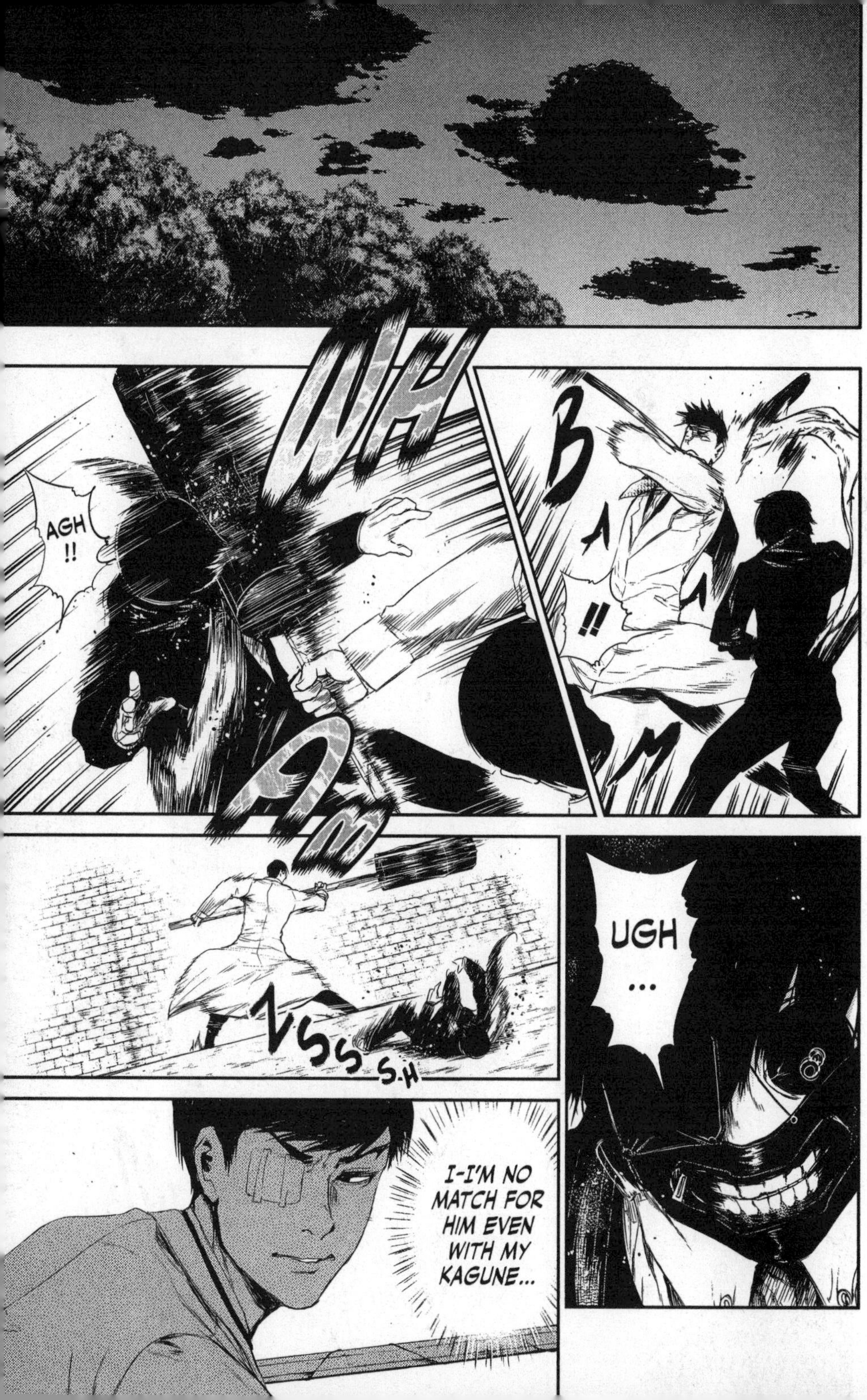
AGH !!
UGH ...
I-I'M NO MATCH FOR HIM EVEN WITH MY KAGUNE...

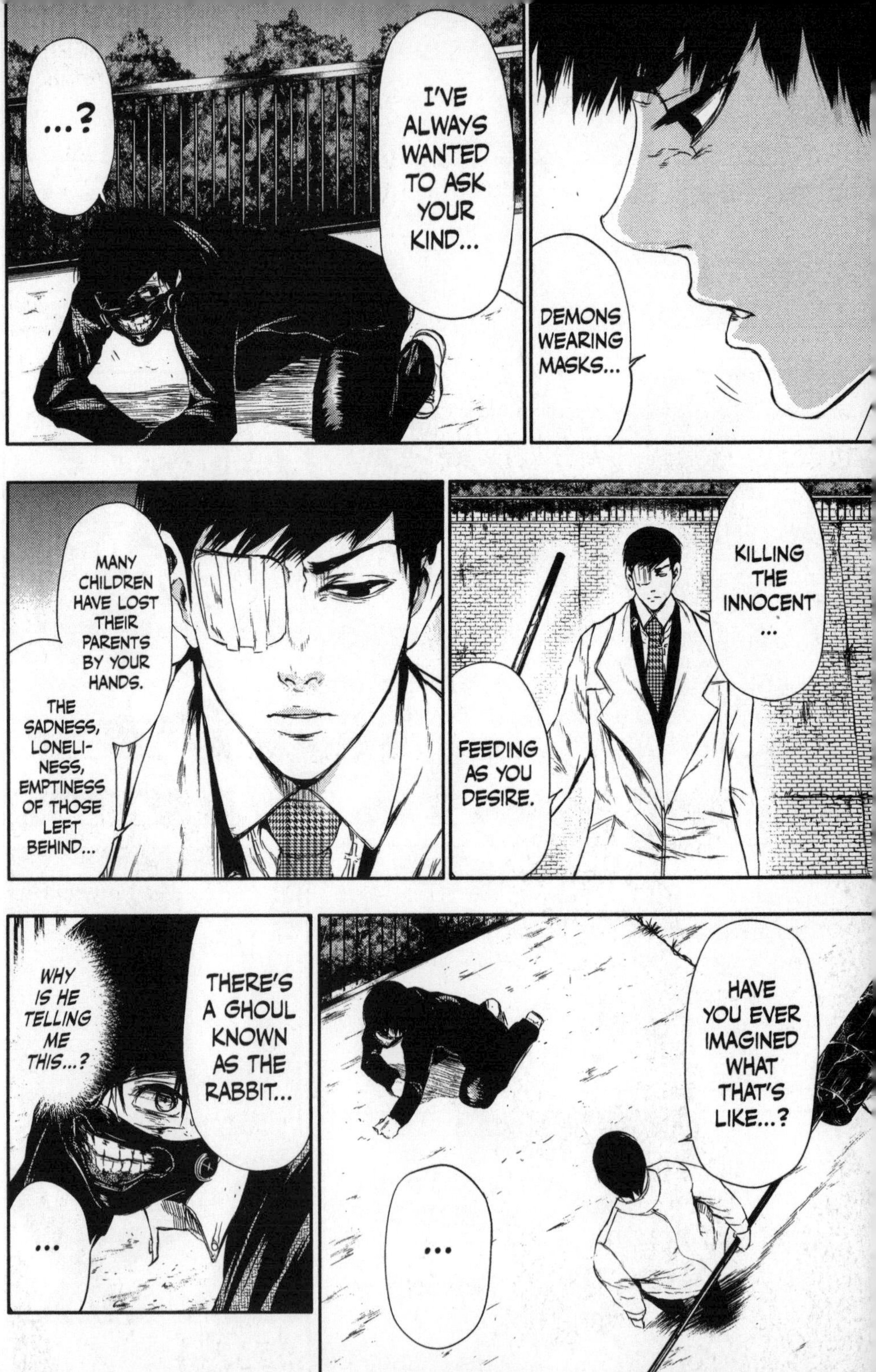
DEMONS WEARING MASKS...
I'VE ALWAYS WANTED TO ASK YOUR KIND...
...?
KILLING THE INNOCENT...
FEEDING AS YOU DESIRE.
MANY CHILDREN HAVE LOST THEIR PARENTS BY YOUR HANDS.
THE SADNESS, LONELINESS, EMPTINESS OF THOSE LEFT BEHIND...
HAVE YOU EVER IMAGINED WHAT THAT'S LIKE...?
...
THERE'S A GHOUL KNOWN AS THE RABBIT...
WHY IS HE TELLING ME THIS...?
...

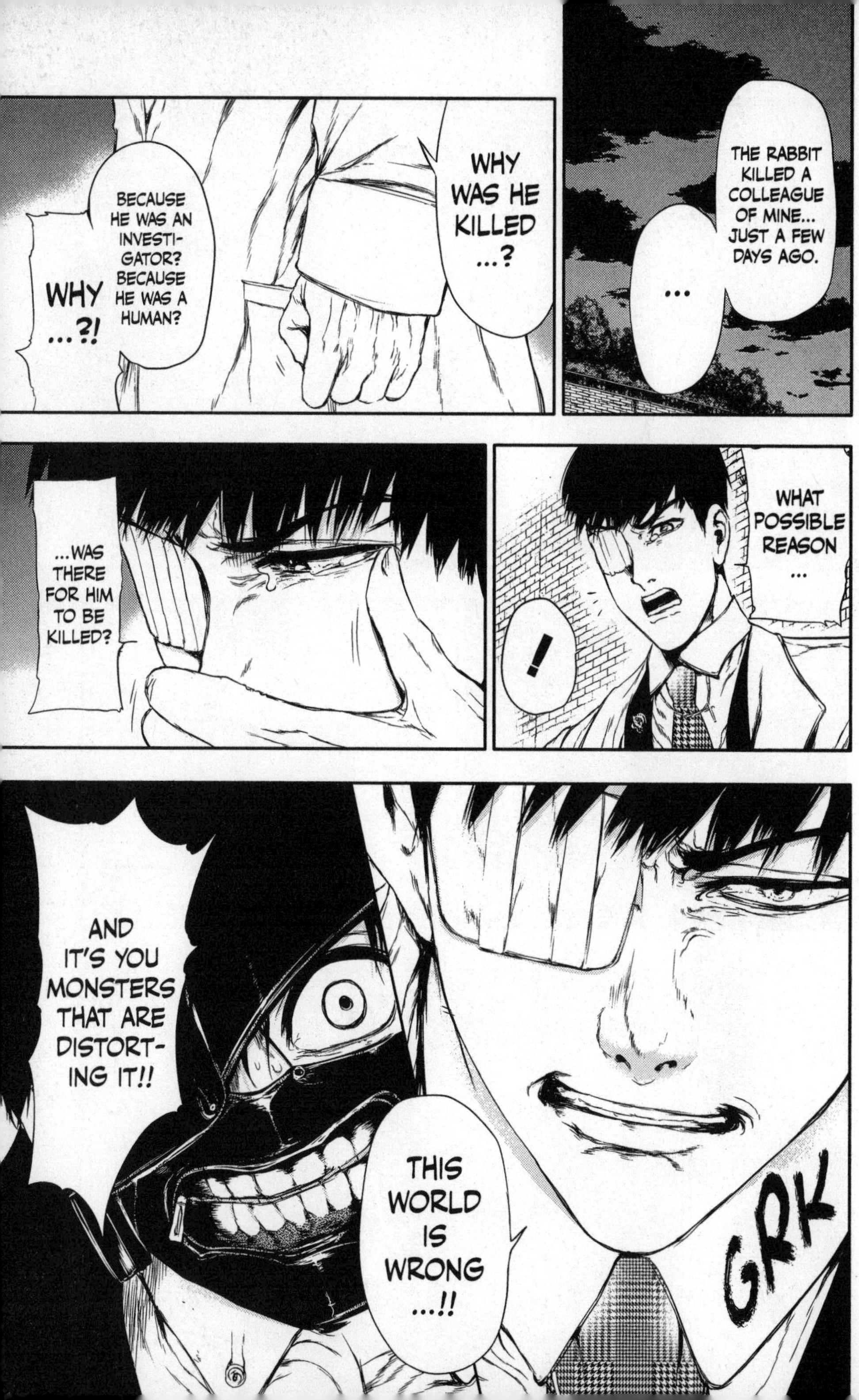

THE RABBIT KILLED A COLLEAGUE OF MINE... JUST A FEW DAYS AGO.
...
WHY WAS HE KILLED ...?
BECAUSE HE WAS AN INVESTI-GATOR? BECAUSE HE WAS A HUMAN?
WHY ...?!
WHAT POSSIBLE REASON ...
!
...WAS THERE FOR HIM TO BE KILLED?
GRK
THIS WORLD IS WRONG ...!!
AND IT'S YOU MONSTERS THAT ARE DISTORT-ING IT!!

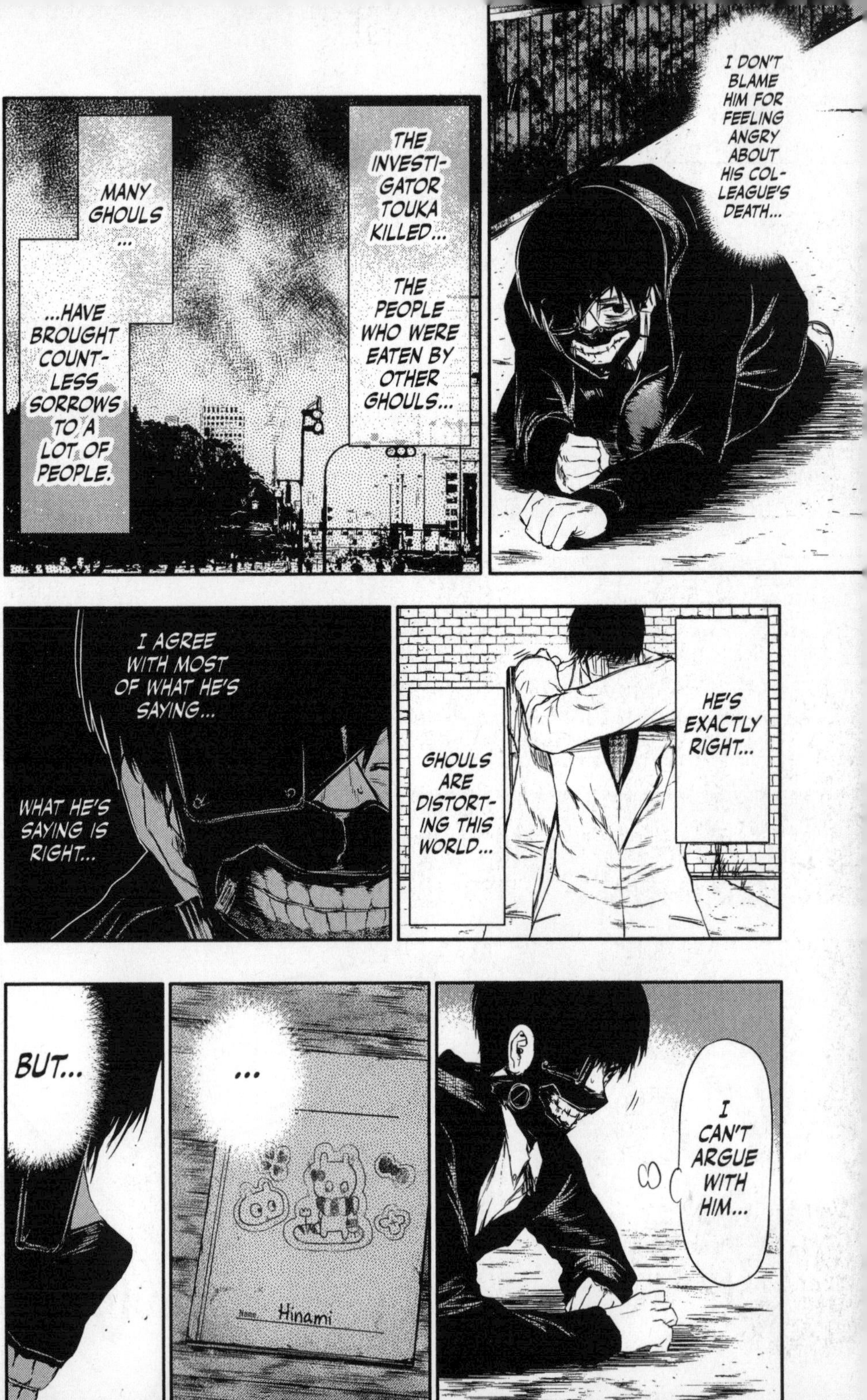
I DON'T BLAME HIM FOR FEELING ANGRY ABOUT HIS COLLEAGUE'S DEATH...
THE INVESTIGATOR TOUKA KILLED...
THE PEOPLE WHO WERE EATEN BY OTHER GHOULS...
MANY GHOULS...
...HAVE BROUGHT COUNTLESS SORROWS TO A LOT OF PEOPLE.
HE'S EXACTLY RIGHT...
GHOULS ARE DISTORTING THIS WORLD...
I AGREE WITH MOST OF WHAT HE'S SAYING...
WHAT HE'S SAYING IS RIGHT...
I CAN'T ARGUE WITH HIM...
...
Name Hinami
BUT...

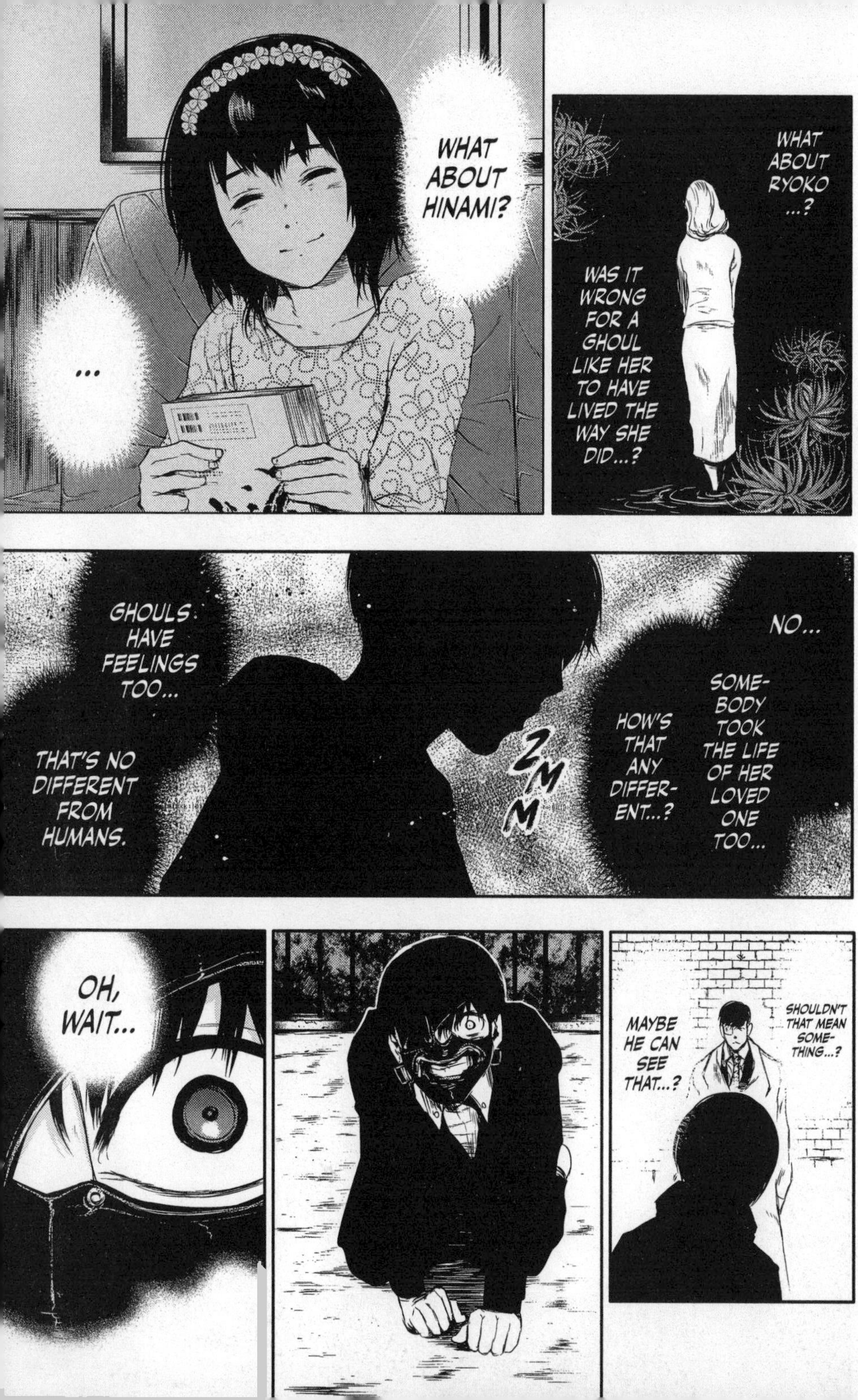
WHAT ABOUT RYOKO ...?
WAS IT WRONG FOR A GHOUL LIKE HER TO HAVE LIVED THE WAY SHE DID...?
WHAT ABOUT HINAMI?
...
NO...
SOME-BODY TOOK THE LIFE OF HER LOVED ONE TOO...
HOW'S THAT ANY DIFFER-ENT...?
ZMM
GHOULS HAVE FEELINGS TOO...
THAT'S NO DIFFERENT FROM HUMANS.
SHOULDN'T THAT MEAN SOME-THING...?
MAYBE HE CAN SEE THAT...?
OH, WAIT...

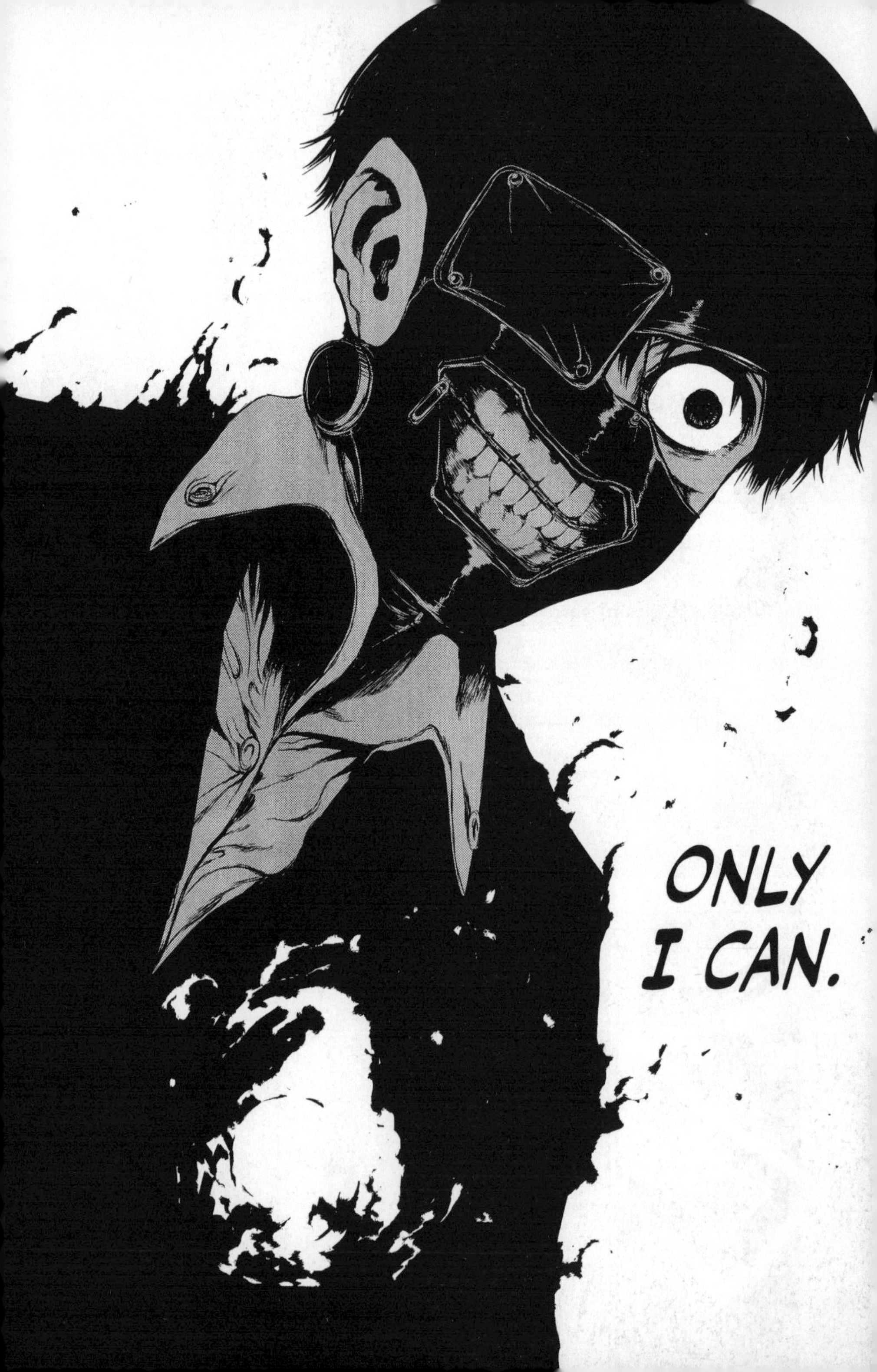
ONLY
I CAN.

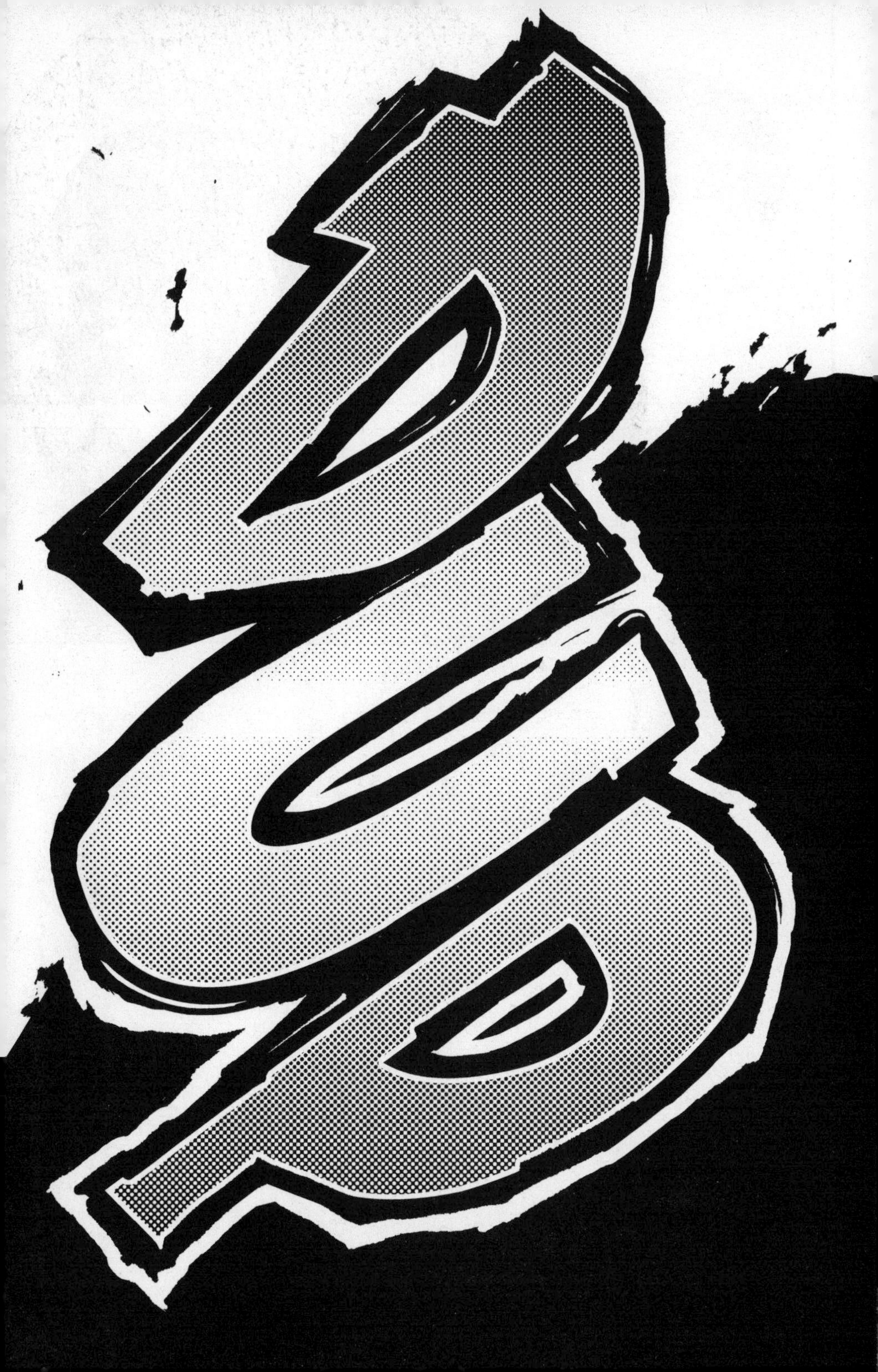

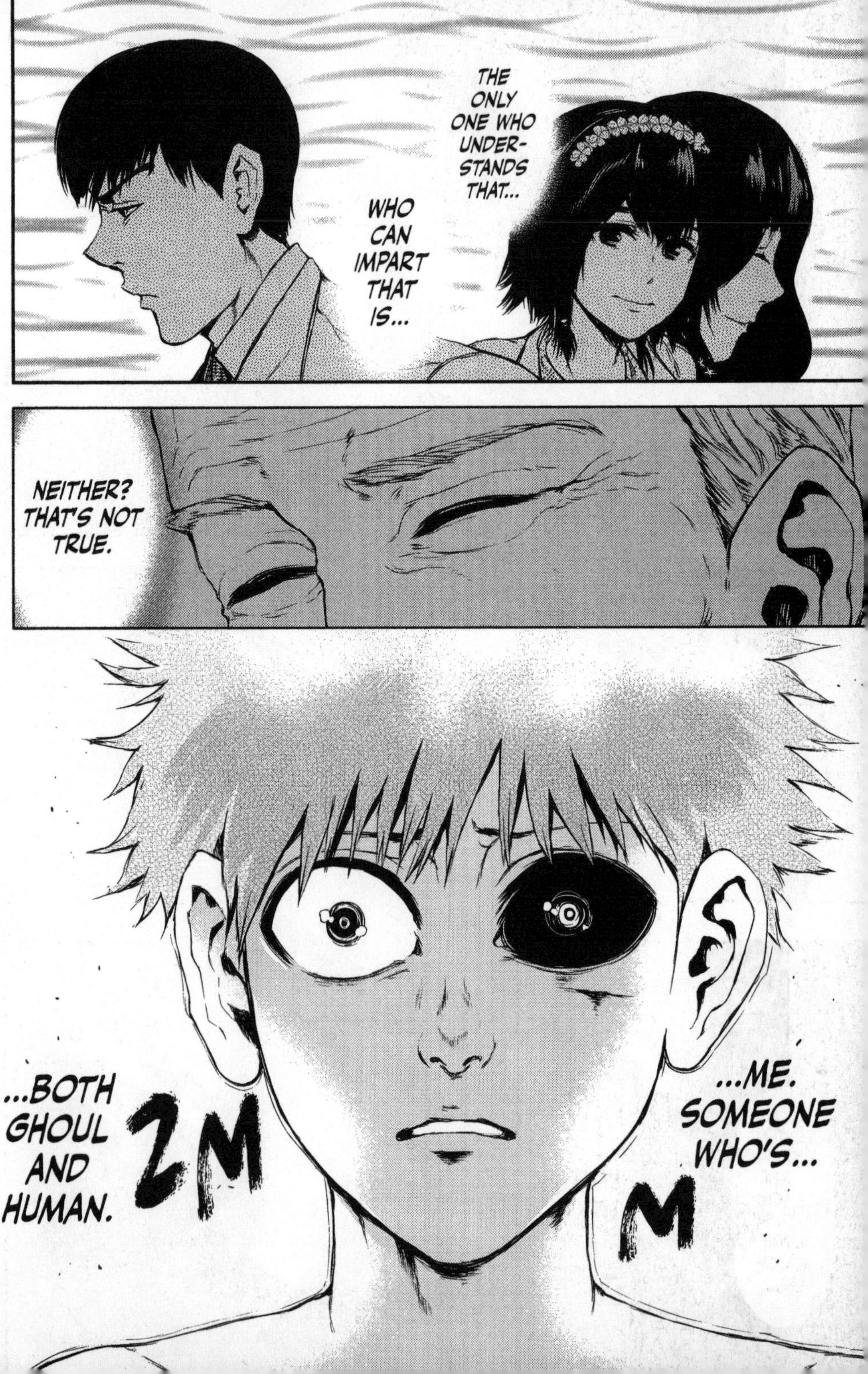
THE ONLY ONE WHO UNDER-STANDS THAT...
WHO CAN IMPART THAT IS...
NEITHER? THAT'S NOT TRUE.
...ME. SOMEONE WHO'S...
M
ZM
...BOTH GHOUL AND HUMAN.

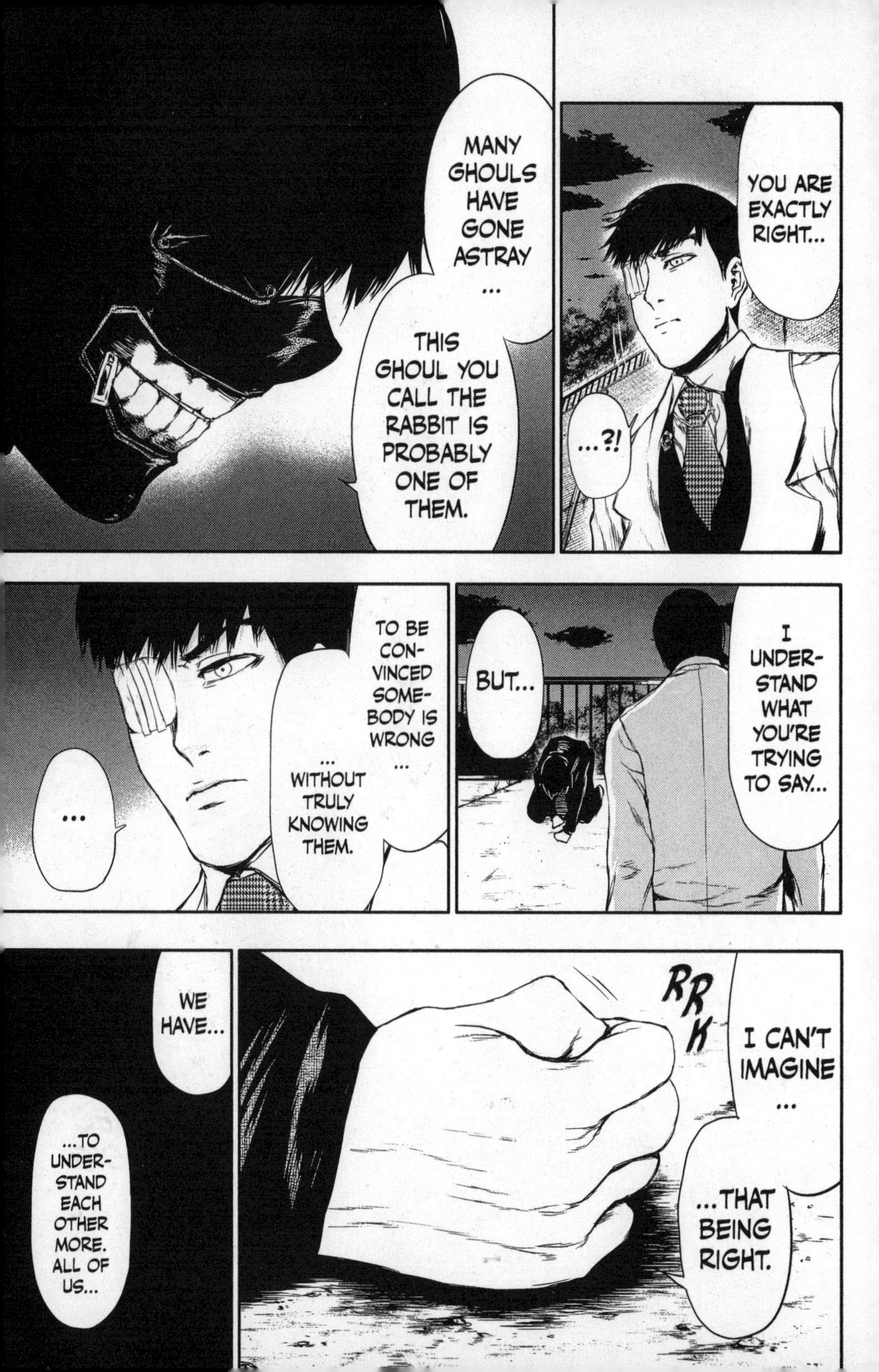
YOU ARE EXACTLY RIGHT...
...?!
MANY GHOULS HAVE GONE ASTRAY ...
THIS GHOUL YOU CALL THE RABBIT IS PROBABLY ONE OF THEM.
I UNDER-STAND WHAT YOU'RE TRYING TO SAY...
BUT...
TO BE CON-VINCED SOME-BODY IS WRONG ... ... WITHOUT TRULY KNOWING THEM.
...
RRK
I CAN'T IMAGINE ...
...THAT BEING RIGHT.
WE HAVE...
...TO UNDER-STAND EACH OTHER MORE. ALL OF US...

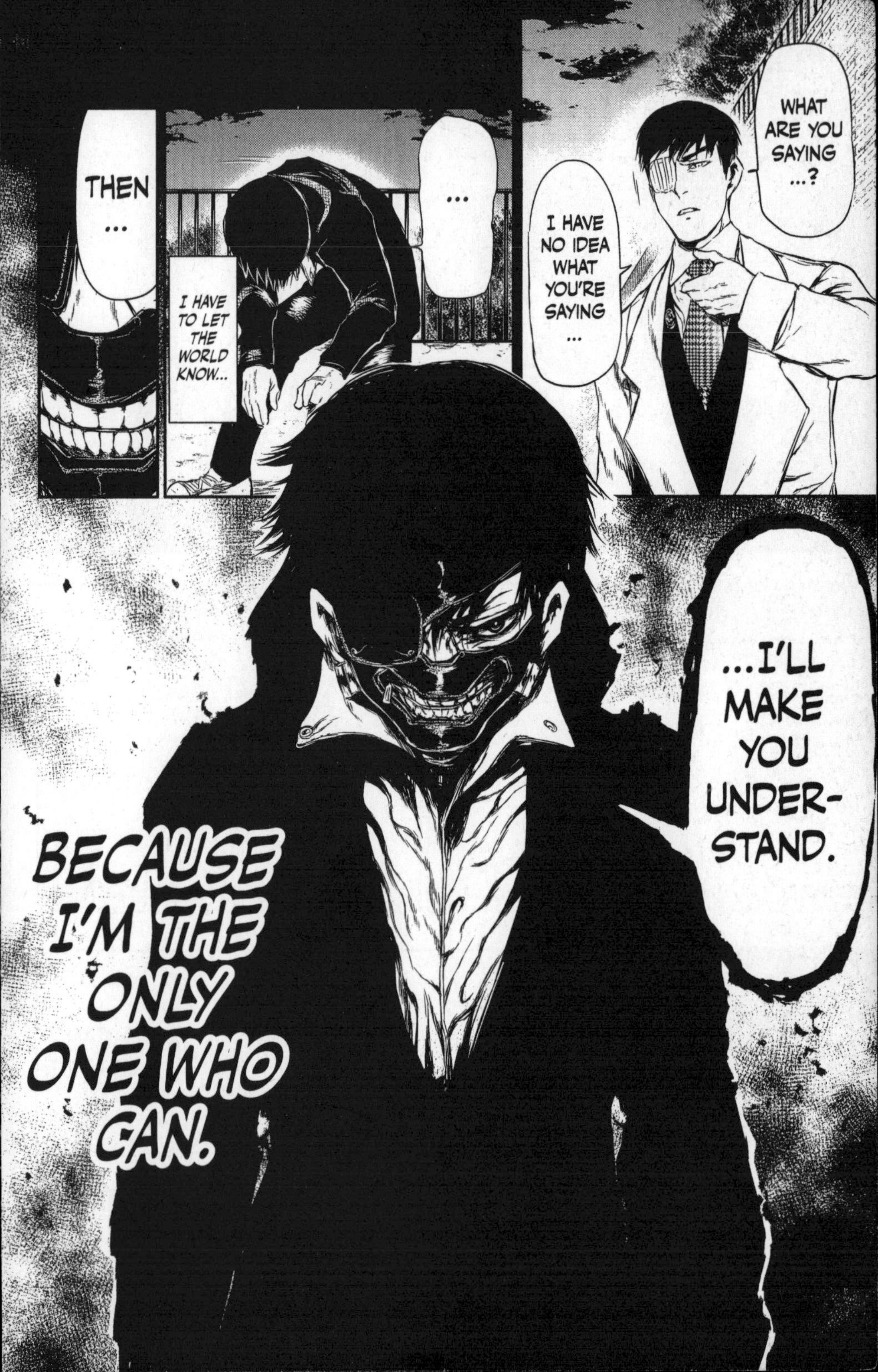
WHAT ARE YOU SAYING ...?
I HAVE NO IDEA WHAT YOU'RE SAYING ...
...
I HAVE TO LET THE WORLD KNOW...
THEN ...
...I'LL MAKE YOU UNDER-STAND.
BECAUSE I'M THE ONLY ONE WHO CAN.

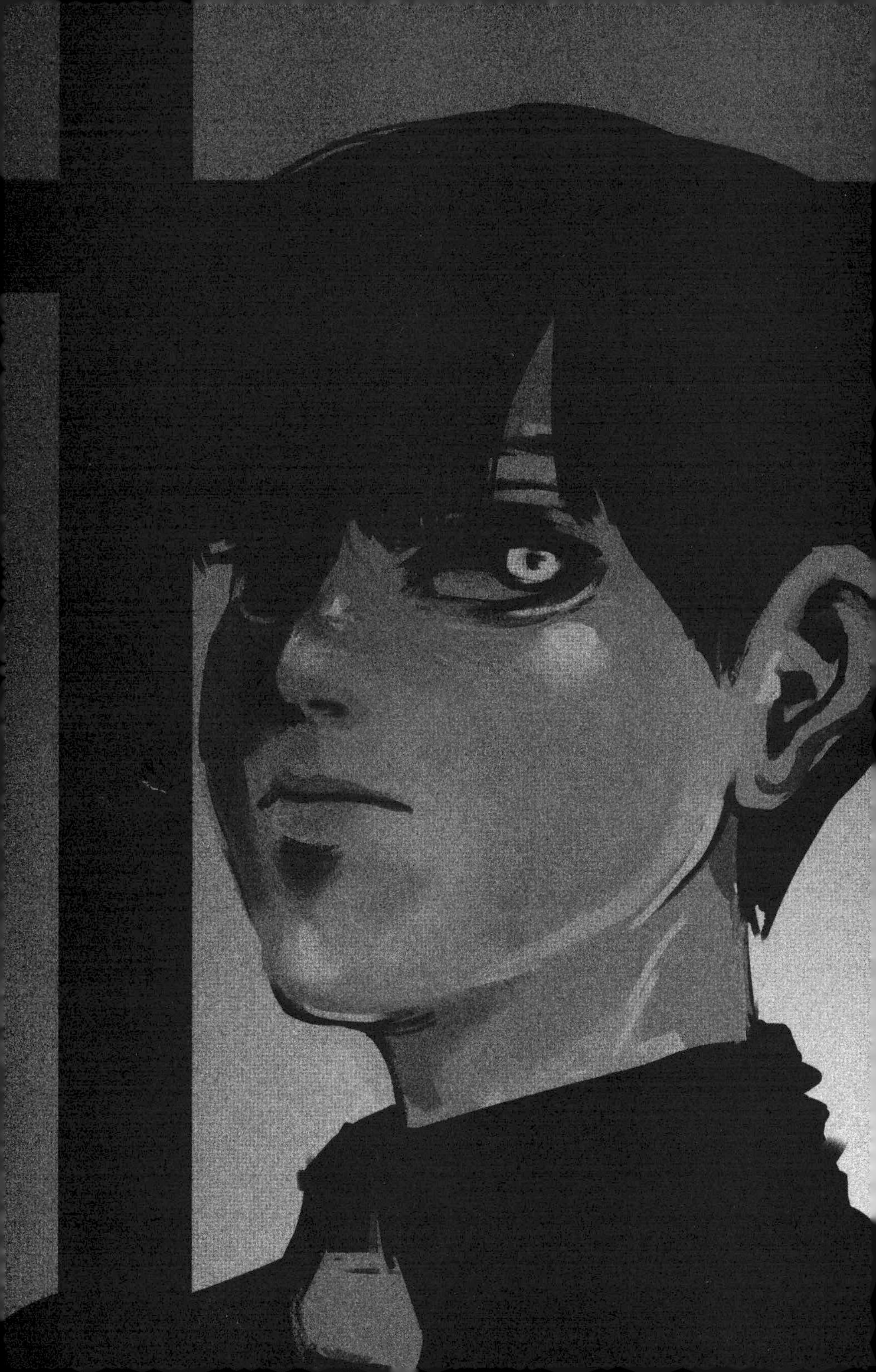

#026

TOKYO GHOUL

[ADVERSARY]

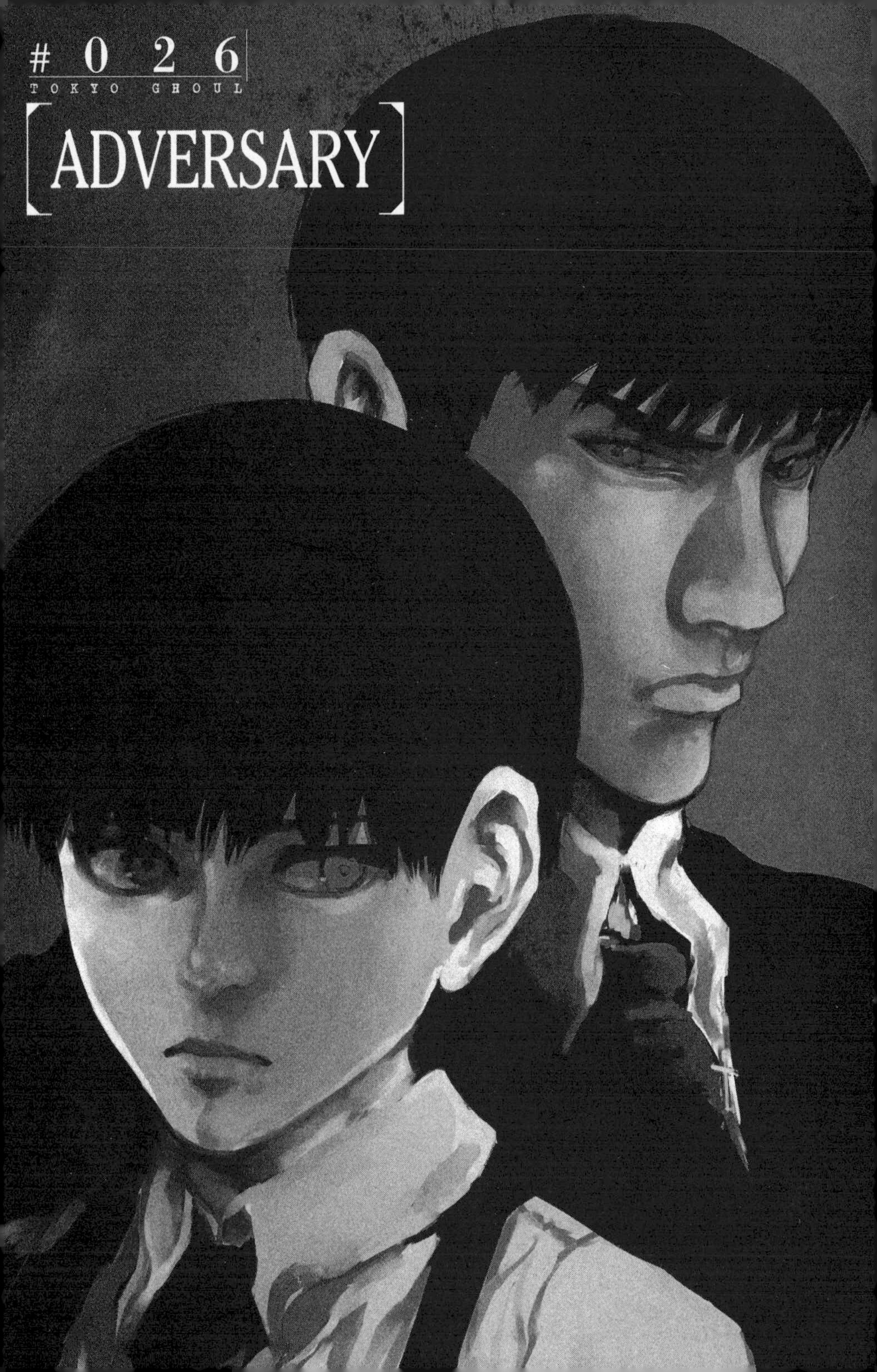

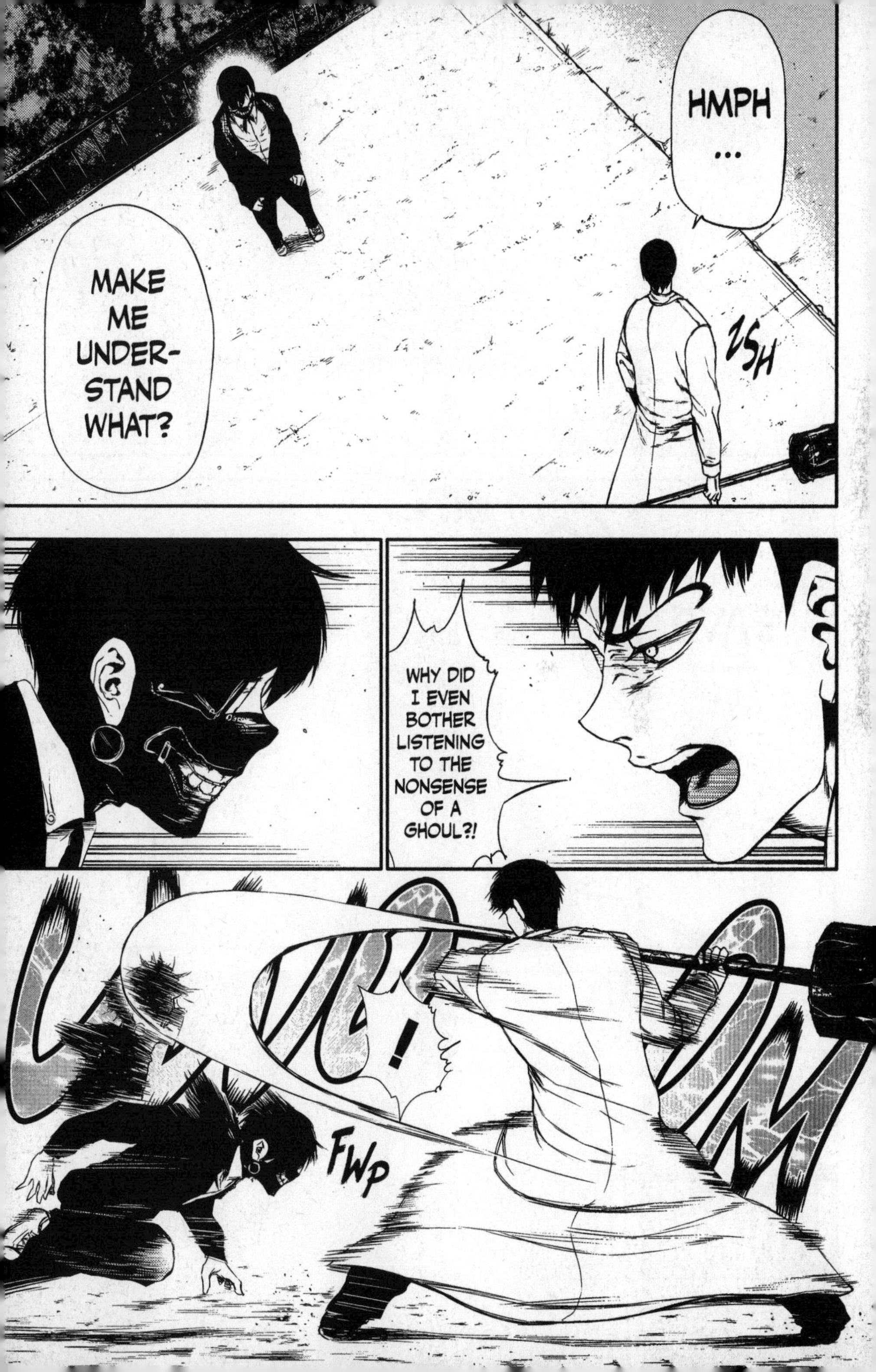
HMPH ...
MAKE ME UNDER-STAND WHAT?
ZSH
WHY DID I EVEN BOTHER LISTENING TO THE NONSENSE OF A GHOUL?!
!
FWP

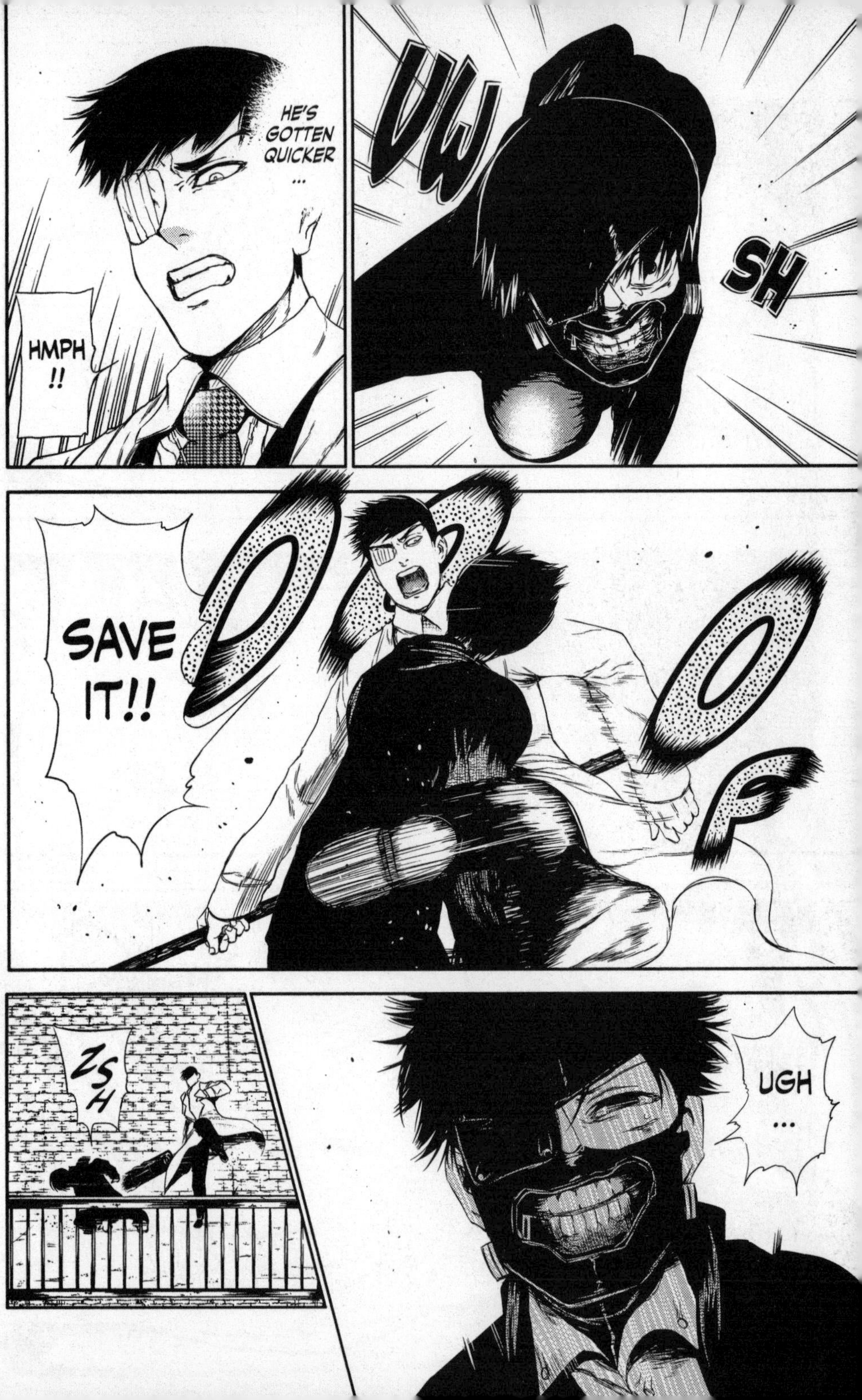
SH
HE'S GOTTEN QUICKER ...
HMPH !!
SAVE IT!!
UGH ...
ZSH

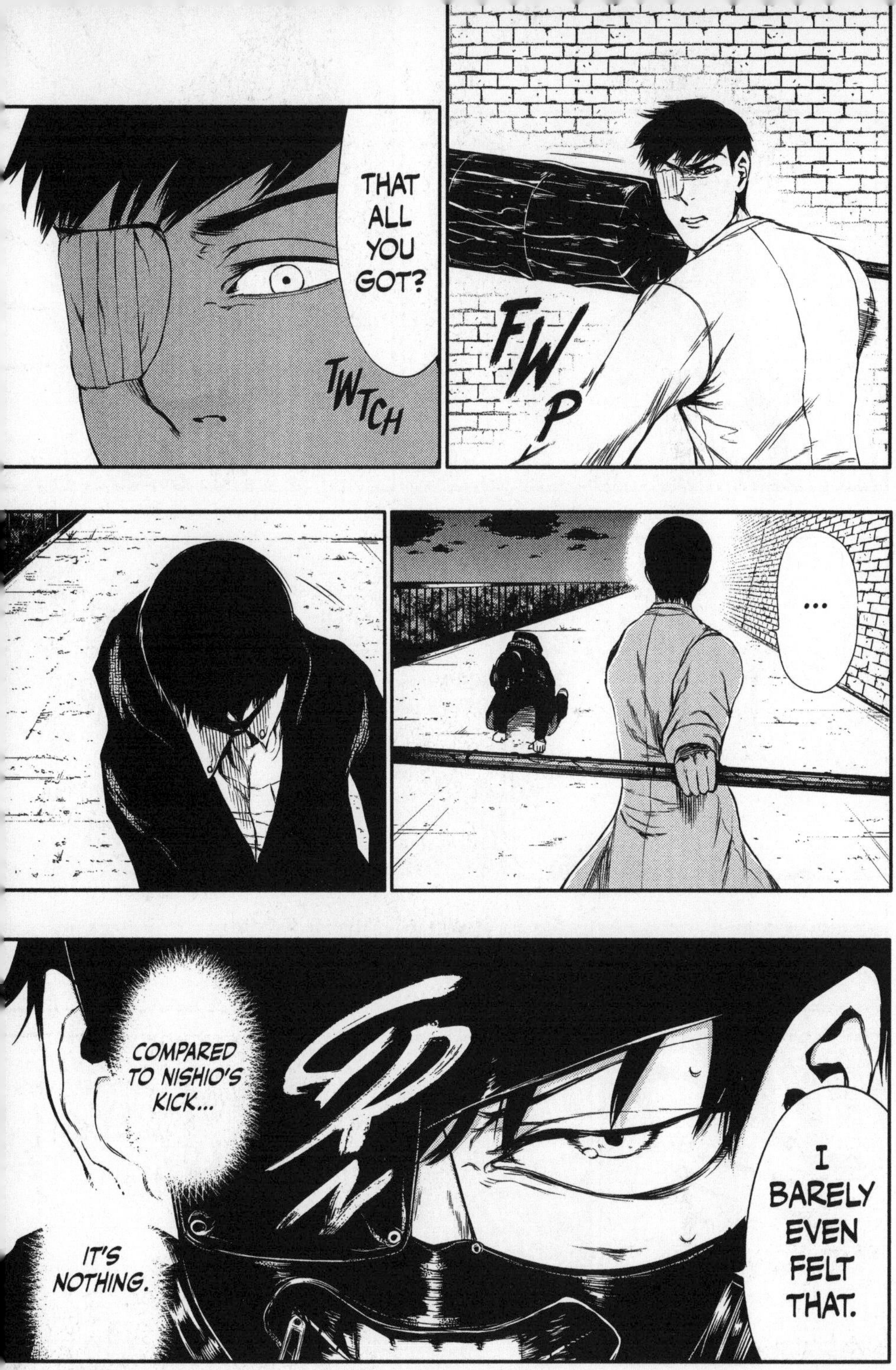
FWP
THAT ALL YOU GOT?
TWTCH
...
I BARELY EVEN FELT THAT.
COMPARED TO NISHIO'S KICK...
IT'S NOTHING.

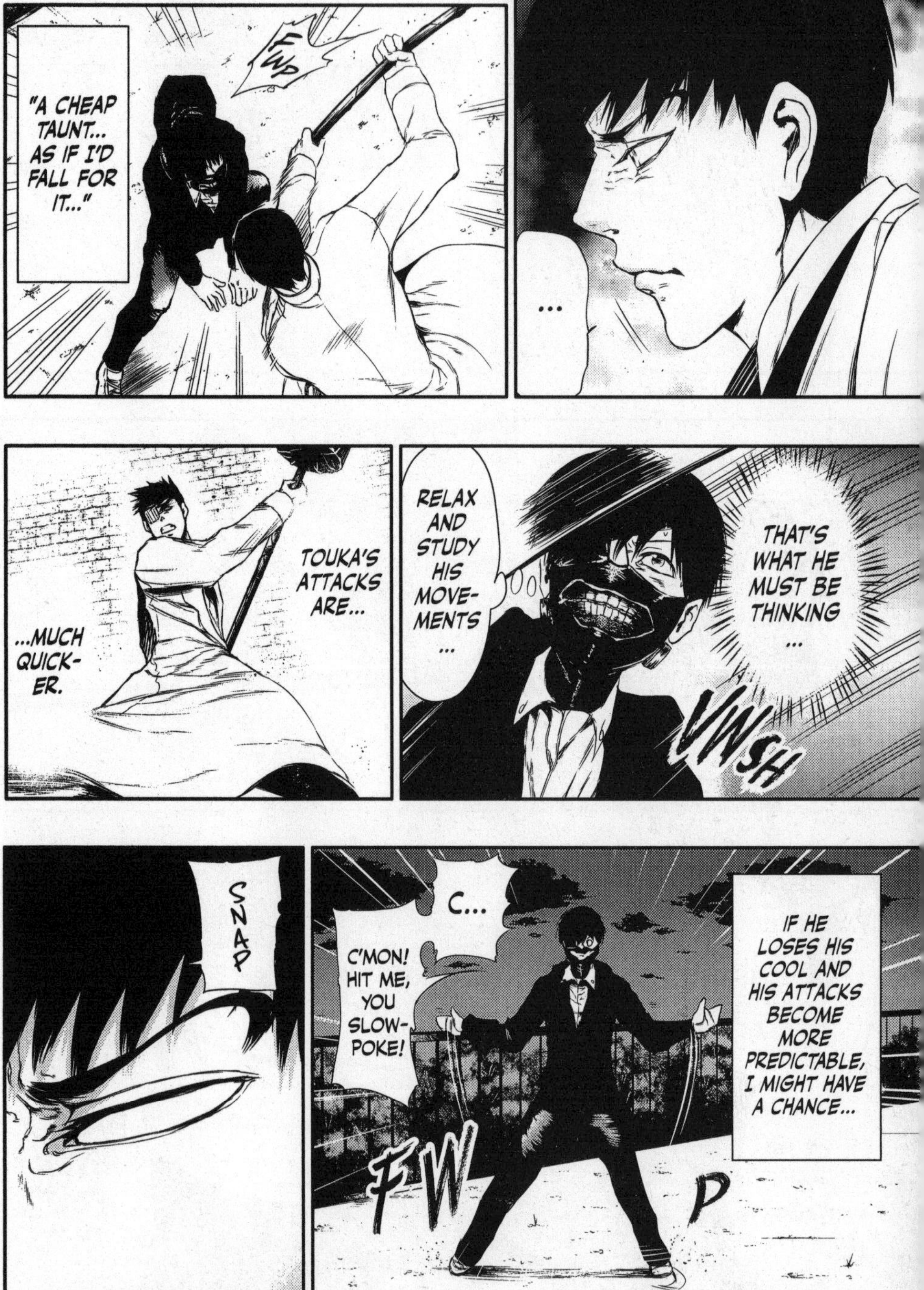
...
"A CHEAP TAUNT... AS IF I'D FALL FOR IT..."
FWP
RELAX AND STUDY HIS MOVE-MENTS...
THAT'S WHAT HE MUST BE THINKING...
VWSH
TOUKA'S ATTACKS ARE...
...MUCH QUICK-ER.
IF HE LOSES HIS COOL AND HIS ATTACKS BECOME MORE PREDICTABLE, I MIGHT HAVE A CHANCE...
C...
C'MON! HIT ME, YOU SLOW-POKE!
FWP
SNAP

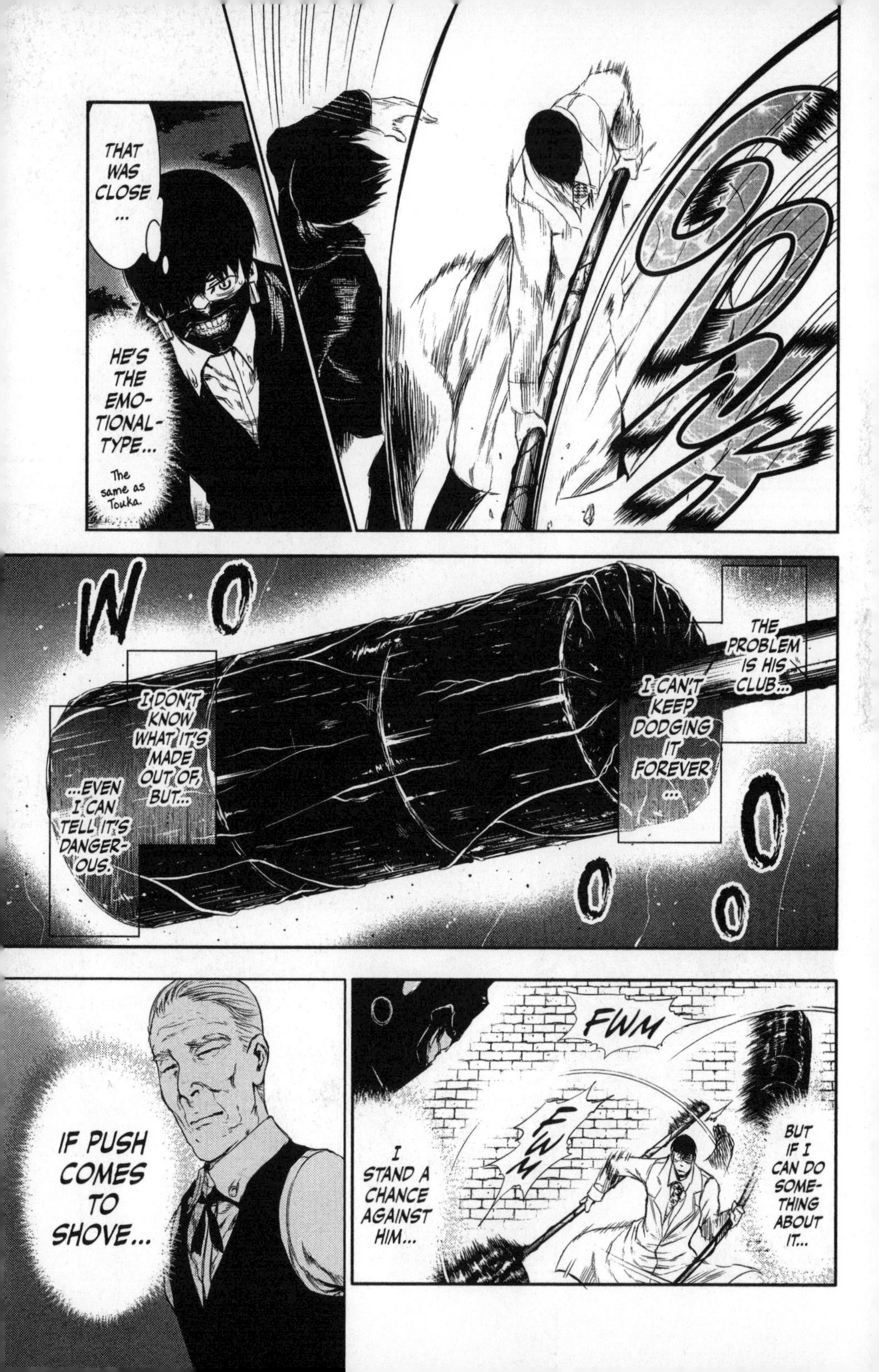
THAT WAS CLOSE...
HE'S THE EMOTIONAL-TYPE...
The same as Touka.
WOOOO
THE PROBLEM IS HIS CLUB...
I CAN'T KEEP DODGING IT FOREVER...
I DON'T KNOW WHAT IT'S MADE OUT OF, BUT...
...EVEN I CAN TELL IT'S DANGEROUS.
FWM
FWM
BUT IF I CAN DO SOMETHING ABOUT IT...
I STAND A CHANCE AGAINST HIM...
IF PUSH COMES TO SHOVE...

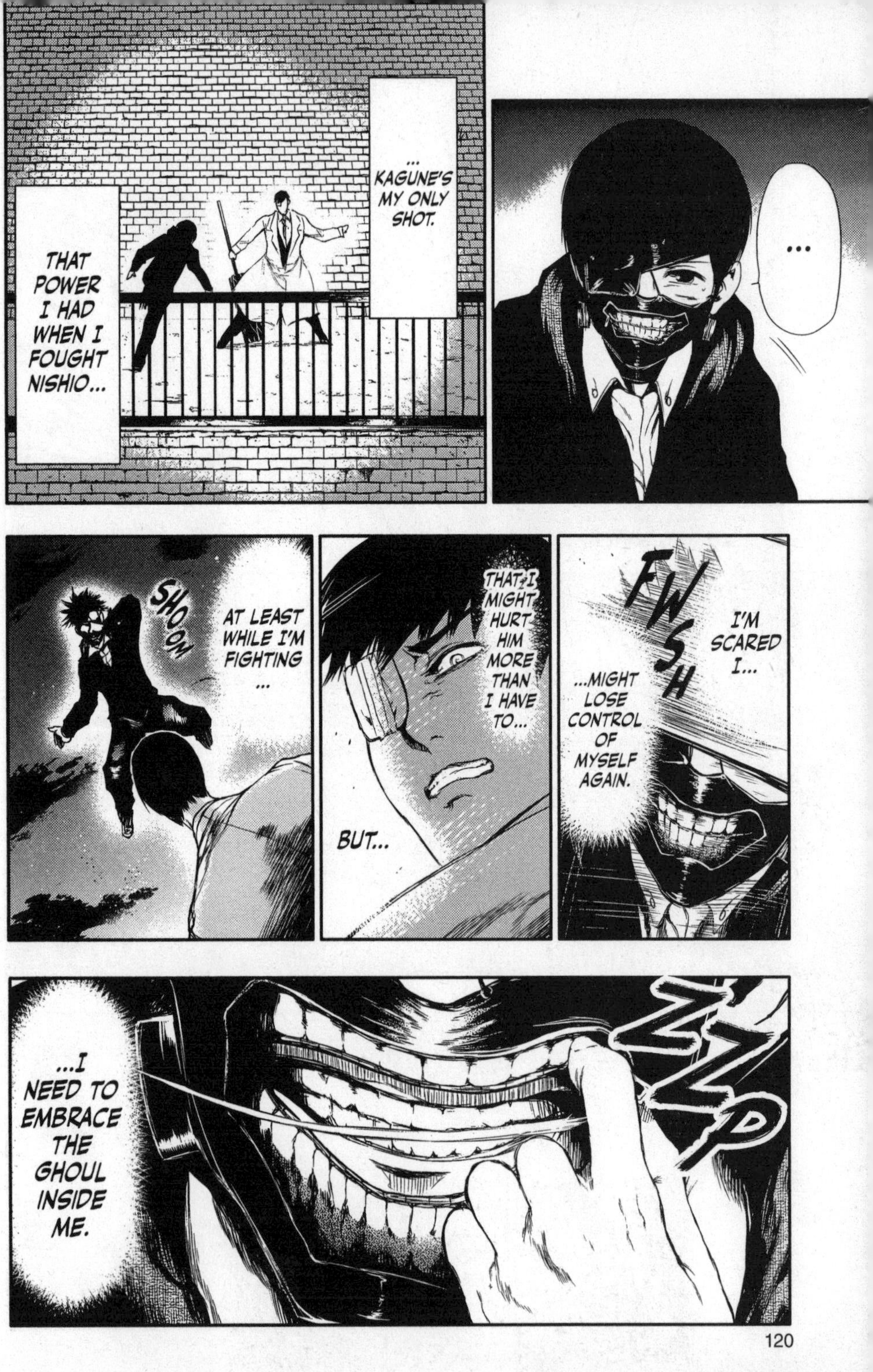
...
...KAGUNE'S MY ONLY SHOT.
THAT POWER I HAD WHEN I FOUGHT NISHIO...
FWSH
I'M SCARED I...
...MIGHT LOSE CONTROL OF MYSELF AGAIN.
THAT I MIGHT HURT HIM MORE THAN I HAVE TO...
BUT...
SHOOM
AT LEAST WHILE I'M FIGHTING...
ZZIP
...I NEED TO EMBRACE THE GHOUL INSIDE ME.

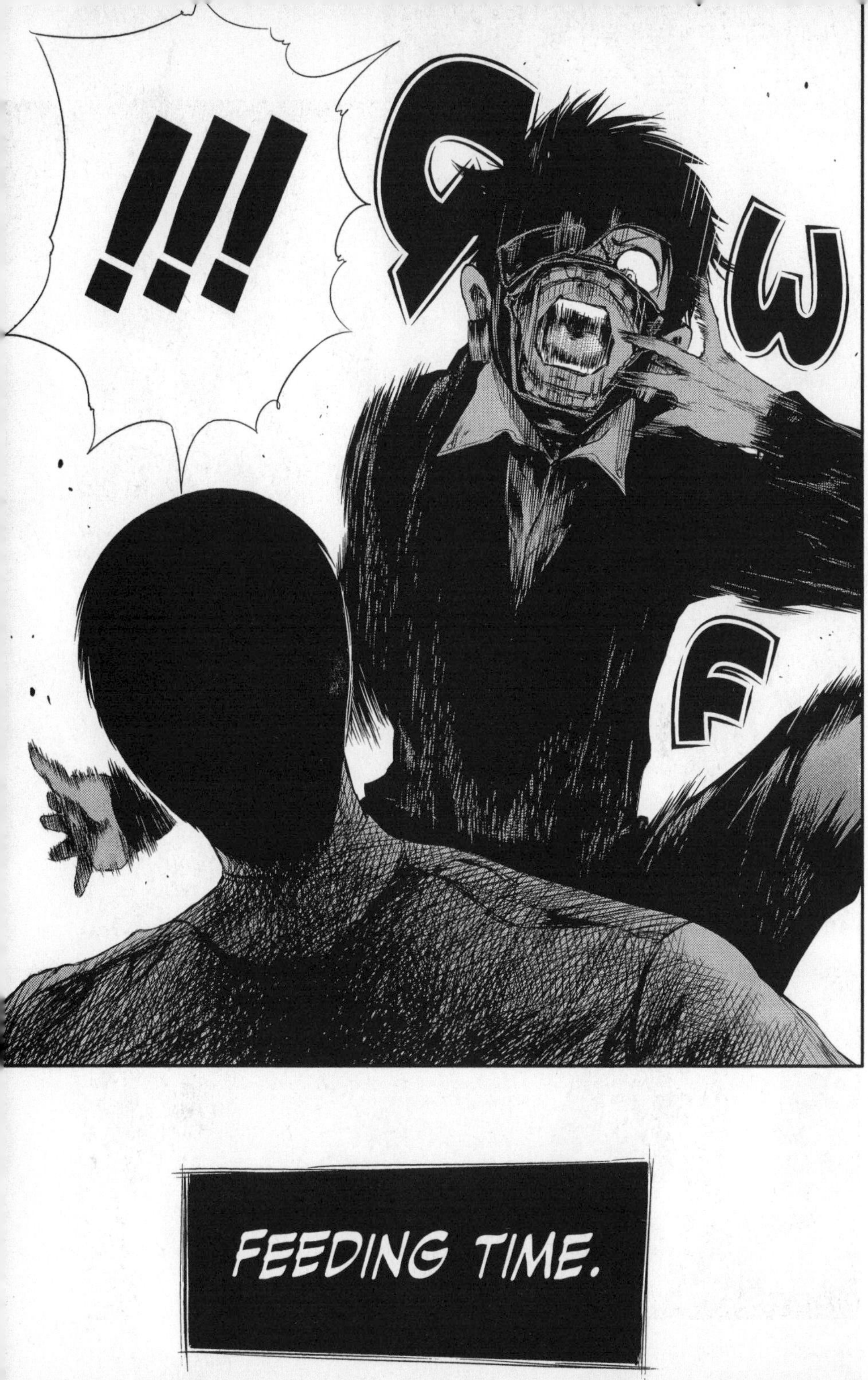
GWF
!!!

FEEDING TIME.

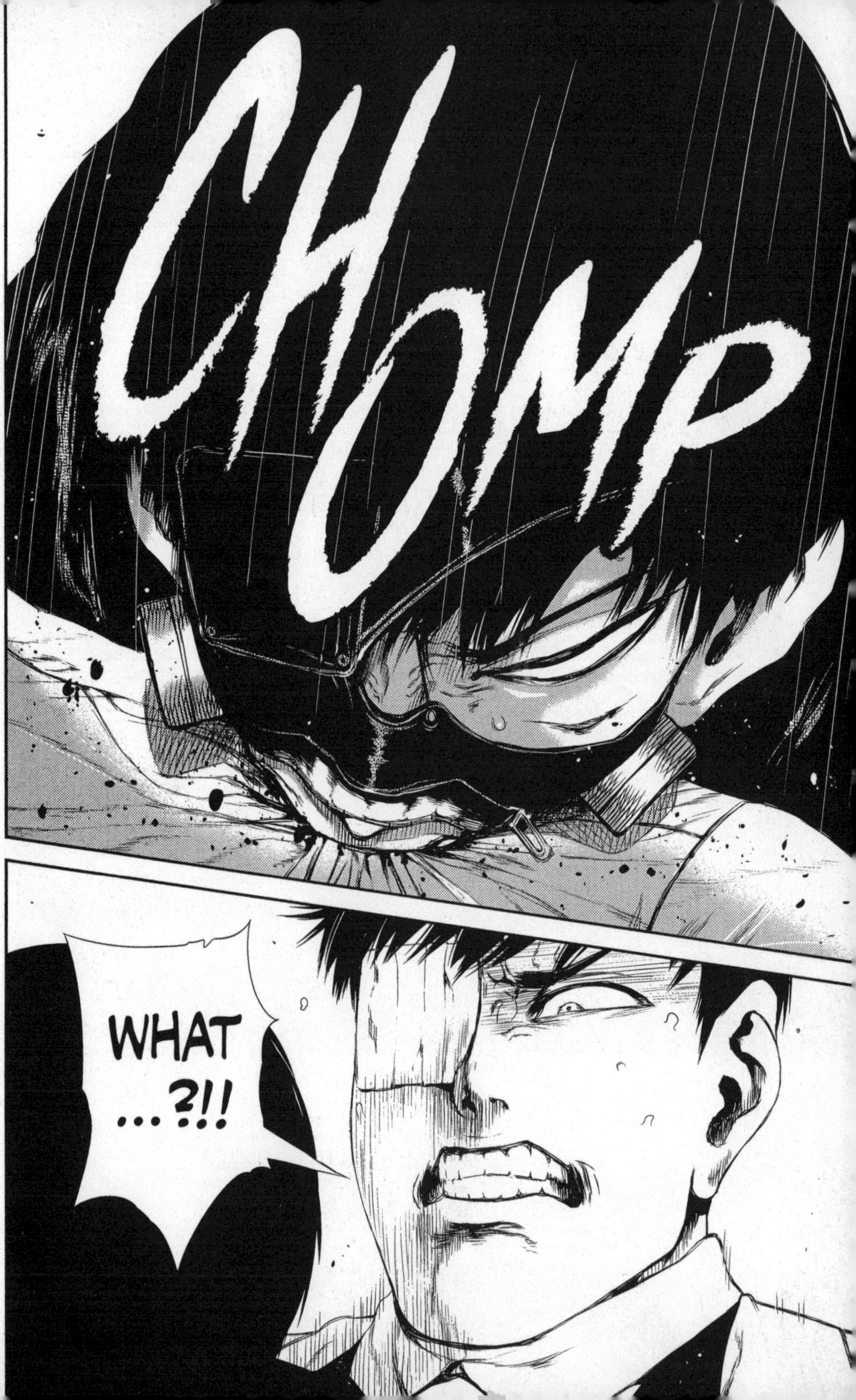
CHOMP
WHAT ...?!!

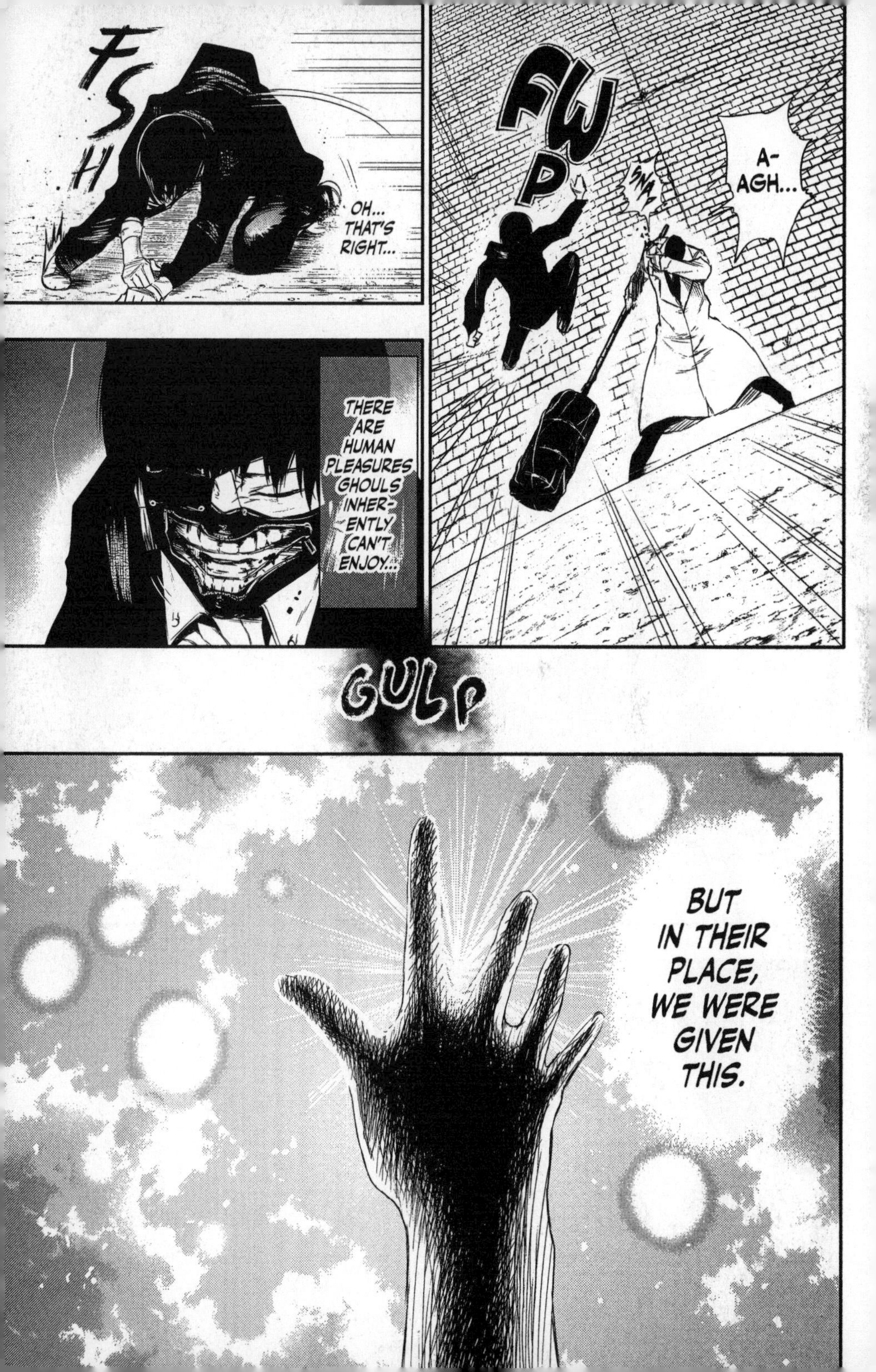
FWP
A-
AGH...
FSH
OH... THAT'S RIGHT...
THERE ARE HUMAN PLEASURES GHOULS INHERENTLY CAN'T ENJOY...
GULP
BUT IN THEIR PLACE, WE WERE GIVEN THIS.

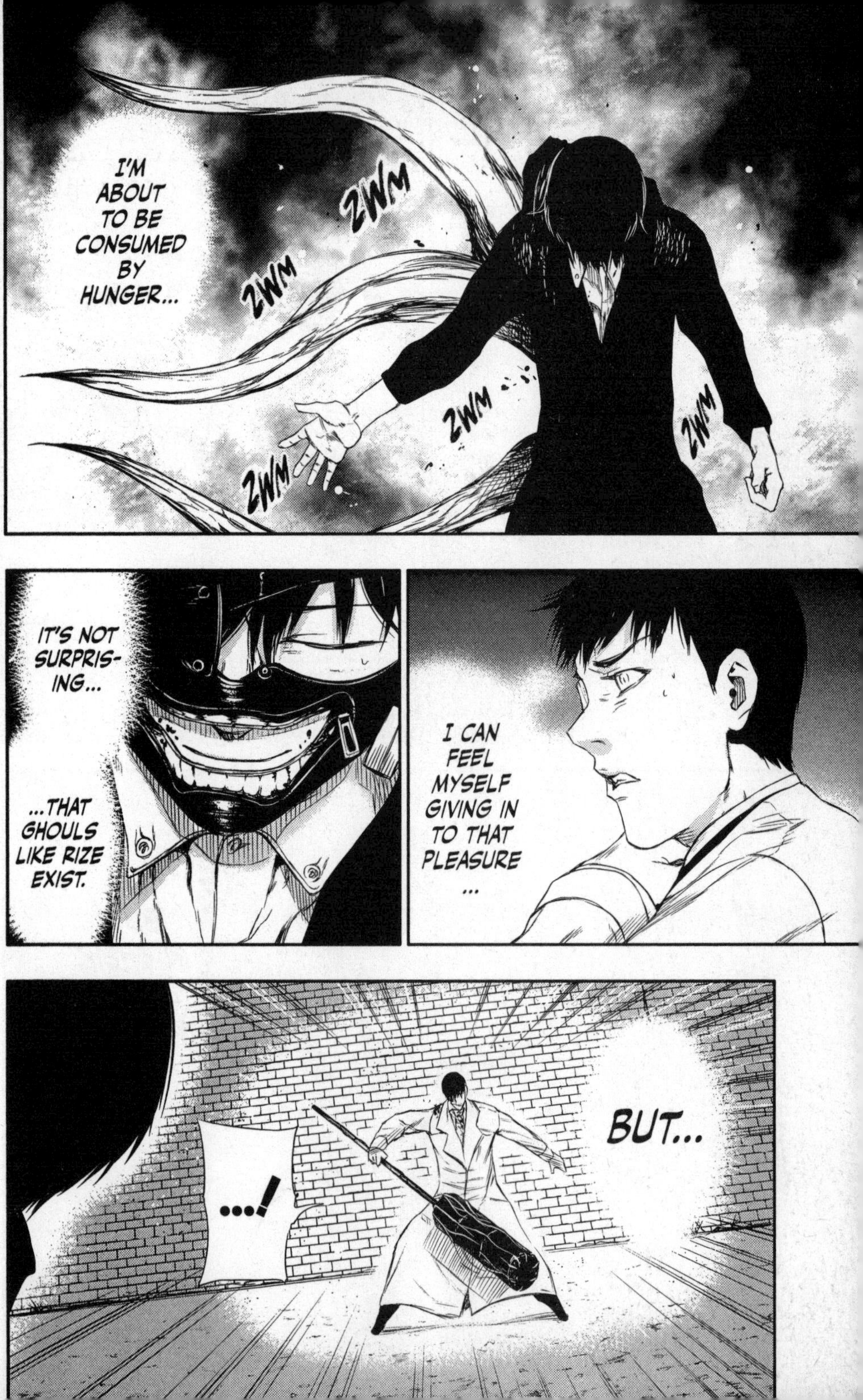
I'M ABOUT TO BE CONSUMED BY HUNGER...
ZWM
ZWM
ZWM
ZWM
ZWM
I CAN FEEL MYSELF GIVING IN TO THAT PLEASURE ...
IT'S NOT SURPRISING...
...THAT GHOULS LIKE RIZE EXIST.
BUT...
...!

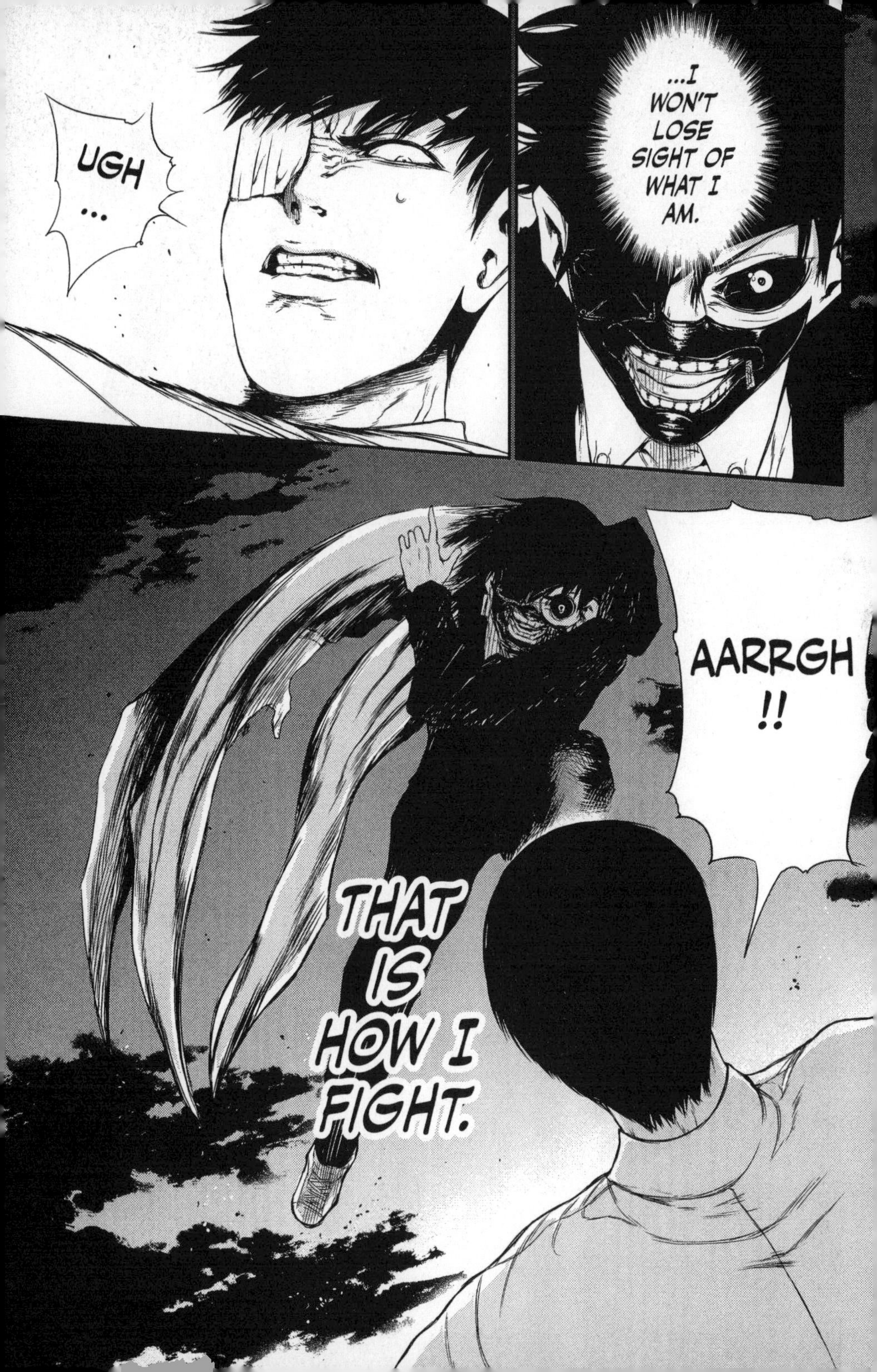
...I WON'T LOSE SIGHT OF WHAT I AM.
UGH ...
AARRGH !!
THAT IS HOW I FIGHT.

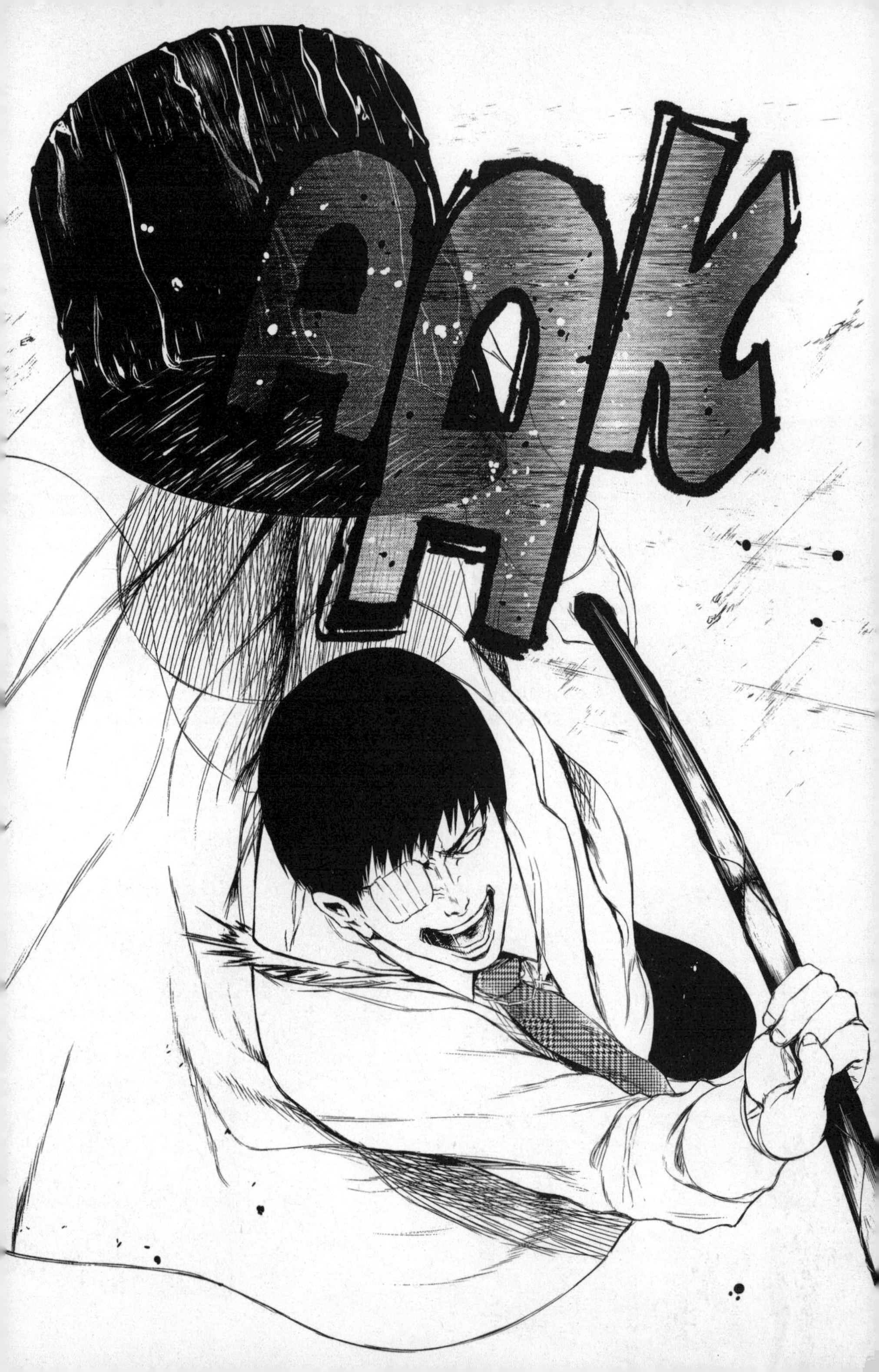

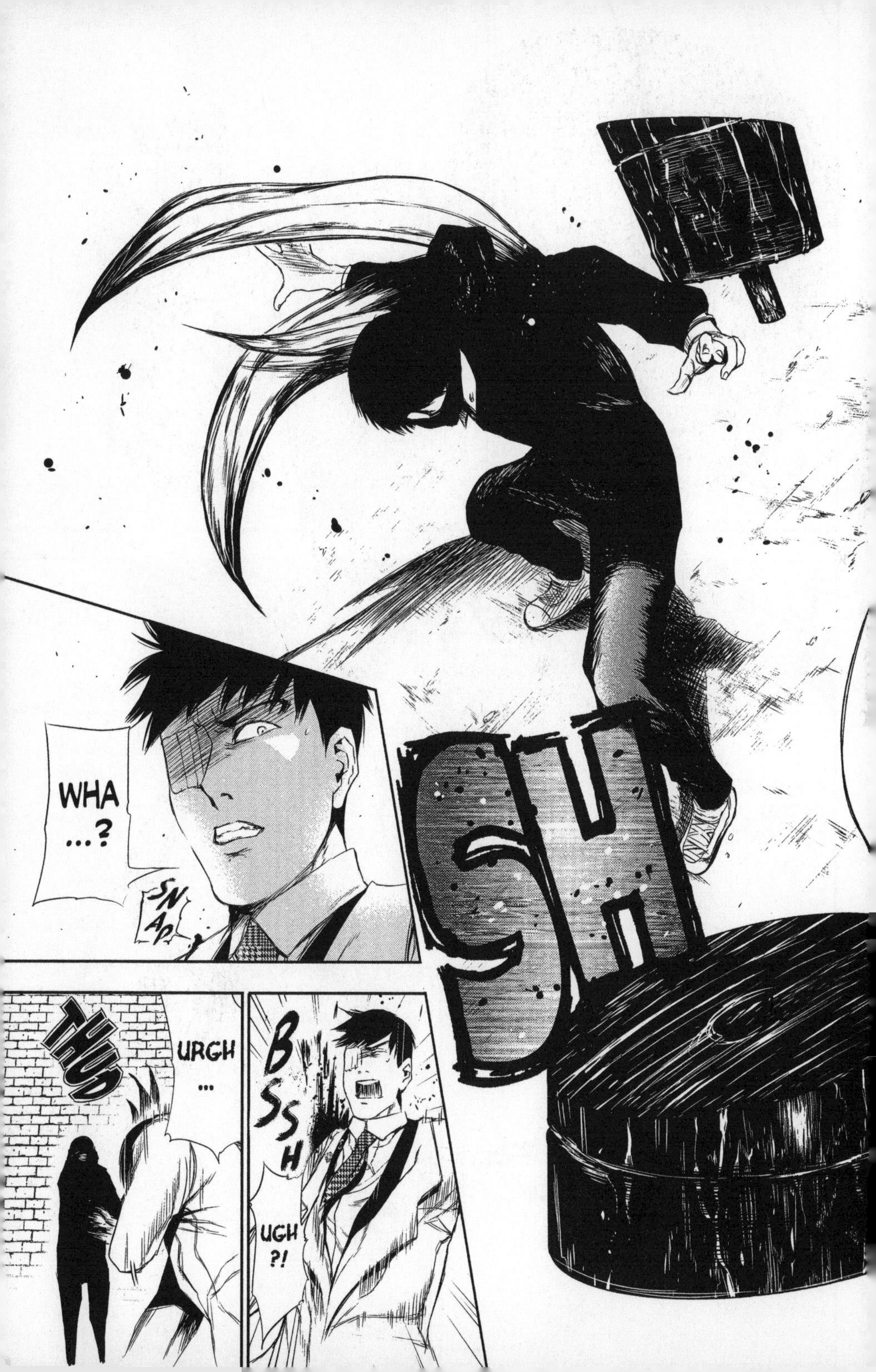
SH
WHA ...?
SNAP
BSSH
UGH ?!
THUD
URGH ...

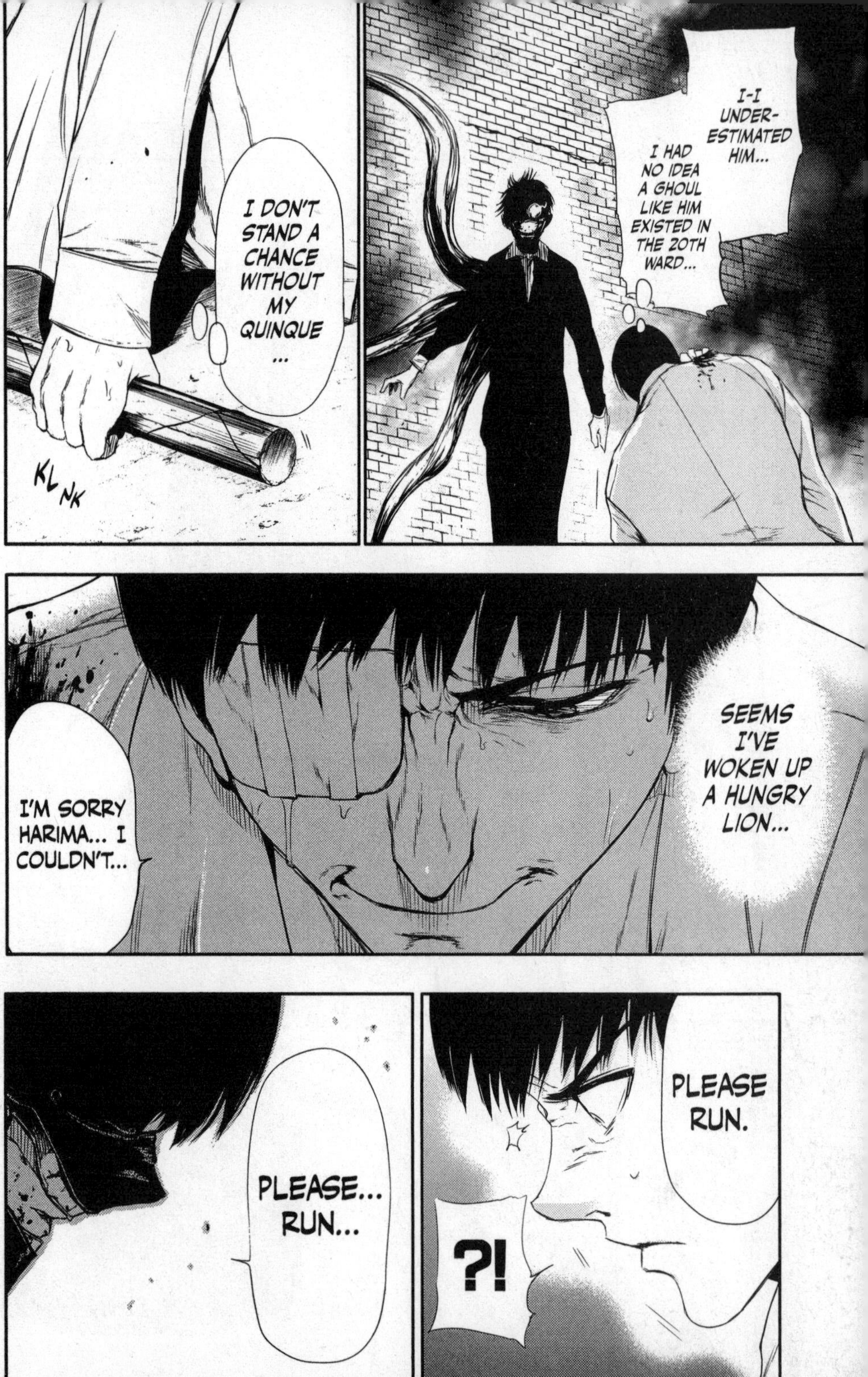
I-I UNDER-ESTIMATED HIM...
I HAD NO IDEA A GHOUL LIKE HIM EXISTED IN THE 20TH WARD...
I DON'T STAND A CHANCE WITHOUT MY QUINQUE ...
KLUNK
SEEMS I'VE WOKEN UP A HUNGRY LION...
I'M SORRY HARIMA... I COULDN'T...
PLEASE RUN.
?!
PLEASE... RUN...

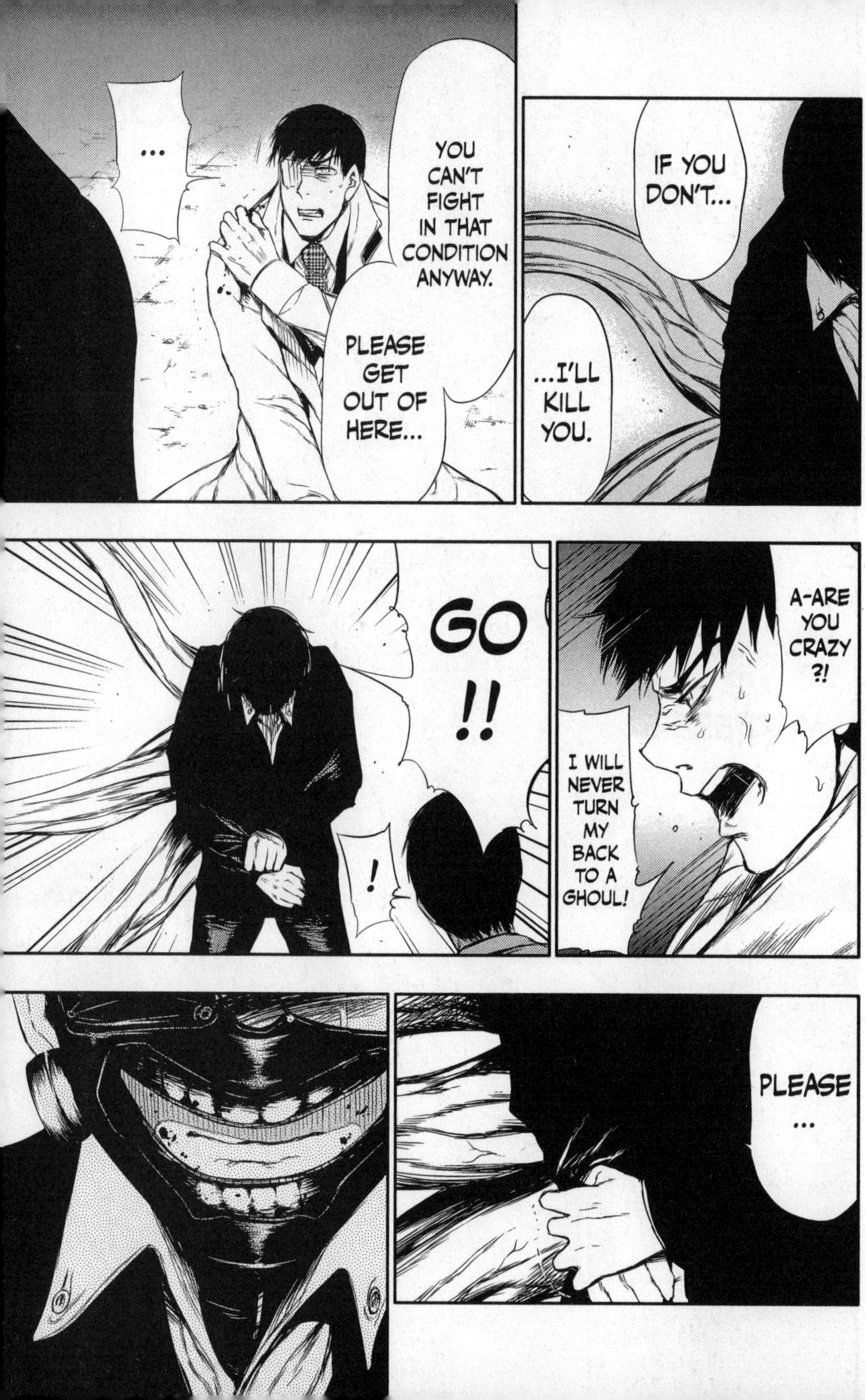
IF YOU DON'T...
...I'LL KILL YOU.
YOU CAN'T FIGHT IN THAT CONDITION ANYWAY.
PLEASE GET OUT OF HERE...
...
A-ARE YOU CRAZY?!
I WILL NEVER TURN MY BACK TO A GHOUL!
GO!!
!
PLEASE...

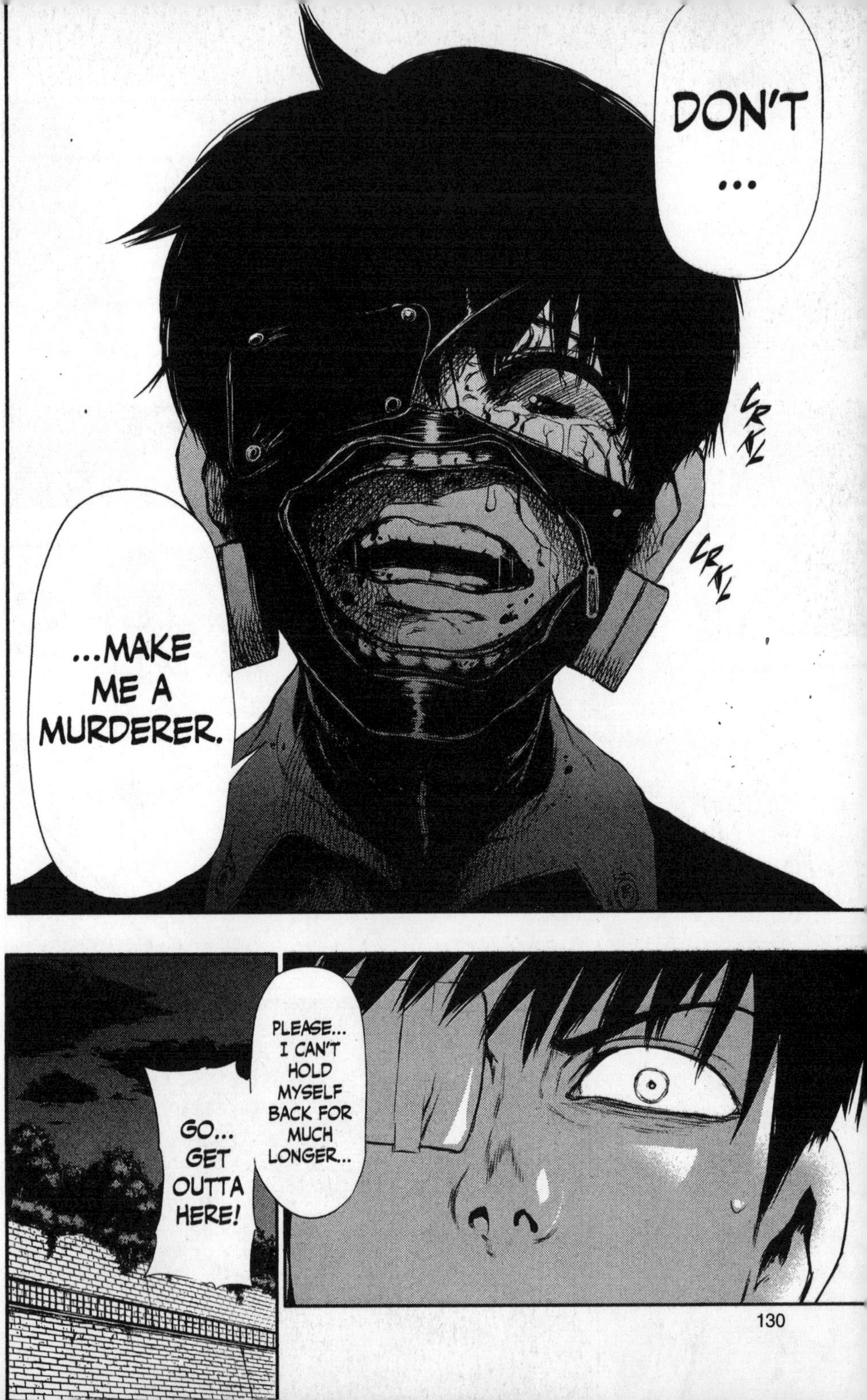
DON'T ...
CRKL
CRKL
...MAKE ME A MURDERER.
PLEASE... I CAN'T HOLD MYSELF BACK FOR MUCH LONGER...
GO... GET OUTTA HERE!

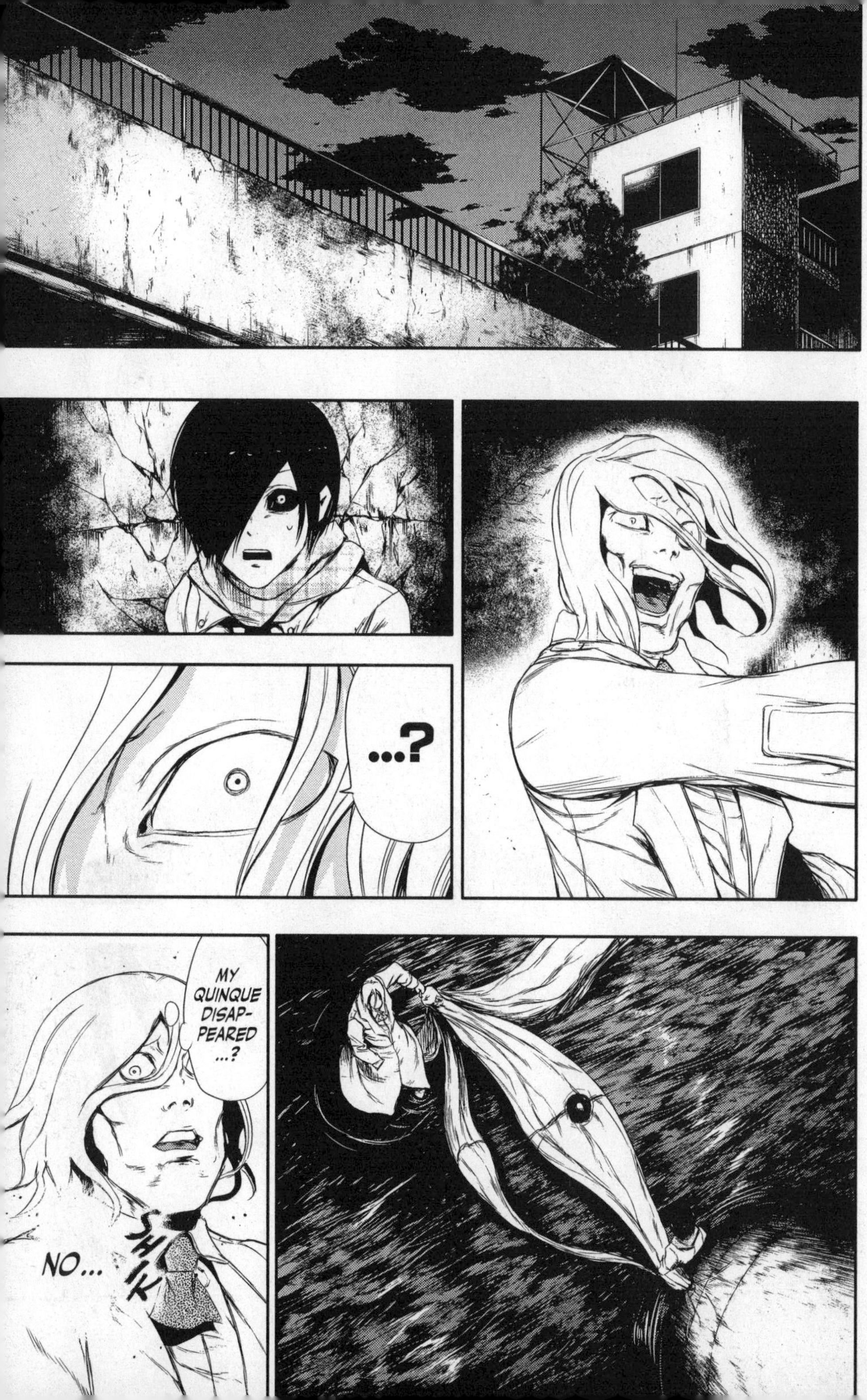
...?
MY QUINQUE DISAP-PEARED ...?
SHIK
NO...

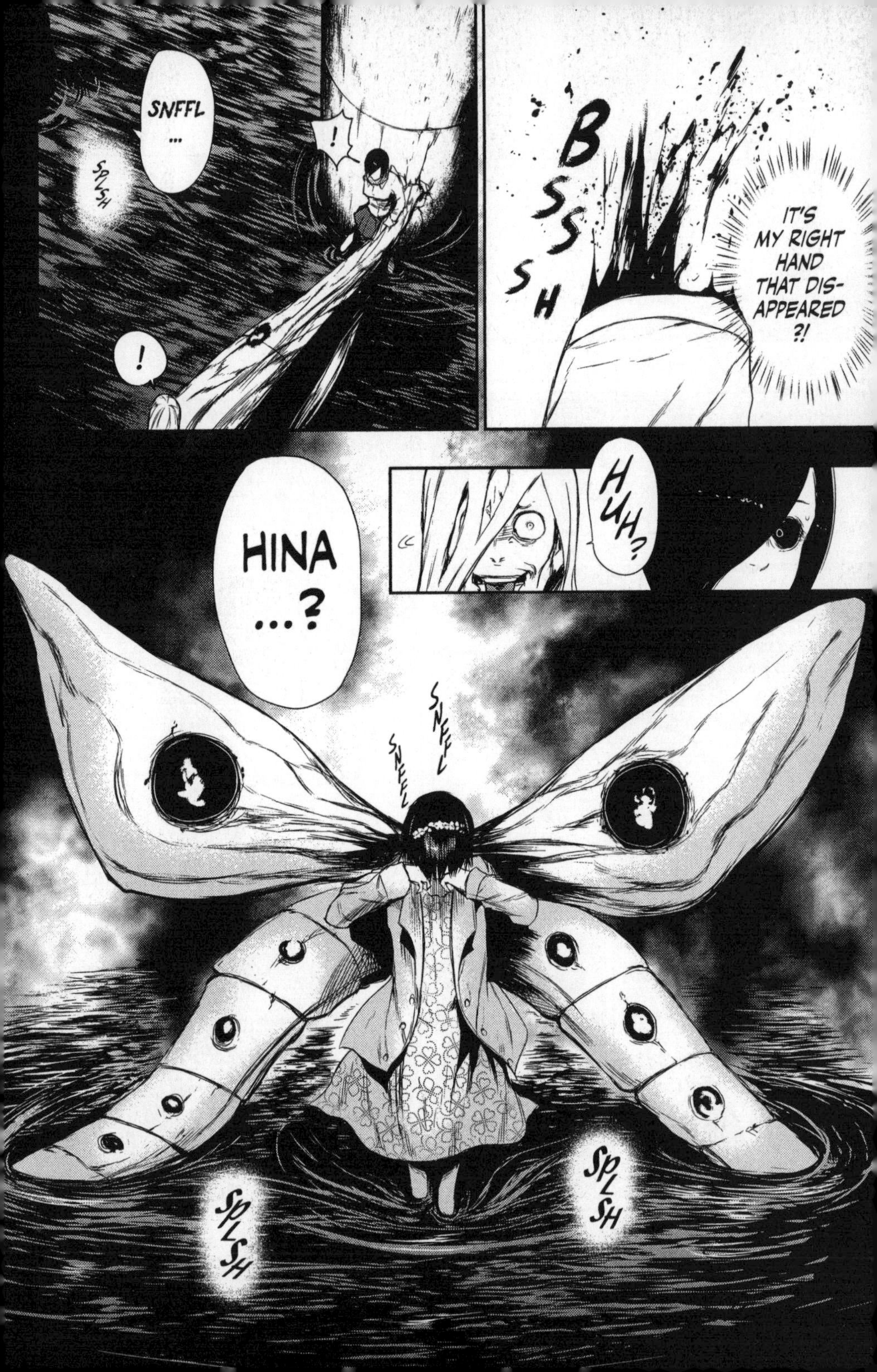
BSSSH
IT'S MY RIGHT HAND THAT DIS-APPEARED?!
!
SNFFL...
SPLSH
!
HUH?
HINA...?
SNFFL
SNFFL
SPLSH
SPLSH

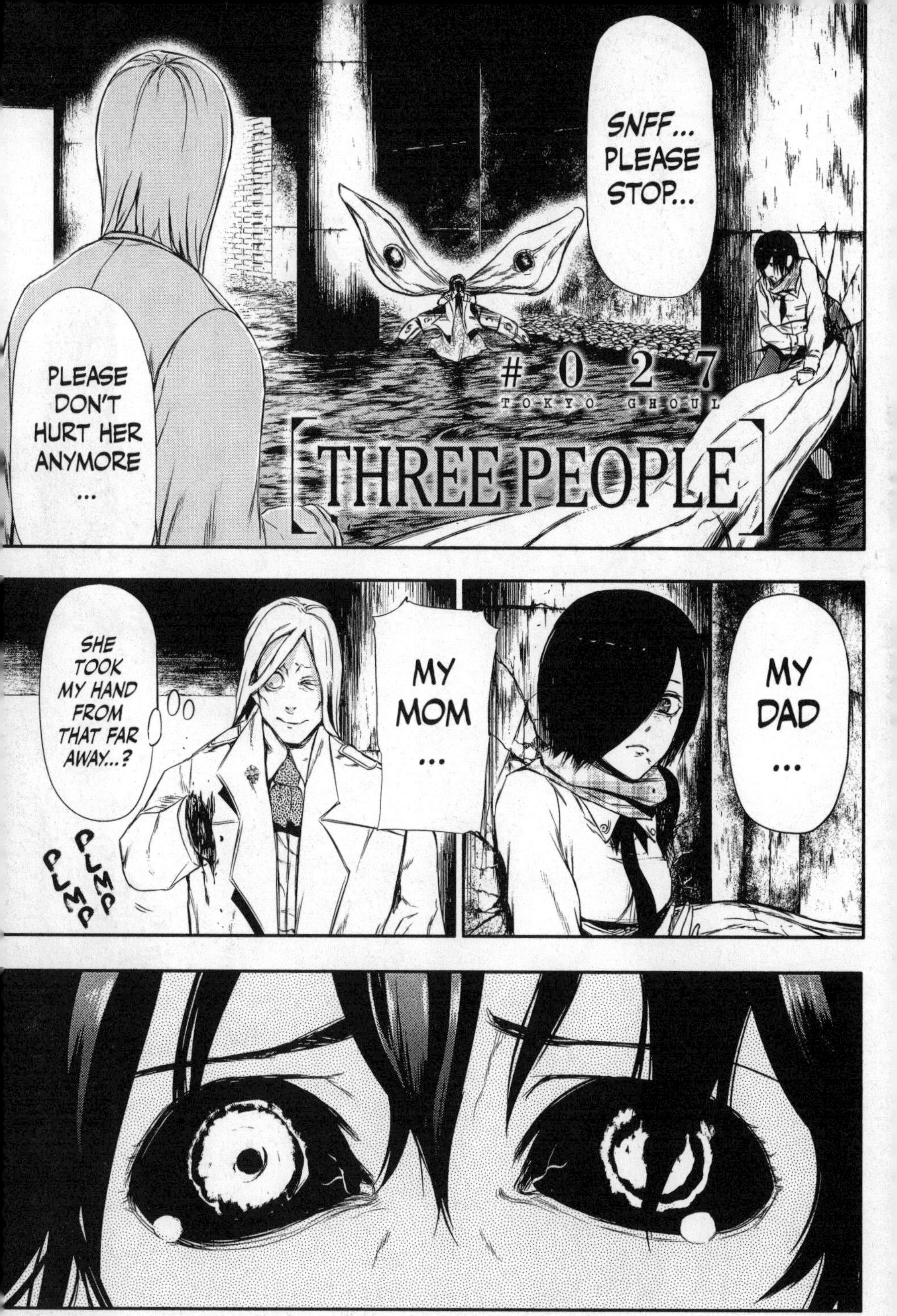
SNFF... PLEASE STOP...
#027
TOKYO GHOUL
THREE PEOPLE
PLEASE DON'T HURT HER ANYMORE ...
MY DAD ...
MY MOM ...
SHE TOOK MY HAND FROM THAT FAR AWAY...?
PLMP PLMP

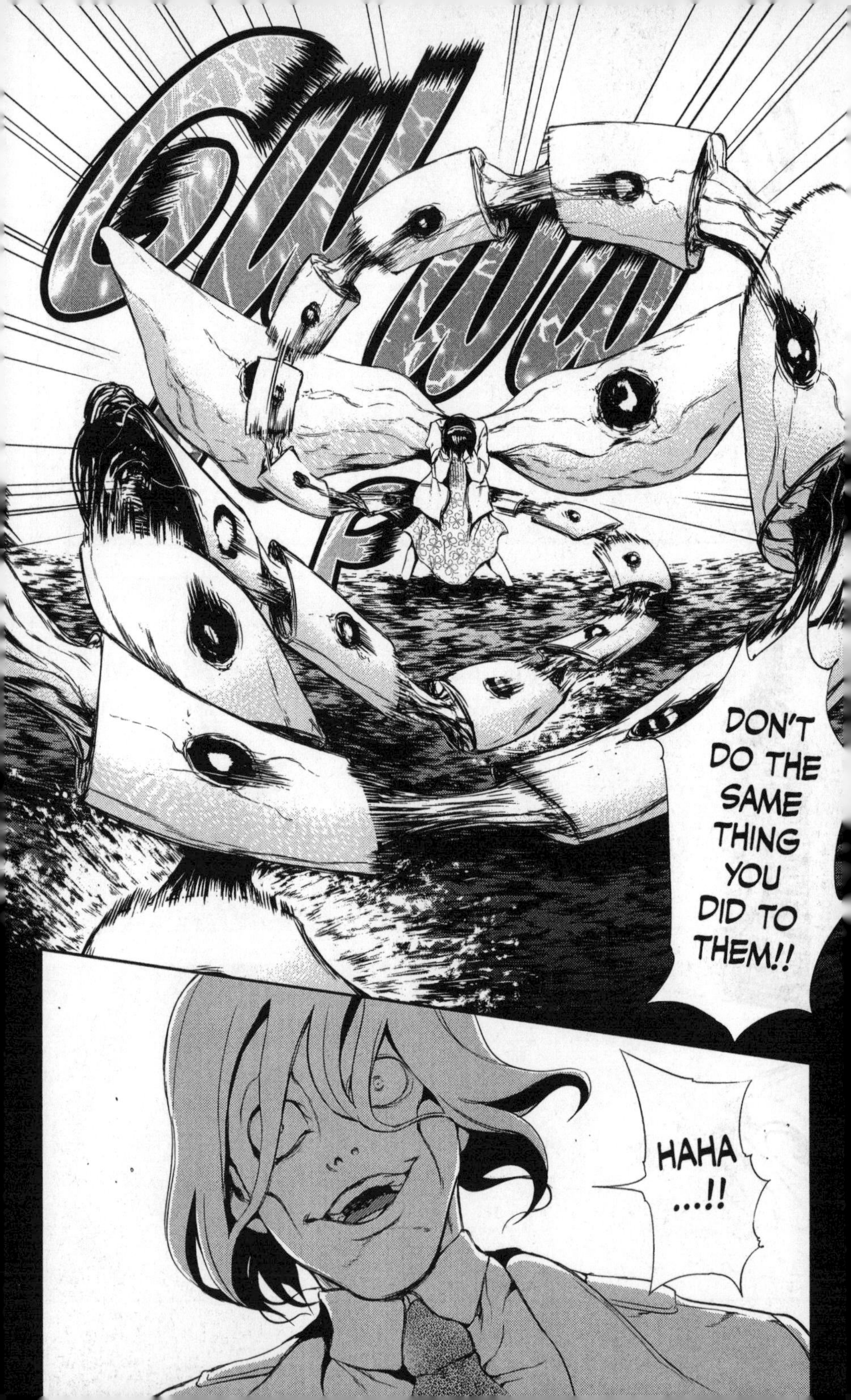
DON'T DO THE SAME THING YOU DID TO THEM!!
HAHA ...!!

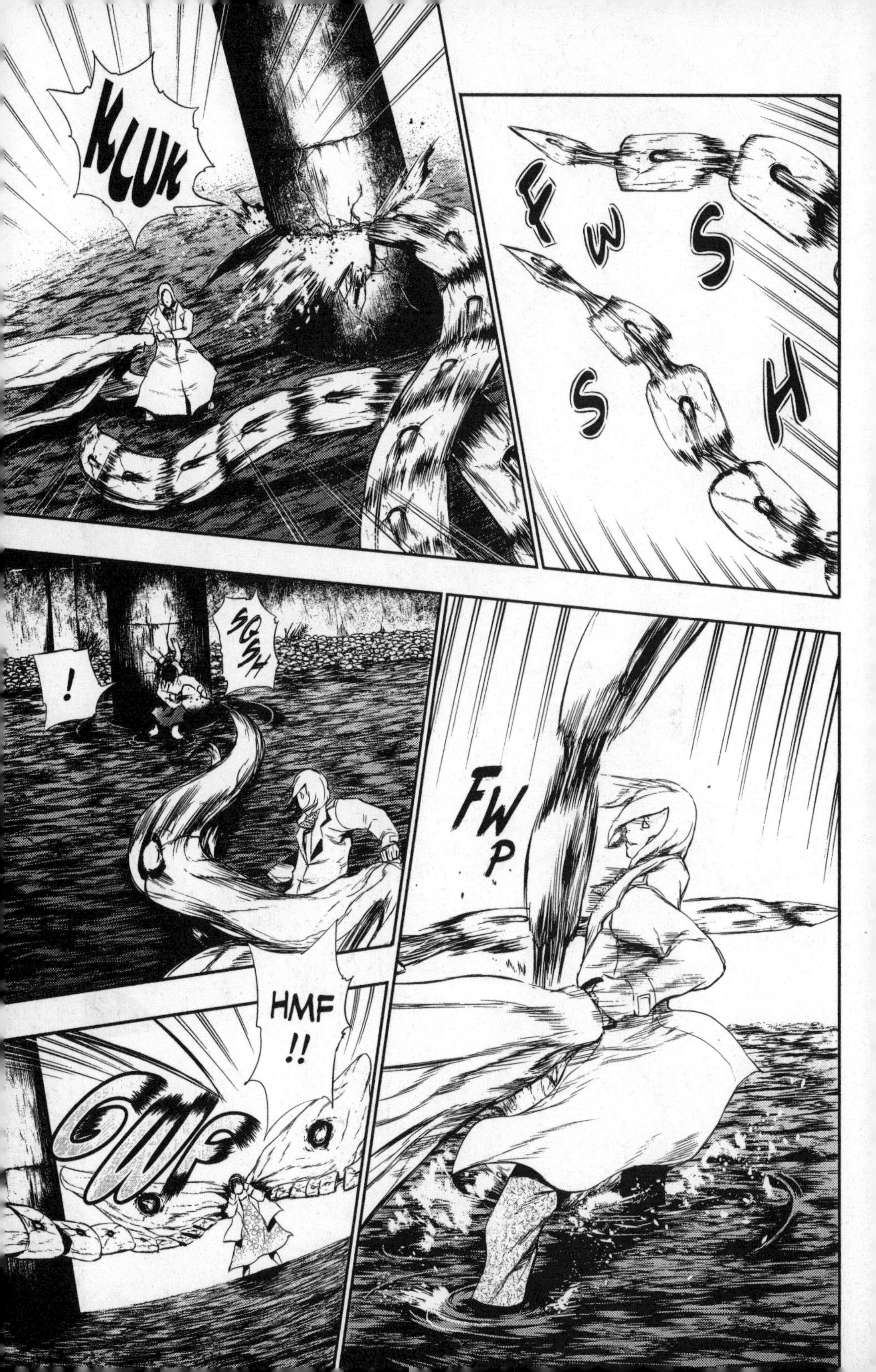
FWSSH
KLUK
FWP
SGSH
!
HMF !!

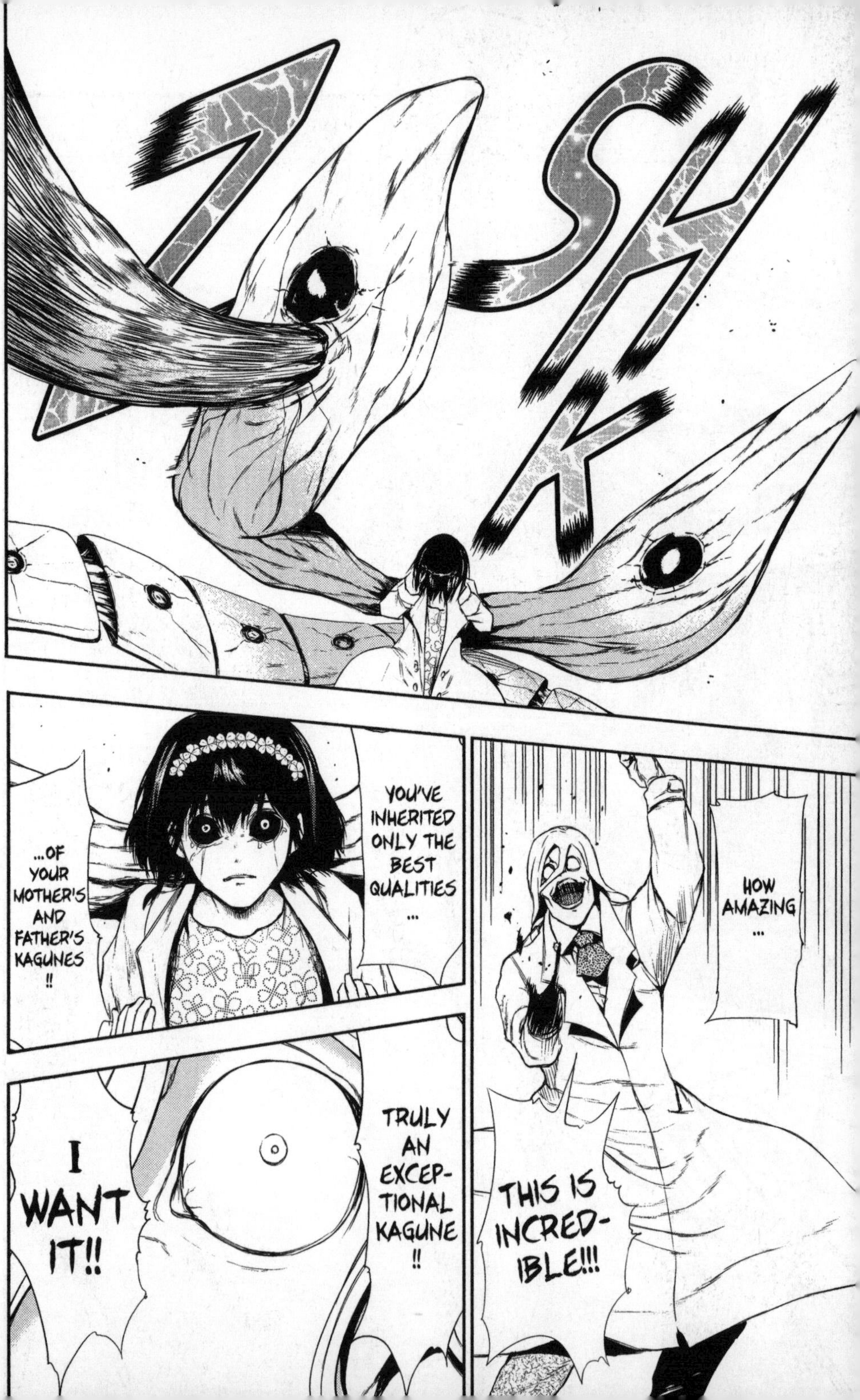
ZSHK
HOW AMAZING...
THIS IS INCREDIBLE!!!
YOU'VE INHERITED ONLY THE BEST QUALITIES...
...OF YOUR MOTHER'S AND FATHER'S KAGUNES!!
TRULY AN EXCEPTIONAL KAGUNE!!
I WANT IT!!

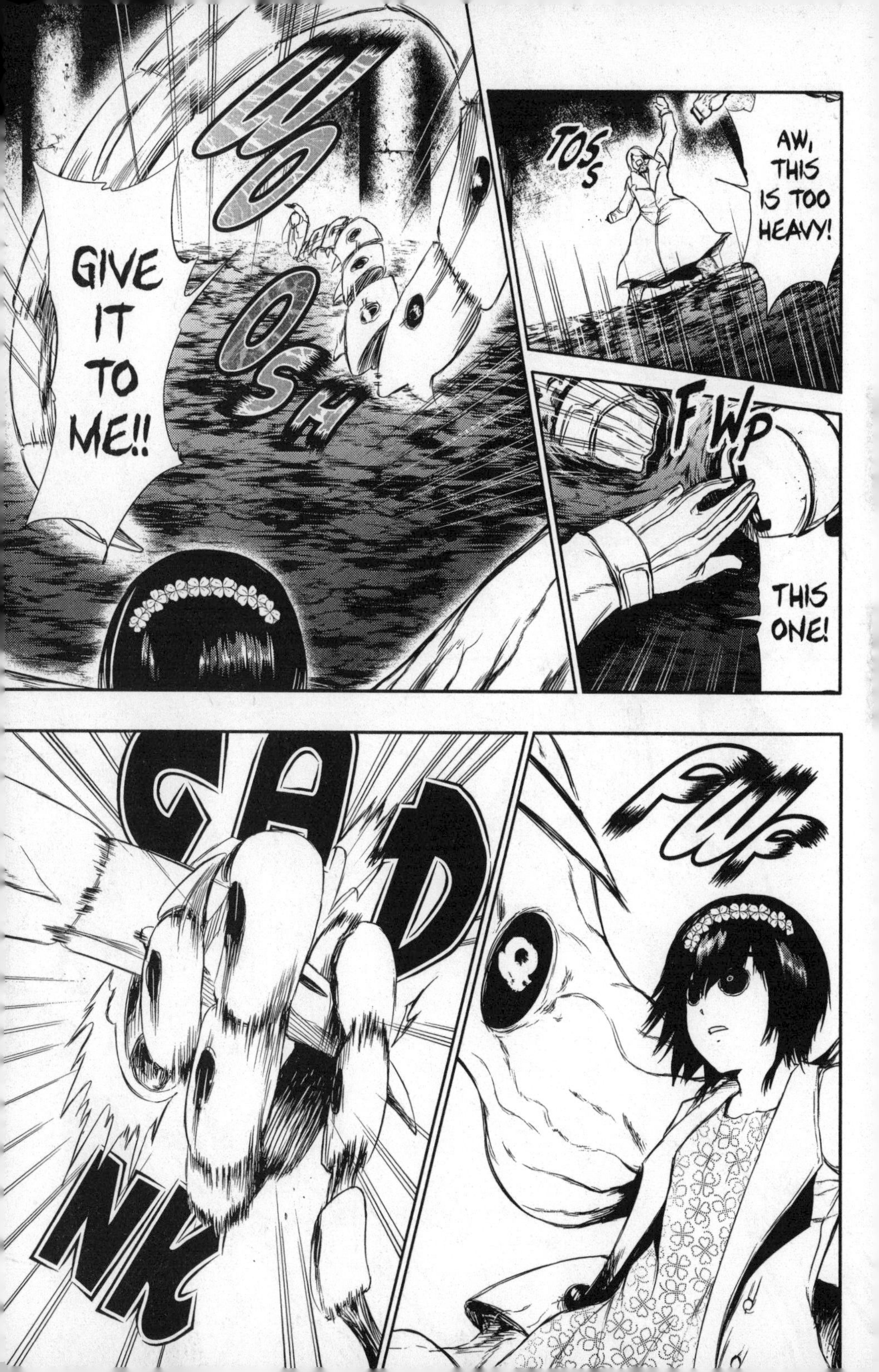
TOSS
AW, THIS IS TOO HEAVY!
FWP
THIS ONE!
GIVE IT TO ME!!

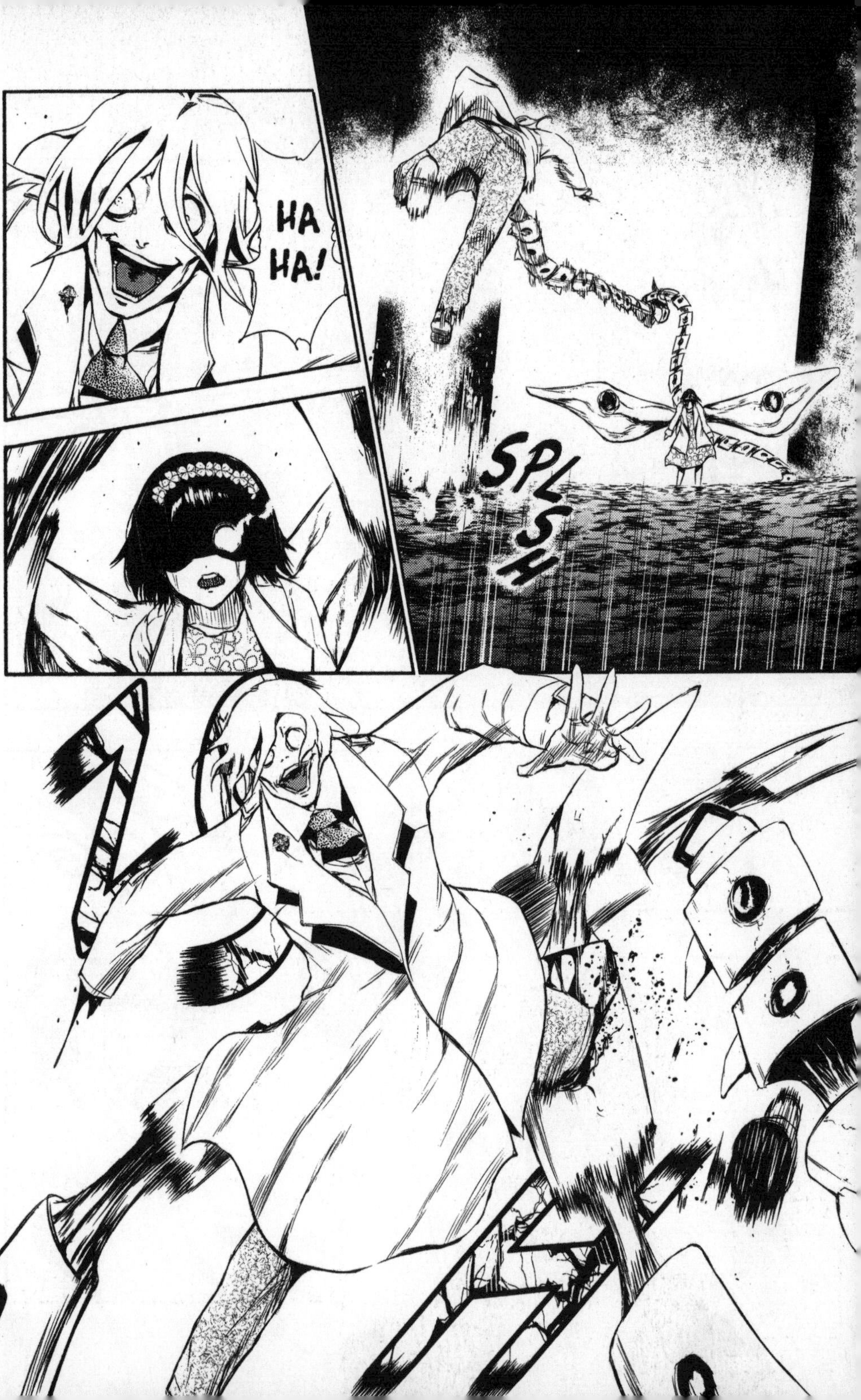
SPLSH
HA HA!

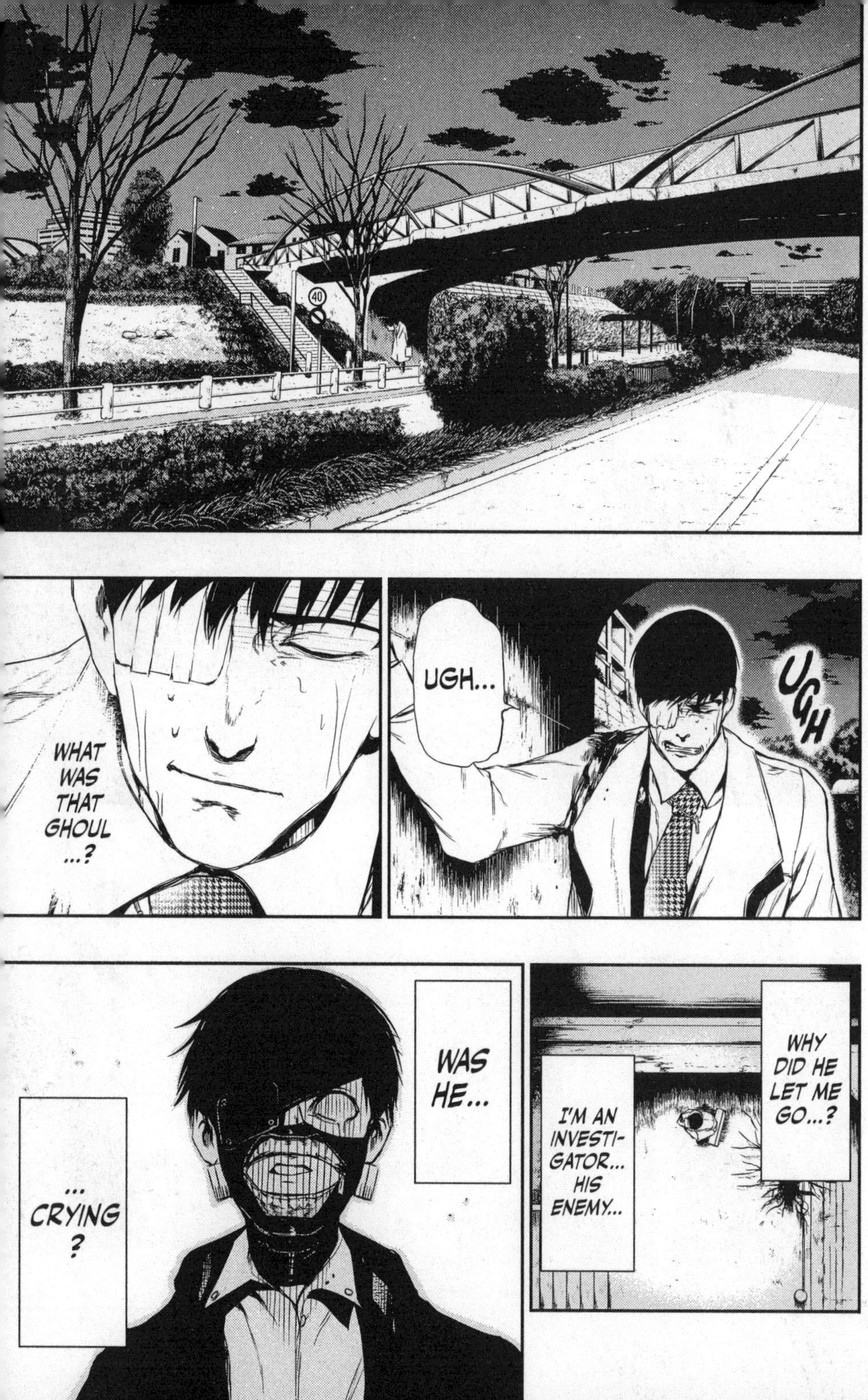
40
UGH...
UGH
WHAT WAS THAT GHOUL ...?
WHY DID HE LET ME GO...?
I'M AN INVESTIGATOR... HIS ENEMY...
WAS HE...
... CRYING?

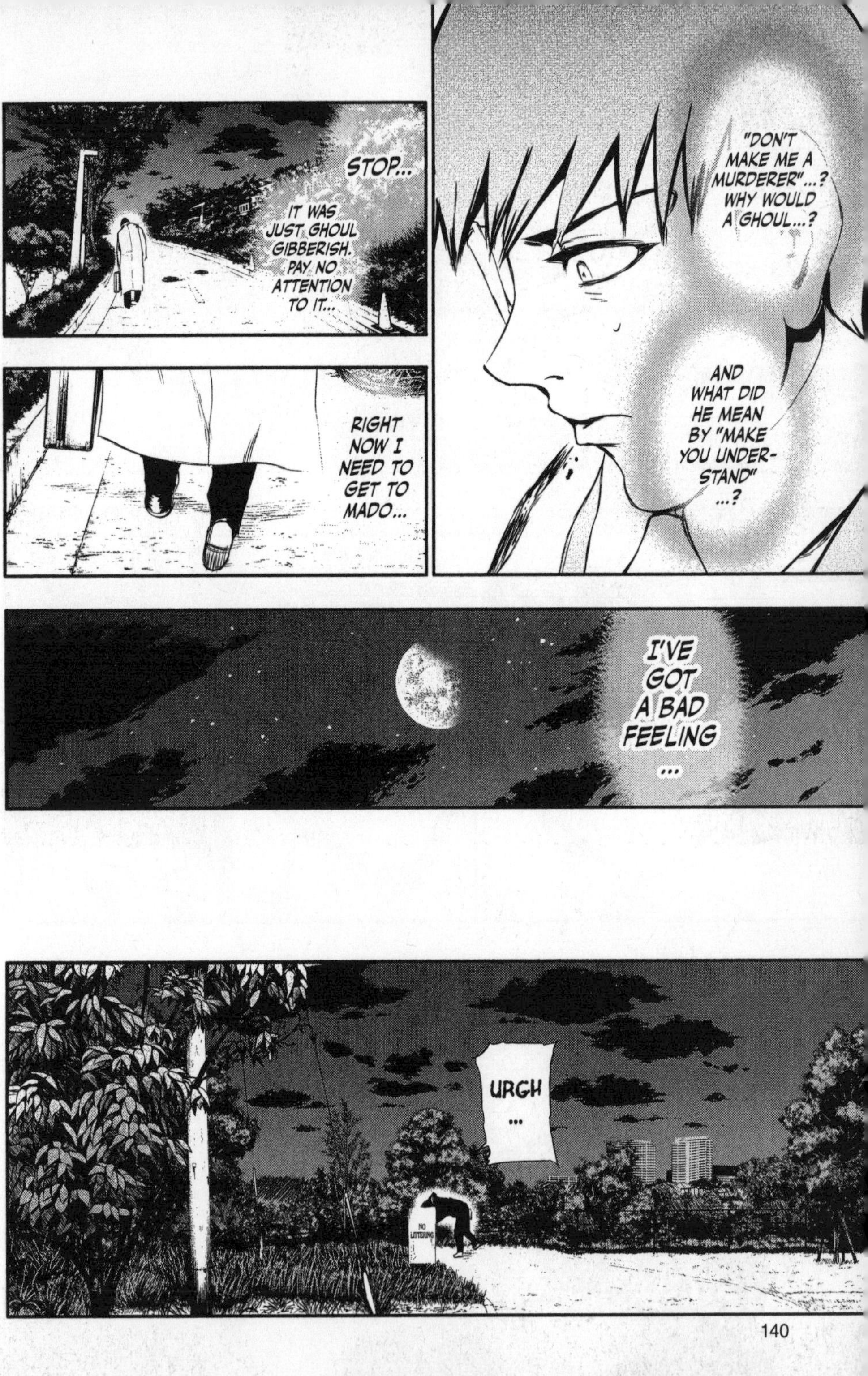
"DON'T MAKE ME A MURDERER"...? WHY WOULD A GHOUL...?
AND WHAT DID HE MEAN BY "MAKE YOU UNDER-STAND"...?
STOP...
IT WAS JUST GHOUL GIBBERISH. PAY NO ATTENTION TO IT...
RIGHT NOW I NEED TO GET TO MADO...
I'VE GOT A BAD FEELING...
URGH...
NO LITTERING

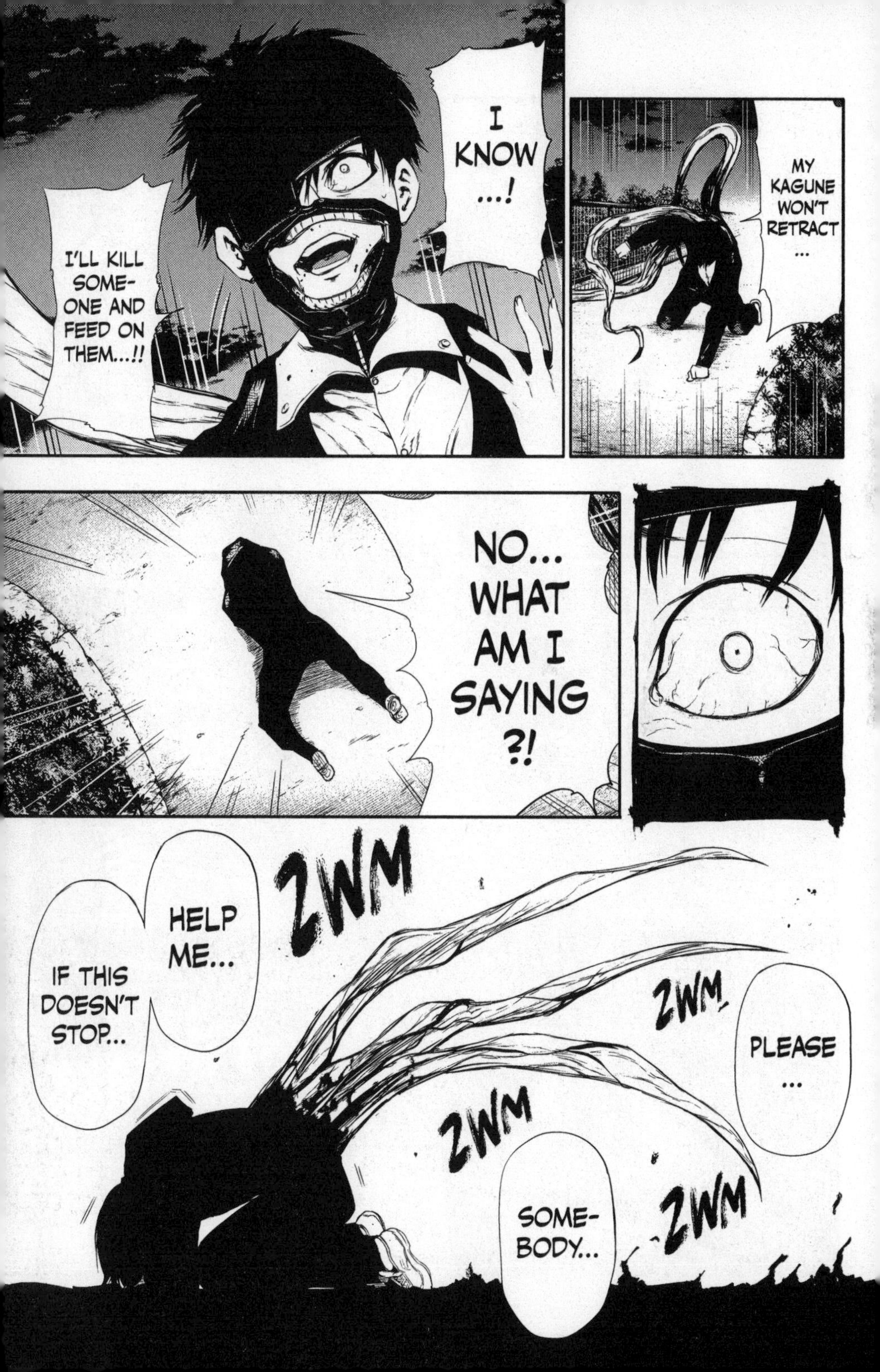
MY KAGUNE WON'T RETRACT ...
I KNOW ...!
I'LL KILL SOME-ONE AND FEED ON THEM...!!
NO... WHAT AM I SAYING ?!
ZWM
PLEASE ...
ZWM
ZWM
SOME-BODY...
ZWM
HELP ME...
IF THIS DOESN'T STOP...

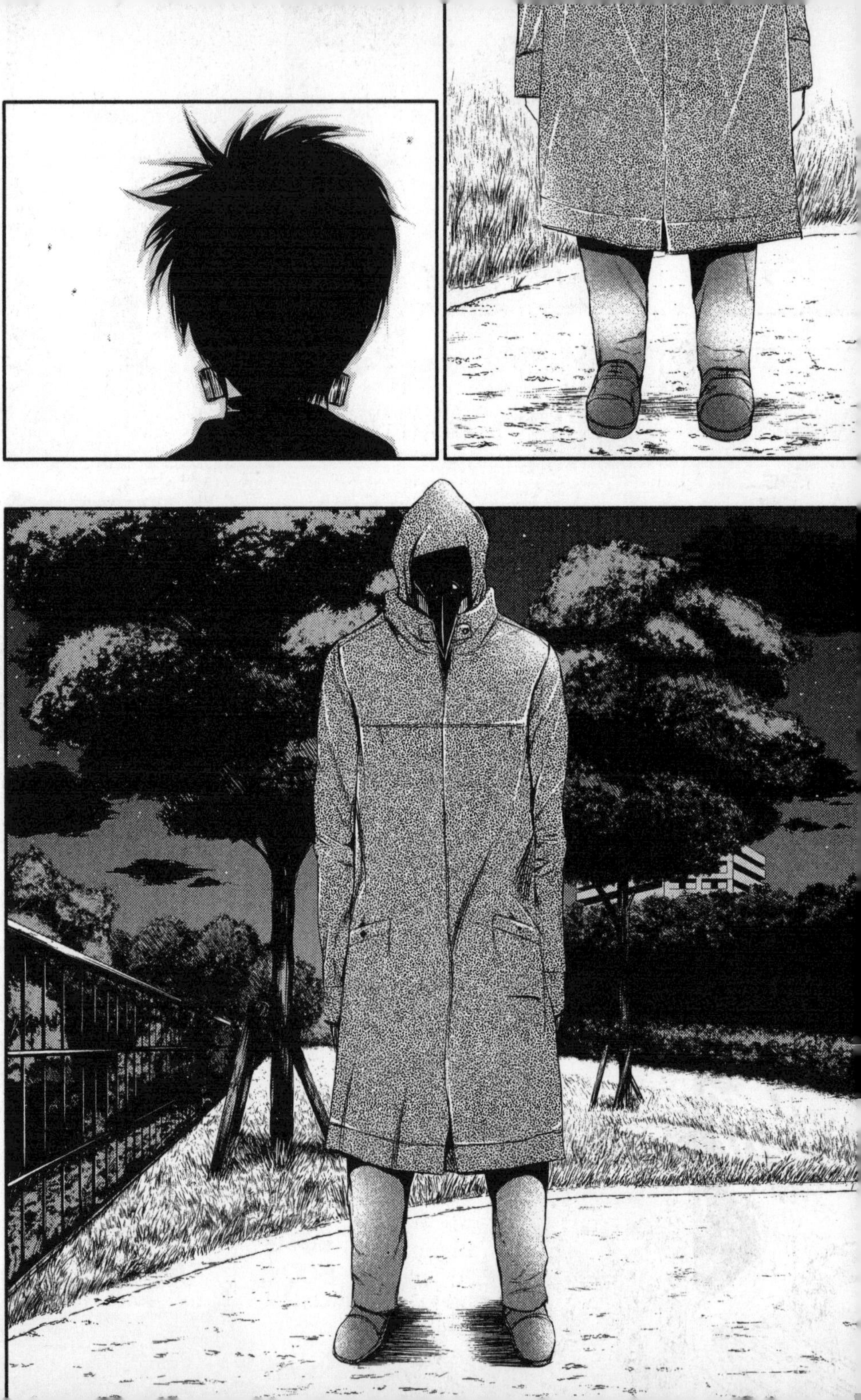

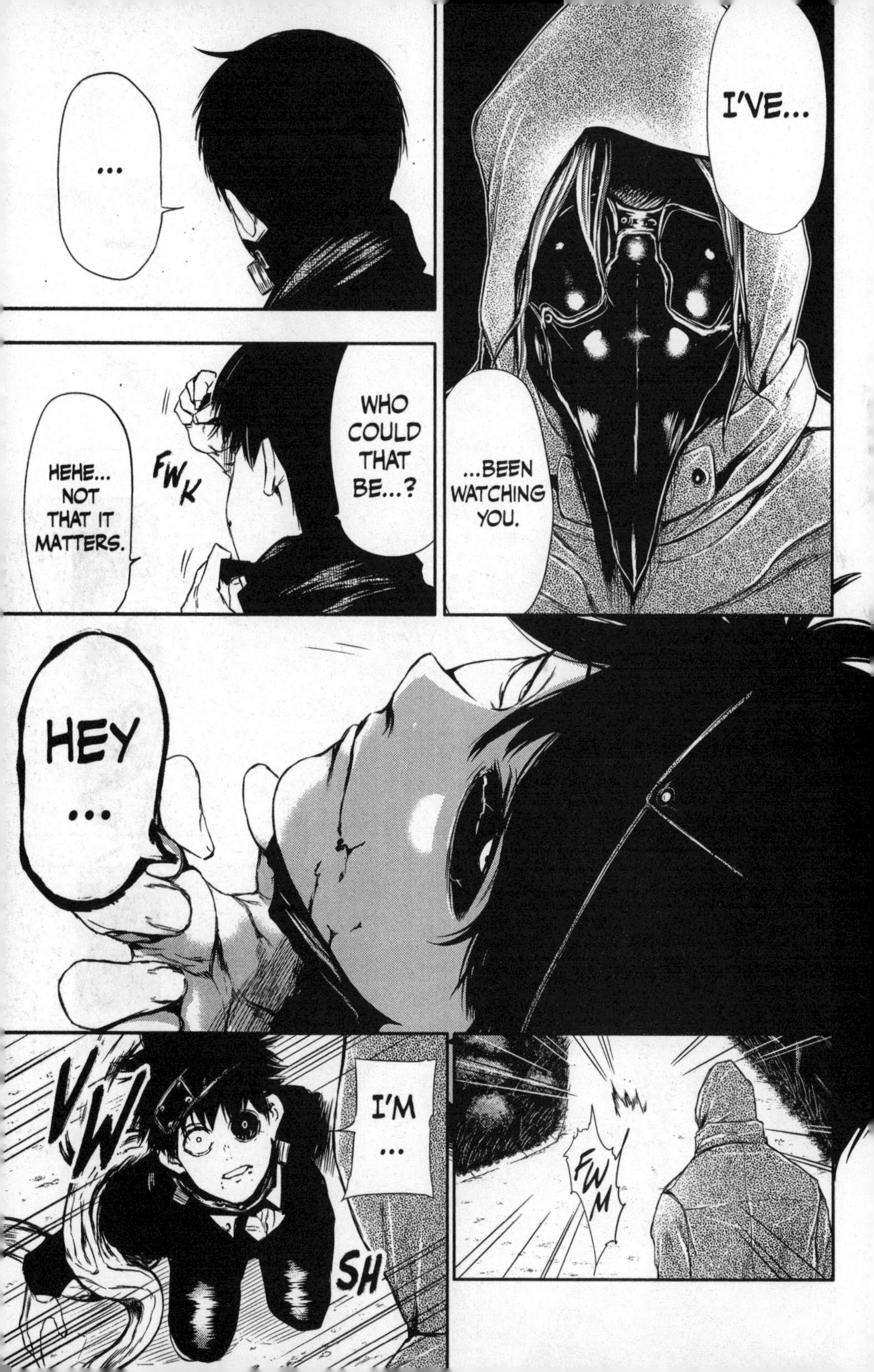
I'VE...
...BEEN WATCHING YOU.
...
WHO COULD THAT BE...?
FWK
HEHE... NOT THAT IT MATTERS.
HEY...
FWM
I'M...
VW
SH

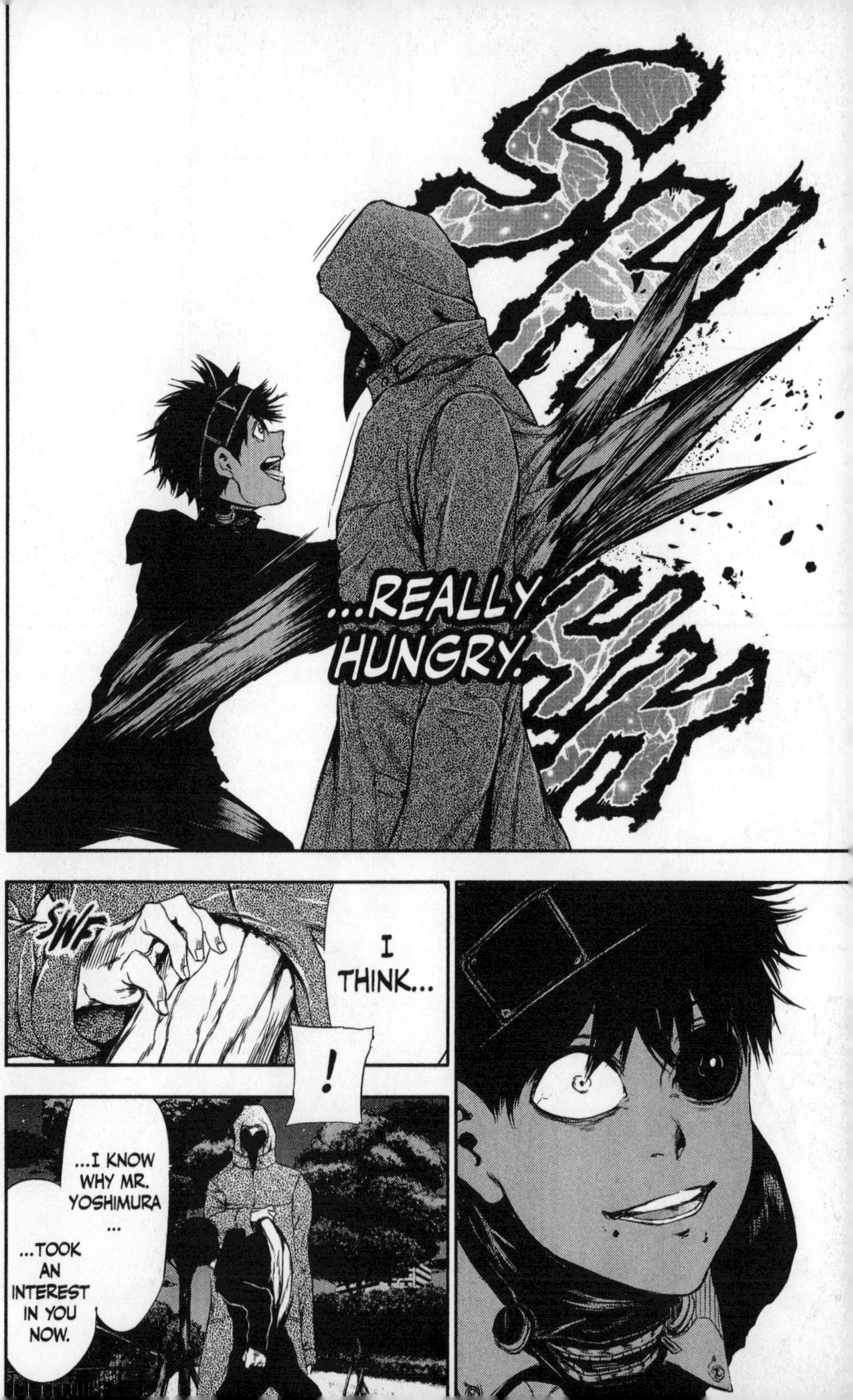
...REALLY HUNGRY.
SWF
I THINK...
!
...I KNOW WHY MR. YOSHIMURA ...
...TOOK AN INTEREST IN YOU NOW.

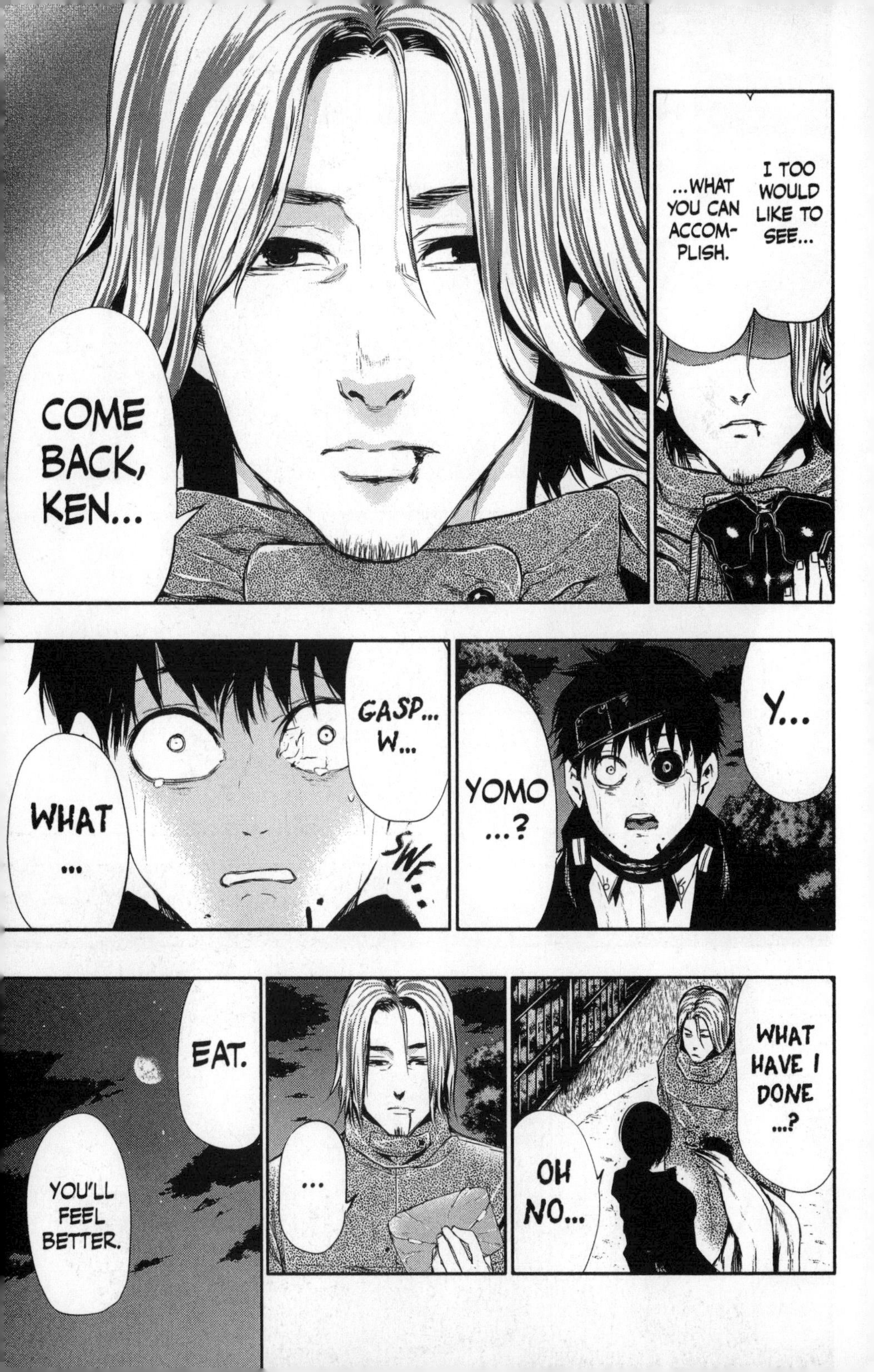
I TOO WOULD LIKE TO SEE...
...WHAT YOU CAN ACCOMPLISH.
COME BACK, KEN...
Y...
YOMO...?
GASP... W...
SWF...
WHAT...
WHAT HAVE I DONE...?
OH NO...
...
EAT.
YOU'LL FEEL BETTER.

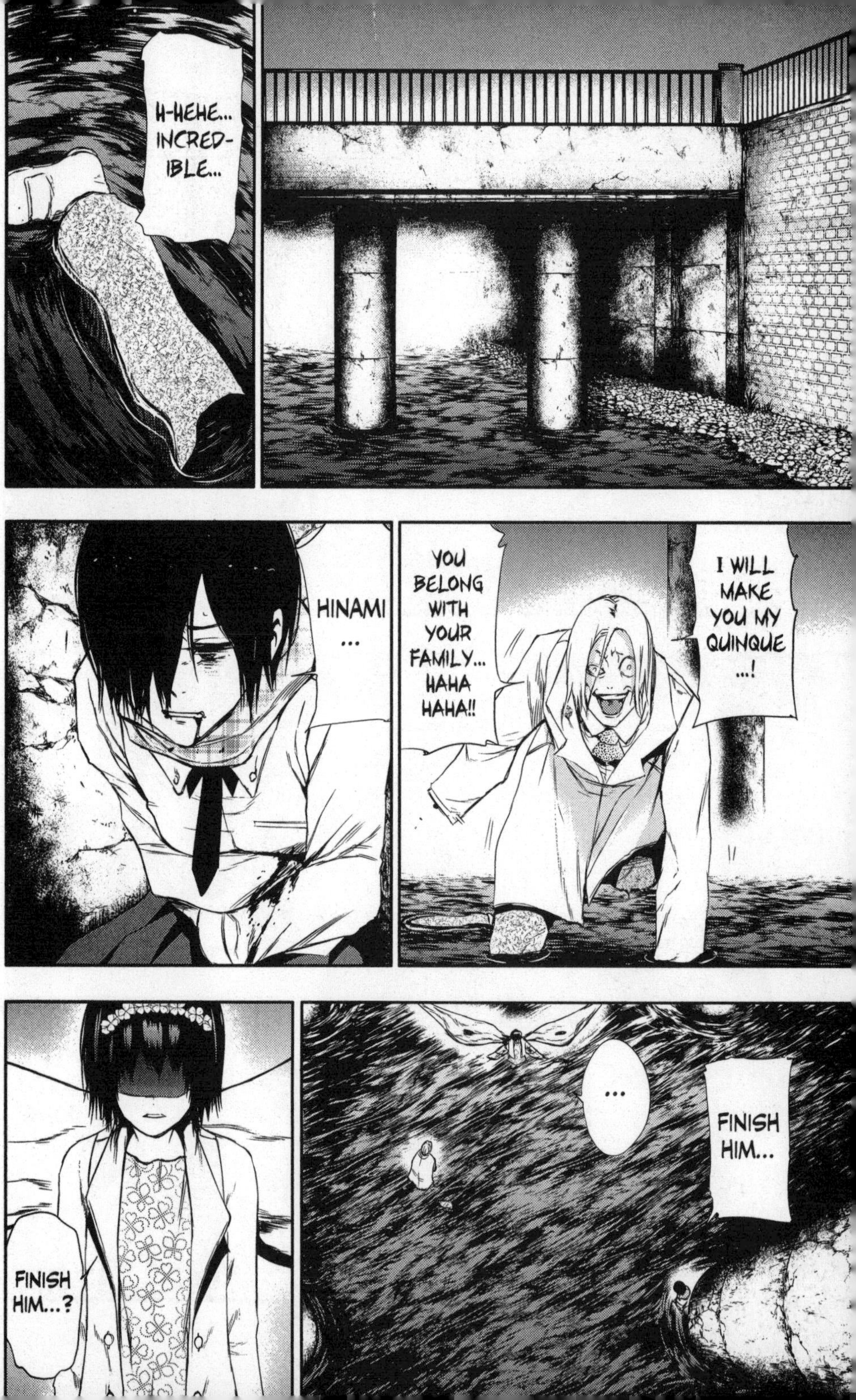
H-HEHE... INCRED-IBLE...
I WILL MAKE YOU MY QUINQUE ...!
YOU BELONG WITH YOUR FAMILY... HAHA HAHA!!
HINAMI ...
FINISH HIM...
...
FINISH HIM...?

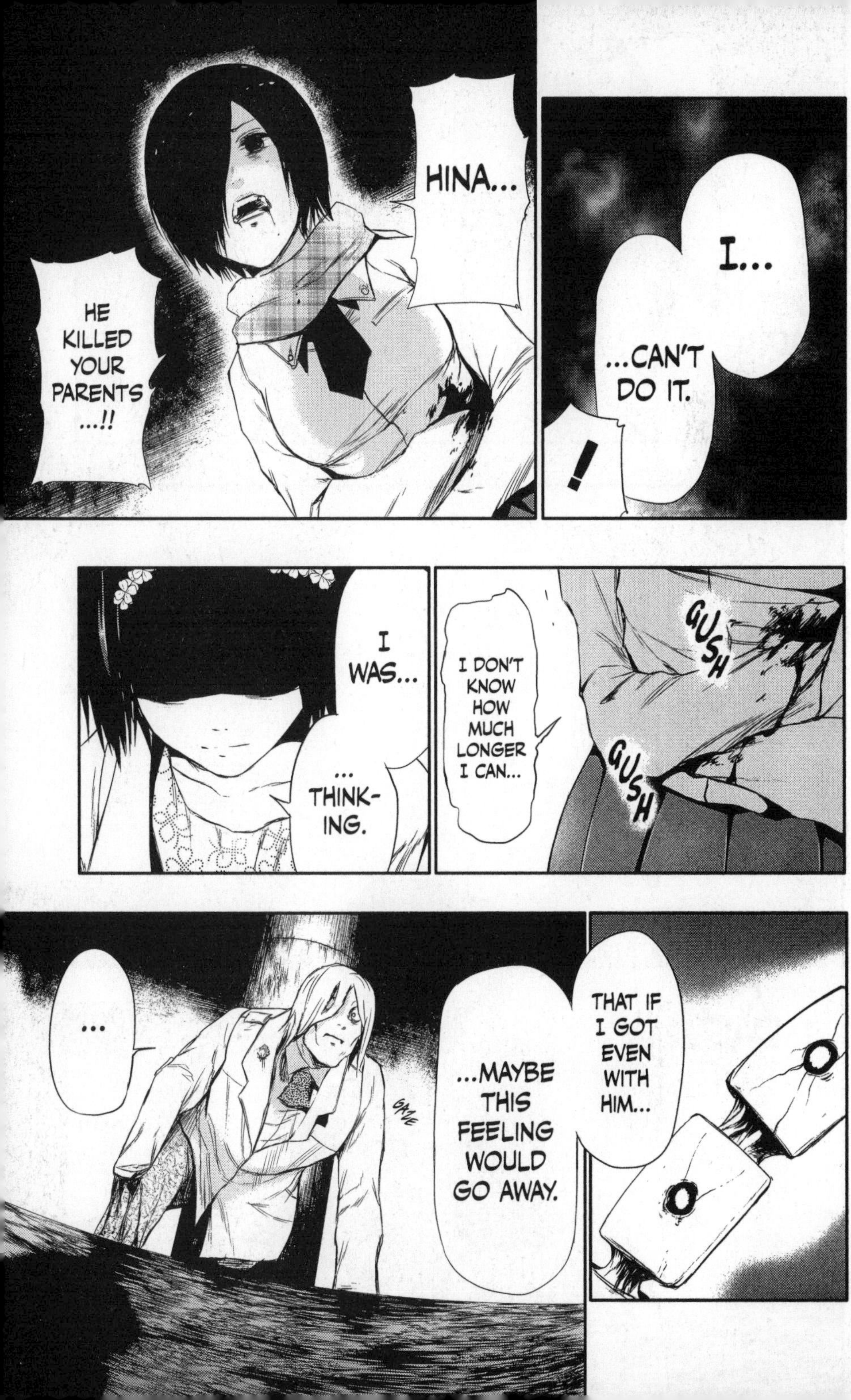
I...
...CAN'T DO IT.
!
HINA...
HE KILLED YOUR PARENTS ...!!
GUSH
GUSH
I DON'T KNOW HOW MUCH LONGER I CAN...
I WAS...
... THINKING.
THAT IF I GOT EVEN WITH HIM...
...MAYBE THIS FEELING WOULD GO AWAY.
GAZE
...

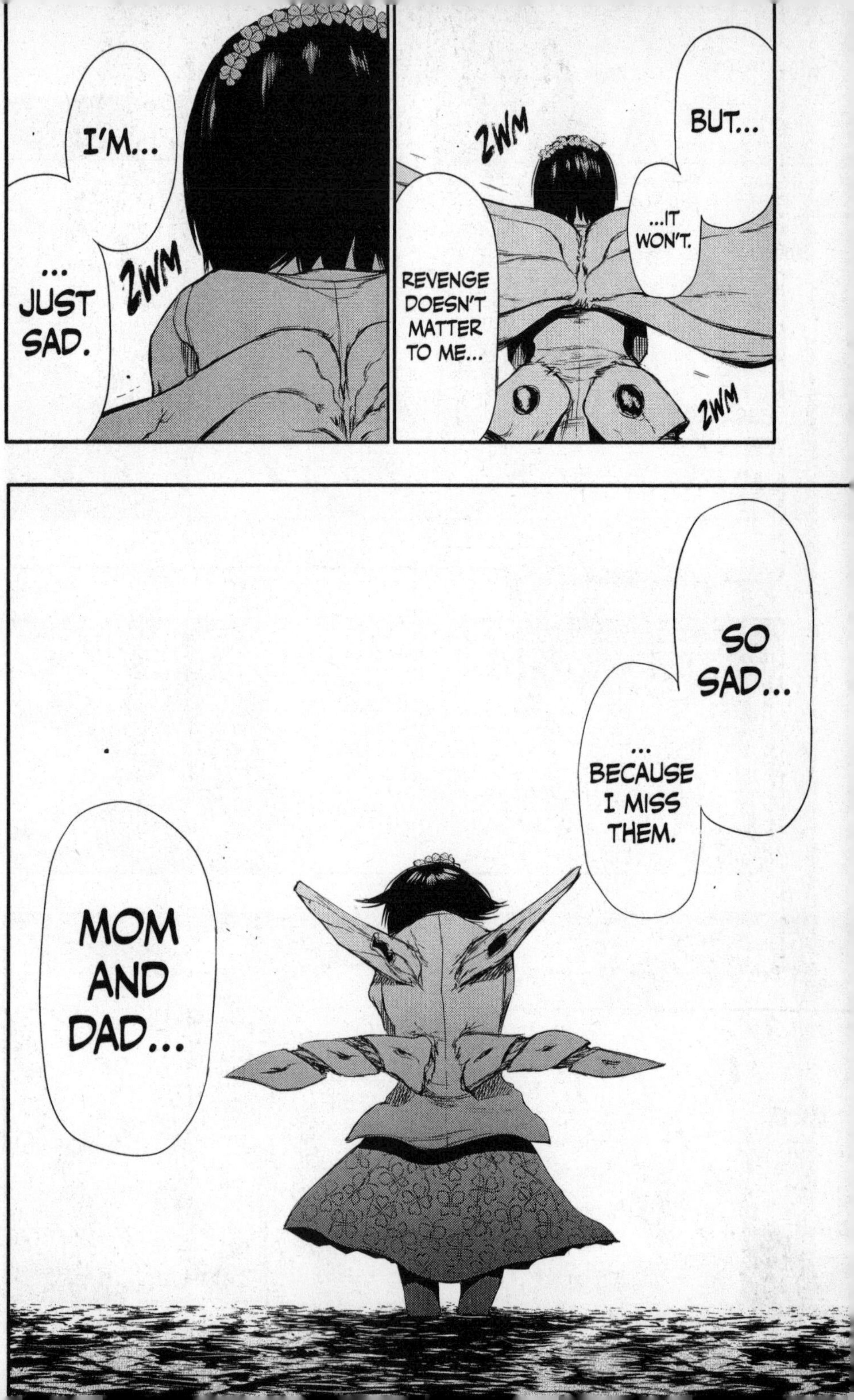
BUT...
...IT WON'T.
ZWM
REVENGE DOESN'T MATTER TO ME...
ZWM
I'M...
... JUST SAD.
ZWM
SO SAD...
... BECAUSE I MISS THEM.
MOM AND DAD...

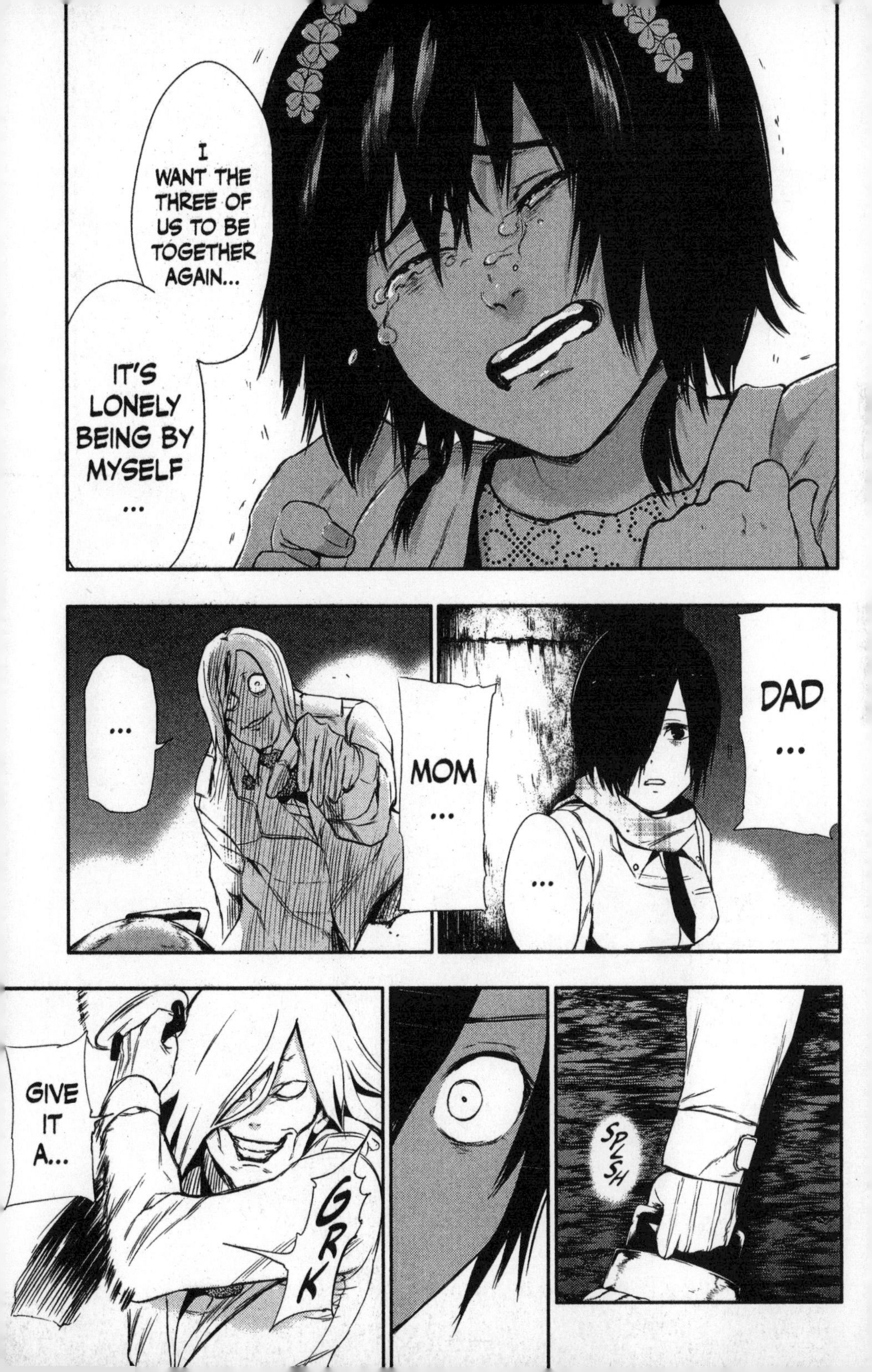
I WANT THE THREE OF US TO BE TOGETHER AGAIN...
IT'S LONELY BEING BY MYSELF ...
DAD ...
MOM ...
...
...
SPLSH
GIVE IT A...
GRK

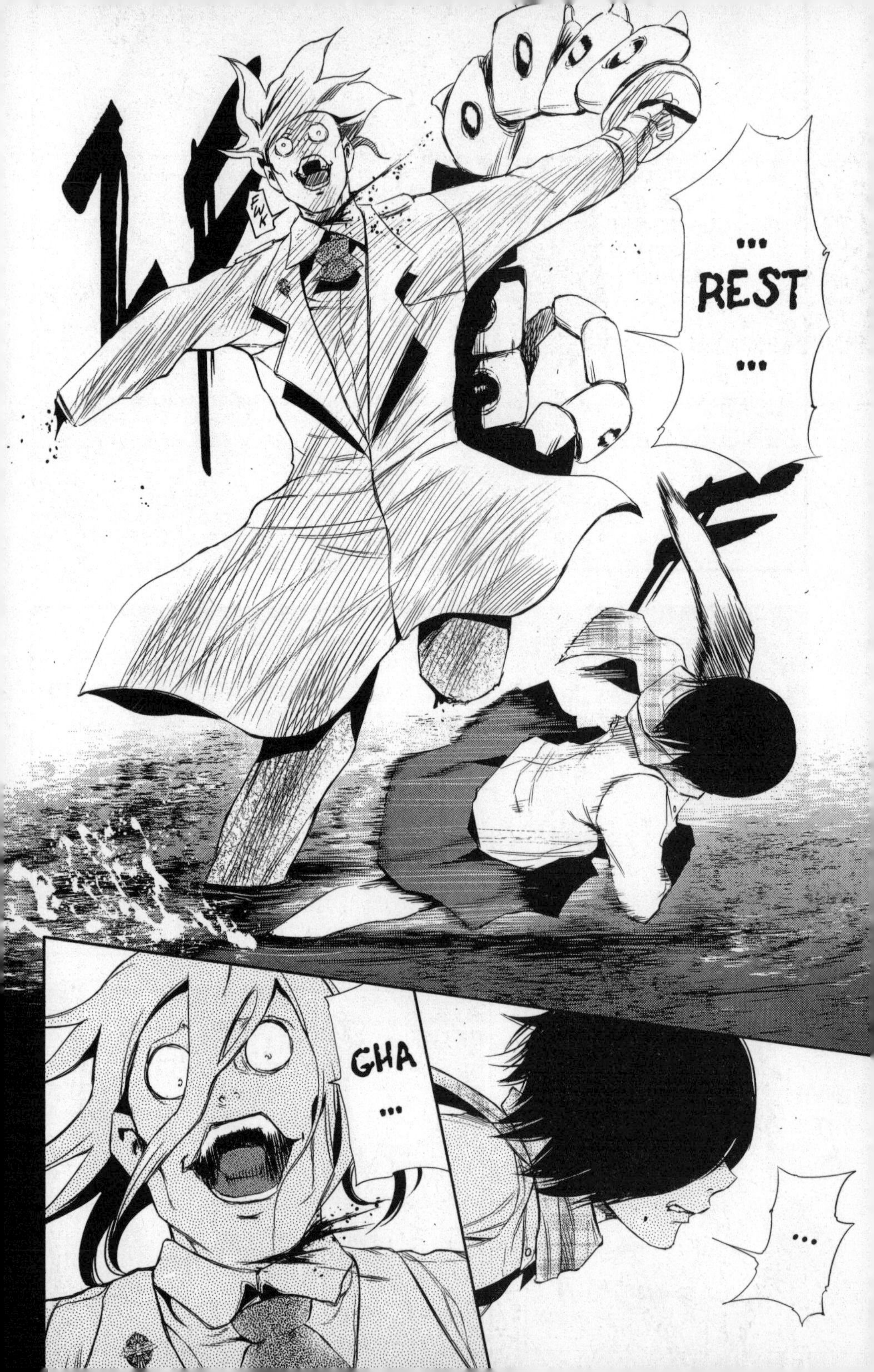
... REST ...
FWK
...
GHA ...

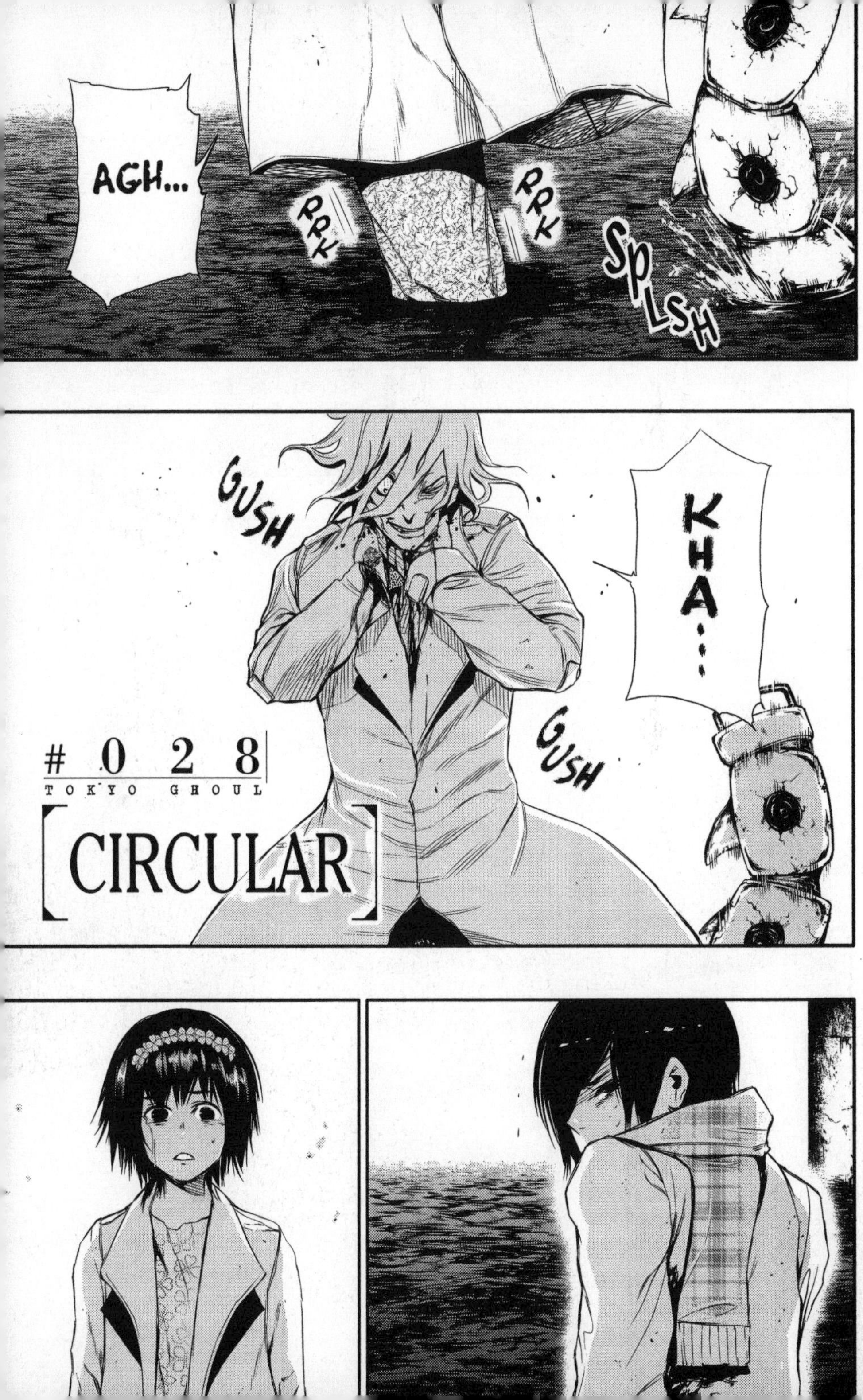
SPLSH
RRK
RRK
AGH...
KHA...
GUSH
GUSH
#028
TOKYO GHOUL
CIRCULAR

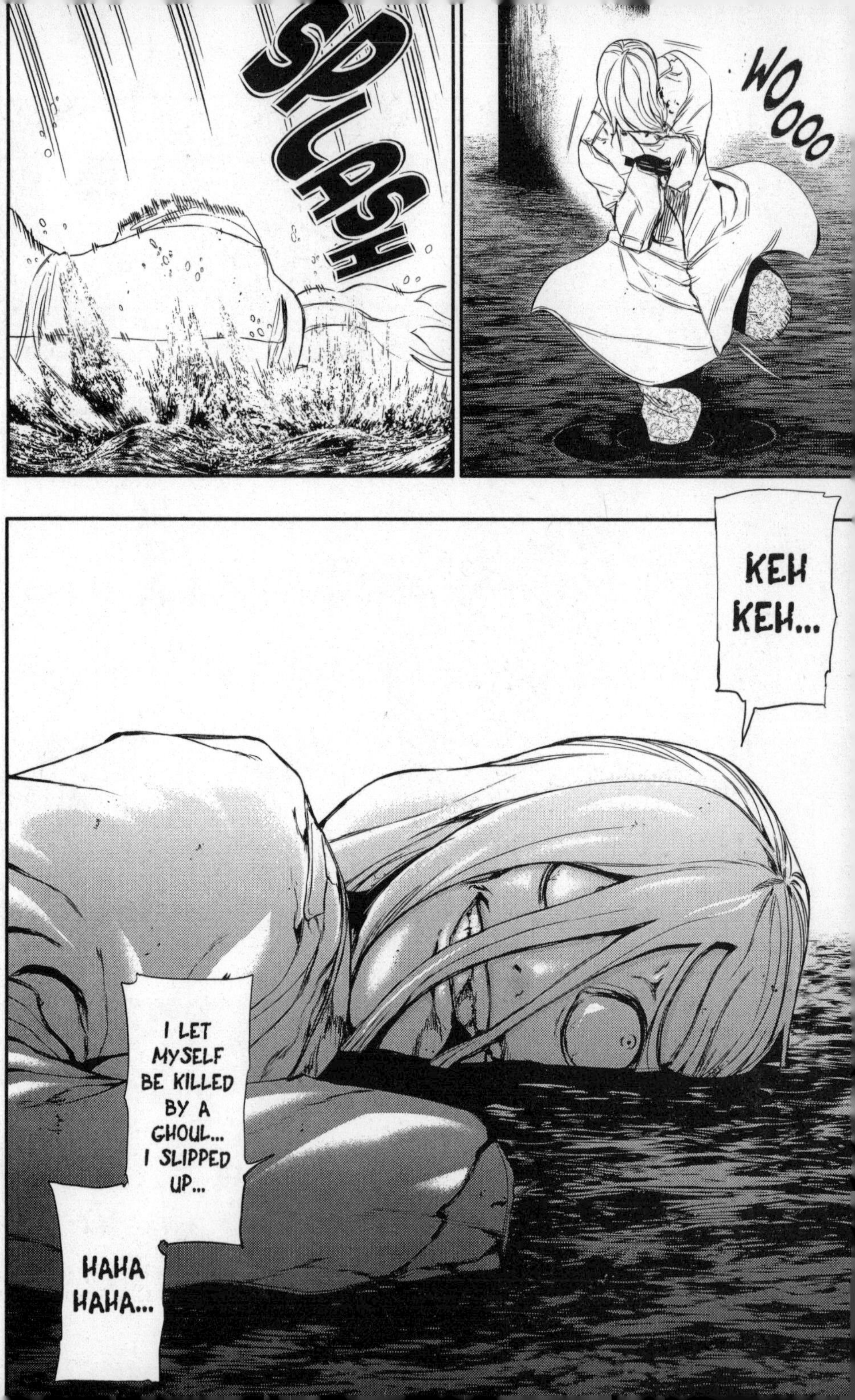
WOOOO
SPLASH
KEH KEH...
I LET MYSELF BE KILLED BY A GHOUL... I SLIPPED UP...
HAHA HAHA...

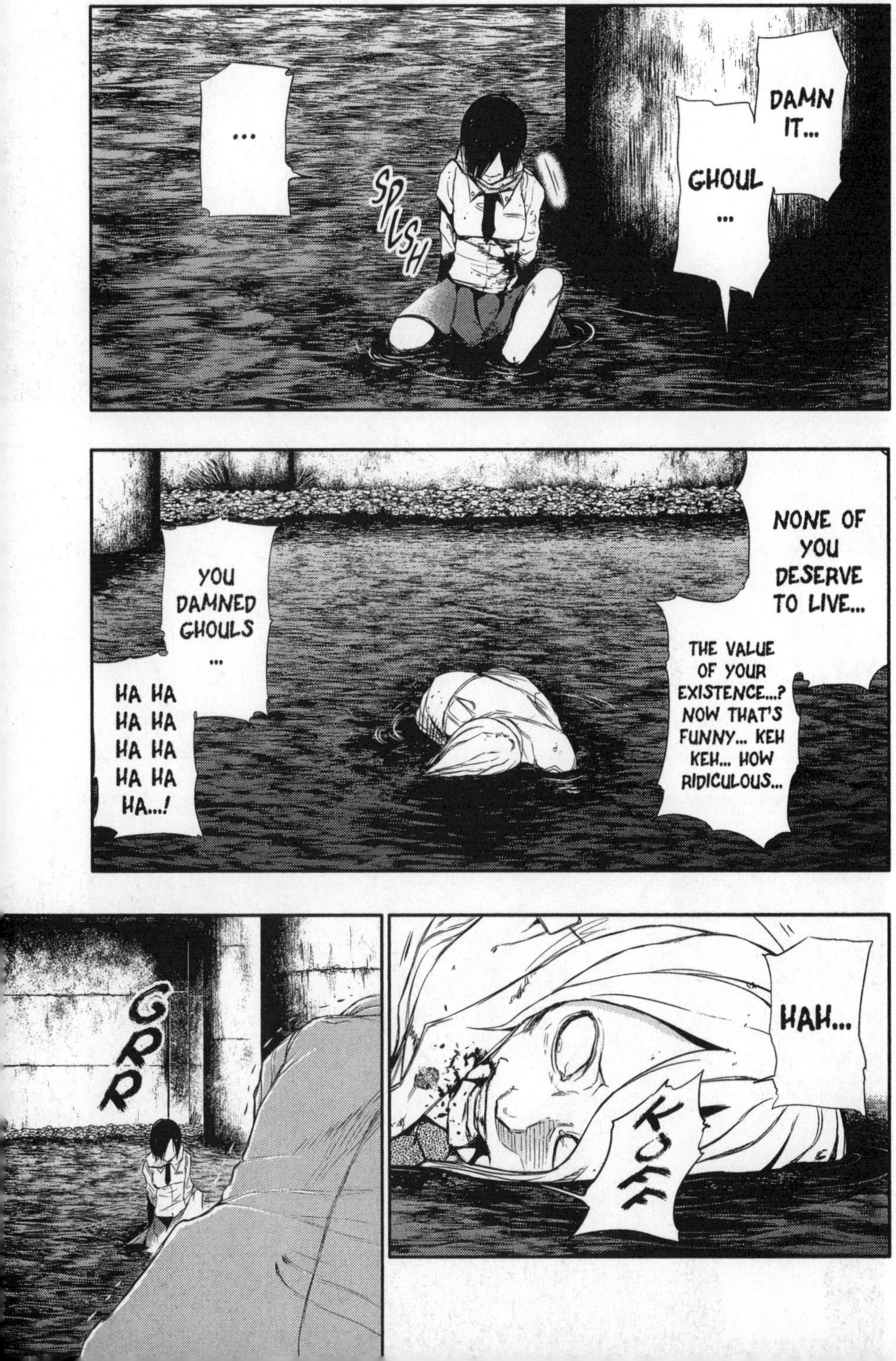
DAMN IT...
GHOUL ...
...
SPLSH
NONE OF YOU DESERVE TO LIVE...
THE VALUE OF YOUR EXISTENCE...? NOW THAT'S FUNNY... KEH KEH... HOW RIDICULOUS...
YOU DAMNED GHOULS ...
HA HA HA HA HA HA HA HA HA...!
HAH...
KOFF
GRR

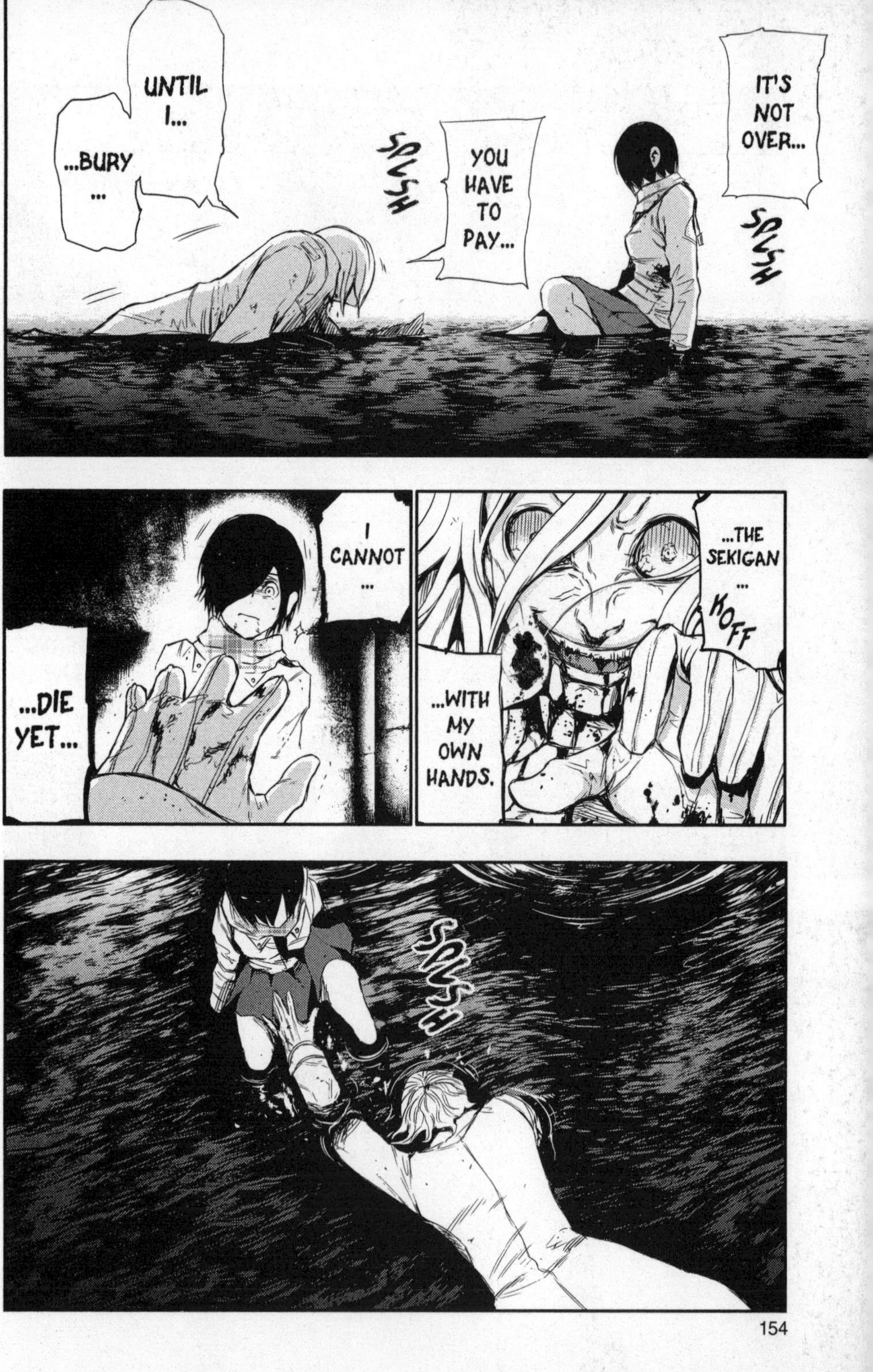
IT'S NOT OVER...
SPLSH
YOU HAVE TO PAY...
SPLSH
UNTIL I...
...BURY ...
...THE SEKIGAN ...
KOFF
...WITH MY OWN HANDS.
I CANNOT ...
...DIE YET...
SPLSH

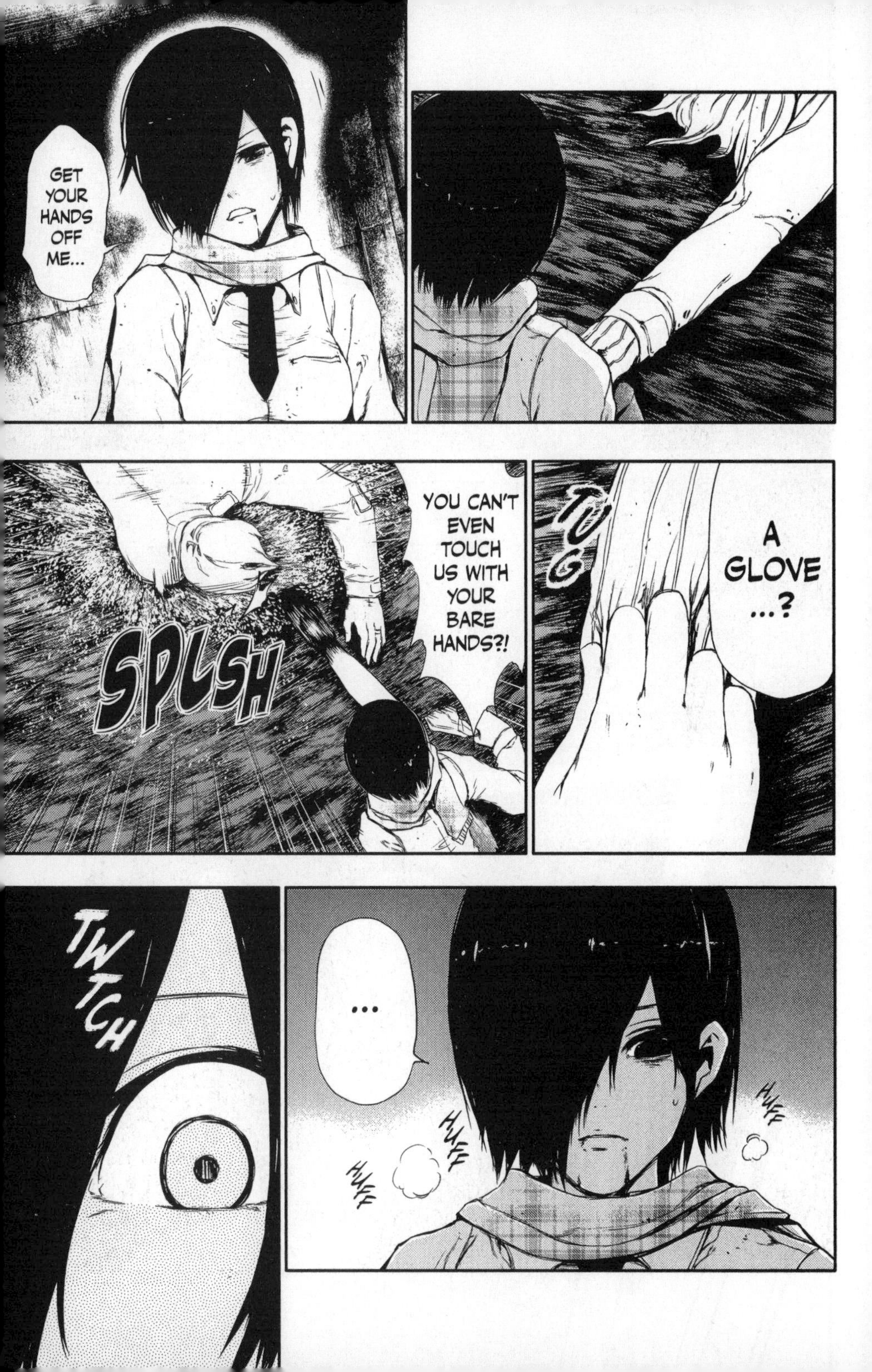
GET YOUR HANDS OFF ME...
TUG
A GLOVE ...?
YOU CAN'T EVEN TOUCH US WITH YOUR BARE HANDS?!
SPLSH
...
HUFF
HUFF
HUFF
TWTCH

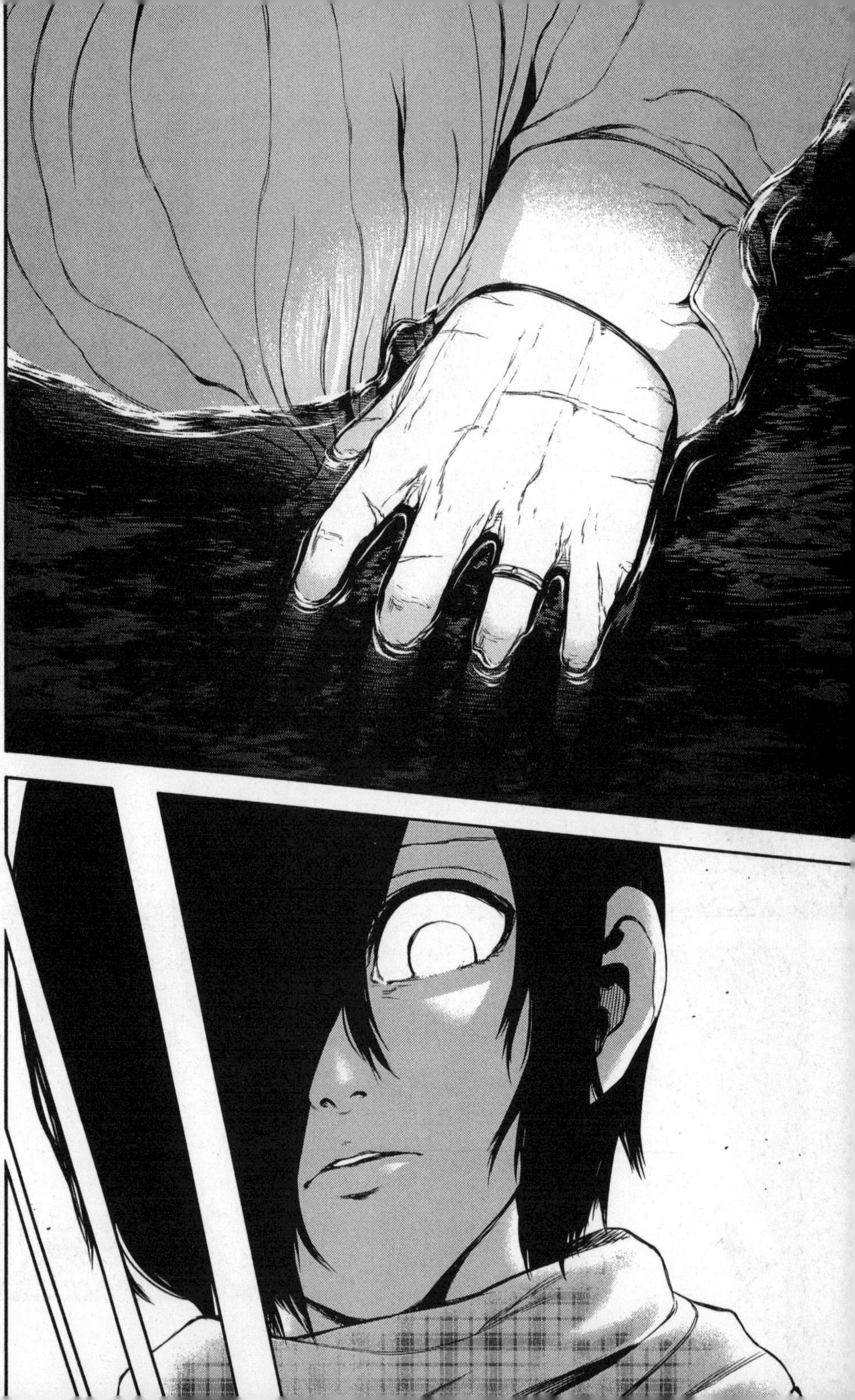

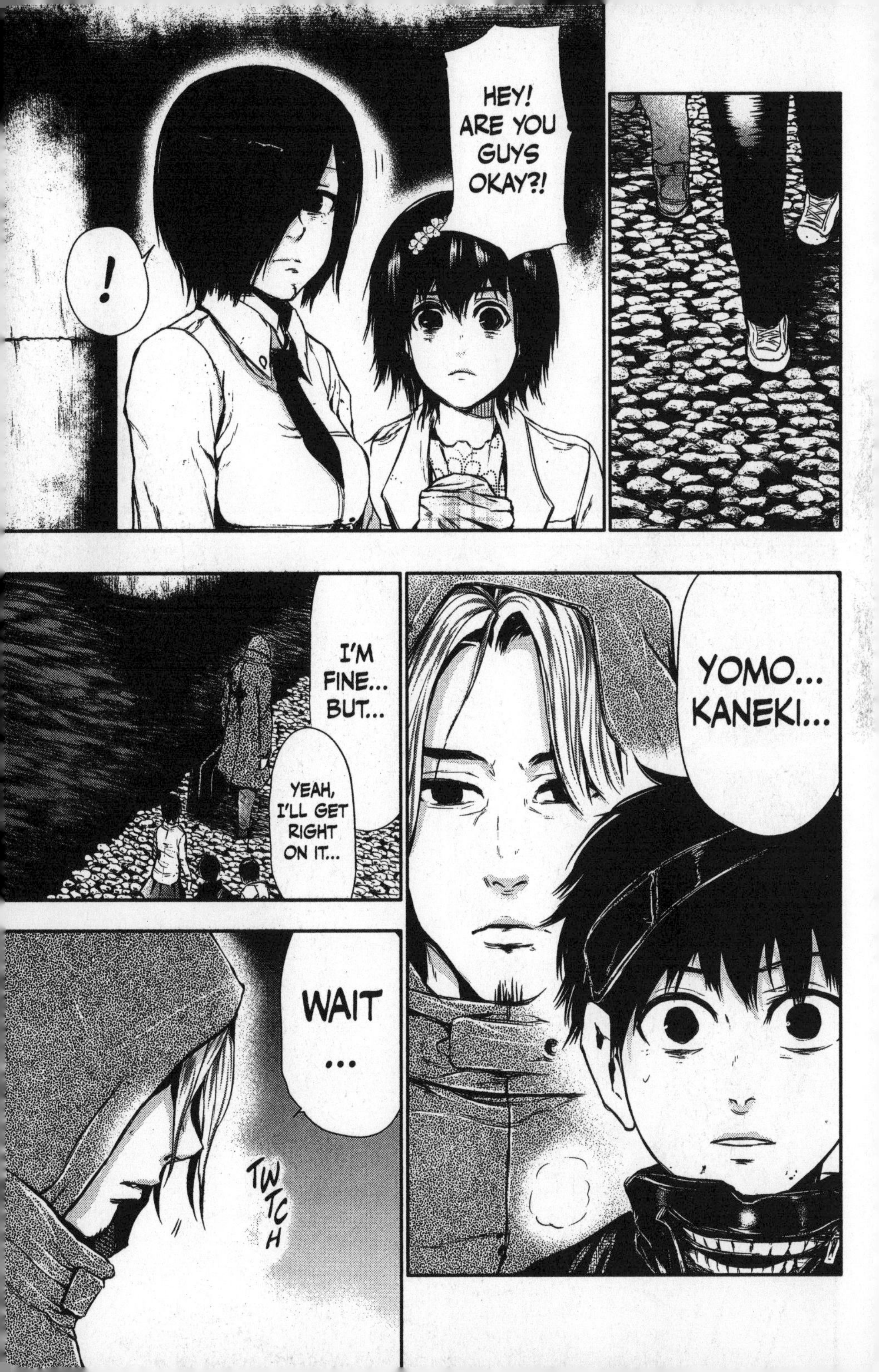
HEY! ARE YOU GUYS OKAY?!
!
YOMO... KANEKI...
I'M FINE... BUT...
YEAH, I'LL GET RIGHT ON IT...
WAIT ...
TWTCH

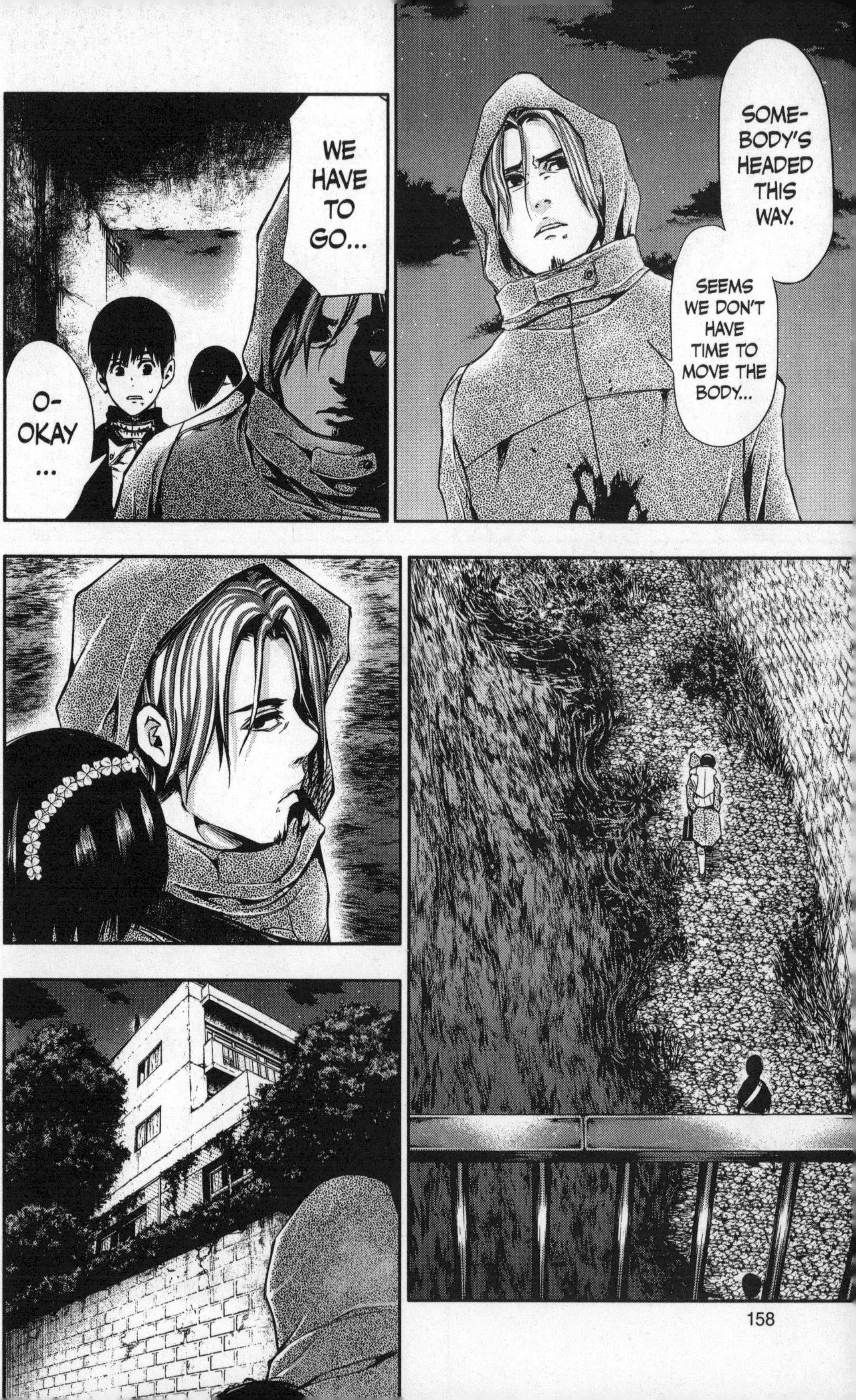
SOME-BODY'S HEADED THIS WAY.
SEEMS WE DON'T HAVE TIME TO MOVE THE BODY...
WE HAVE TO GO...
O-OKAY ...

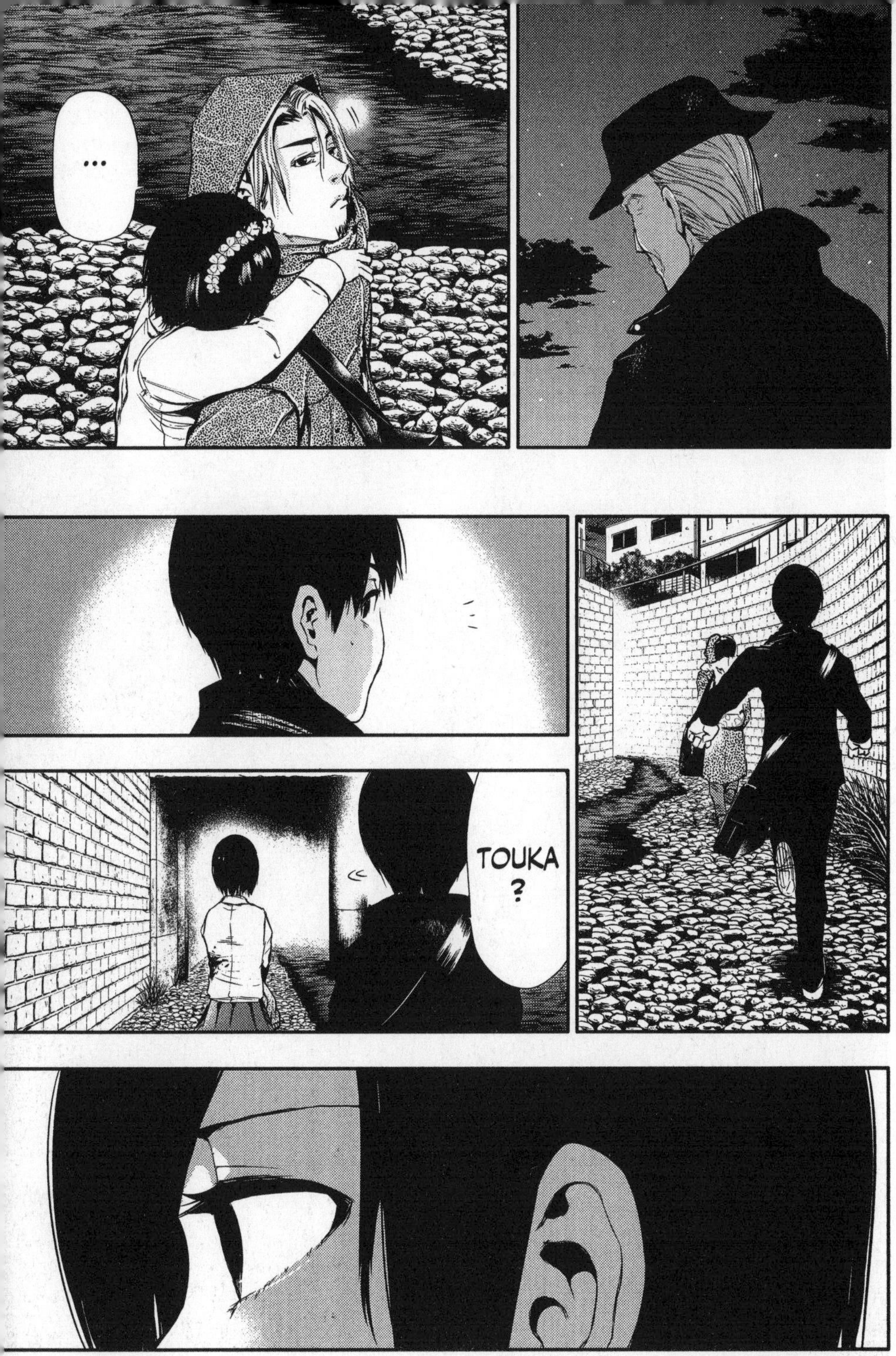
...
TOUKA ?

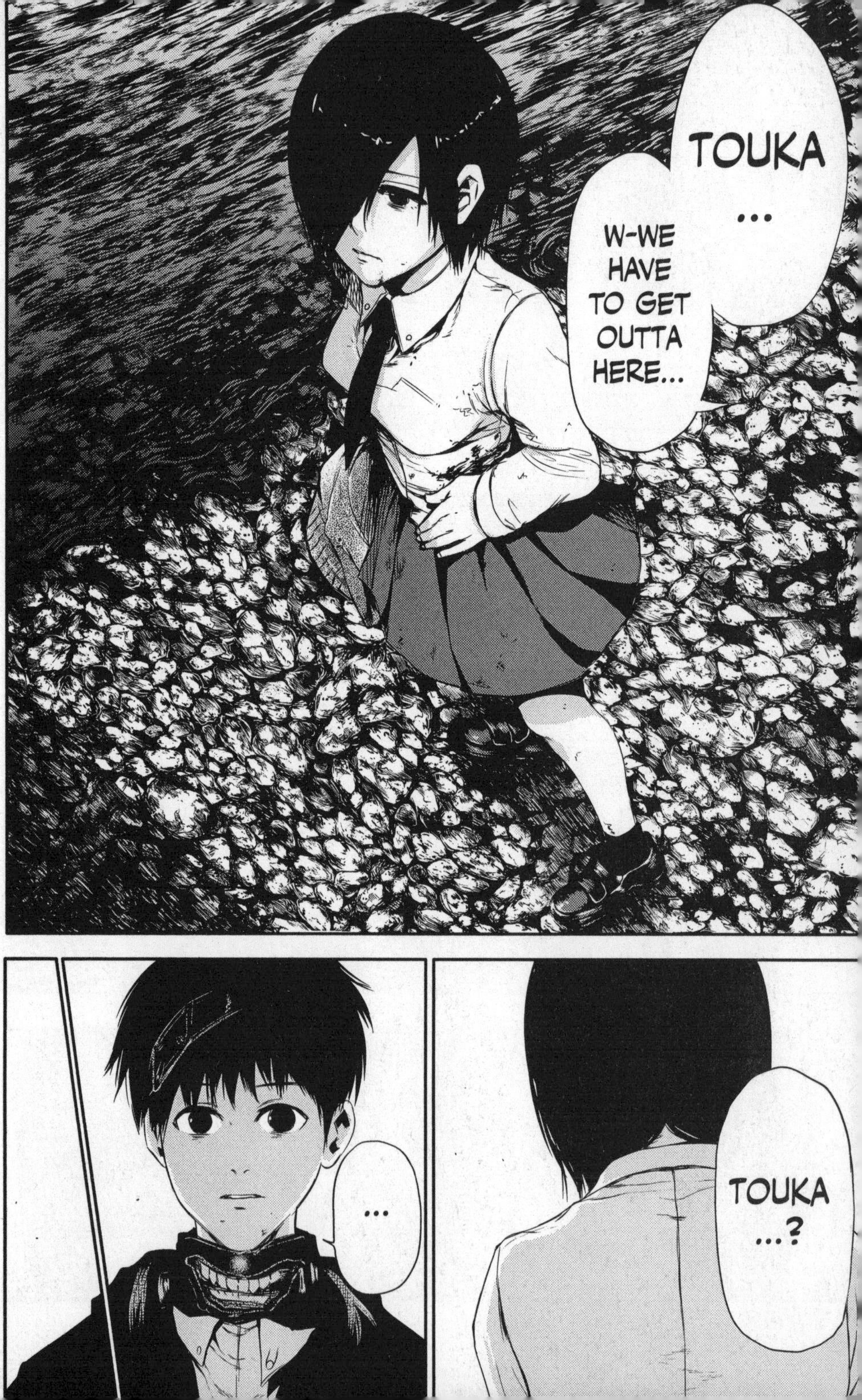
TOUKA ...
W-WE HAVE TO GET OUTTA HERE...
TOUKA ...?
...

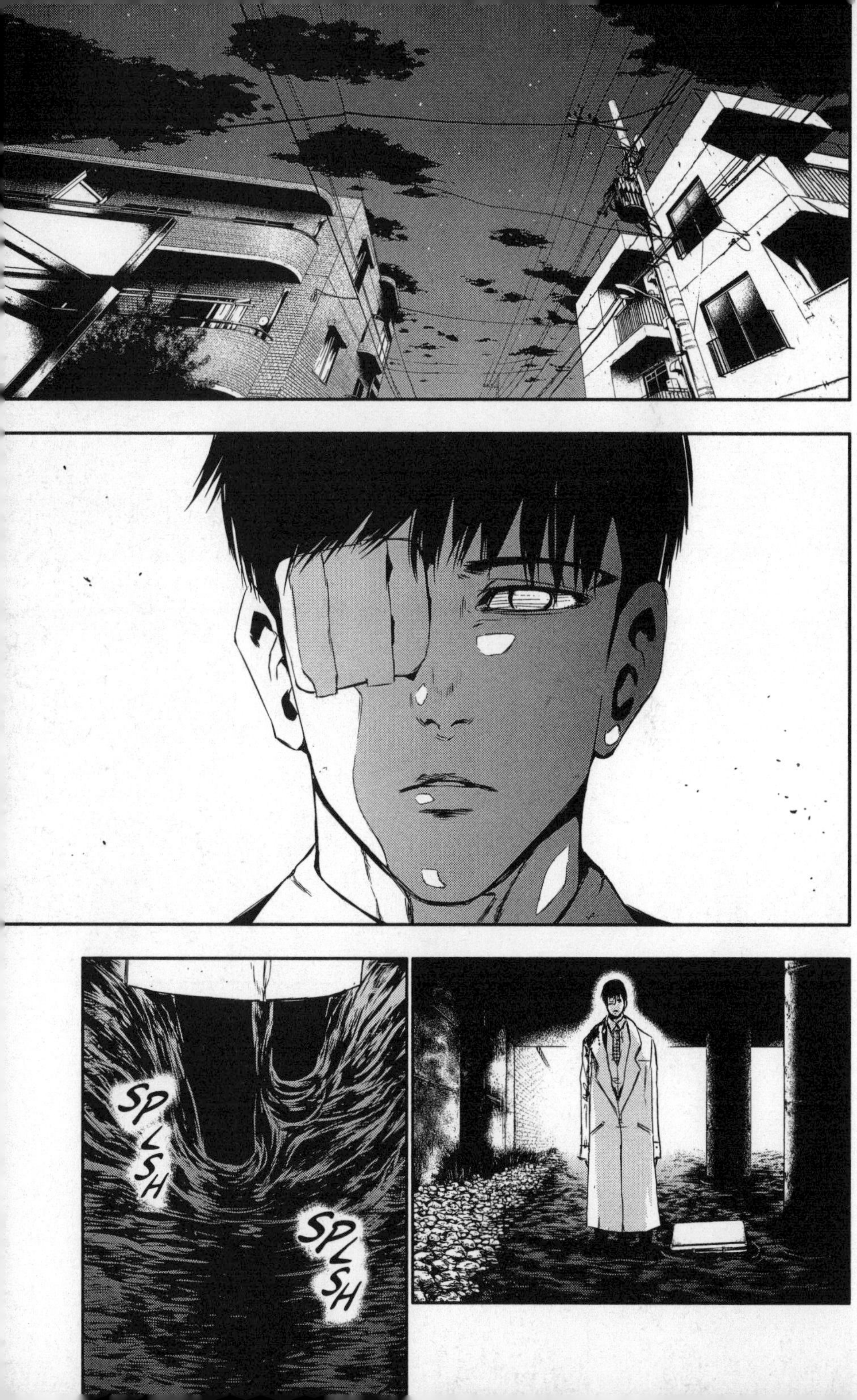
SPLSH
SPLSH

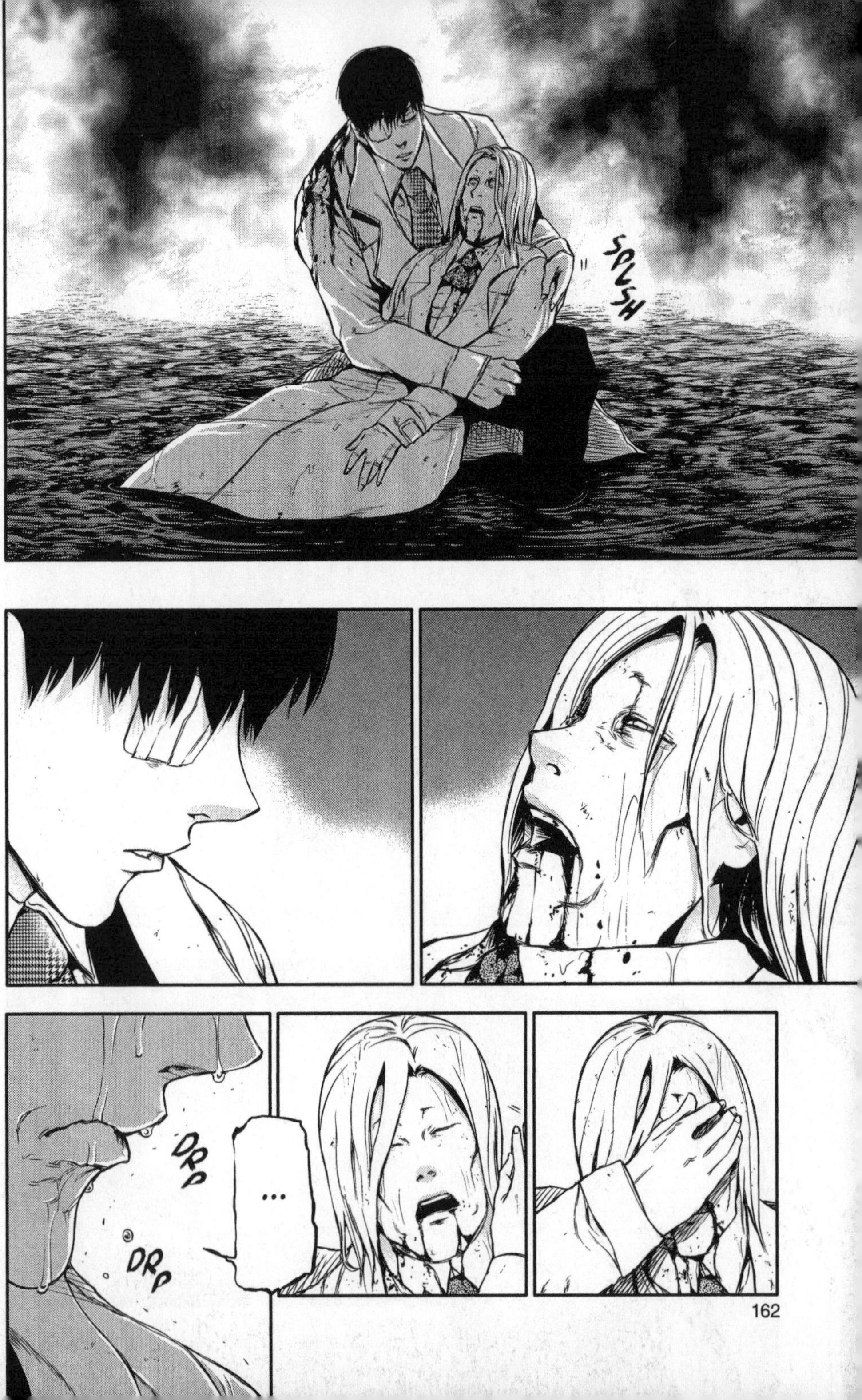
SPLSH
...
DRP
DRP

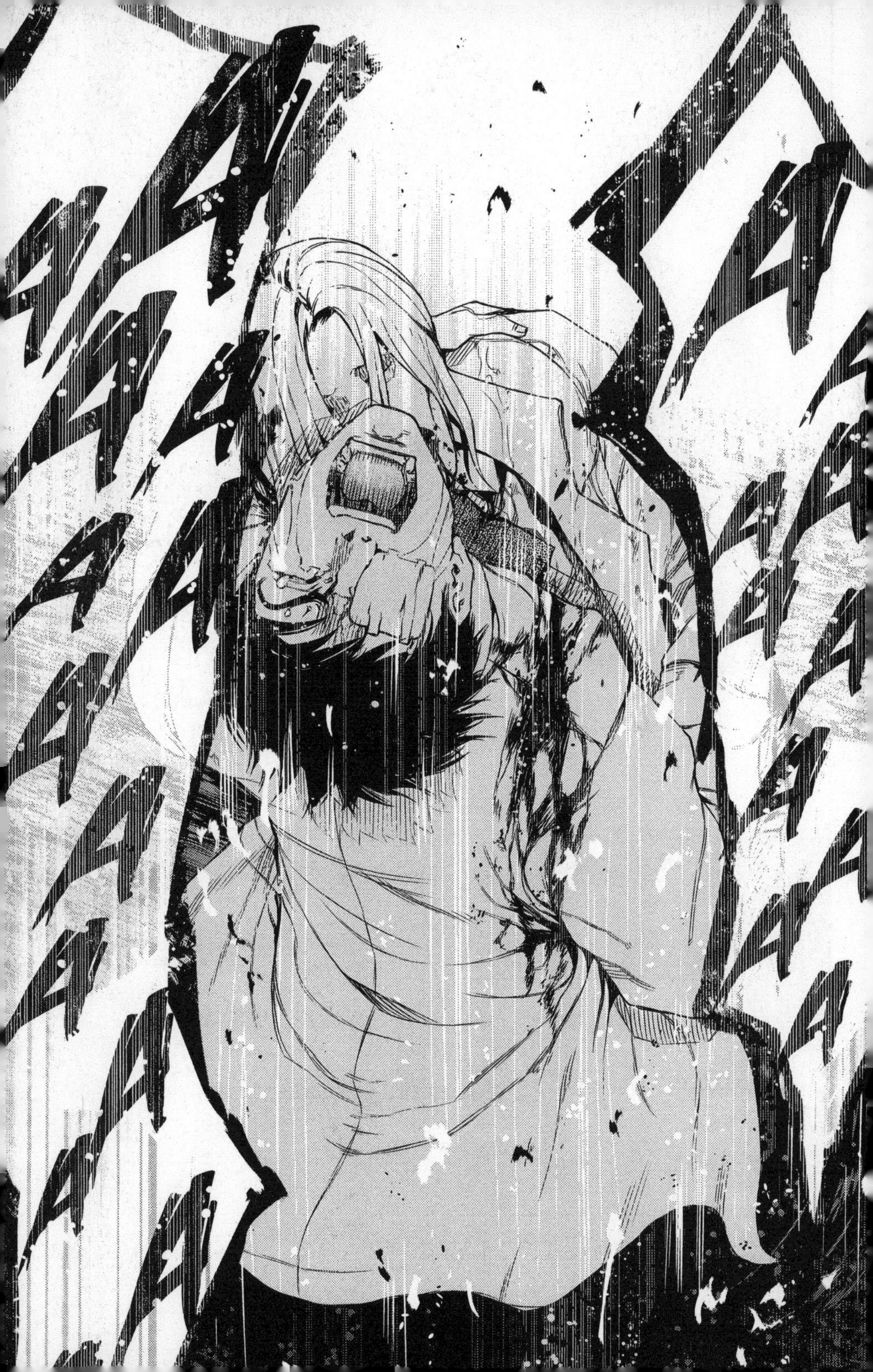
AAAAAAAAAAAAA
AAAAAAAAAAAAAA

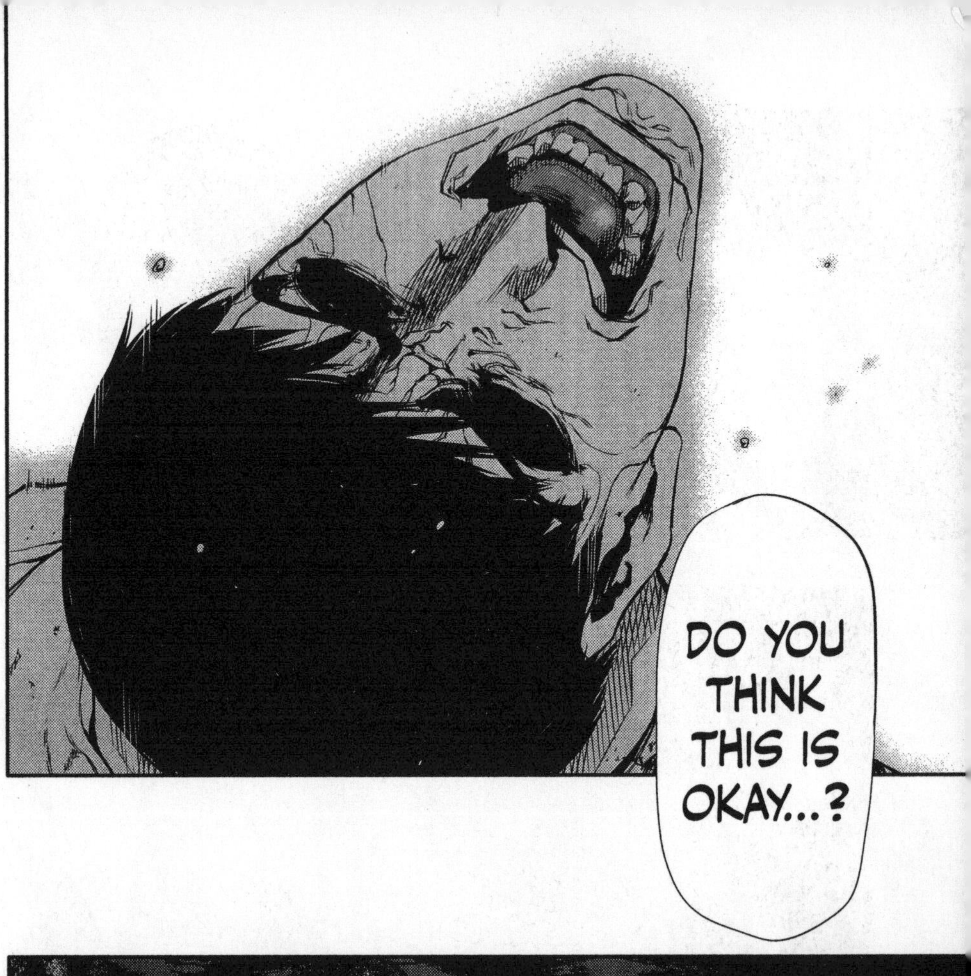
DO YOU THINK THIS IS OKAY...?

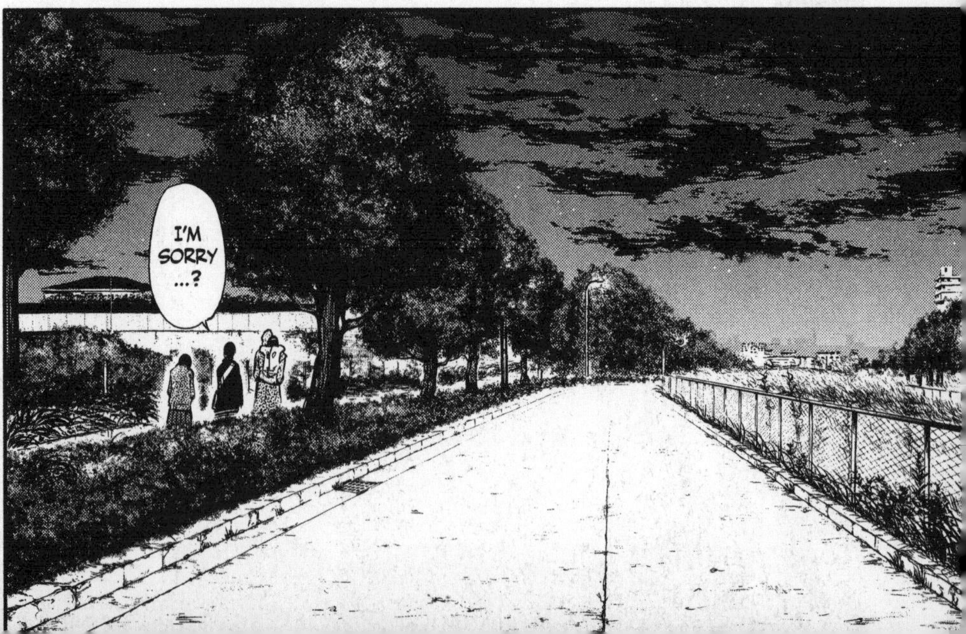
I'M SORRY ...?

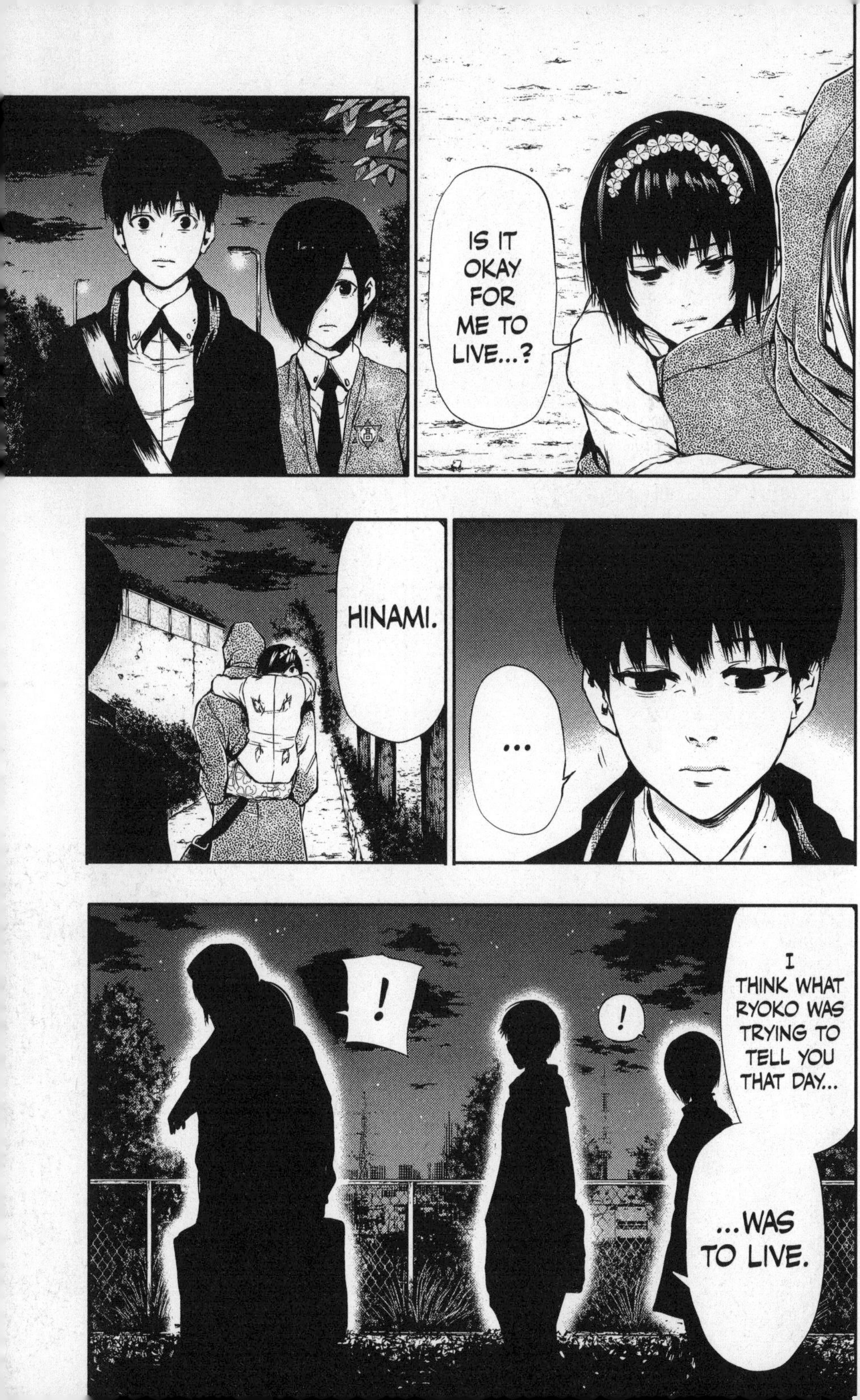
IS IT OKAY FOR ME TO LIVE...?
...
HINAMI.
I THINK WHAT RYOKO WAS TRYING TO TELL YOU THAT DAY...
!
!
...WAS TO LIVE.

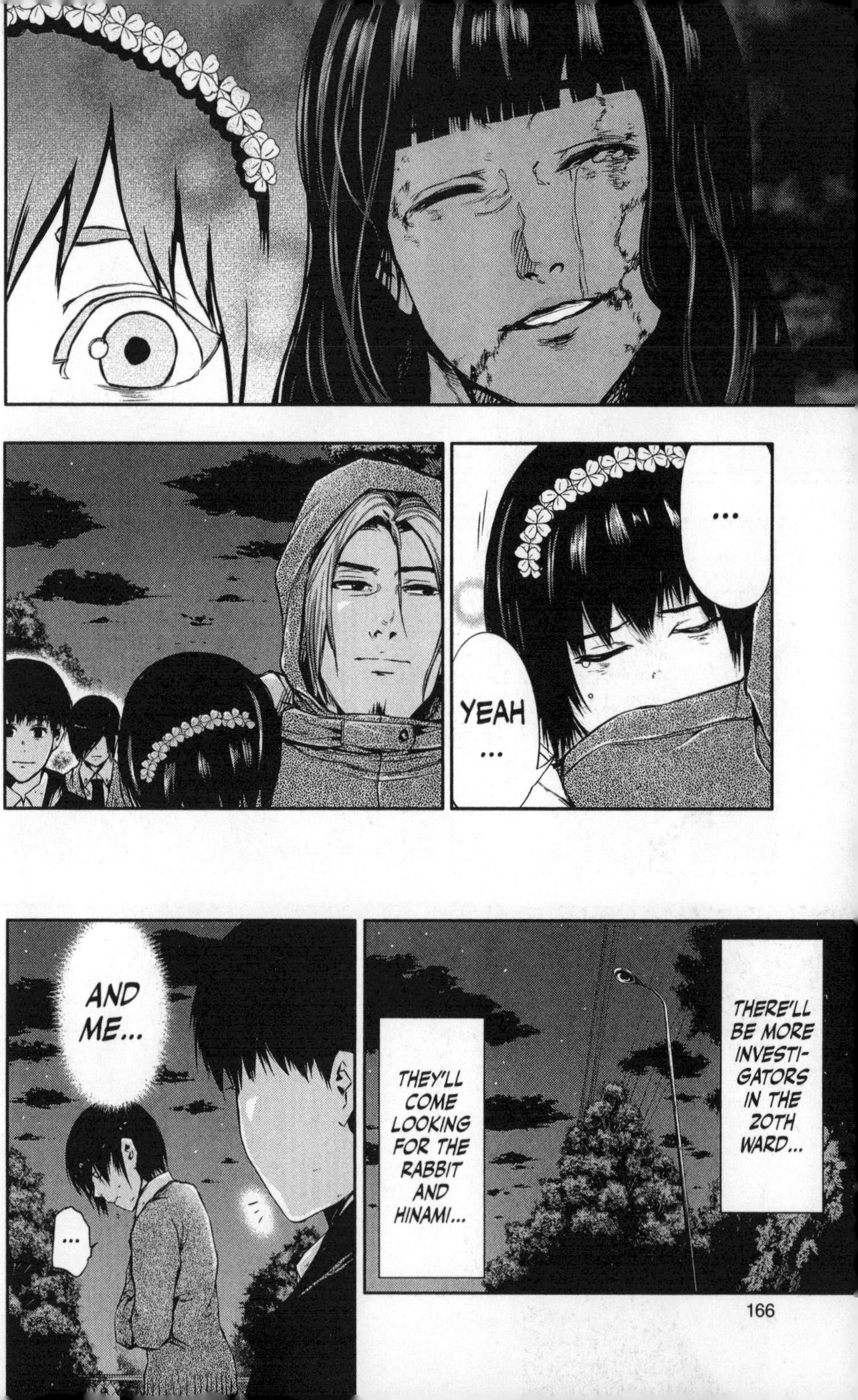
...
YEAH ...
THERE'LL BE MORE INVESTIGATORS IN THE 20TH WARD...
THEY'LL COME LOOKING FOR THE RABBIT AND HINAMI...
AND ME...
...

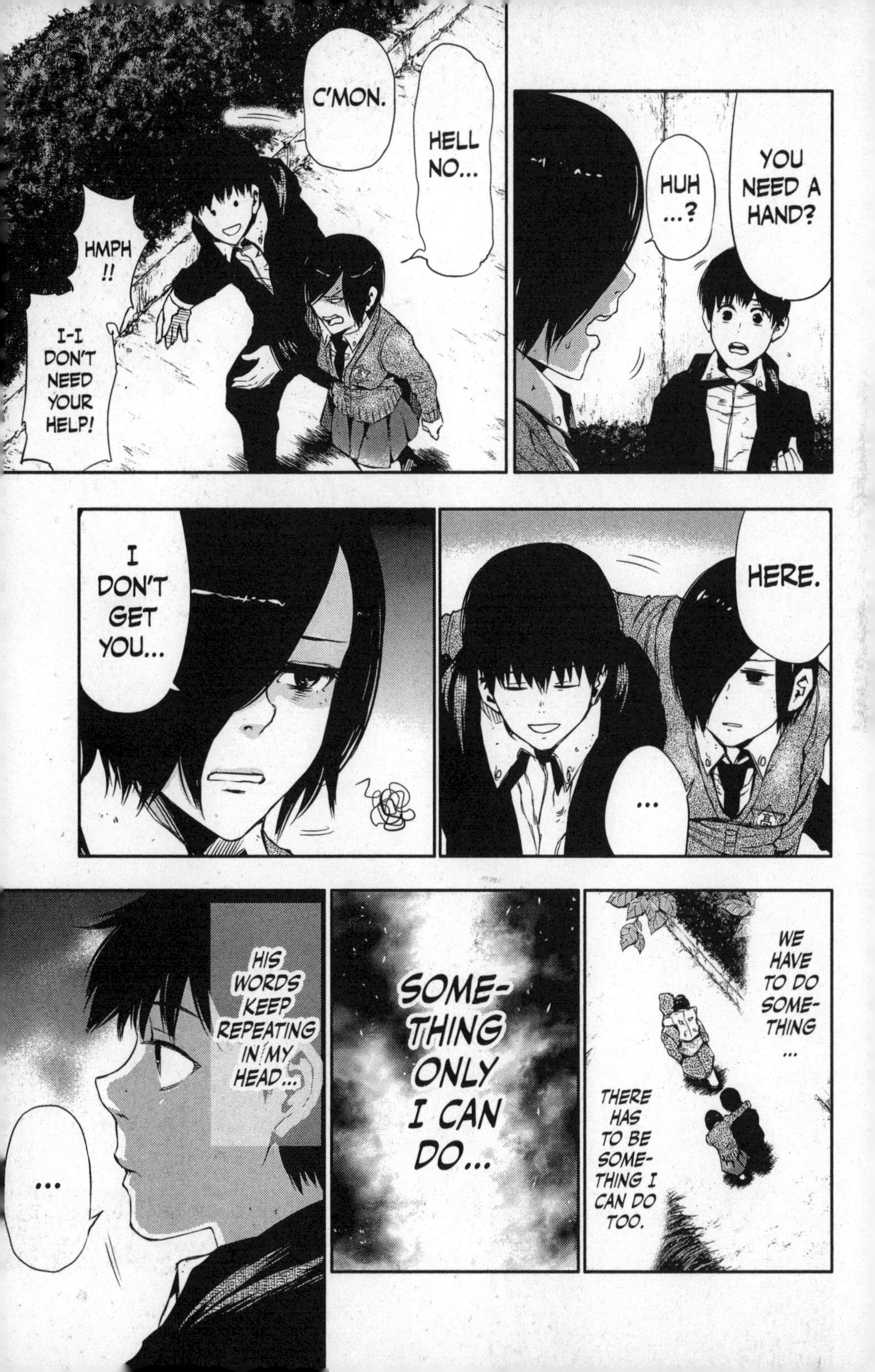
YOU NEED A HAND?
HUH ...?
HELL NO...
C'MON.
HMPH !!
I-I DON'T NEED YOUR HELP!
HERE.
...
I DON'T GET YOU...
WE HAVE TO DO SOMETHING ...
THERE HAS TO BE SOMETHING I CAN DO TOO.
SOMETHING ONLY I CAN DO...
HIS WORDS KEEP REPEATING IN MY HEAD...
...

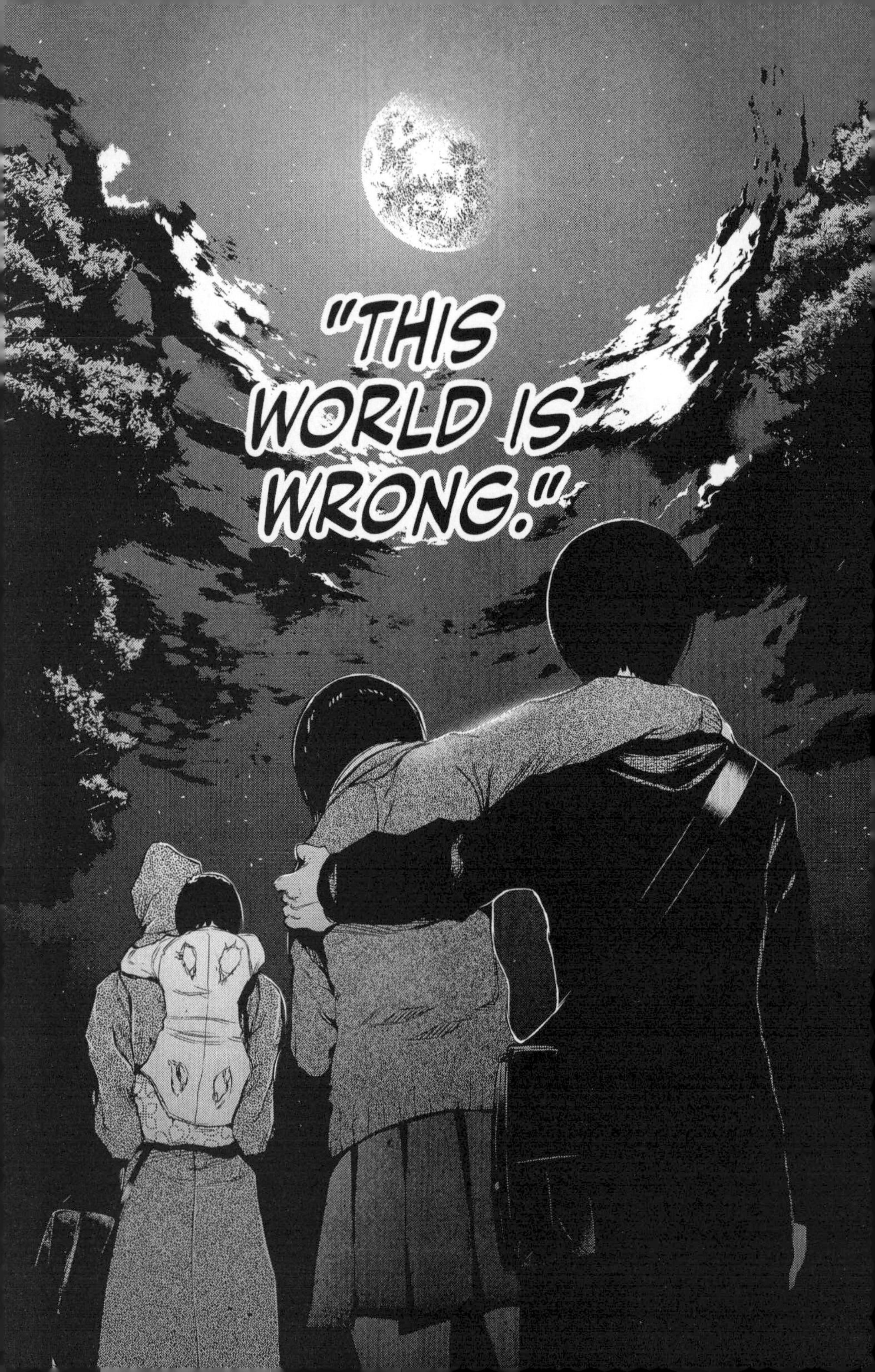
"THIS WORLD IS WRONG."

東京喰種
トーキョーグール
Tokyo
Ghoul

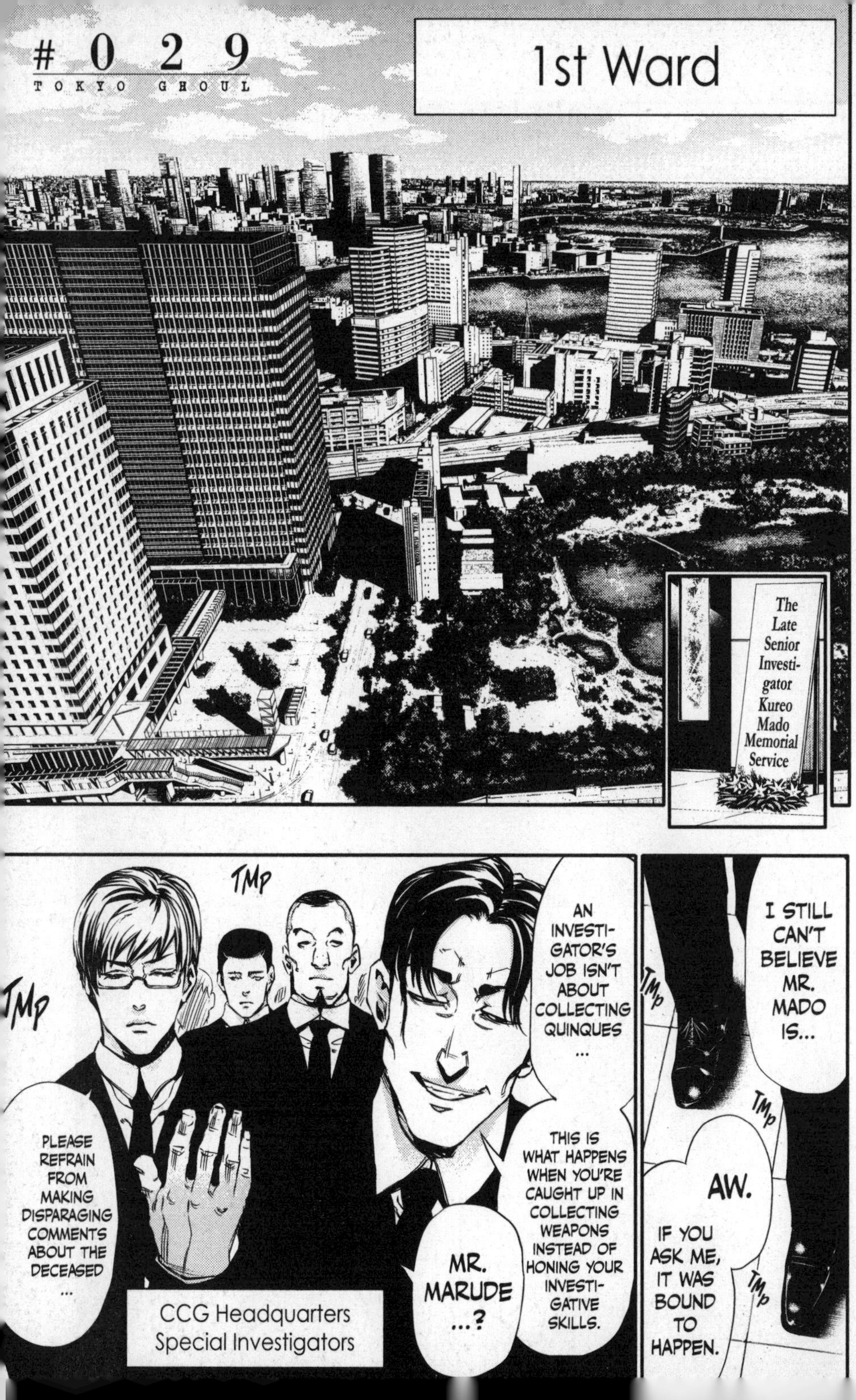
#029
TOKYO GHOUL
1st Ward
The Late Senior Investigator Kureo Mado Memorial Service
I STILL CAN'T BELIEVE MR. MADO IS...
TMP
TMP
AW.
IF YOU ASK ME, IT WAS BOUND TO HAPPEN.
TMP
TMP
AN INVESTIGATOR'S JOB ISN'T ABOUT COLLECTING QUINQUES ...
THIS IS WHAT HAPPENS WHEN YOU'RE CAUGHT UP IN COLLECTING WEAPONS INSTEAD OF HONING YOUR INVESTIGATIVE SKILLS.
MR. MARUDE ...?
TMP
PLEASE REFRAIN FROM MAKING DISPARAGING COMMENTS ABOUT THE DECEASED ...
TMP
CCG Headquarters Special Investigators

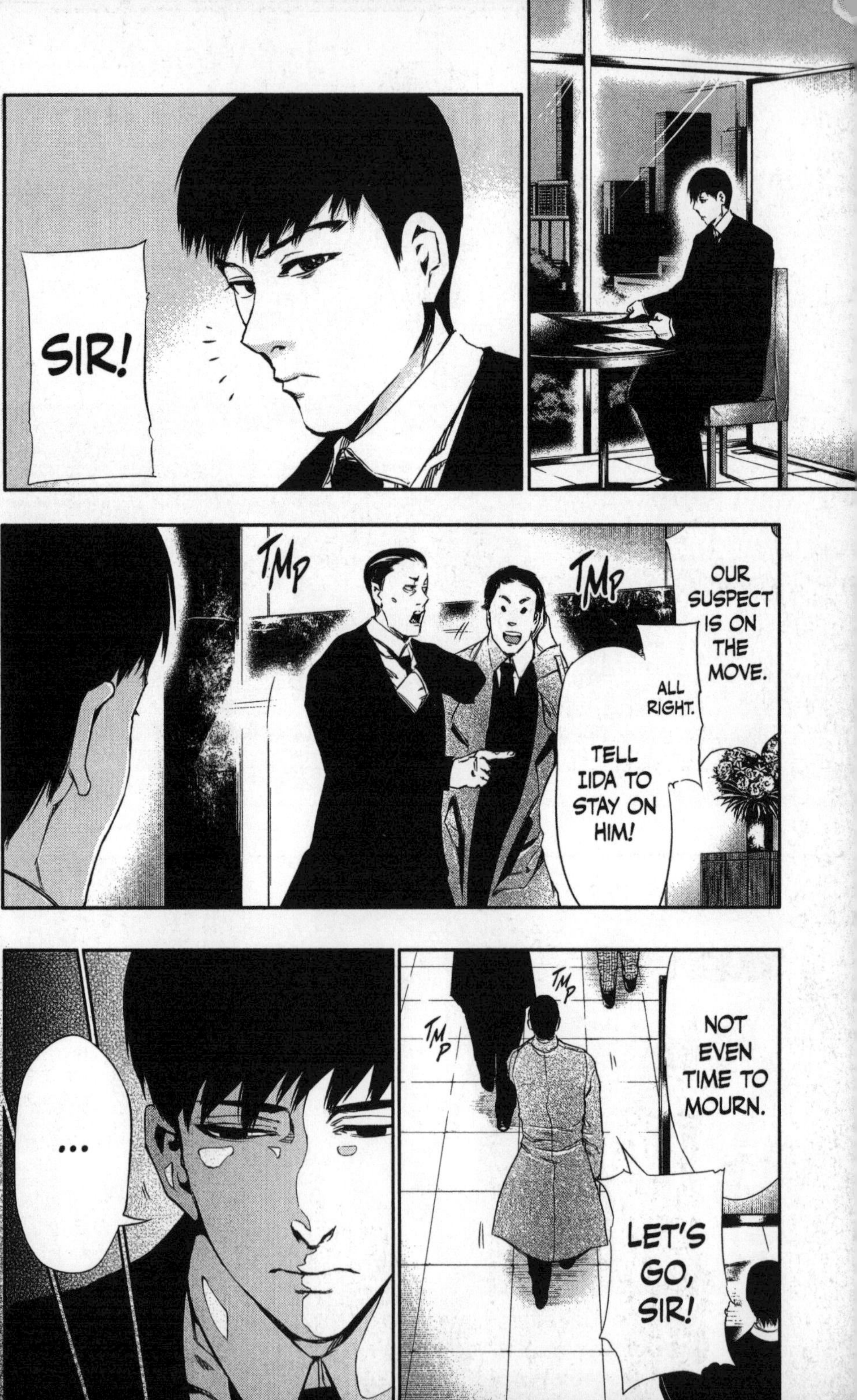
SIR!
TMP
TMP
OUR SUSPECT IS ON THE MOVE.
ALL RIGHT.
TELL IIDA TO STAY ON HIM!
TMP
TMP
NOT EVEN TIME TO MOURN.
LET'S GO, SIR!
...

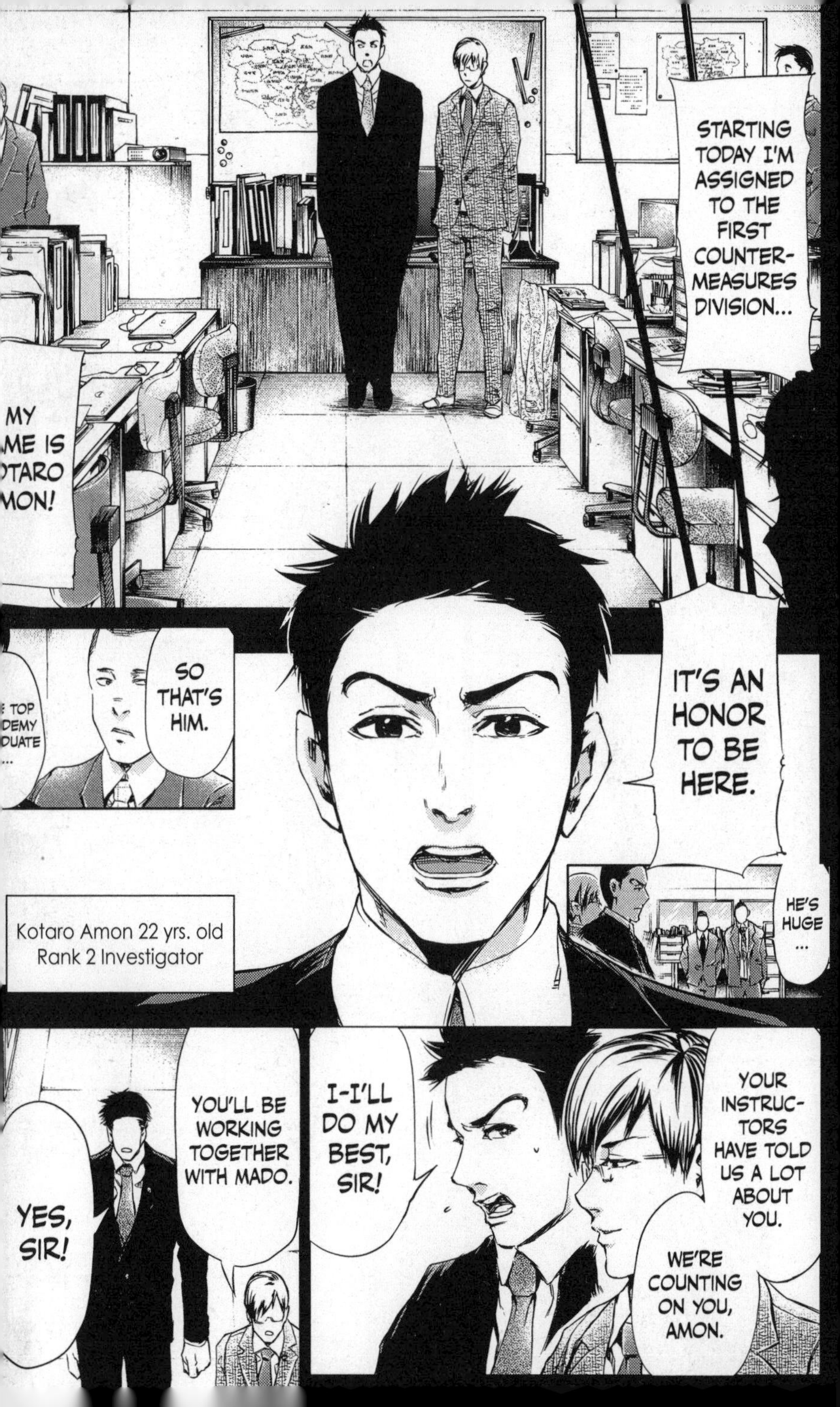
STARTING TODAY I'M ASSIGNED TO THE FIRST COUNTER-MEASURES DIVISION...
MY ME IS OTARO MON!
IT'S AN HONOR TO BE HERE.
HE'S HUGE ...
SO THAT'S HIM.
Kotaro Amon 22 yrs. old Rank 2 Investigator
YOUR INSTRUCTORS HAVE TOLD US A LOT ABOUT YOU.
WE'RE COUNTING ON YOU, AMON.
I-I'LL DO MY BEST, SIR!
YOU'LL BE WORKING TOGETHER WITH MADO.
YES, SIR!

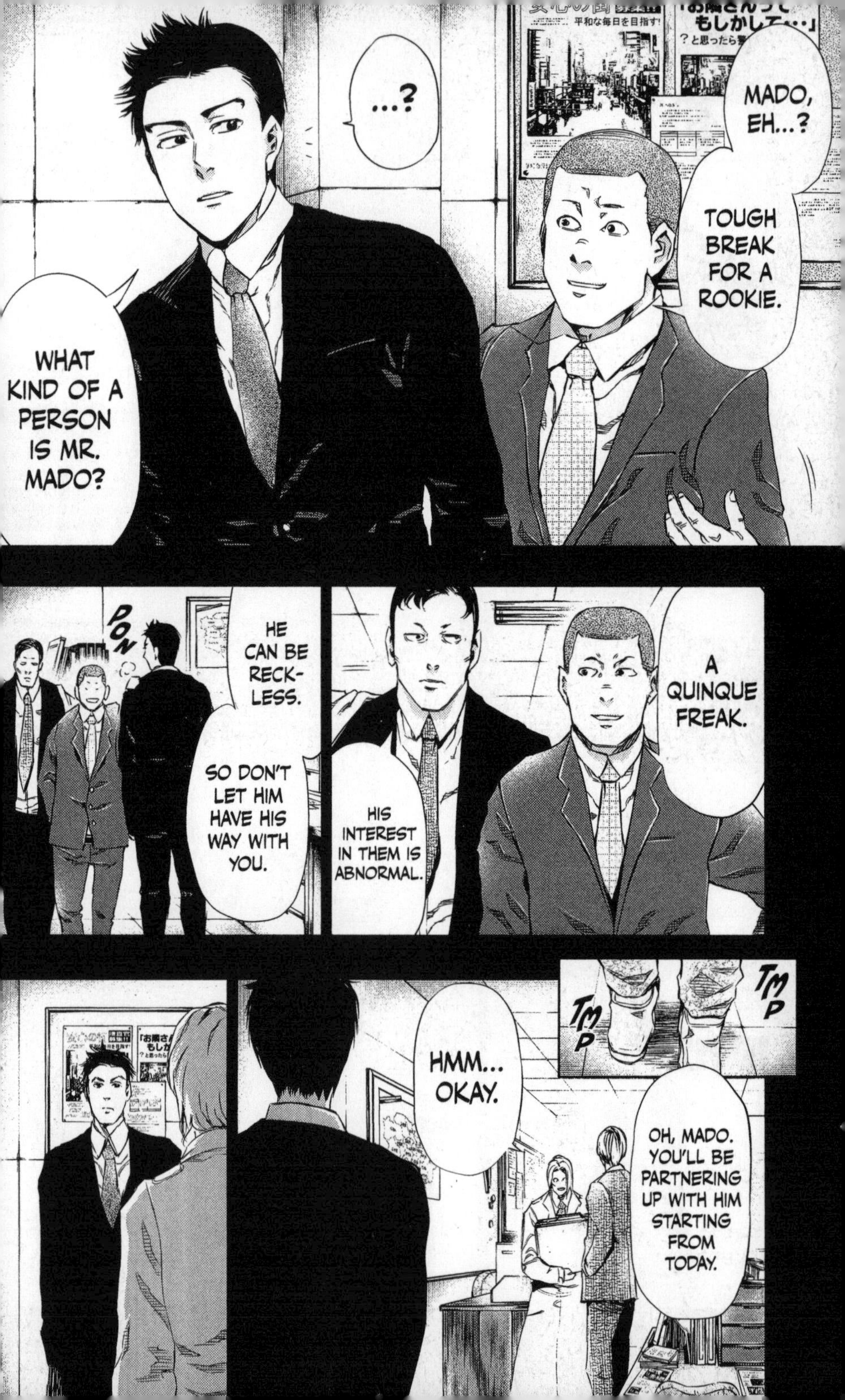
平和な毎日を目指す!
MADO, EH...?
TOUGH BREAK FOR A ROOKIE.
...?
WHAT KIND OF A PERSON IS MR. MADO?
A QUINQUE FREAK.
HIS INTEREST IN THEM IS ABNORMAL.
PON
HE CAN BE RECK-LESS.
SO DON'T LET HIM HAVE HIS WAY WITH YOU.
TMP
TMP
OH, MADO. YOU'LL BE PARTNERING UP WITH HIM STARTING FROM TODAY.
HMM... OKAY.

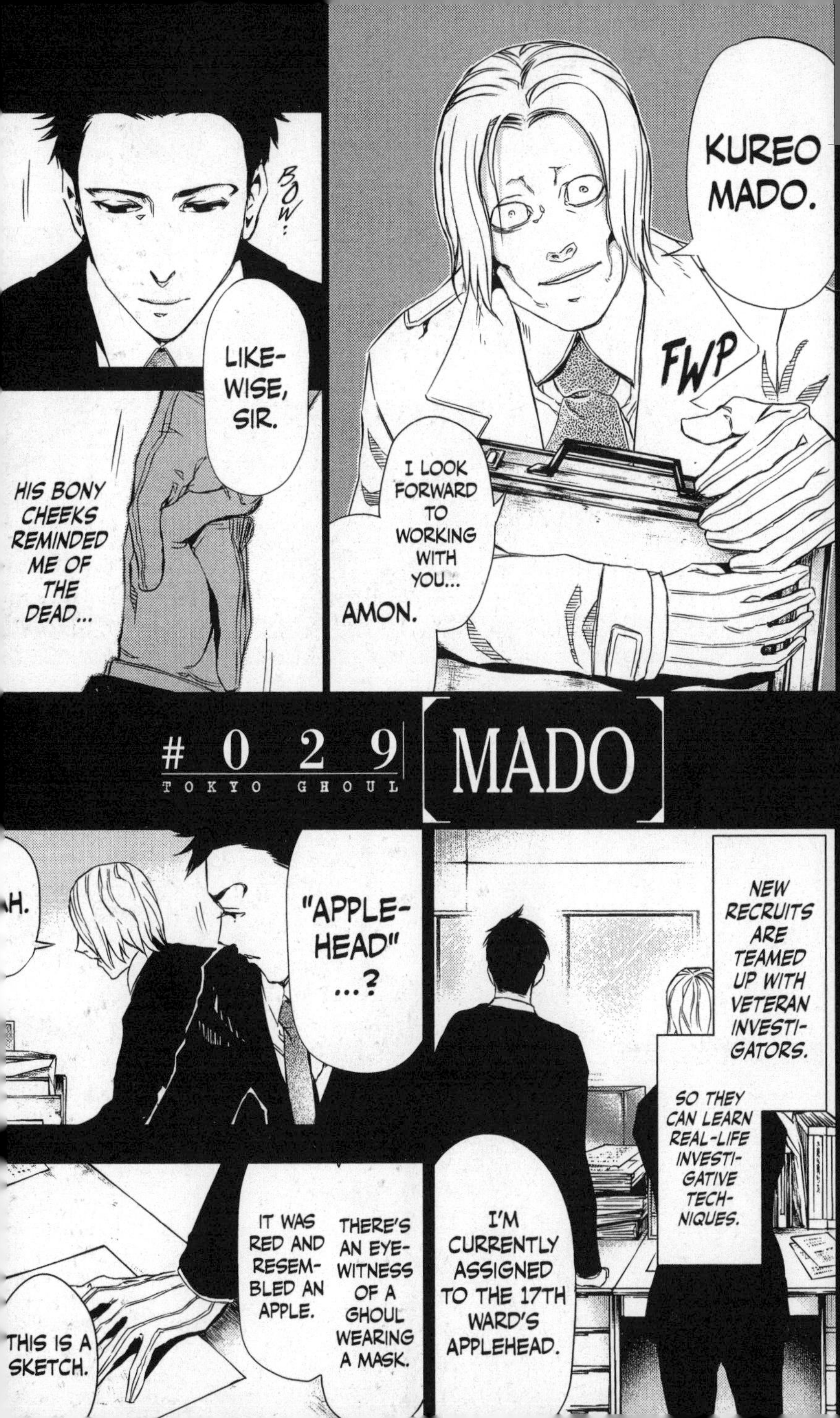
KUREO MADO.
FWP
I LOOK FORWARD TO WORKING WITH YOU...
AMON.
BOW!
LIKE-WISE, SIR.
HIS BONY CHEEKS REMINDED ME OF THE DEAD...
#029 TOKYO GHOUL
MADO
NEW RECRUITS ARE TEAMED UP WITH VETERAN INVESTI-GATORS.
SO THEY CAN LEARN REAL-LIFE INVESTI-GATIVE TECH-NIQUES.
I'M CURRENTLY ASSIGNED TO THE 17TH WARD'S APPLEHEAD.
"APPLE-HEAD" ...?
THERE'S AN EYE-WITNESS OF A GHOUL WEARING A MASK.
IT WAS RED AND RESEM-BLED AN APPLE.
THIS IS A SKETCH.

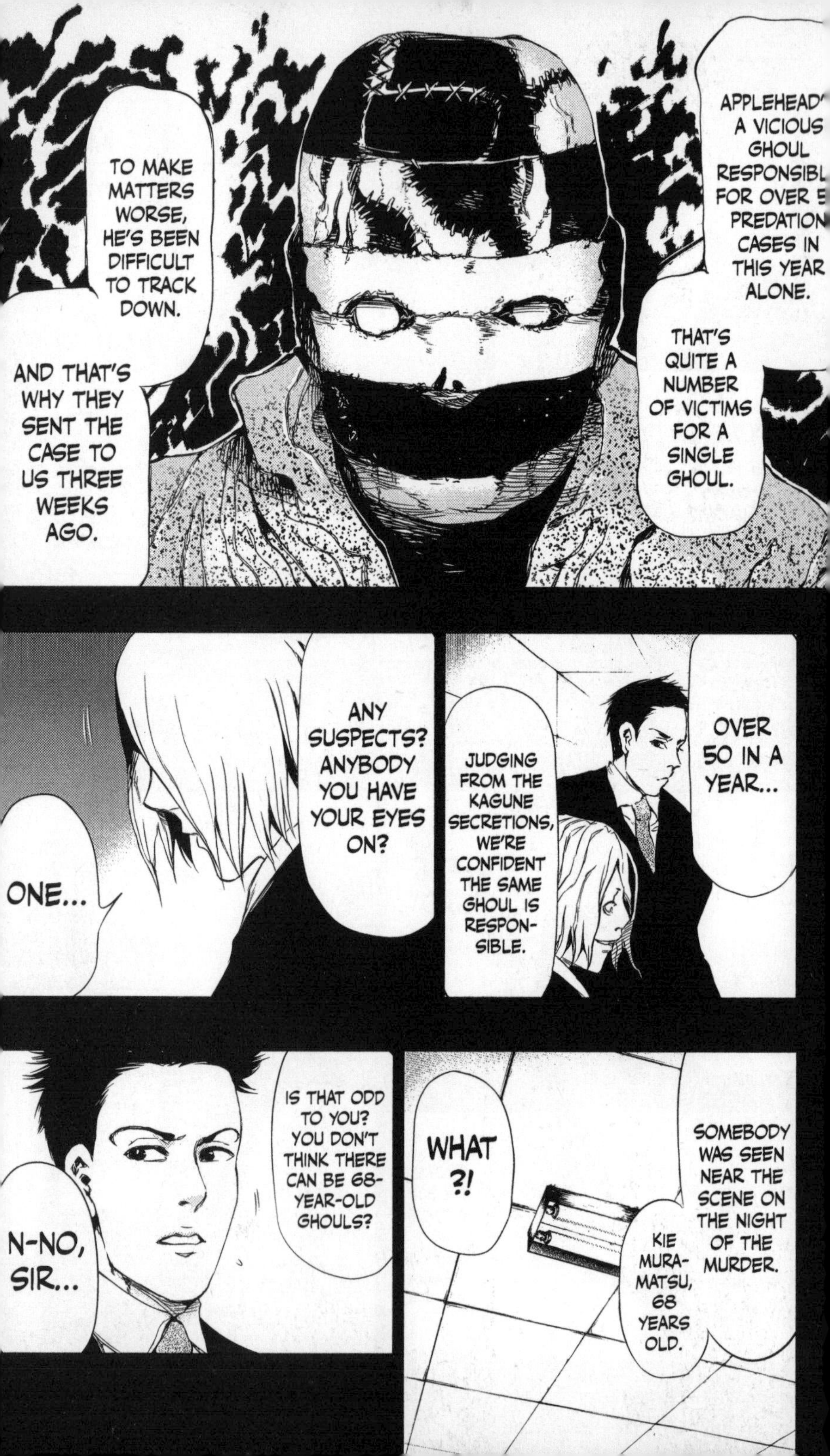
APPLEHEAD' A VICIOUS GHOUL RESPONSIBL FOR OVER 5 PREDATION CASES IN THIS YEAR ALONE.
THAT'S QUITE A NUMBER OF VICTIMS FOR A SINGLE GHOUL.
TO MAKE MATTERS WORSE, HE'S BEEN DIFFICULT TO TRACK DOWN.
AND THAT'S WHY THEY SENT THE CASE TO US THREE WEEKS AGO.
OVER 50 IN A YEAR...
JUDGING FROM THE KAGUNE SECRETIONS, WE'RE CONFIDENT THE SAME GHOUL IS RESPONSIBLE.
ANY SUSPECTS? ANYBODY YOU HAVE YOUR EYES ON?
ONE...
SOMEBODY WAS SEEN NEAR THE SCENE ON THE NIGHT OF THE MURDER.
KIE MURAMATSU, 68 YEARS OLD.
WHAT?!
IS THAT ODD TO YOU? YOU DON'T THINK THERE CAN BE 68-YEAR-OLD GHOULS?
N-NO, SIR...

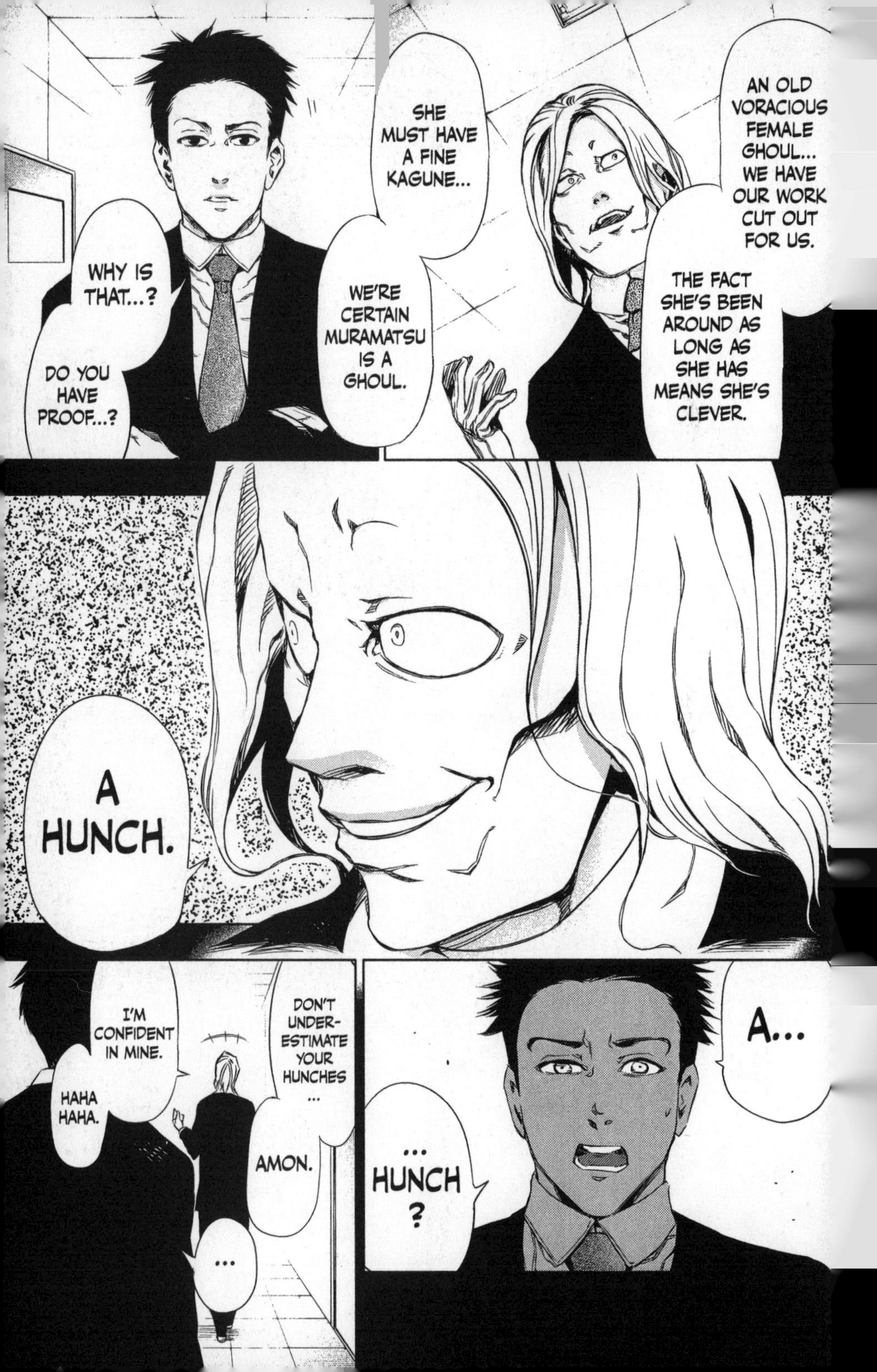
AN OLD VORACIOUS FEMALE GHOUL... WE HAVE OUR WORK CUT OUT FOR US.
THE FACT SHE'S BEEN AROUND AS LONG AS SHE HAS MEANS SHE'S CLEVER.
SHE MUST HAVE A FINE KAGUNE...
WE'RE CERTAIN MURAMATSU IS A GHOUL.
WHY IS THAT...?
DO YOU HAVE PROOF...?
A HUNCH.
A...
...HUNCH?
DON'T UNDER-ESTIMATE YOUR HUNCHES...
AMON.
I'M CONFIDENT IN MINE.
HAHA HAHA.
...

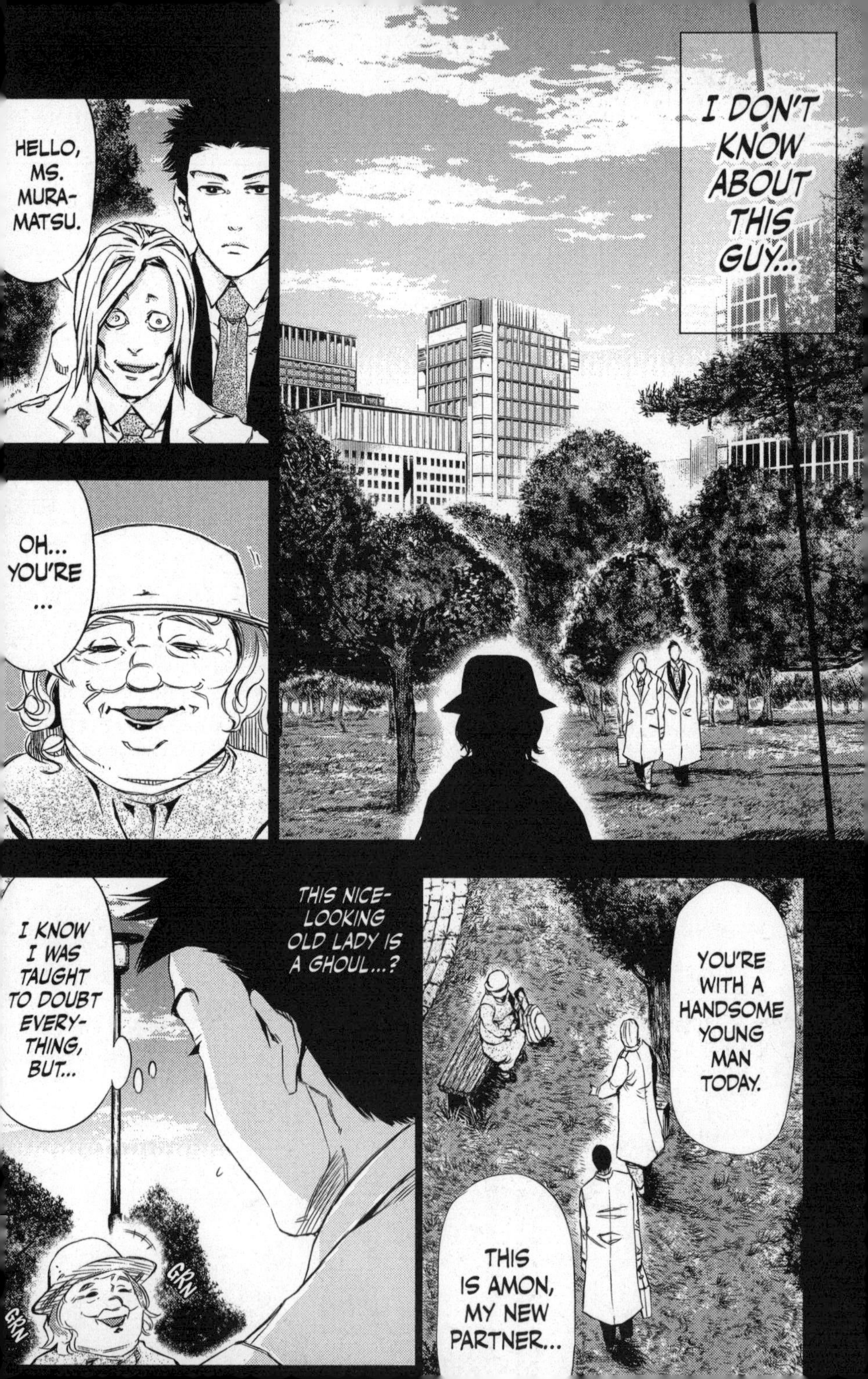
I DON'T KNOW ABOUT THIS GUY...
HELLO, MS. MURA-MATSU.
OH... YOU'RE ...
YOU'RE WITH A HANDSOME YOUNG MAN TODAY.
THIS IS AMON, MY NEW PARTNER...
THIS NICE-LOOKING OLD LADY IS A GHOUL...?
I KNOW I WAS TAUGHT TO DOUBT EVERY-THING, BUT...
GRN
GRN

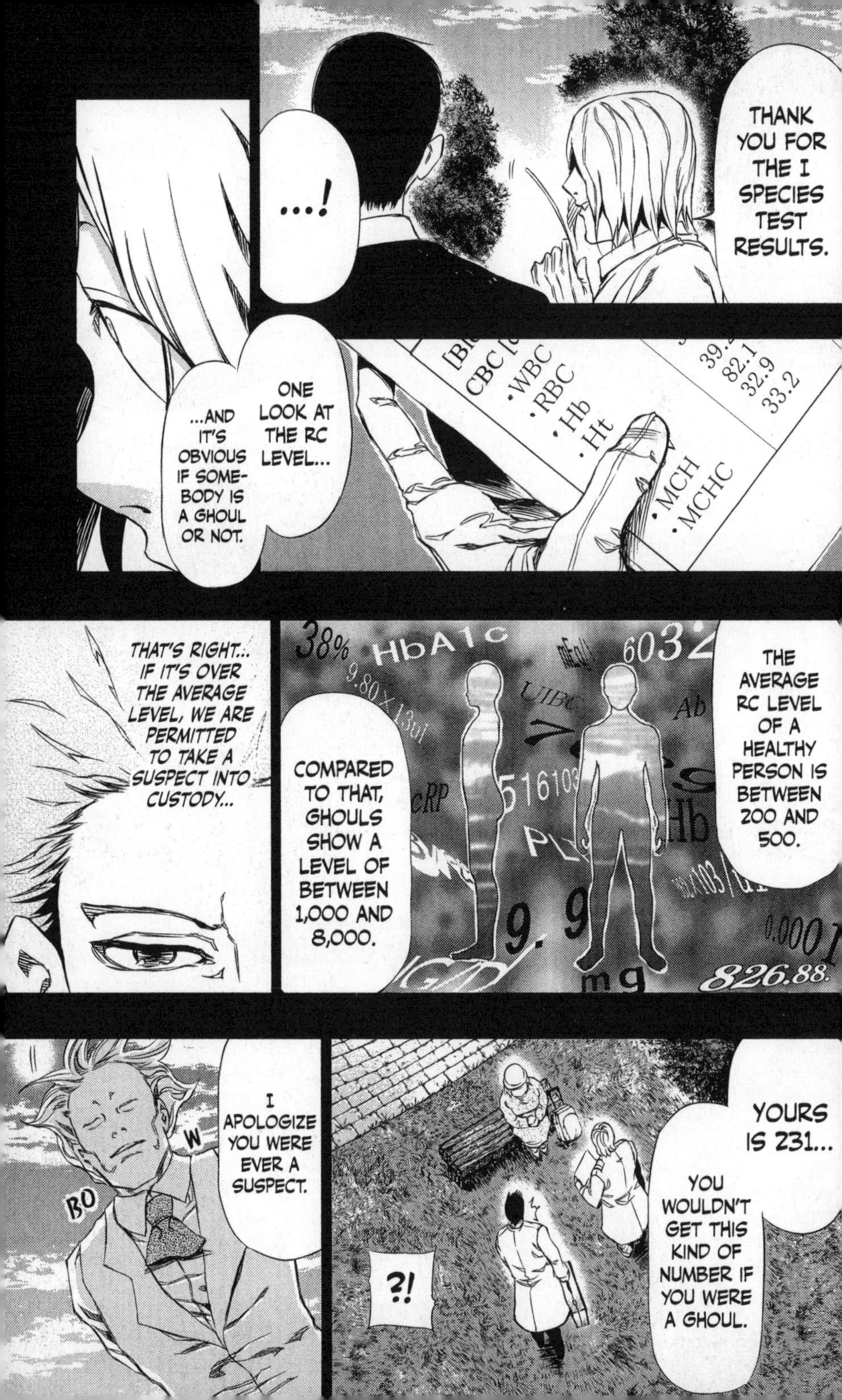
THANK YOU FOR THE I SPECIES TEST RESULTS.
...!
ONE LOOK AT THE RC LEVEL...
...AND IT'S OBVIOUS IF SOMEBODY IS A GHOUL OR NOT.
THE AVERAGE RC LEVEL OF A HEALTHY PERSON IS BETWEEN 200 AND 500.
COMPARED TO THAT, GHOULS SHOW A LEVEL OF BETWEEN 1,000 AND 8,000.
THAT'S RIGHT... IF IT'S OVER THE AVERAGE LEVEL, WE ARE PERMITTED TO TAKE A SUSPECT INTO CUSTODY...
YOURS IS 231...
YOU WOULDN'T GET THIS KIND OF NUMBER IF YOU WERE A GHOUL.
?!
I APOLOGIZE YOU WERE EVER A SUSPECT.
W
BO

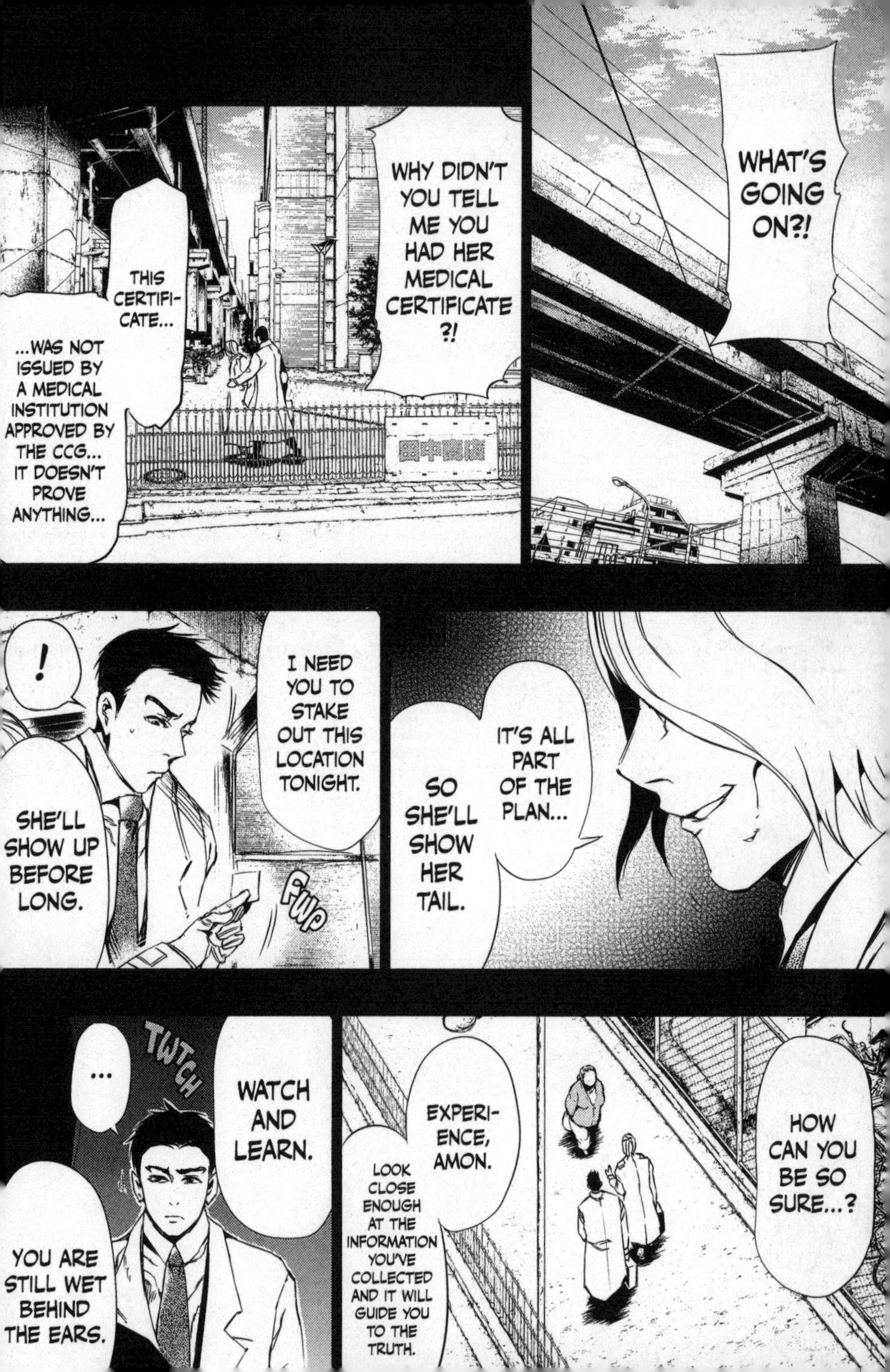
WHAT'S GOING ON?!
WHY DIDN'T YOU TELL ME YOU HAD HER MEDICAL CERTIFICATE?!
THIS CERTIFI-CATE...
...WAS NOT ISSUED BY A MEDICAL INSTITUTION APPROVED BY THE CCG... IT DOESN'T PROVE ANYTHING...
IT'S ALL PART OF THE PLAN...
SO SHE'LL SHOW HER TAIL.
I NEED YOU TO STAKE OUT THIS LOCATION TONIGHT.
!
FWP
SHE'LL SHOW UP BEFORE LONG.
HOW CAN YOU BE SO SURE...?
EXPERI-ENCE, AMON.
LOOK CLOSE ENOUGH AT THE INFORMATION YOU'VE COLLECTED AND IT WILL GUIDE YOU TO THE TRUTH.
WATCH AND LEARN.
...
TWTCH
YOU ARE STILL WET BEHIND THE EARS.

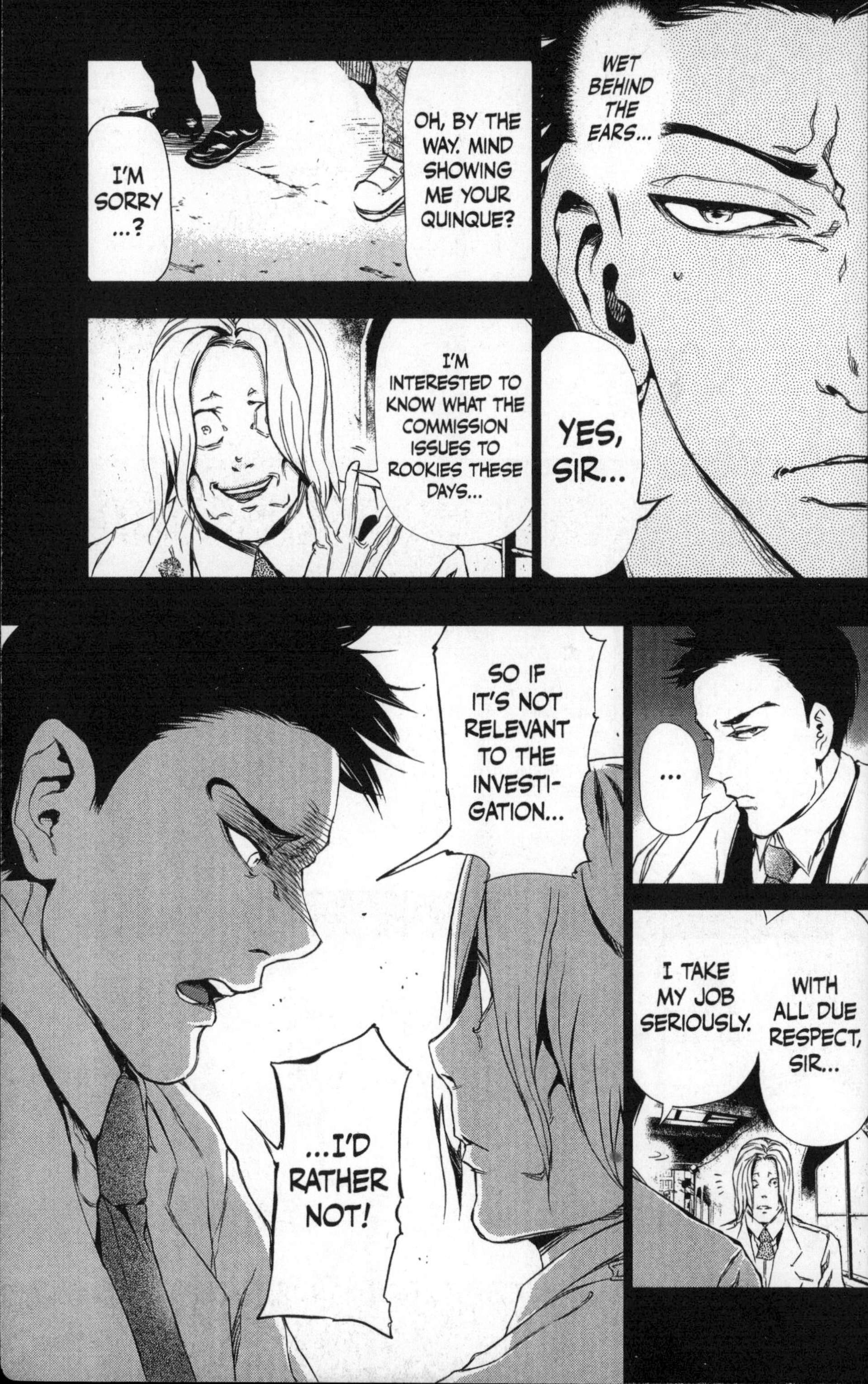
WET BEHIND THE EARS...
YES, SIR...
OH, BY THE WAY. MIND SHOWING ME YOUR QUINQUE?
I'M SORRY ...?
I'M INTERESTED TO KNOW WHAT THE COMMISSION ISSUES TO ROOKIES THESE DAYS...
...
WITH ALL DUE RESPECT, SIR...
I TAKE MY JOB SERIOUSLY.
SO IF IT'S NOT RELEVANT TO THE INVESTIGATION...
...I'D RATHER NOT!

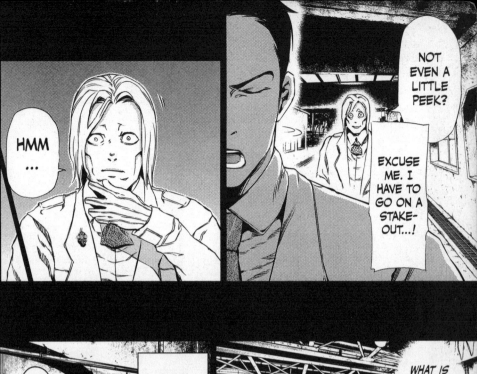

NOT EVEN A LITTLE PEEK?
EXCUSE ME. I HAVE TO GO ON A STAKE-OUT...!
HMM ...
WHAT IS THAT MAN THINKING ...?!
WHY DOES THE MAIN OFFICE ALLOW HIM TO BE THAT WAY...?
I WISH I COULD'VE WORKED WITH SOMEBODY LIKE SENIOR INVESTIGATOR ARIMA, WHOM I DEEPLY RESPECT...
...!
MS. MURA-MATSU ...?
OOF
OOF
WADDLE
WADDLE
HER BAGS LOOK HEAVY...
MS. MURA-MATSU !!

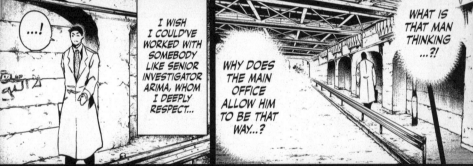

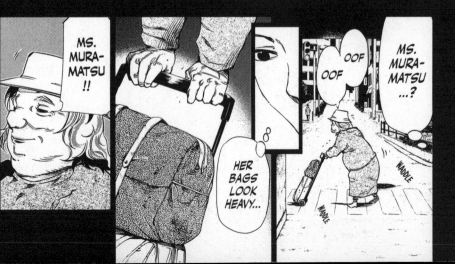

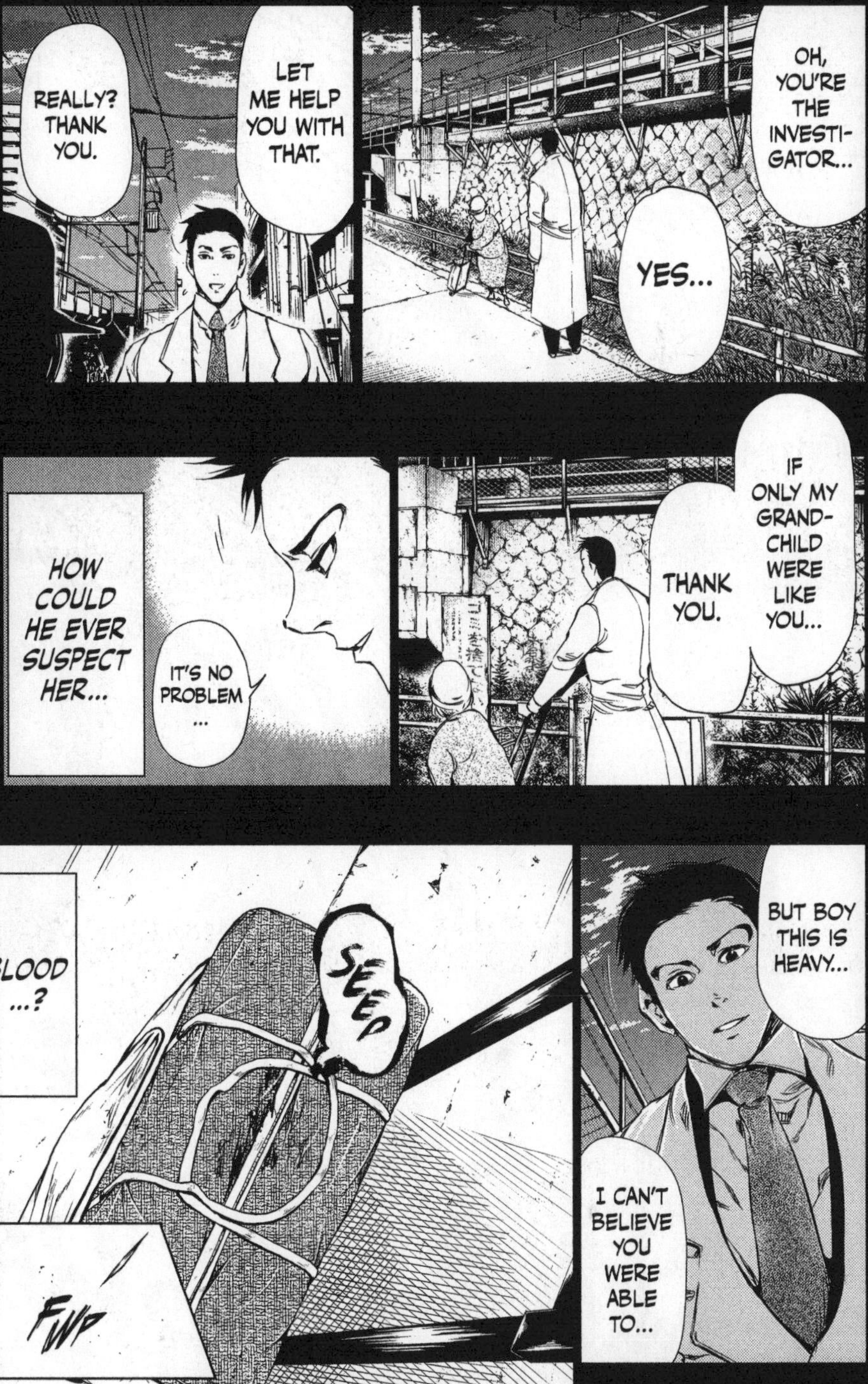
OH, YOU'RE THE INVESTI-GATOR...
YES...
LET ME HELP YOU WITH THAT.
REALLY? THANK YOU.
IF ONLY MY GRAND-CHILD WERE LIKE YOU...
THANK YOU.
IT'S NO PROBLEM ...
HOW COULD HE EVER SUSPECT HER...
BUT BOY THIS IS HEAVY...
I CAN'T BELIEVE YOU WERE ABLE TO...
SEEP
BLOOD ...?
FWP

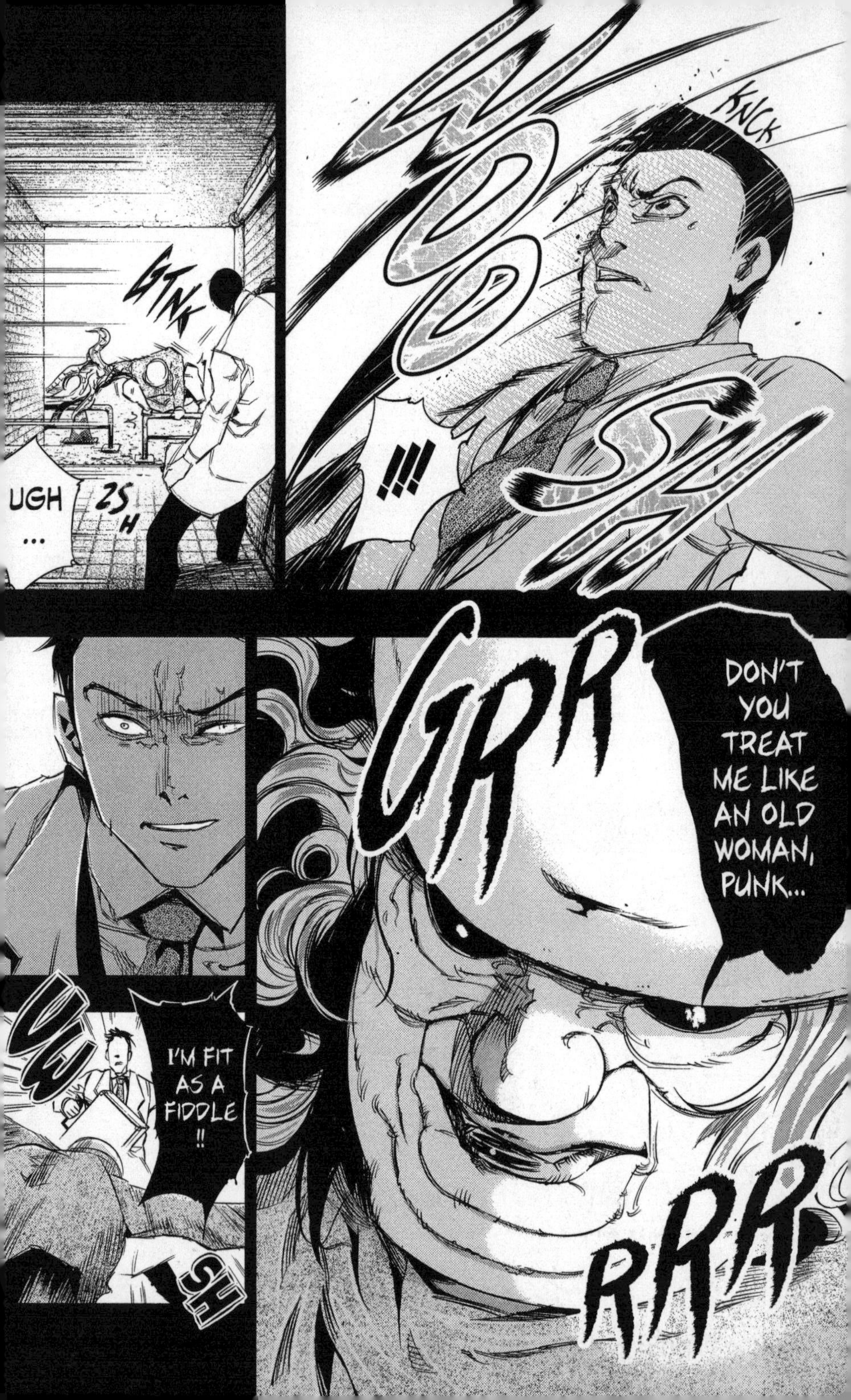
WOOSH
KNCK
!!!
CLINK
UGH...
ZSH
GRRRRR
DON'T YOU TREAT ME LIKE AN OLD WOMAN, PUNK...
I'M FIT AS A FIDDLE!!
SH

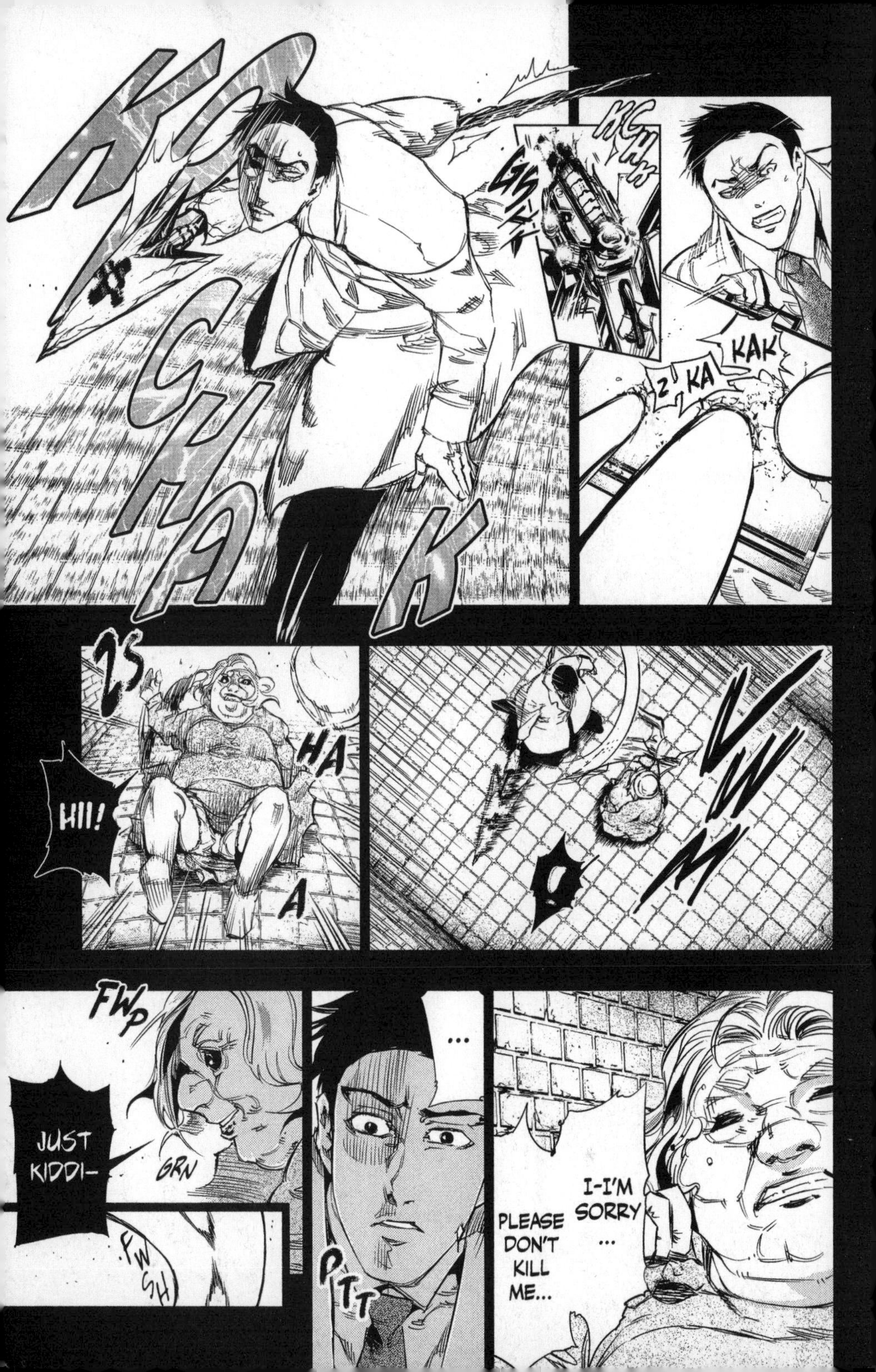
KCHAK
GSK
Z KA KAK
KCHAK
VWM
ZS
HA
A
HII!
I-I'M SORRY ...
PLEASE DON'T KILL ME...
...
PTTT
FWP
JUST KIDDI-
GRN
FWSH

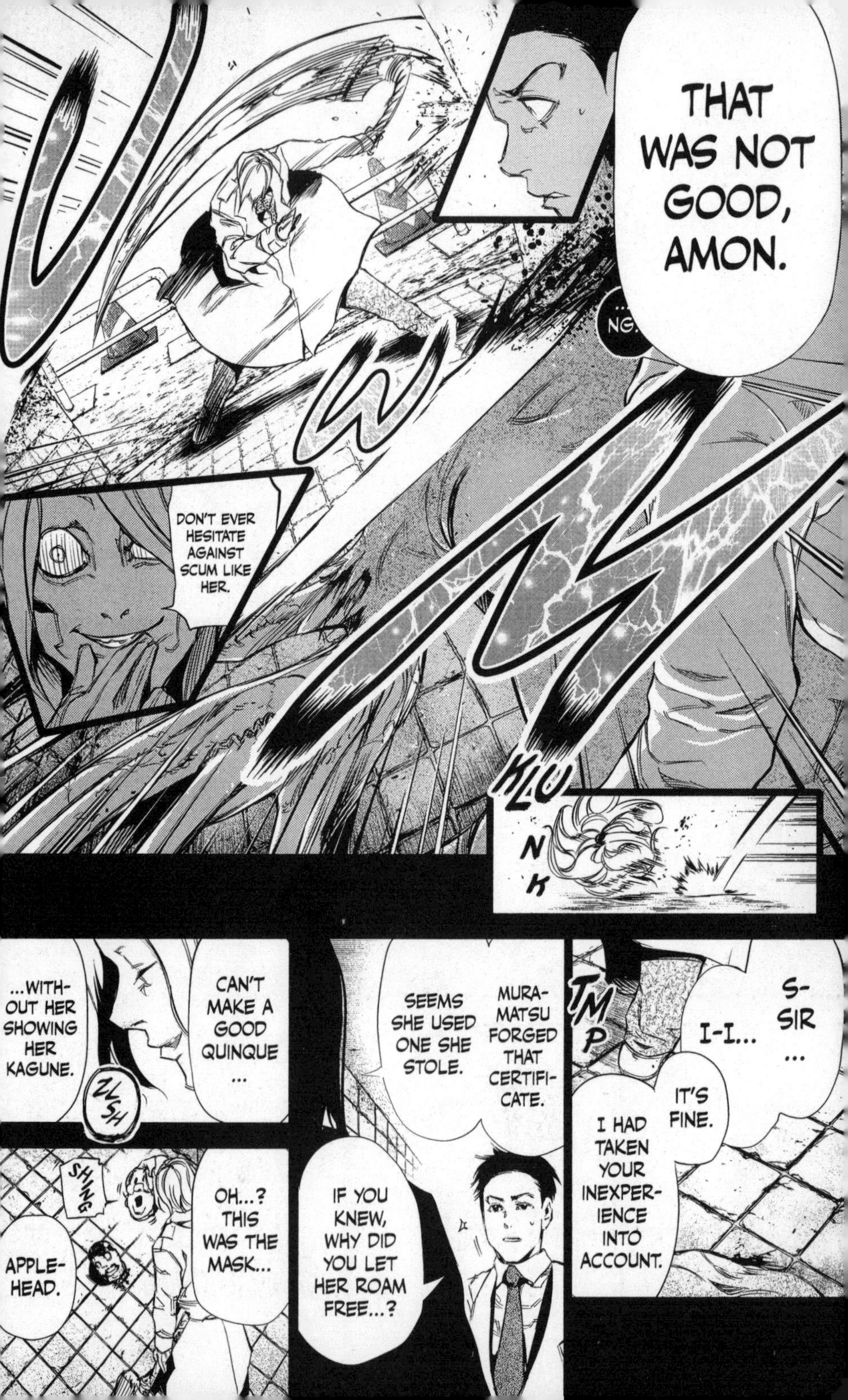
THAT WAS NOT GOOD, AMON.
...NG.
DON'T EVER HESITATE AGAINST SCUM LIKE HER.
KLUNK
S-SIR...
I-I...
TMP
IT'S FINE.
I HAD TAKEN YOUR INEXPERIENCE INTO ACCOUNT.
MURAMATSU FORGED THAT CERTIFICATE.
SEEMS SHE USED ONE SHE STOLE.
IF YOU KNEW, WHY DID YOU LET HER ROAM FREE...?
CAN'T MAKE A GOOD QUINQUE...
...WITHOUT HER SHOWING HER KAGUNE.
ZLSH
OH...? THIS WAS THE MASK...
SHING
APPLEHEAD.

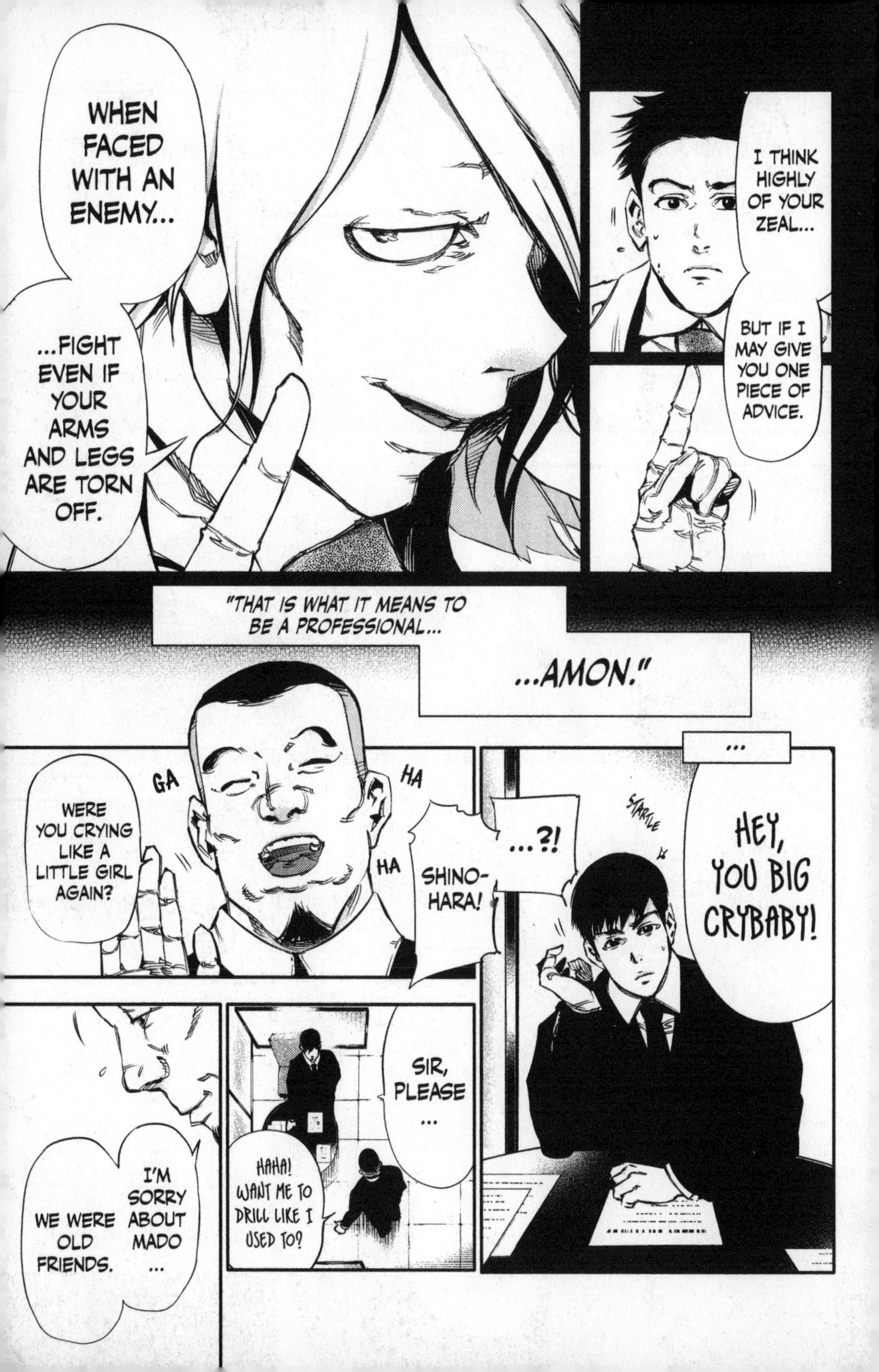
I THINK HIGHLY OF YOUR ZEAL...
BUT IF I MAY GIVE YOU ONE PIECE OF ADVICE.
WHEN FACED WITH AN ENEMY...
...FIGHT EVEN IF YOUR ARMS AND LEGS ARE TORN OFF.
"THAT IS WHAT IT MEANS TO BE A PROFESSIONAL...
...AMON."
...
HEY, YOU BIG CRYBABY!
STARTLE
...?!
SHINO-HARA!
GA
HA
HA
WERE YOU CRYING LIKE A LITTLE GIRL AGAIN?
SIR, PLEASE ...
HAHA! WANT ME TO DRILL LIKE I USED TO?
I'M SORRY ABOUT MADO ...
WE WERE OLD FRIENDS.

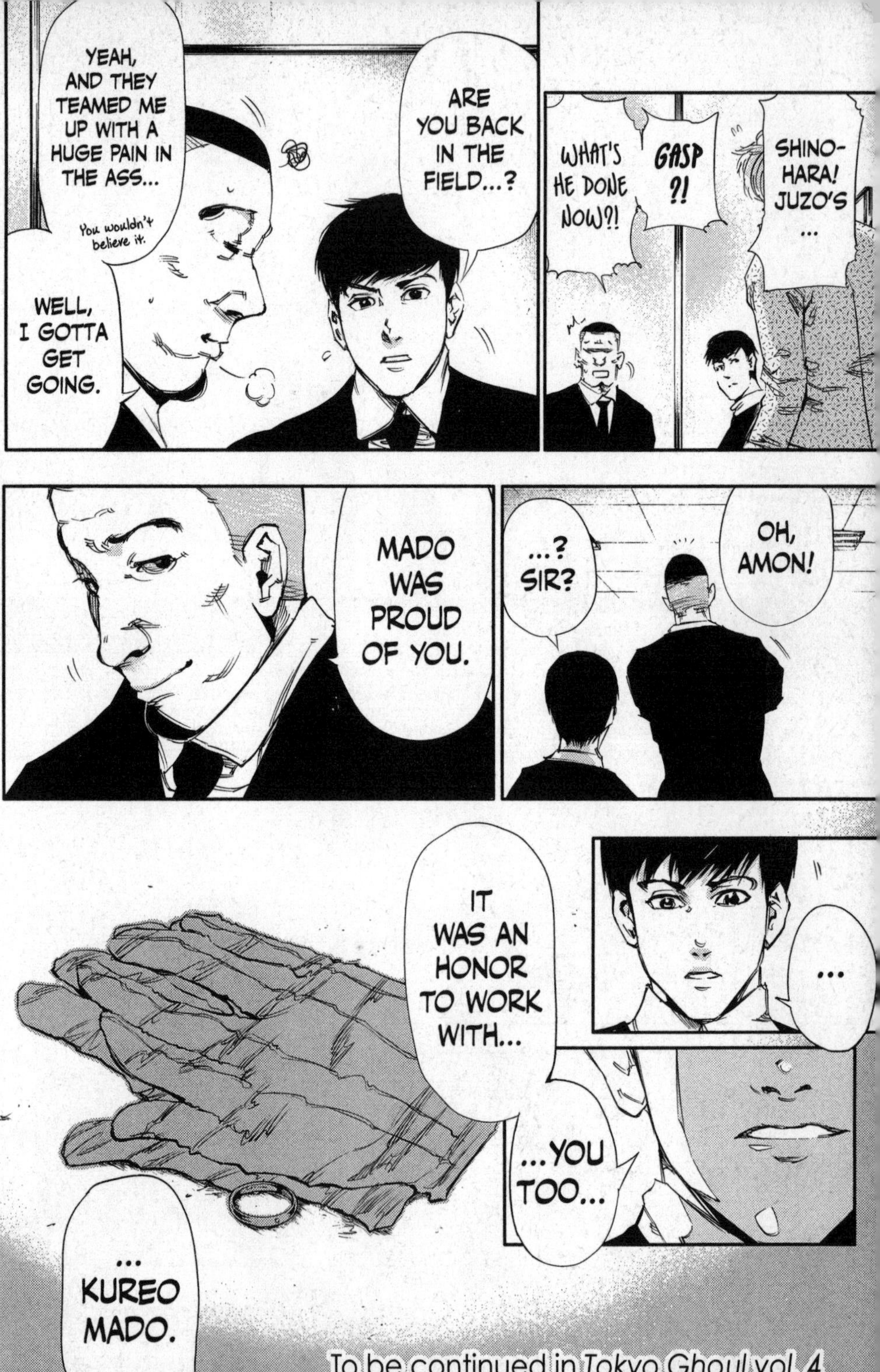
SHINO-HARA! JUZO'S ...
GASP ?!
WHAT'S HE DONE NOW?!
ARE YOU BACK IN THE FIELD...?
YEAH, AND THEY TEAMED ME UP WITH A HUGE PAIN IN THE ASS...
You wouldn't believe it.
WELL, I GOTTA GET GOING.
OH, AMON!
...? SIR?
MADO WAS PROUD OF YOU.
...
IT WAS AN HONOR TO WORK WITH...
...YOU TOO...
... KUREO MADO.

To be continued in *Tokyo Ghoul* vol. 4

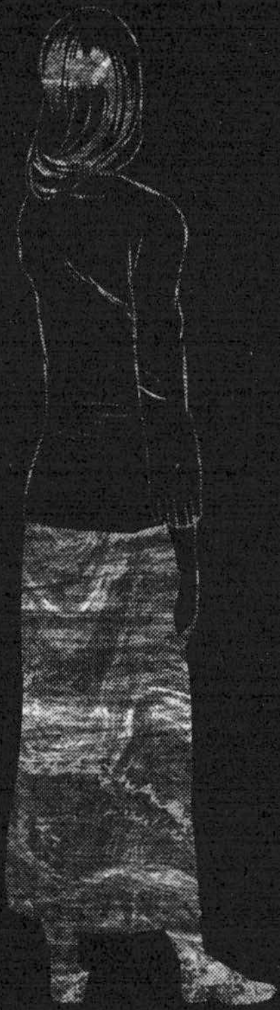

Tokyo Ghoul

Sui Ishida

Assistants
Eda
Ryuji Miyamoto

Help
Mizuki Ide
Matsuzaki

Editor
Jumpei Matsuo

Design
Hideaki Shimada

Cover
Miyuki Takaoka (pocket)

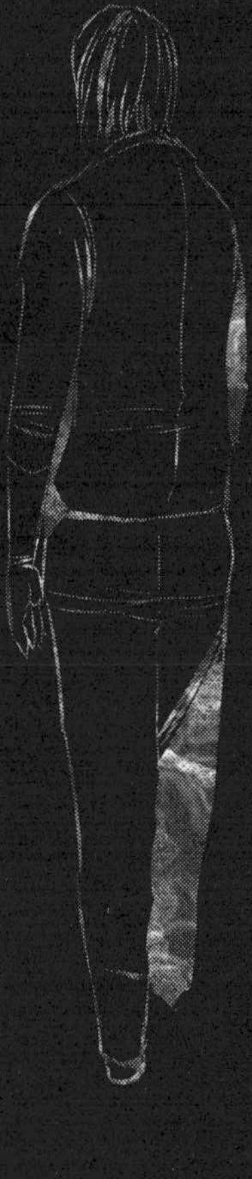

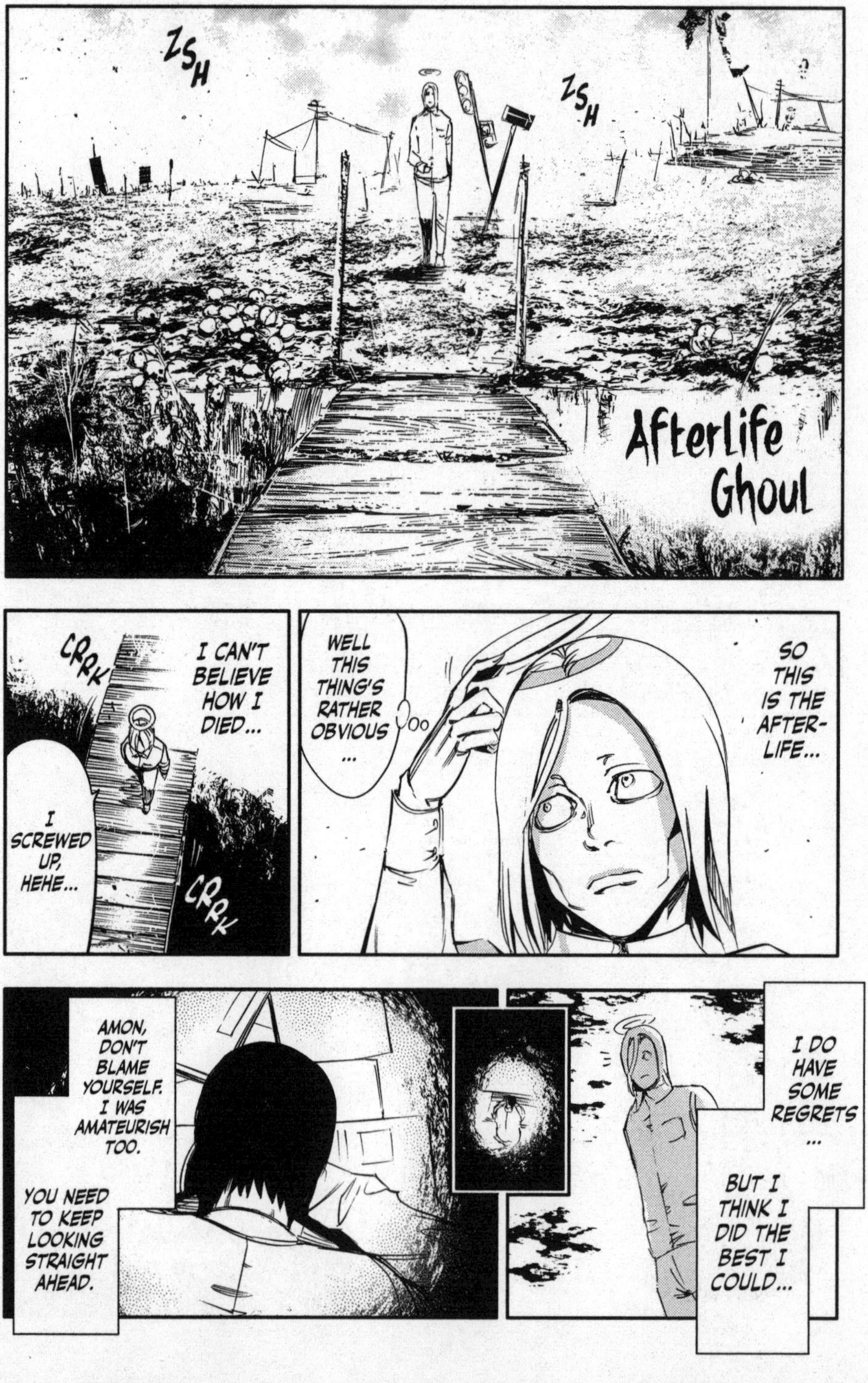
ZSH
ZSH
Afterlife Ghoul
SO THIS IS THE AFTER-LIFE...
WELL THIS THING'S RATHER OBVIOUS ...
I CAN'T BELIEVE HOW I DIED...
CRRK
I SCREWED UP, HEHE...
CRRK
I DO HAVE SOME REGRETS ...
BUT I THINK I DID THE BEST I COULD...
AMON, DON'T BLAME YOURSELF. I WAS AMATEURISH TOO.
YOU NEED TO KEEP LOOKING STRAIGHT AHEAD.

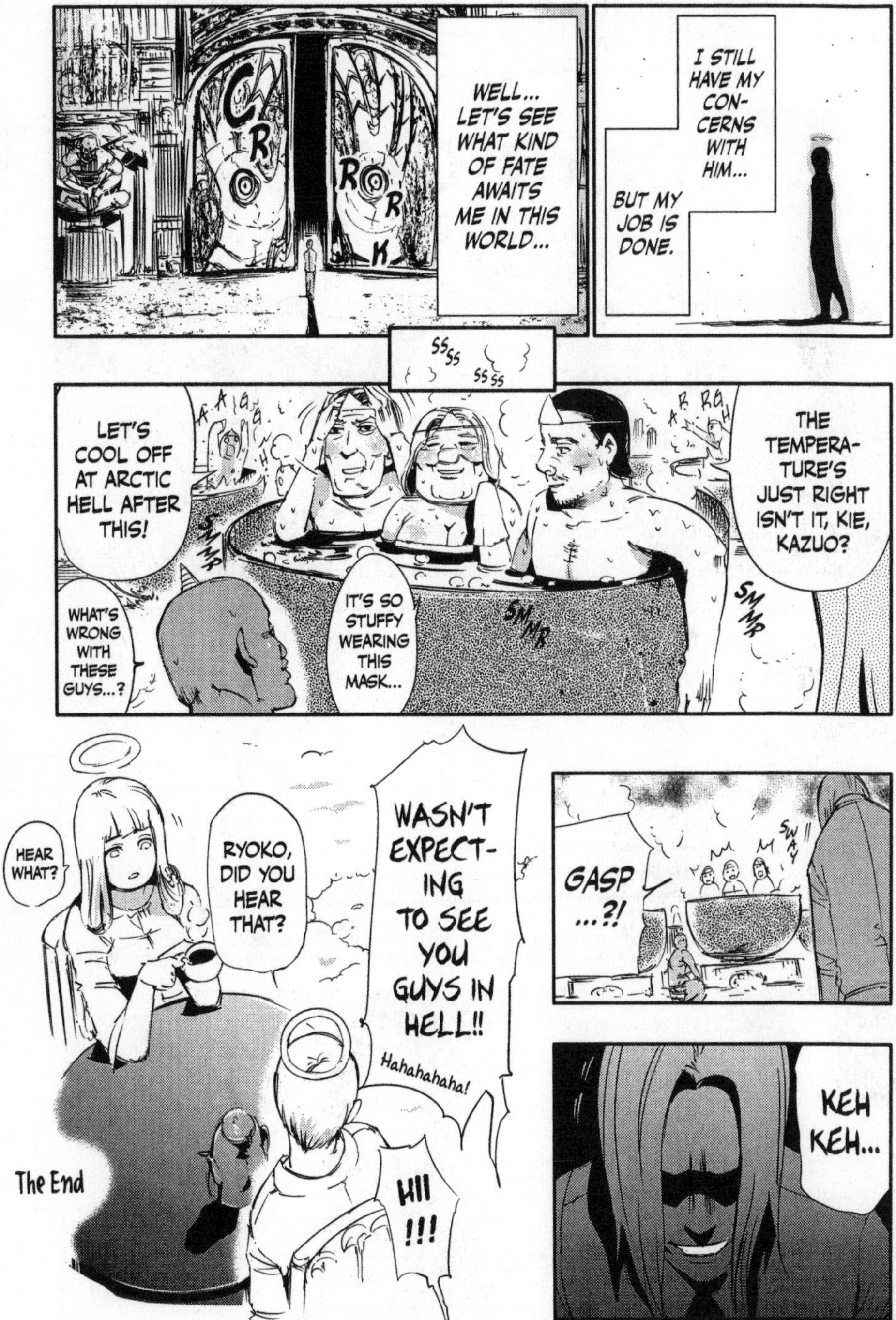
I STILL HAVE MY CONCERNS WITH HIM...
BUT MY JOB IS DONE.
CRO RORK
WELL... LET'S SEE WHAT KIND OF FATE AWAITS ME IN THIS WORLD...
SSSS SSSS
THE TEMPERATURE'S JUST RIGHT ISN'T IT, KIE, KAZUO?
ARRGH
SMMR
IT'S SO STUFFY WEARING THIS MASK...
SMMR
LET'S COOL OFF AT ARCTIC HELL AFTER THIS!
AAGGH
SMMR
WHAT'S WRONG WITH THESE GUYS...?
SWAY
MMM
GASP ...?!
KEH KEH...
WASN'T EXPECTING TO SEE YOU GUYS IN HELL!!
RYOKO, DID YOU HEAR THAT?
HEAR WHAT?
Hahahahaha!
HII !!!
The End

[THIS IS THE LAST PAGE]

TOKYO GHOUL
READS
RIGHT TO LEFT

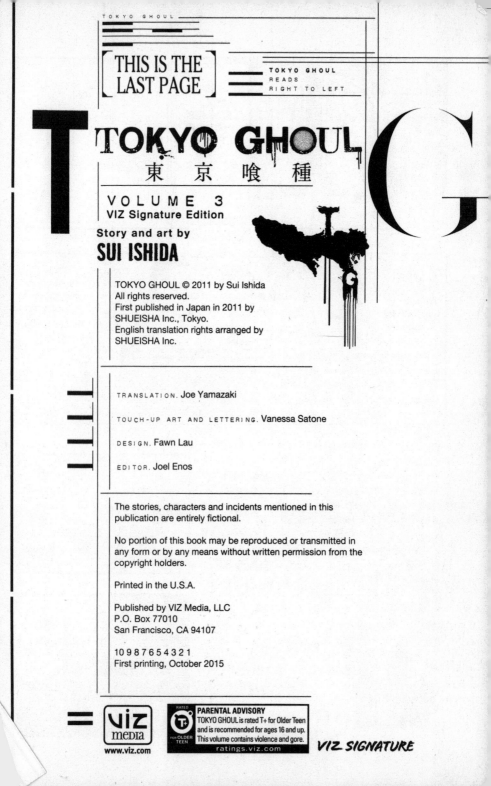

TOKYO GHOUL

東 京 喰 種

VOLUME 3
VIZ Signature Edition

Story and art by
SUI ISHIDA

TOKYO GHOUL © 2011 by Sui Ishida
All rights reserved.
First published in Japan in 2011 by
SHUEISHA Inc., Tokyo.
English translation rights arranged by
SHUEISHA Inc.

TRANSLATION. Joe Yamazaki

TOUCH-UP ART AND LETTERING. Vanessa Satone

DESIGN. Fawn Lau

EDITOR. Joel Enos

The stories, characters and incidents mentioned in this
publication are entirely fictional.

Printed in the U.S.A.

Published by VIZ Media, LLC
P.O. Box 77010
San Francisco, CA 94107

10 9 8 7 6 5 4 3 2 1
First printing, October 2015

VIZ MEDIA
www.viz.com

VIZ SIGNATURE